ART
Takeshi Obata

STORY
Tsugumi Ohba

Platinum End

PLATINVM END

2

CONTENTS

2

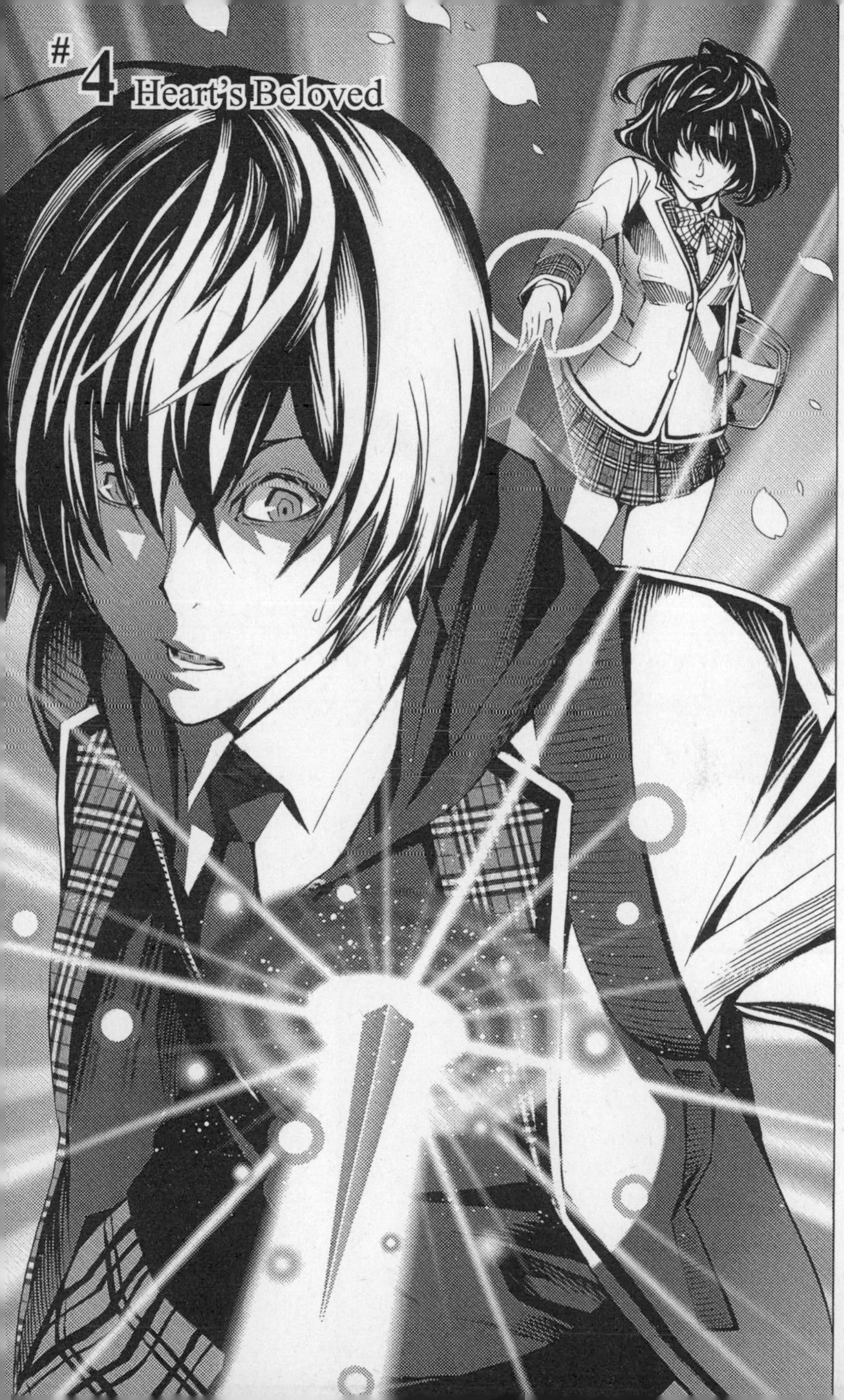

4 Heart's Beloved

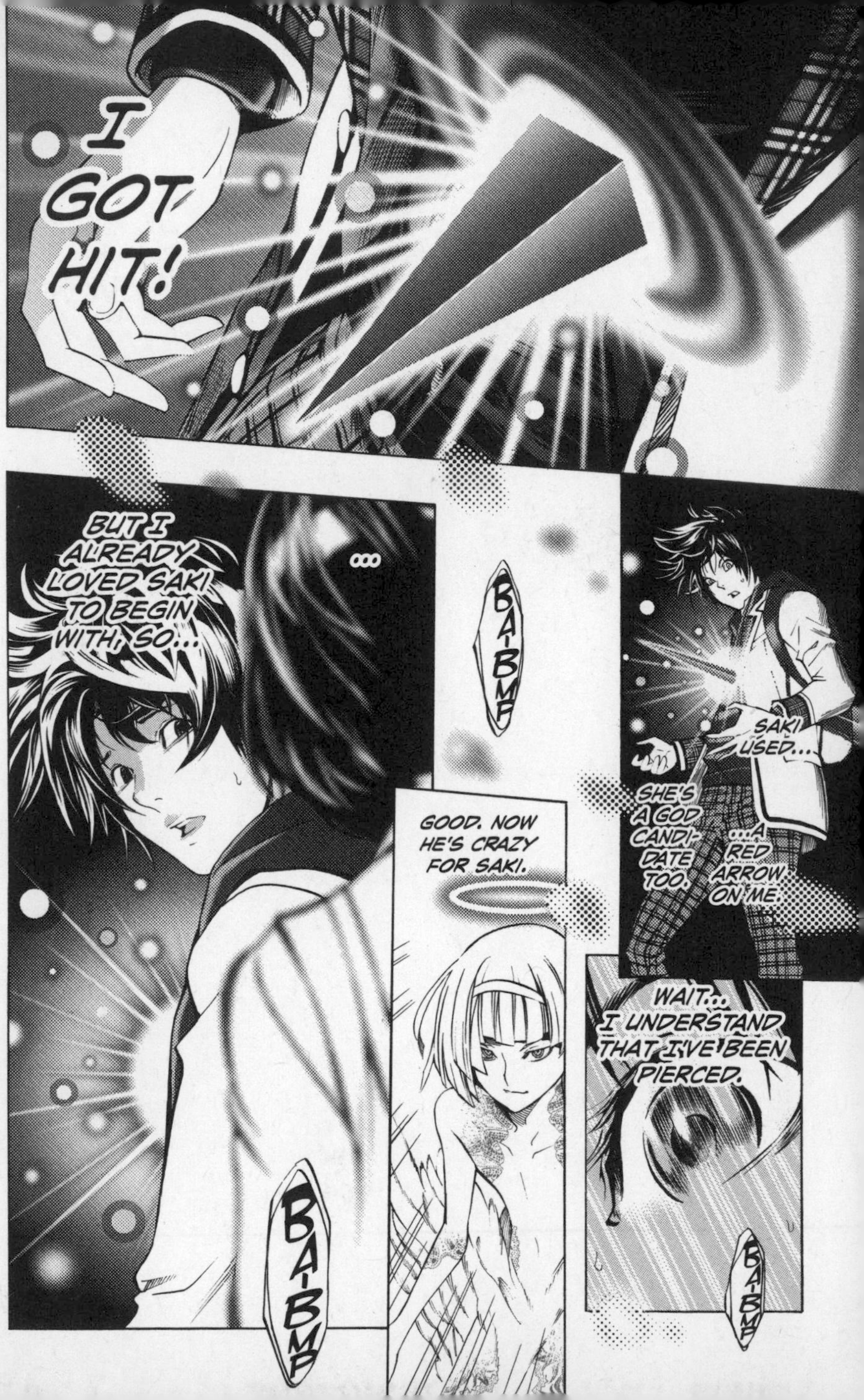
I GOT HIT!
SAKI USED...
...A RED ARROW ON ME.
SHE'S A GOD CANDIDATE TOO.
WAIT... I UNDERSTAND THAT I'VE BEEN PIERCED.
BA-BUMP
BA-BUMP
GOOD. NOW HE'S CRAZY FOR SAKI.
...
BUT I ALREADY LOVED SAKI TO BEGIN WITH, SO...
BA-BUMP

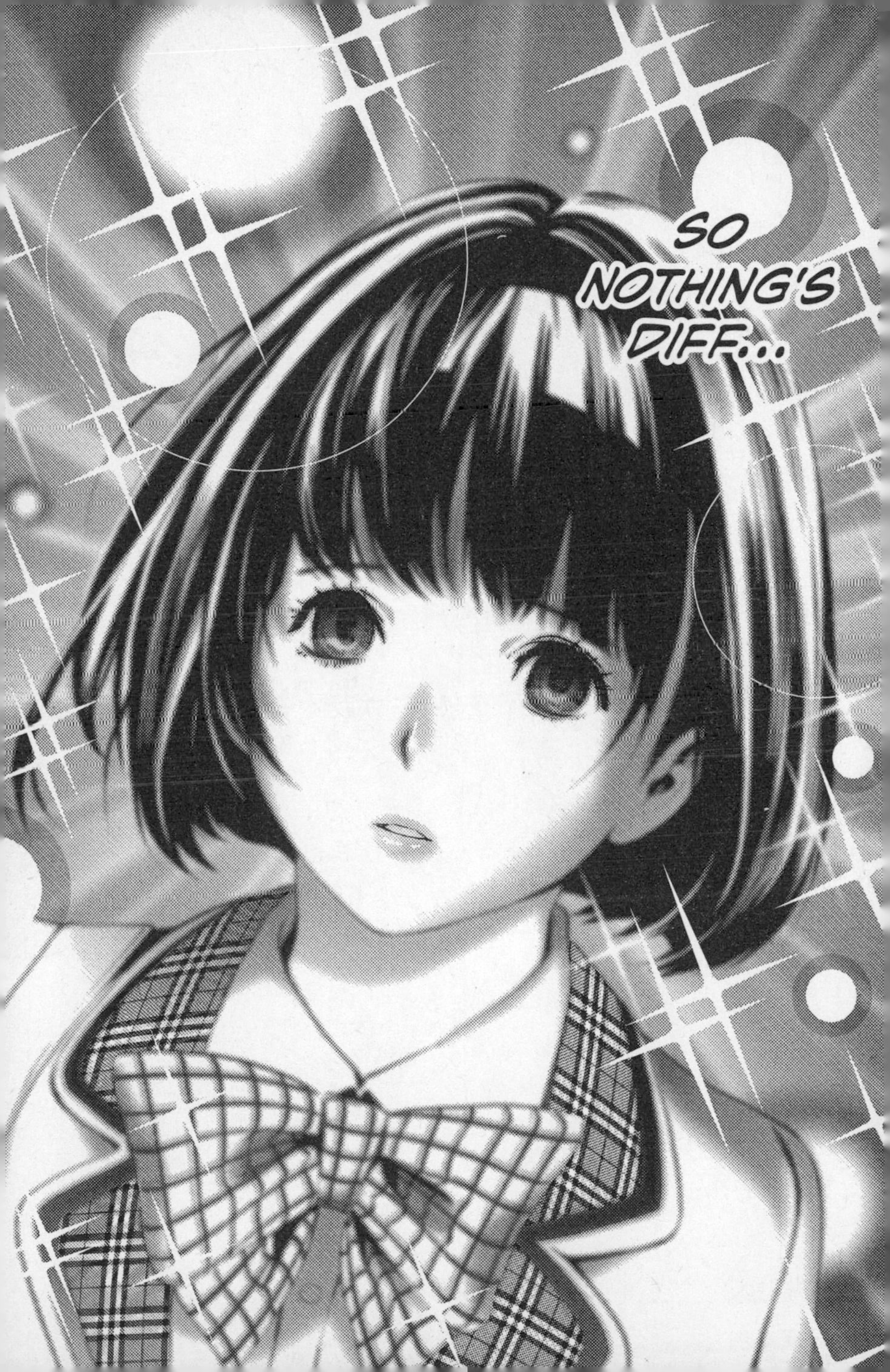
SO NOTHING'S DIFF...

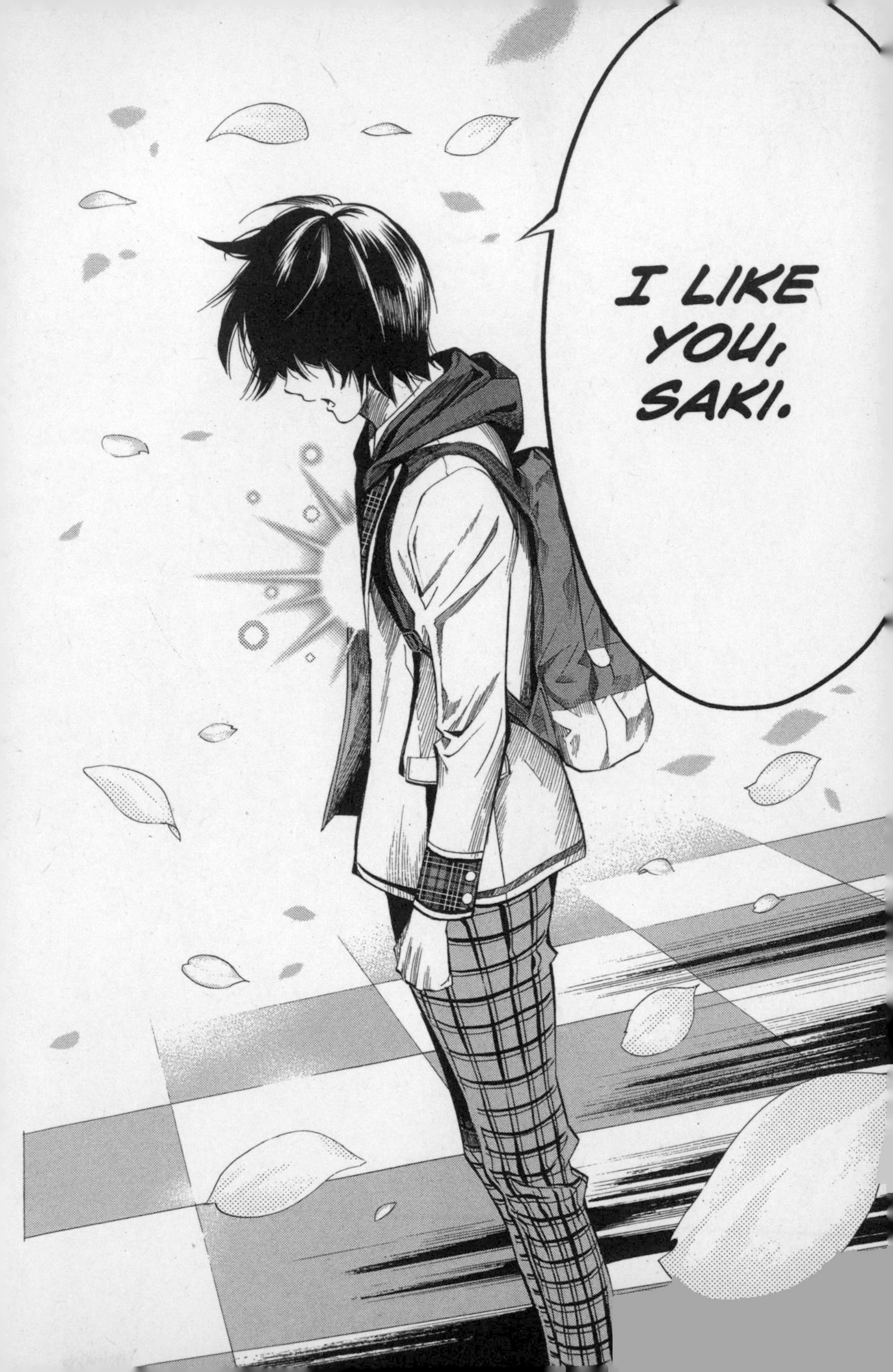
I LIKE YOU, SAKI.

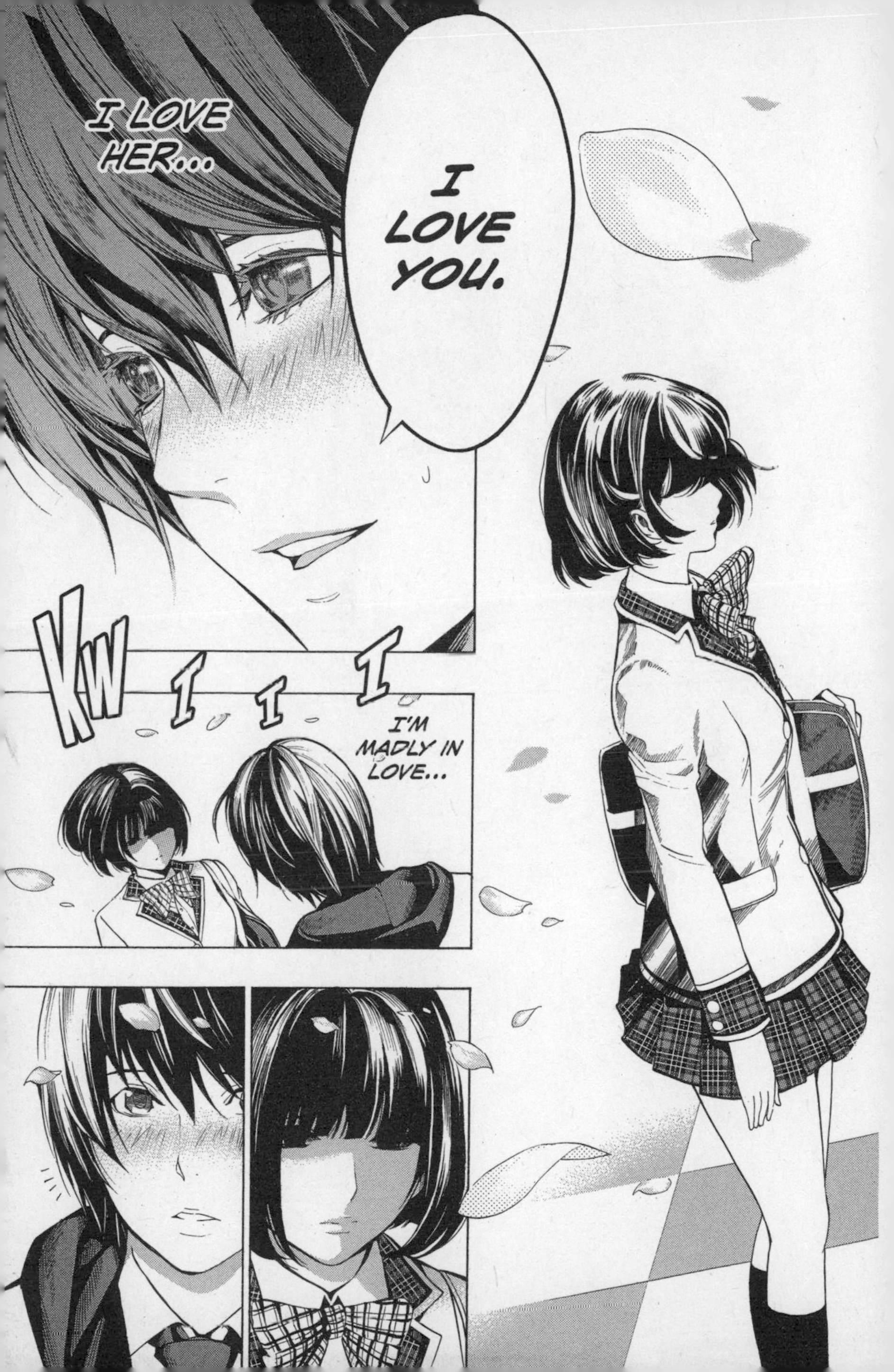
I LOVE YOU.
I LOVE HER...
KWIII
I'M MADLY IN LOVE...

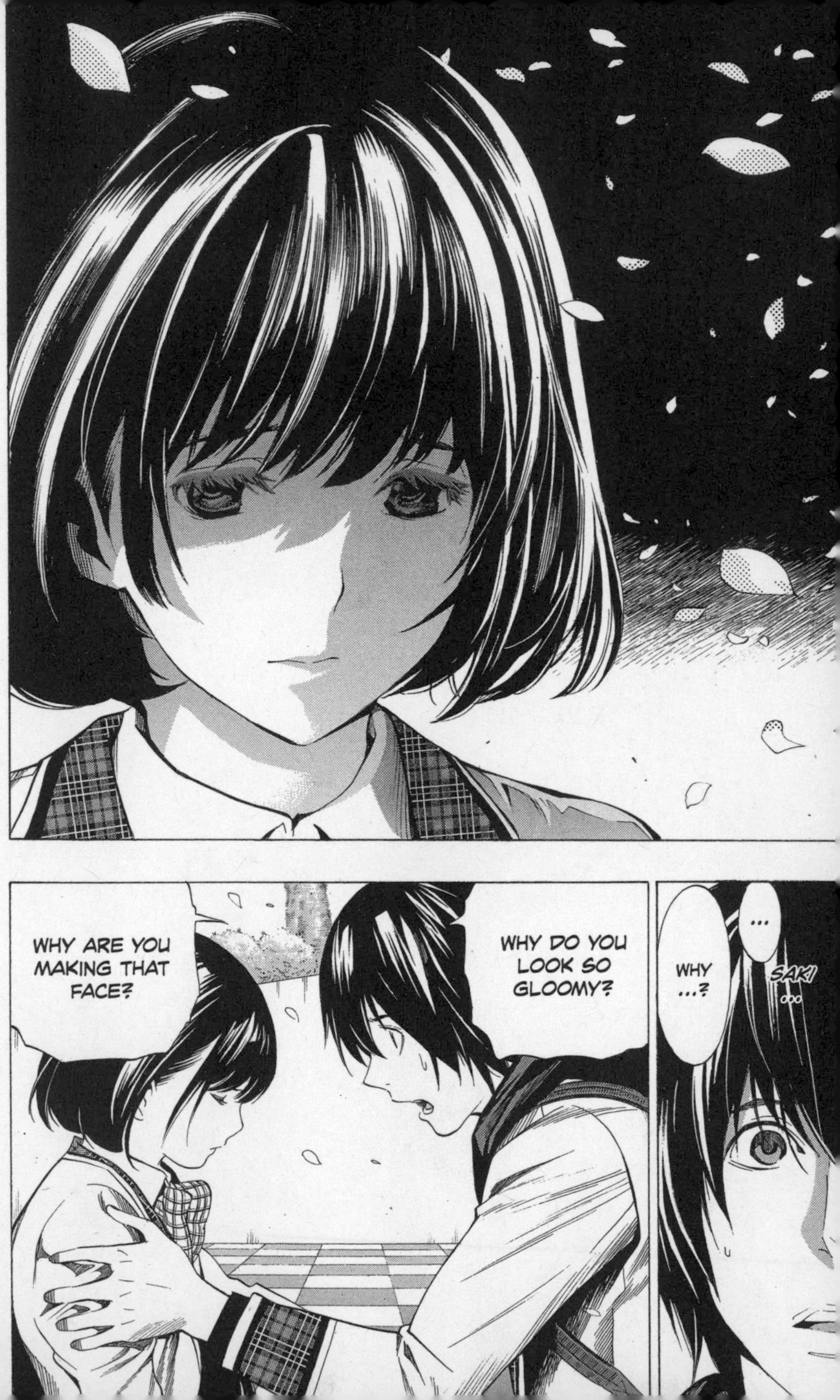
...
SAKI ...
WHY ...?
WHY DO YOU LOOK SO GLOOMY?
WHY ARE YOU MAKING THAT FACE?

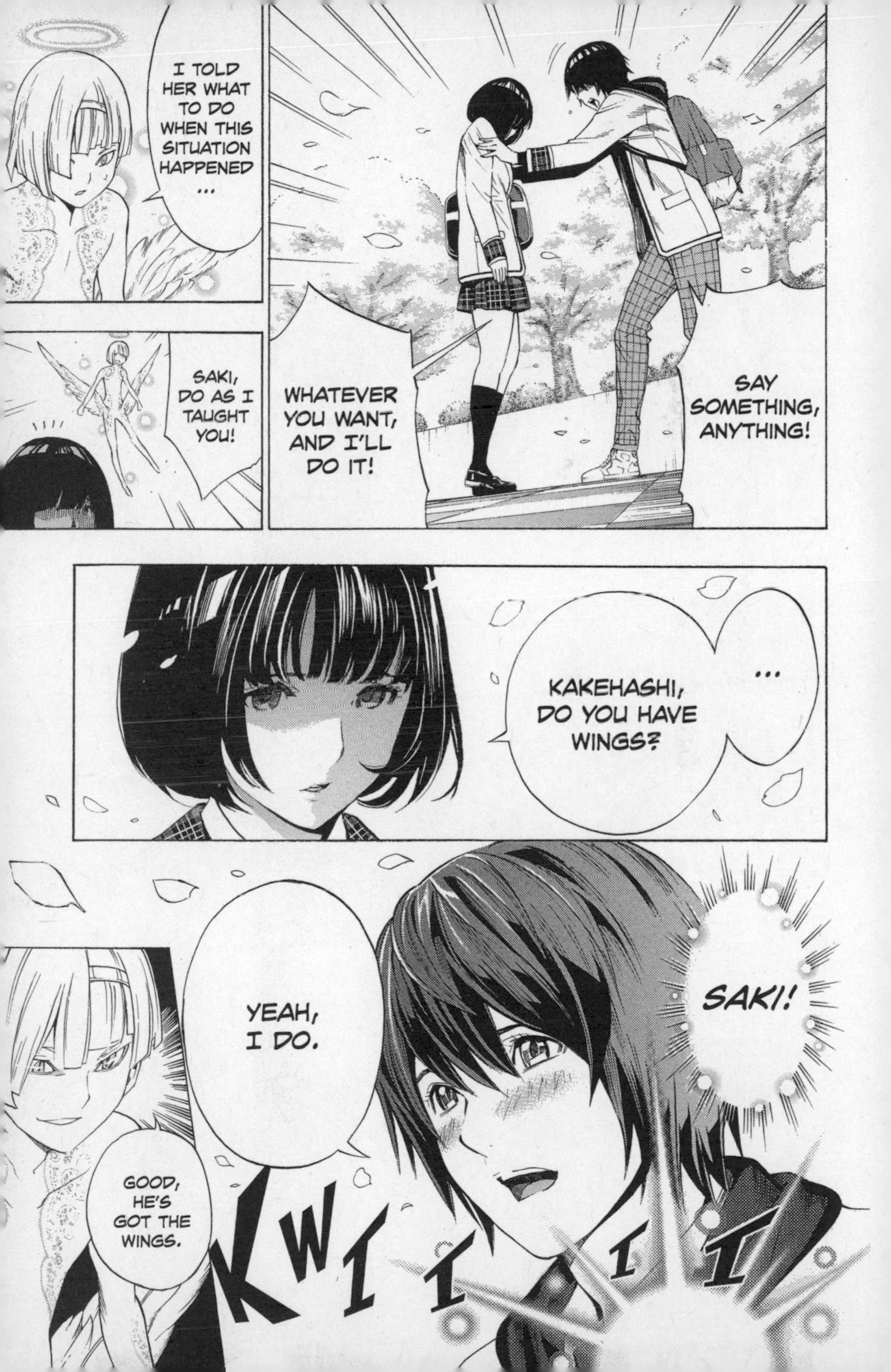
SAY SOMETHING, ANYTHING!
WHATEVER YOU WANT, AND I'LL DO IT!
I TOLD HER WHAT TO DO WHEN THIS SITUATION HAPPENED ...
SAKI, DO AS I TAUGHT YOU!
...
KAKEHASHI, DO YOU HAVE WINGS?
SAKI!
YEAH, I DO.
GOOD, HE'S GOT THE WINGS.
KWIIII

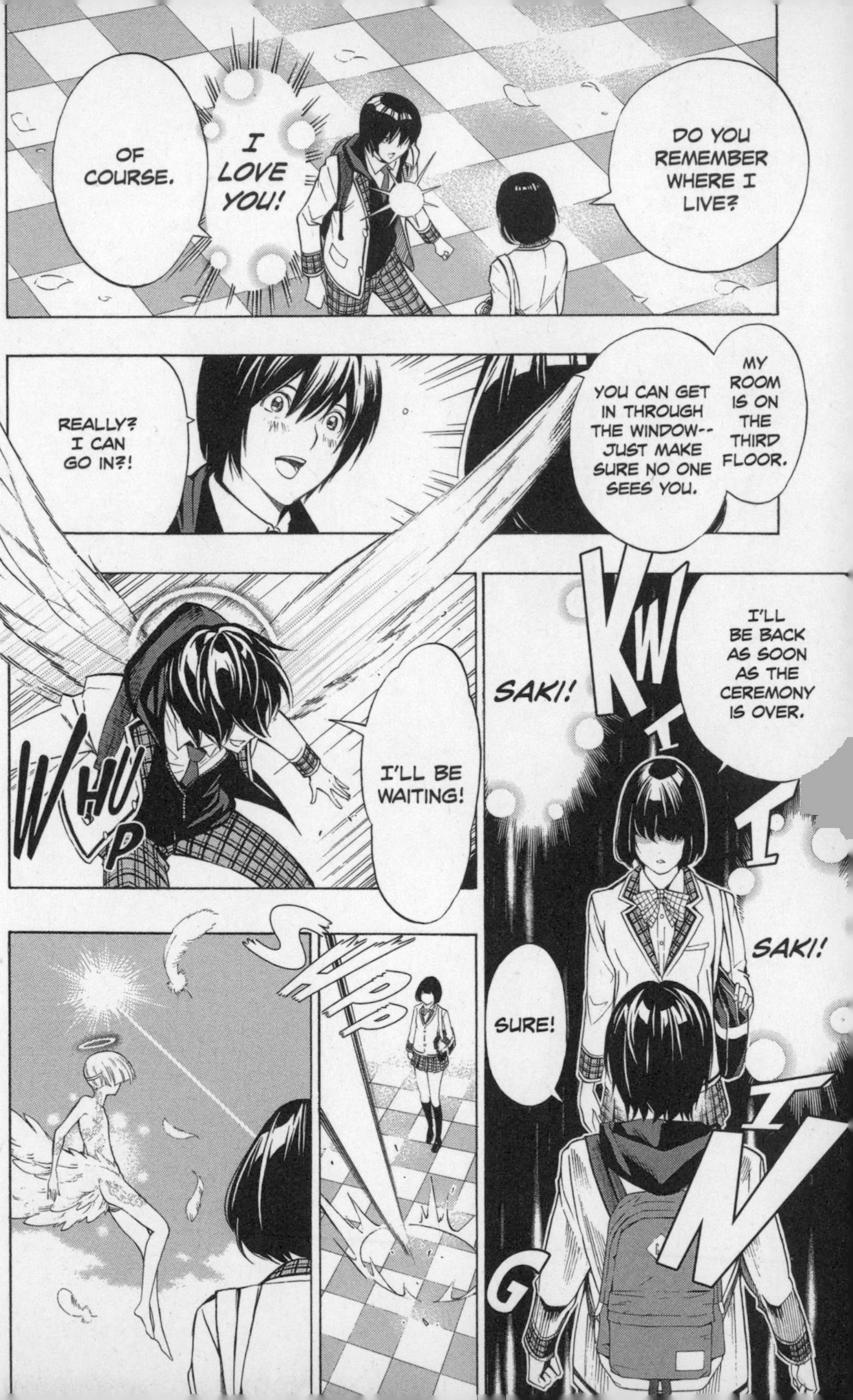
DO YOU REMEMBER WHERE I LIVE?
I LOVE YOU!
OF COURSE.
MY ROOM IS ON THE THIRD FLOOR.
YOU CAN GET IN THROUGH THE WINDOW-- JUST MAKE SURE NO ONE SEES YOU.
REALLY? I CAN GO IN?!
I'LL BE BACK AS SOON AS THE CEREMONY IS OVER.
KWIIING
SAKI!
SAKI!
SURE!
I'LL BE WAITING!
WHUP
SHPP

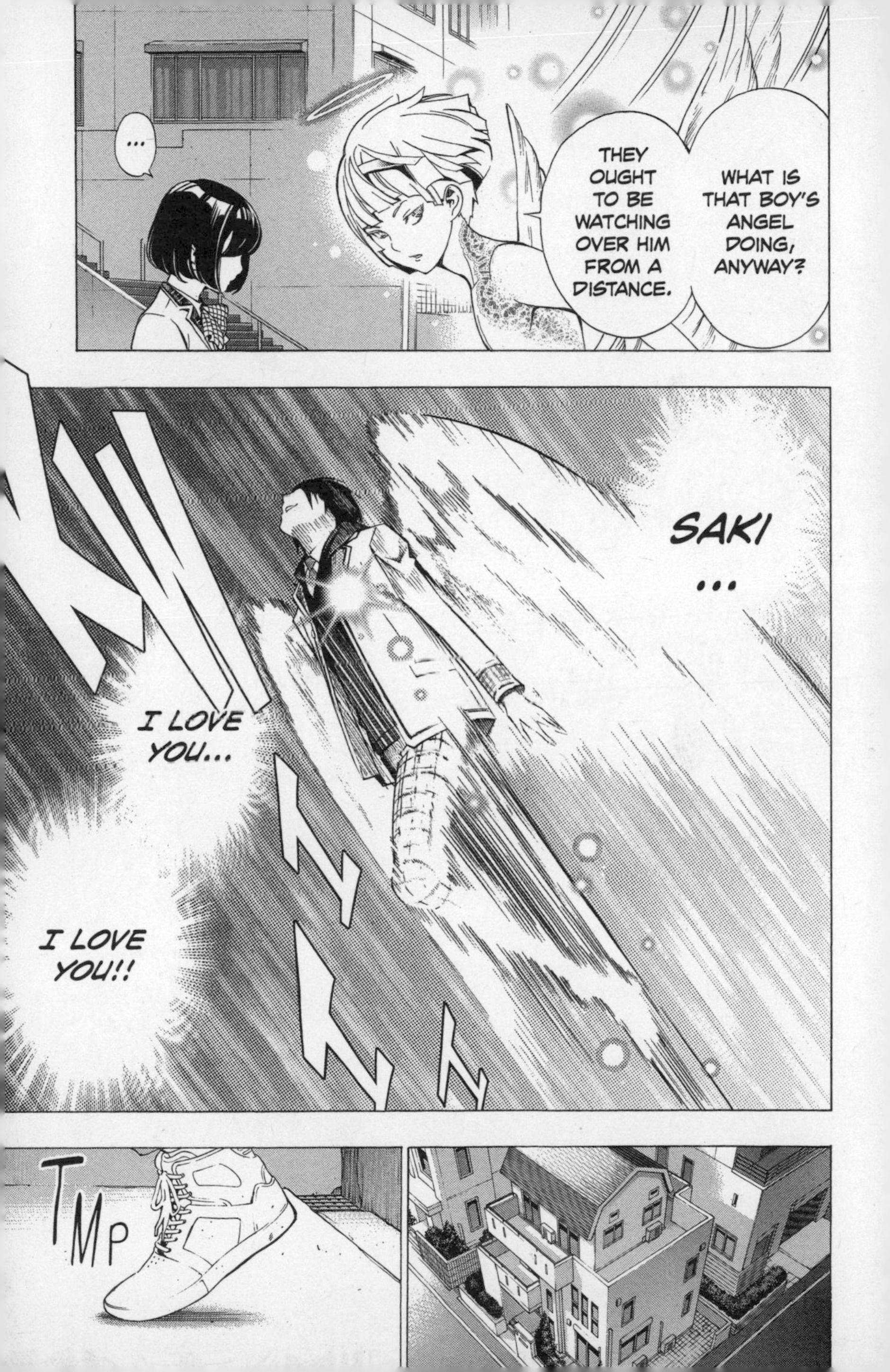
WHAT IS THAT BOY'S ANGEL DOING, ANYWAY?
THEY OUGHT TO BE WATCHING OVER HIM FROM A DISTANCE.
...
SAKI ...
I LOVE YOU...
I LOVE YOU!!
TMP

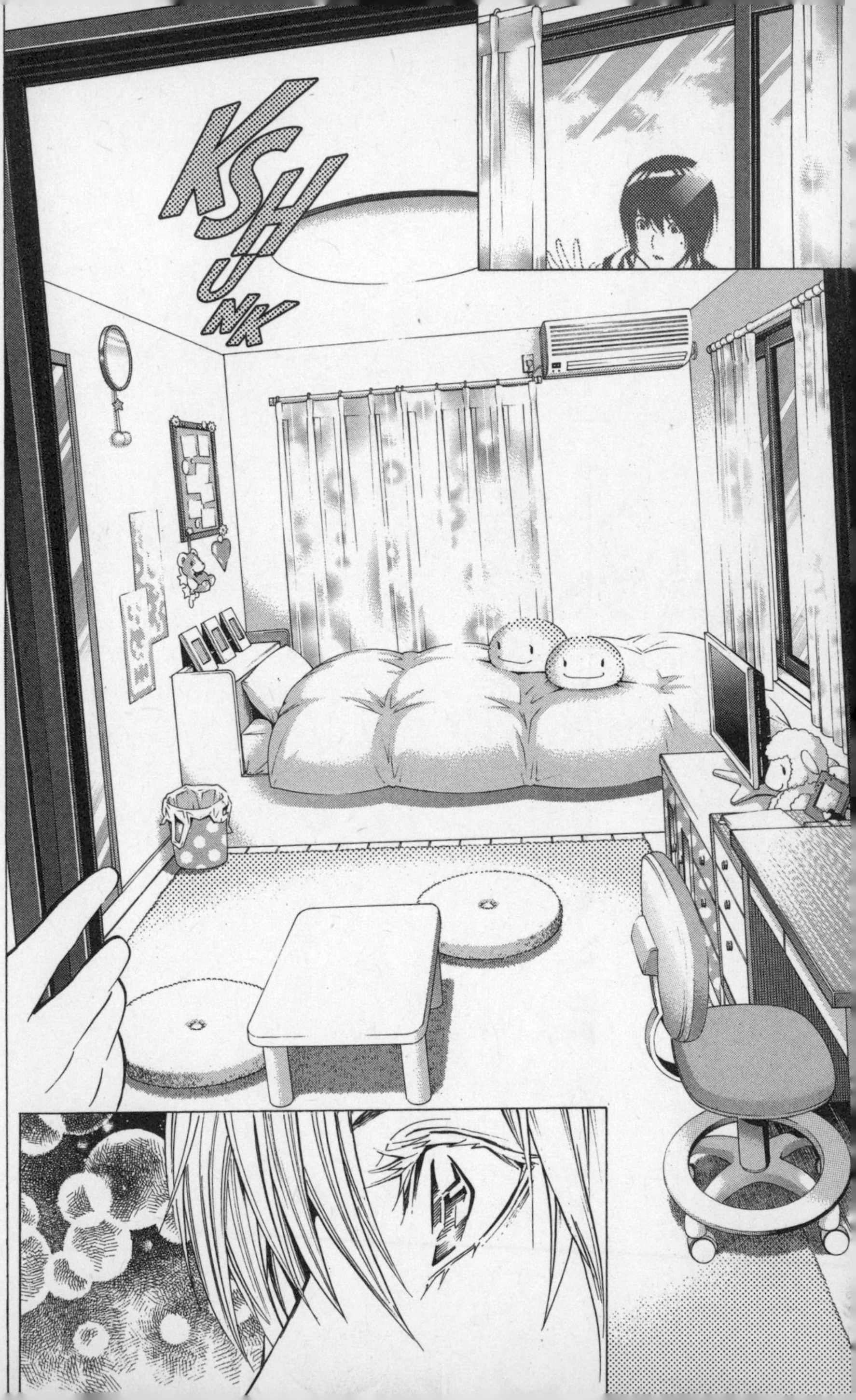
KSHUNK

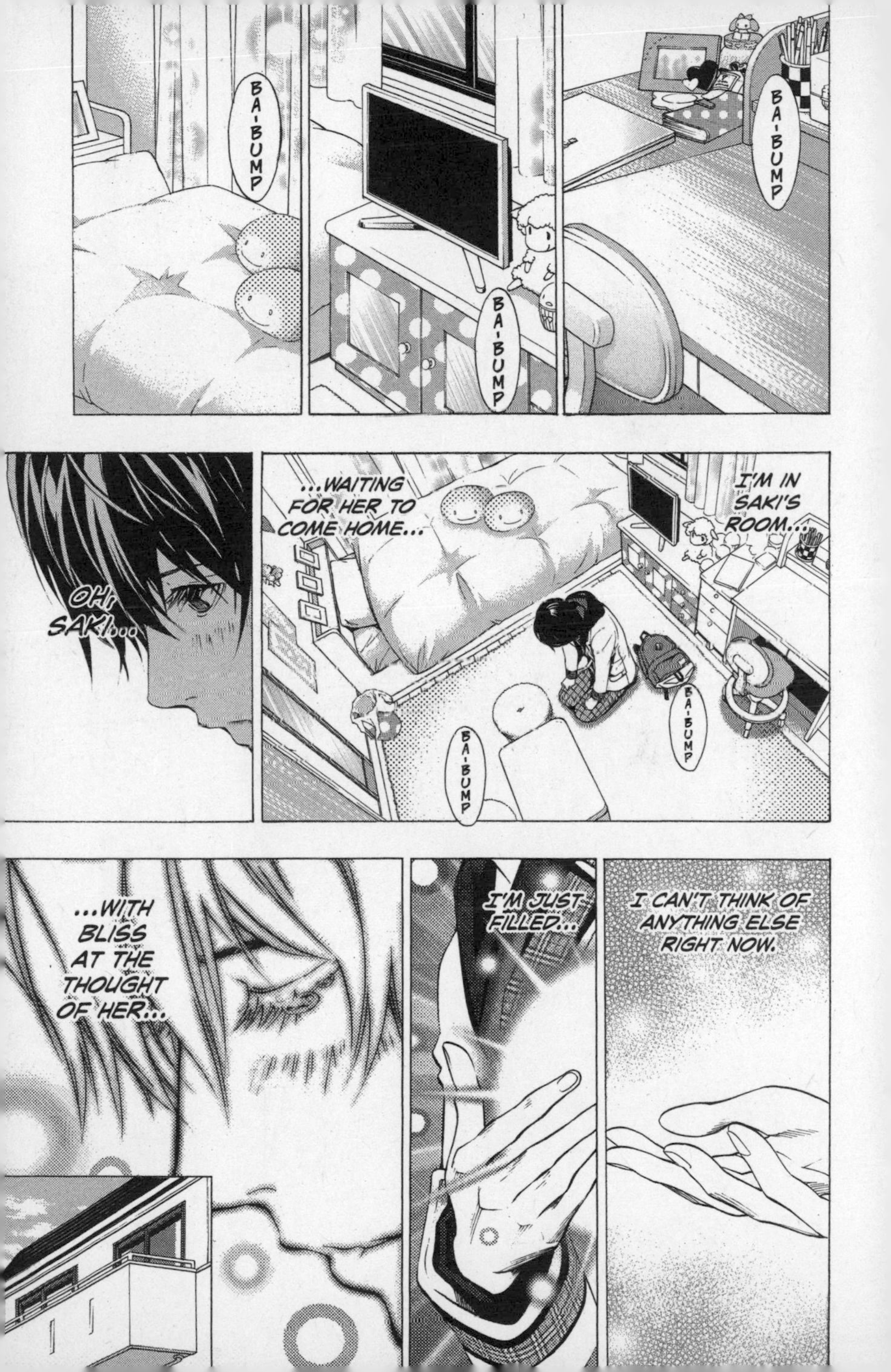

BA-BUMP
BA-BUMP
BA-BUMP
I'M IN SAKI'S ROOM...
...WAITING FOR HER TO COME HOME...
BA-BUMP
BA-BUMP
OH, SAKI...
I CAN'T THINK OF ANYTHING ELSE RIGHT NOW.
I'M JUST FILLED...
...WITH BLISS AT THE THOUGHT OF HER...

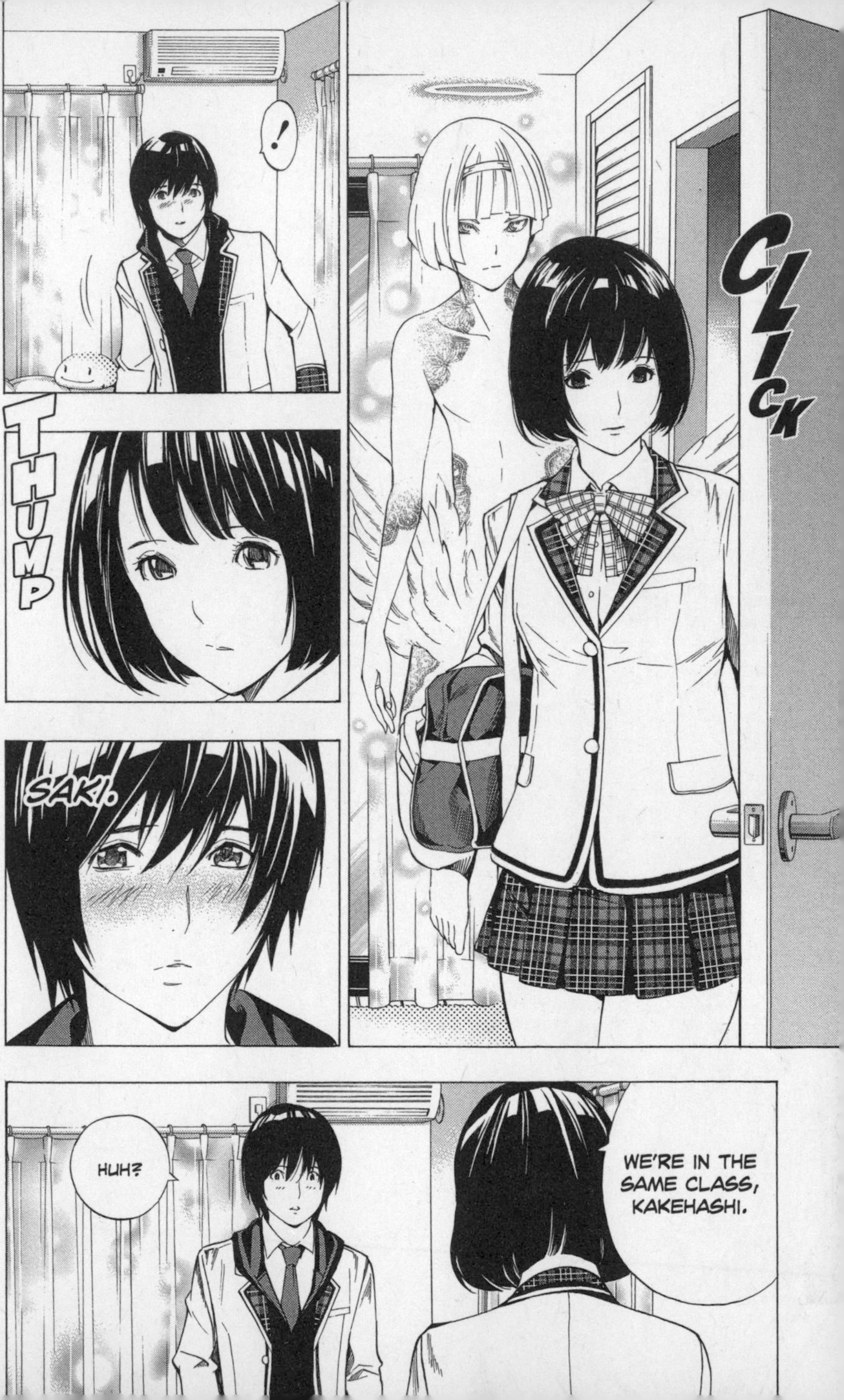
CLICK
!
THUMP
SAKI.
WE'RE IN THE SAME CLASS, KAKEHASHI.
HUH?

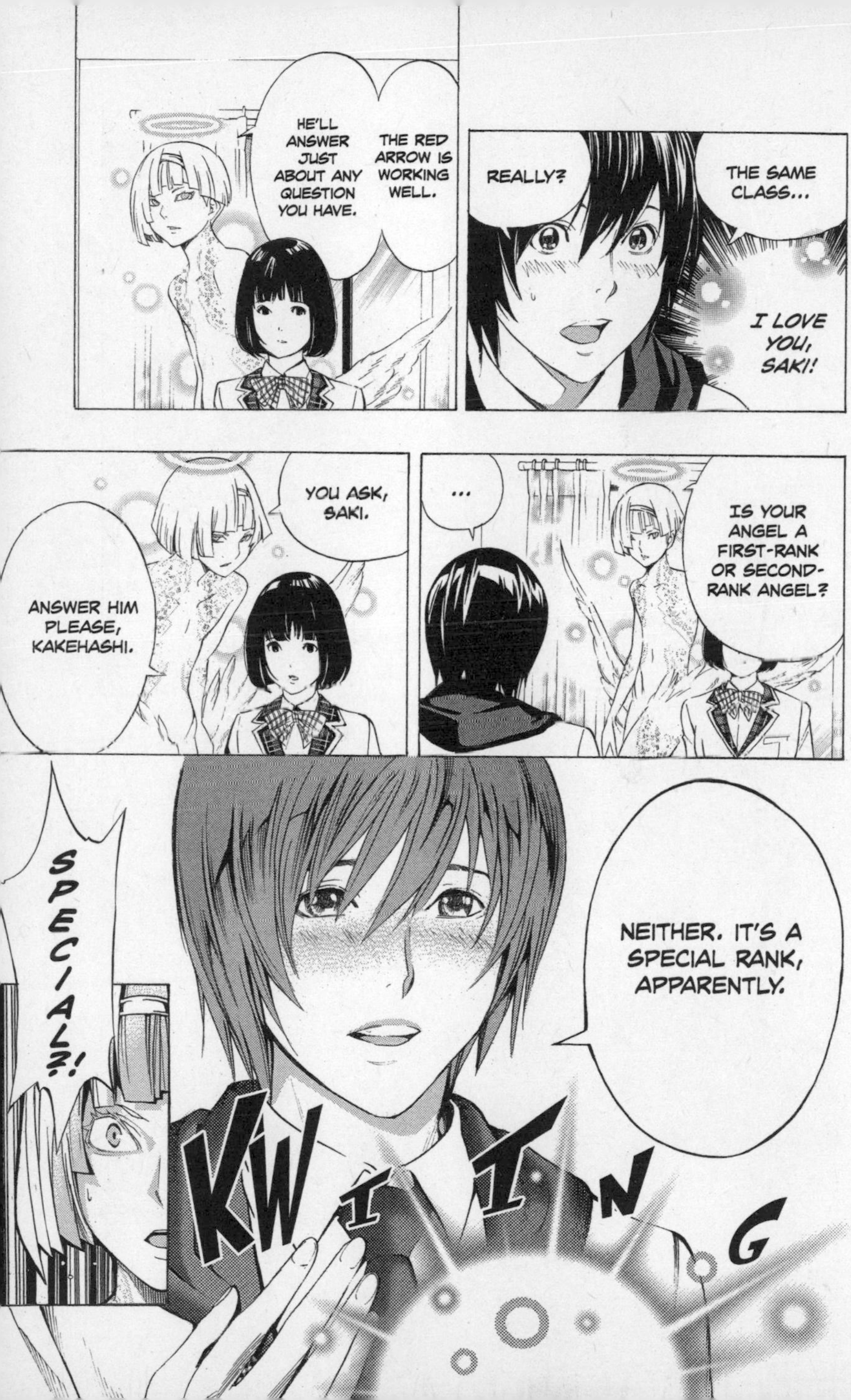
THE SAME CLASS...
REALLY?
I LOVE YOU, SAKI!
THE RED ARROW IS WORKING WELL.
HE'LL ANSWER JUST ABOUT ANY QUESTION YOU HAVE.
IS YOUR ANGEL A FIRST-RANK OR SECOND-RANK ANGEL?
...
YOU ASK, SAKI.
ANSWER HIM PLEASE, KAKEHASHI.
NEITHER. IT'S A SPECIAL RANK, APPARENTLY.
KWIING
SPECIAL?!

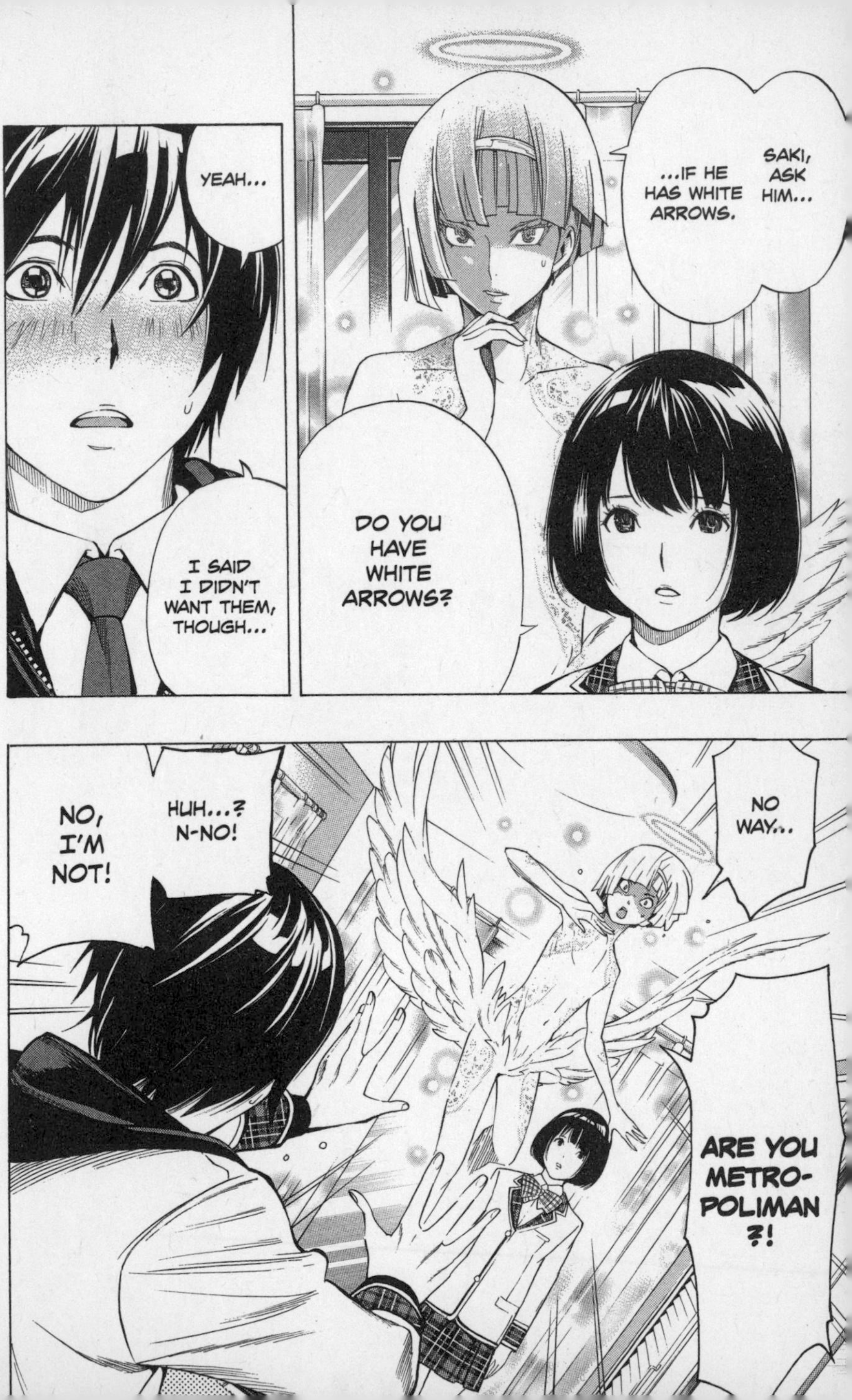
SAKI, ASK HIM...
...IF HE HAS WHITE ARROWS.
DO YOU HAVE WHITE ARROWS?
YEAH...
I SAID I DIDN'T WANT THEM, THOUGH...
NO WAY...
ARE YOU METRO-POLIMAN?!
HUH...? N-NO!
NO, I'M NOT!

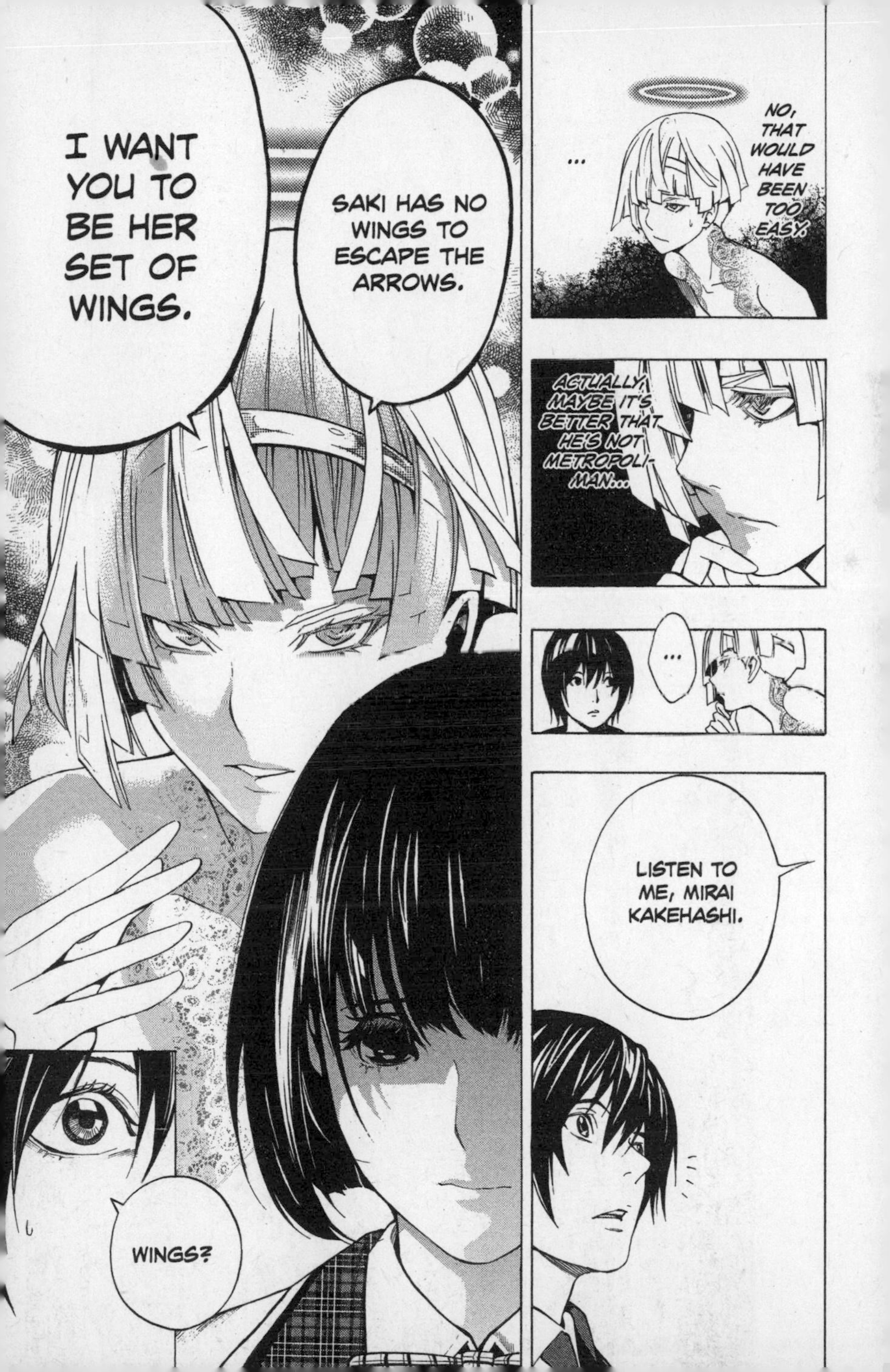
NO, THAT WOULD HAVE BEEN TOO EASY.
...
ACTUALLY, MAYBE IT'S BETTER THAT HE'S NOT METROPOLI-MAN...
...
LISTEN TO ME, MIRAI KAKEHASHI.
SAKI HAS NO WINGS TO ESCAPE THE ARROWS.
I WANT YOU TO BE HER SET OF WINGS.
WINGS?

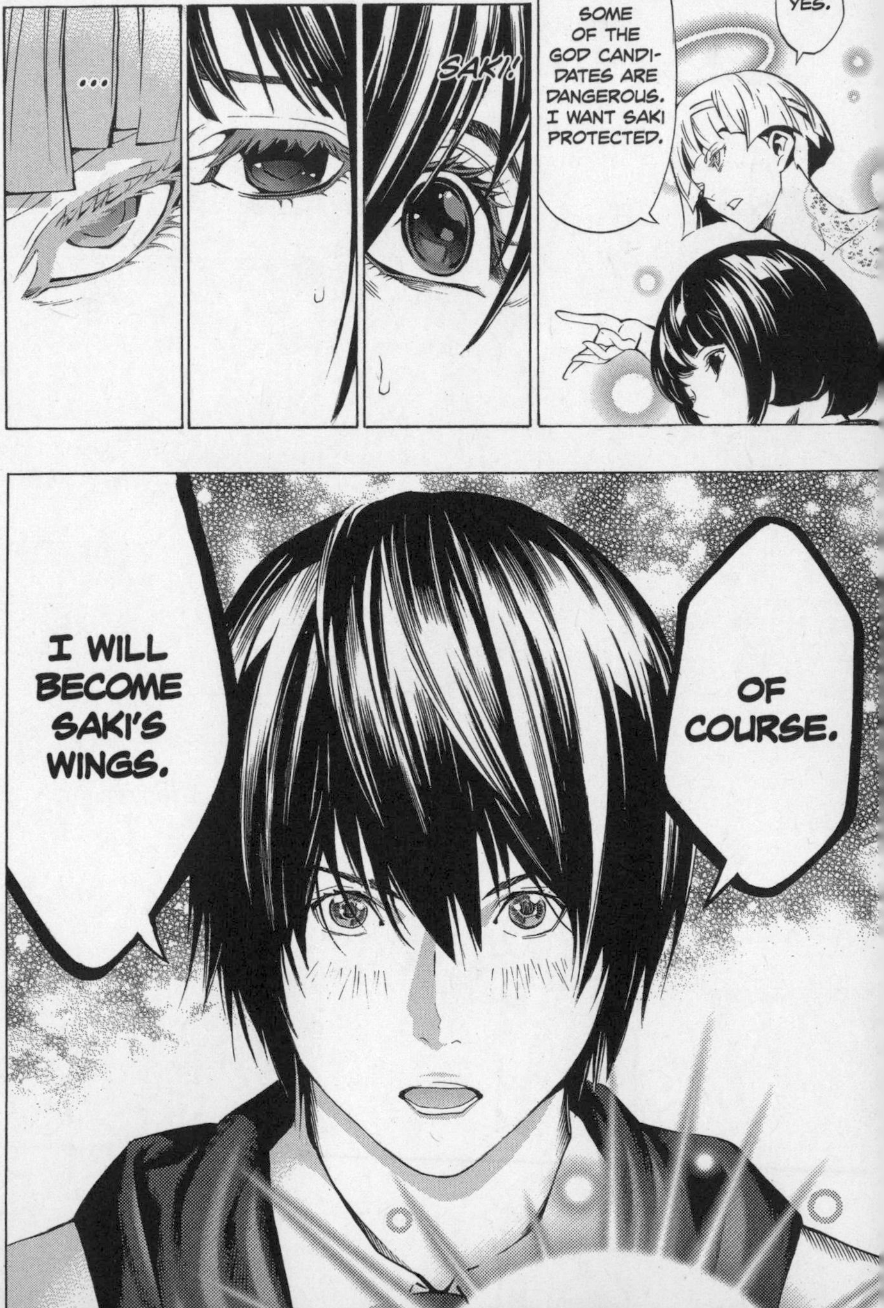
YES.
SOME OF THE GOD CANDIDATES ARE DANGEROUS. I WANT SAKI PROTECTED.
SAKI!
...
OF COURSE.
I WILL BECOME SAKI'S WINGS.

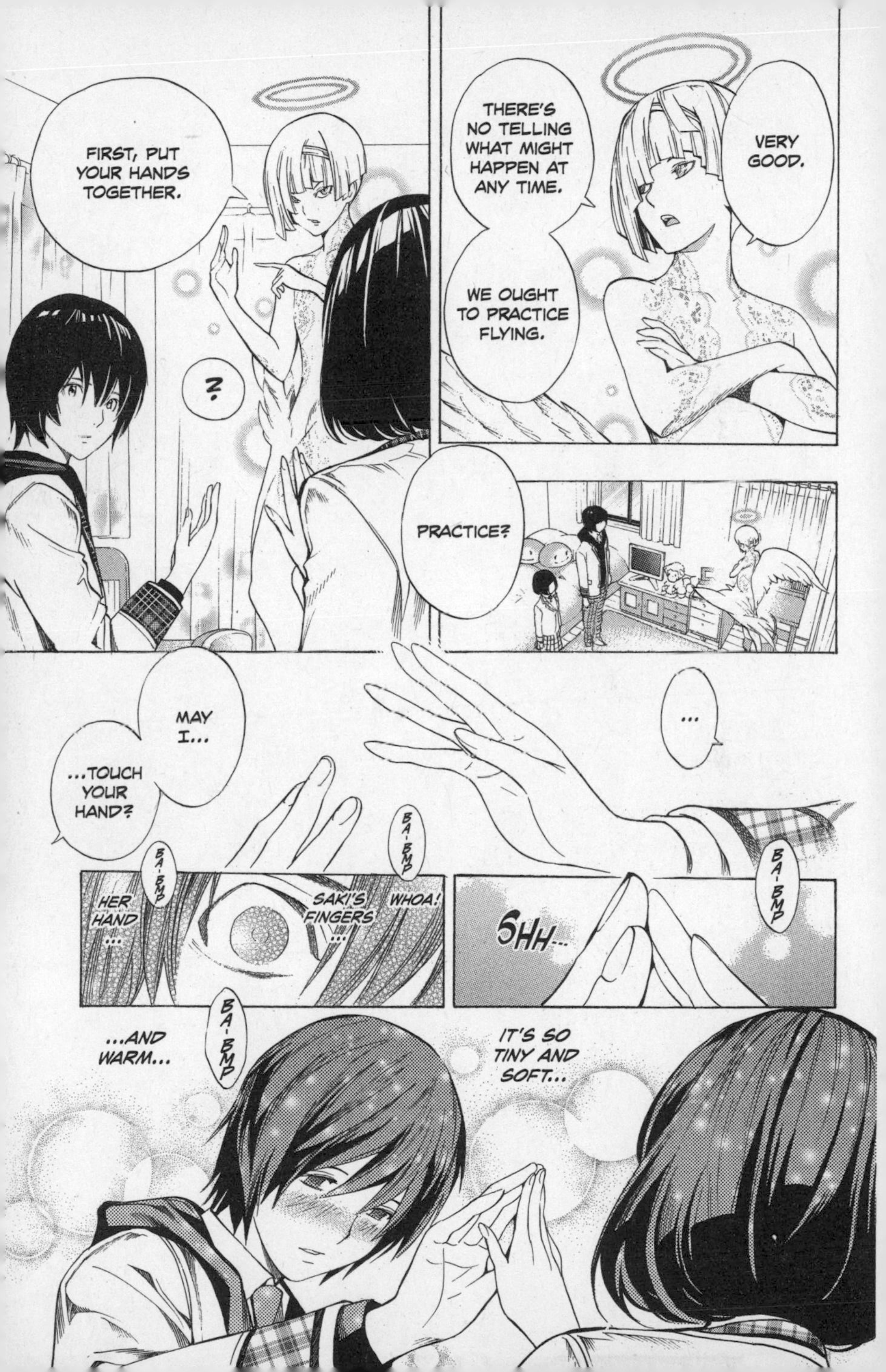
VERY GOOD.
THERE'S NO TELLING WHAT MIGHT HAPPEN AT ANY TIME.
WE OUGHT TO PRACTICE FLYING.
PRACTICE?
FIRST, PUT YOUR HANDS TOGETHER.
?
...
MAY I...
...TOUCH YOUR HAND?
BA-BMP
BA-BMP
SHH...
BA-BMP
WHOA!
SAKI'S FINGERS...
HER HAND...
BA-BMP
IT'S SO TINY AND SOFT...
BA-BMP
...AND WARM...

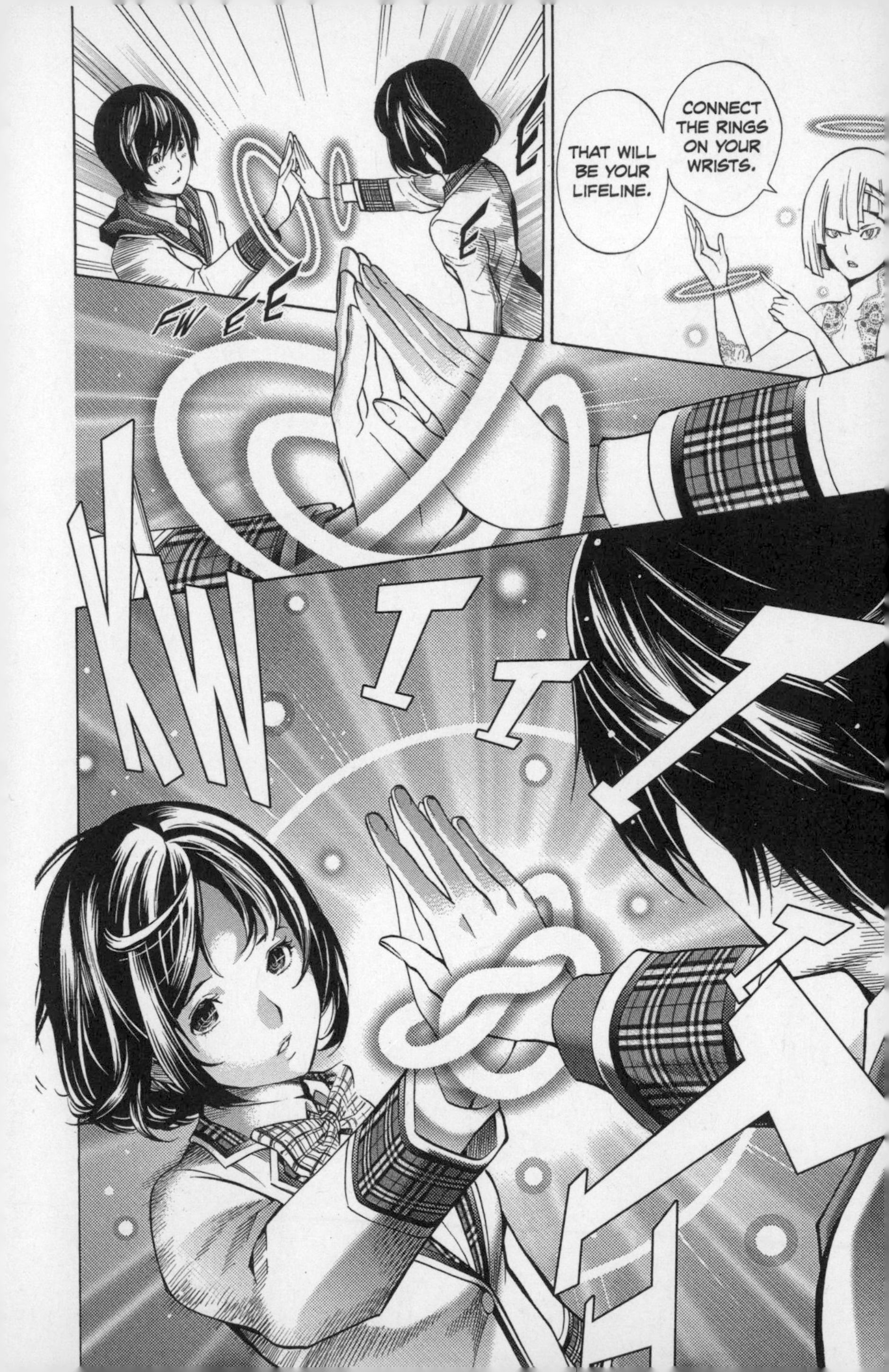
CONNECT THE RINGS ON YOUR WRISTS.
THAT WILL BE YOUR LIFELINE.
FWEEEE
KWII

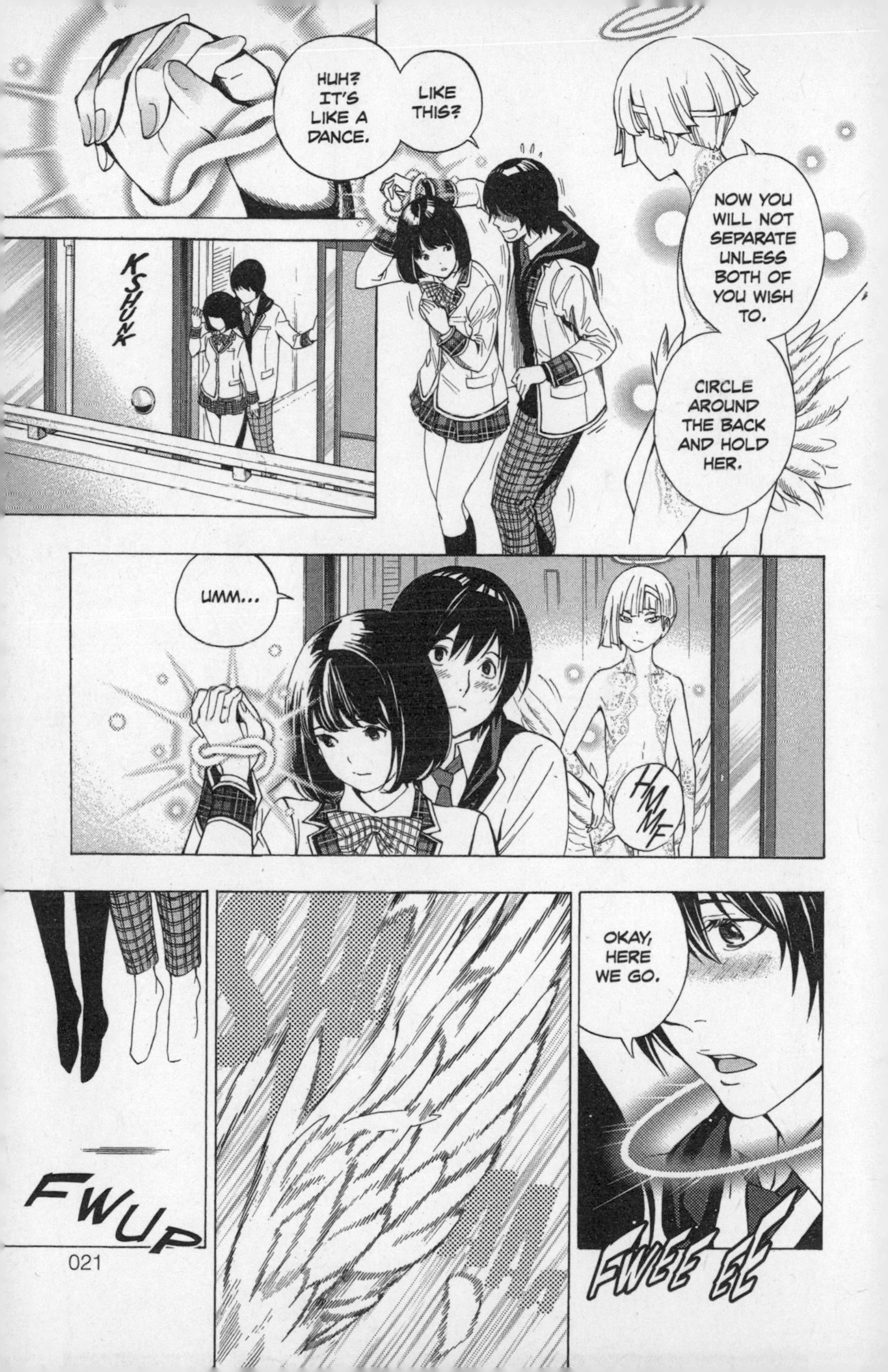
NOW YOU WILL NOT SEPARATE UNLESS BOTH OF YOU WISH TO.
CIRCLE AROUND THE BACK AND HOLD HER.
LIKE THIS?
HUH? IT'S LIKE A DANCE.
KSHUNK
UMM...
HMMF
OKAY, HERE WE GO.
FWEE EE
FWUP

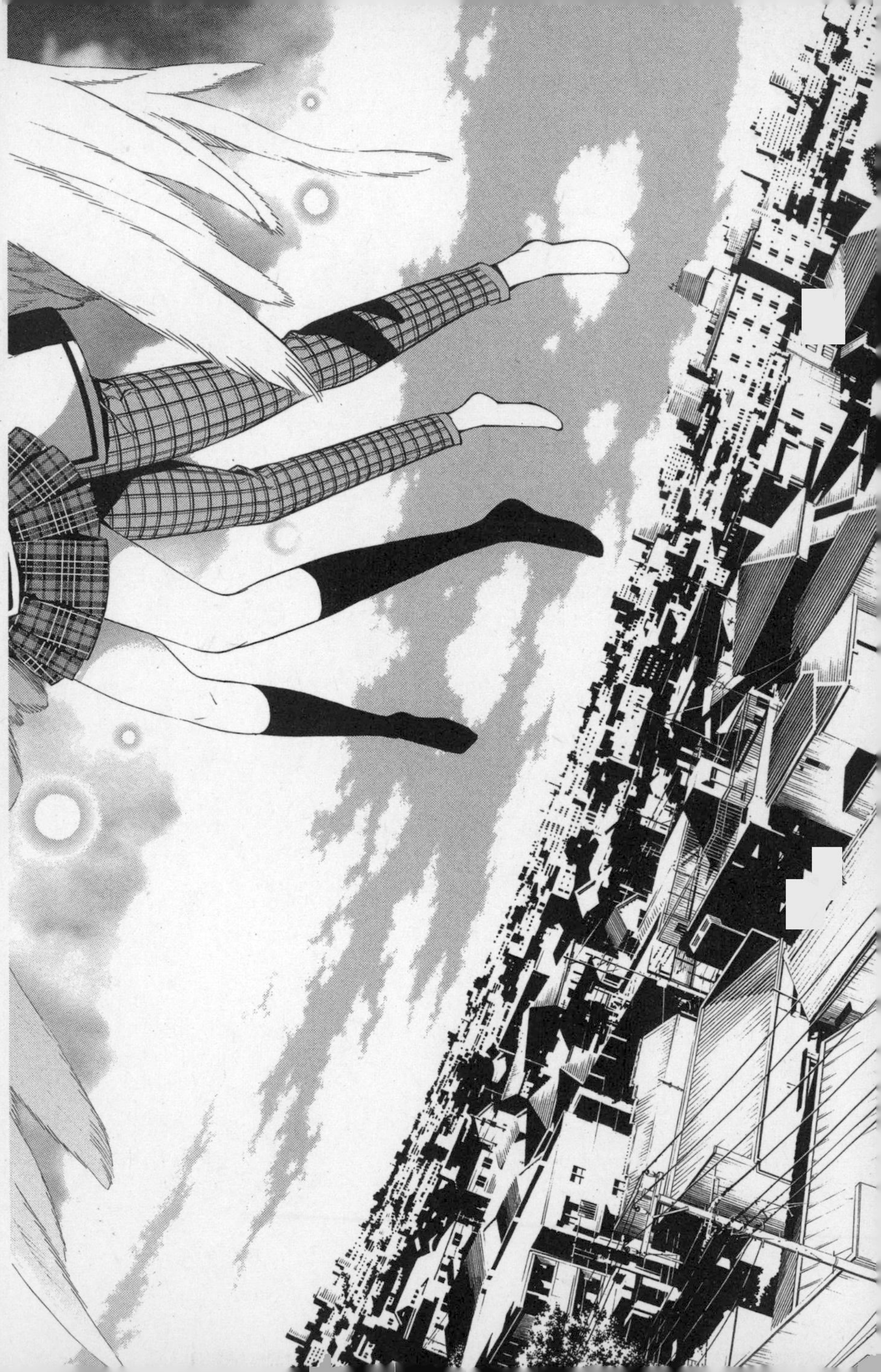

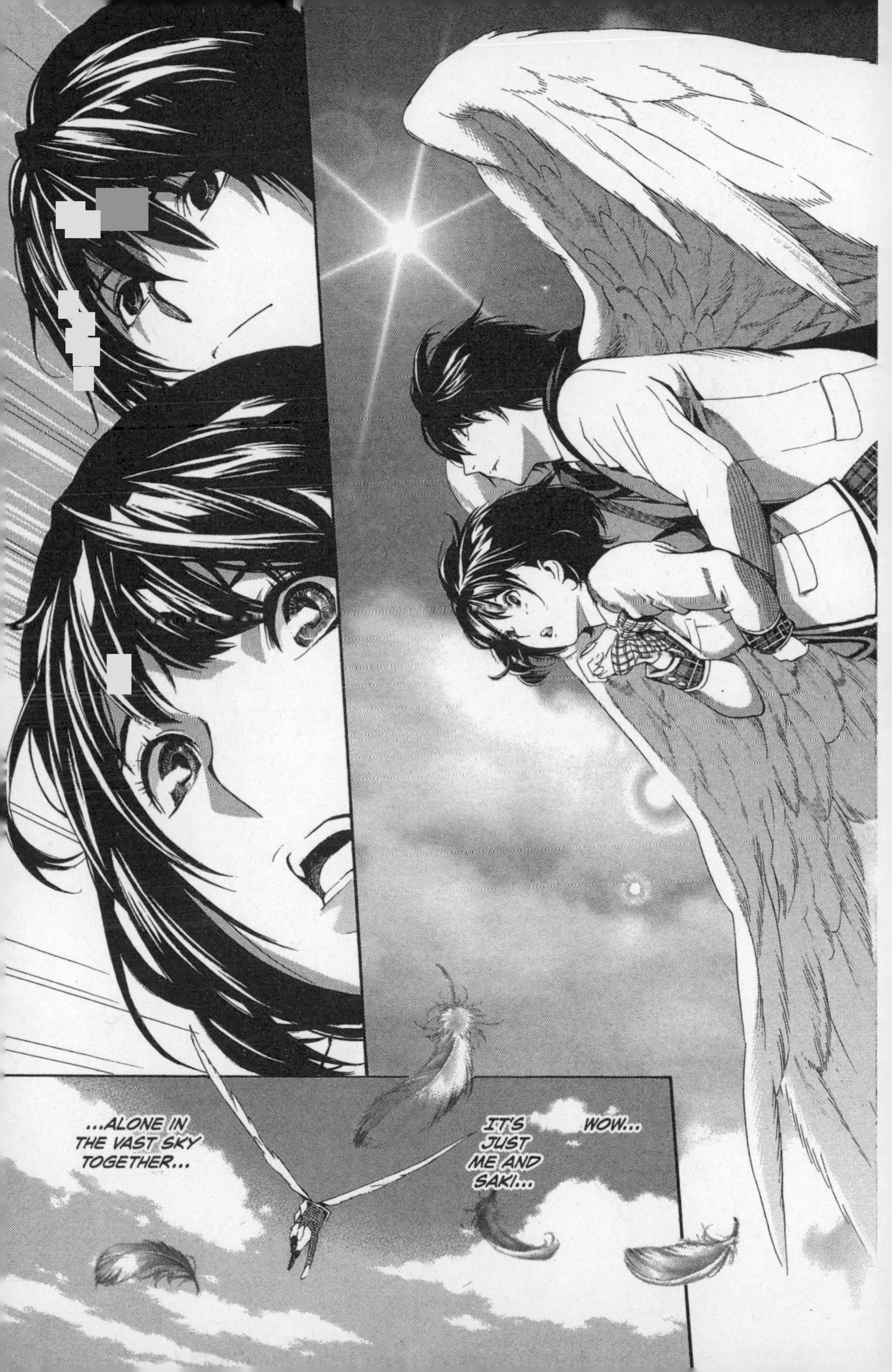
WOW...
IT'S JUST ME AND SAKI...
...ALONE IN THE VAST SKY TOGETHER...

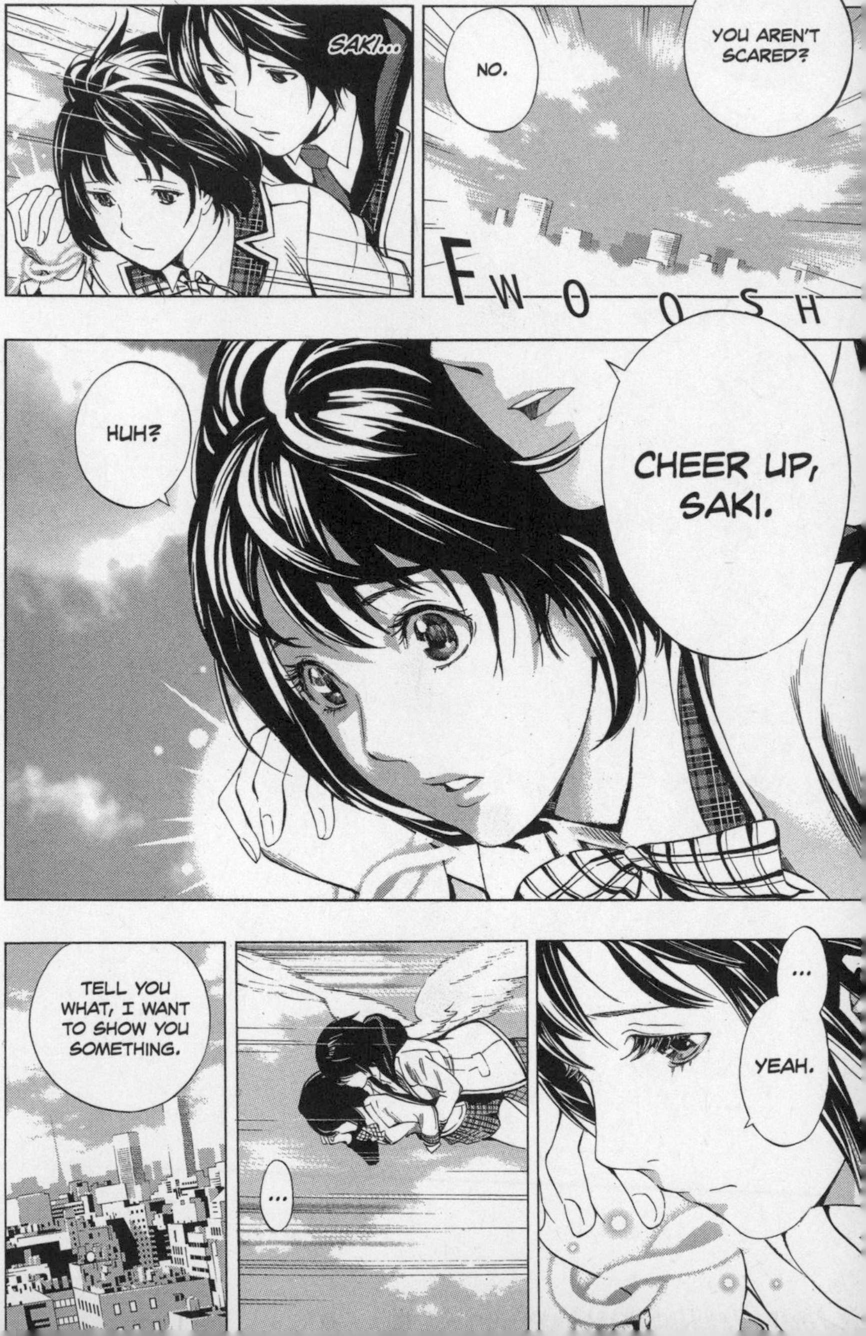
YOU AREN'T SCARED?
NO.
FWOOSH
SAKI...
CHEER UP, SAKI.
HUH?
...
YEAH.
...
TELL YOU WHAT, I WANT TO SHOW YOU SOMETHING.

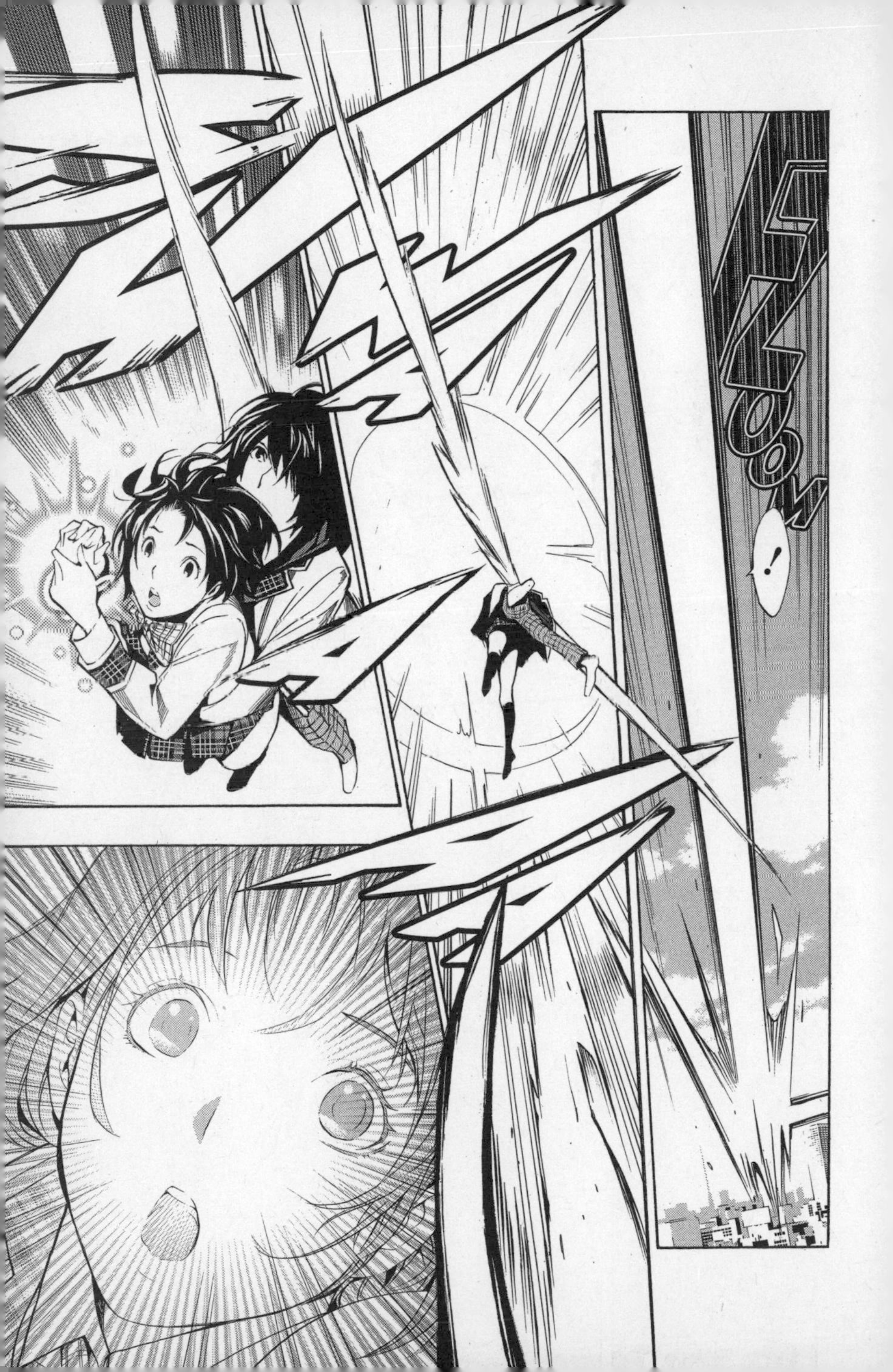
SHOOOM
!

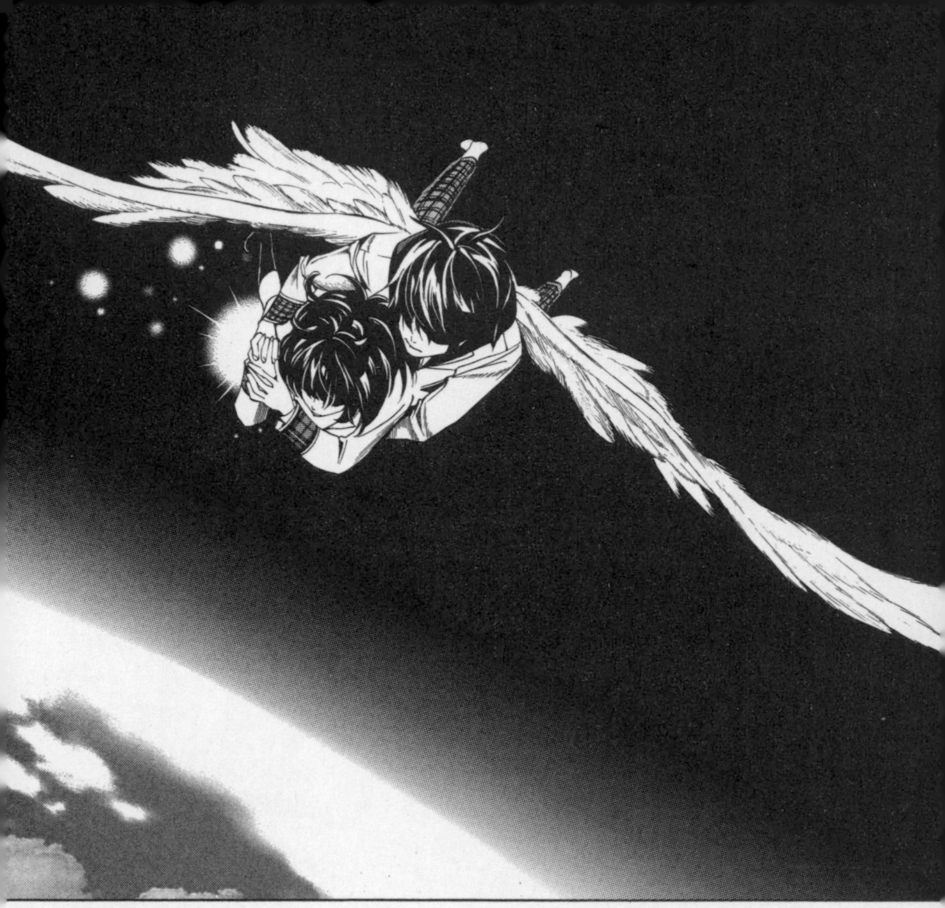
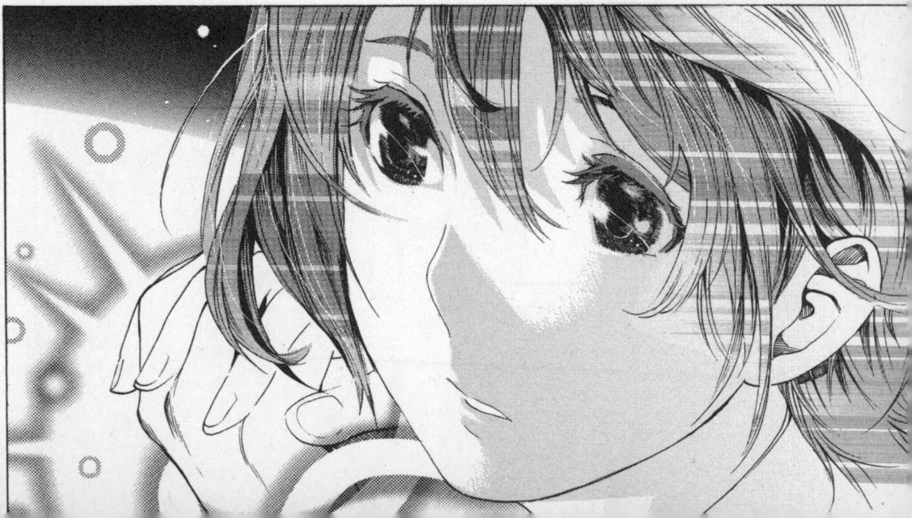

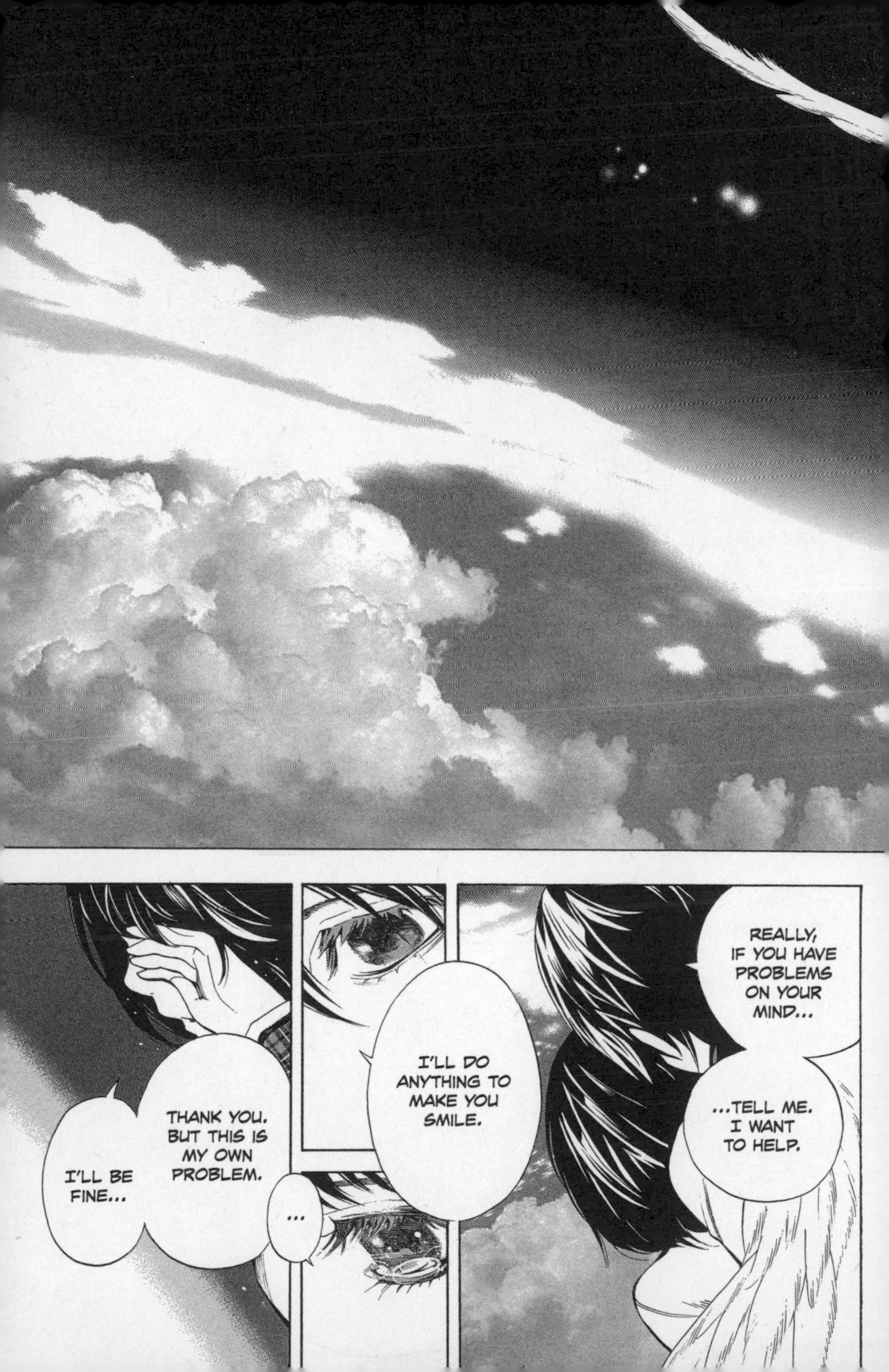
REALLY, IF YOU HAVE PROBLEMS ON YOUR MIND...
...TELL ME. I WANT TO HELP.
I'LL DO ANYTHING TO MAKE YOU SMILE.
...
THANK YOU. BUT THIS IS MY OWN PROBLEM.
I'LL BE FINE...

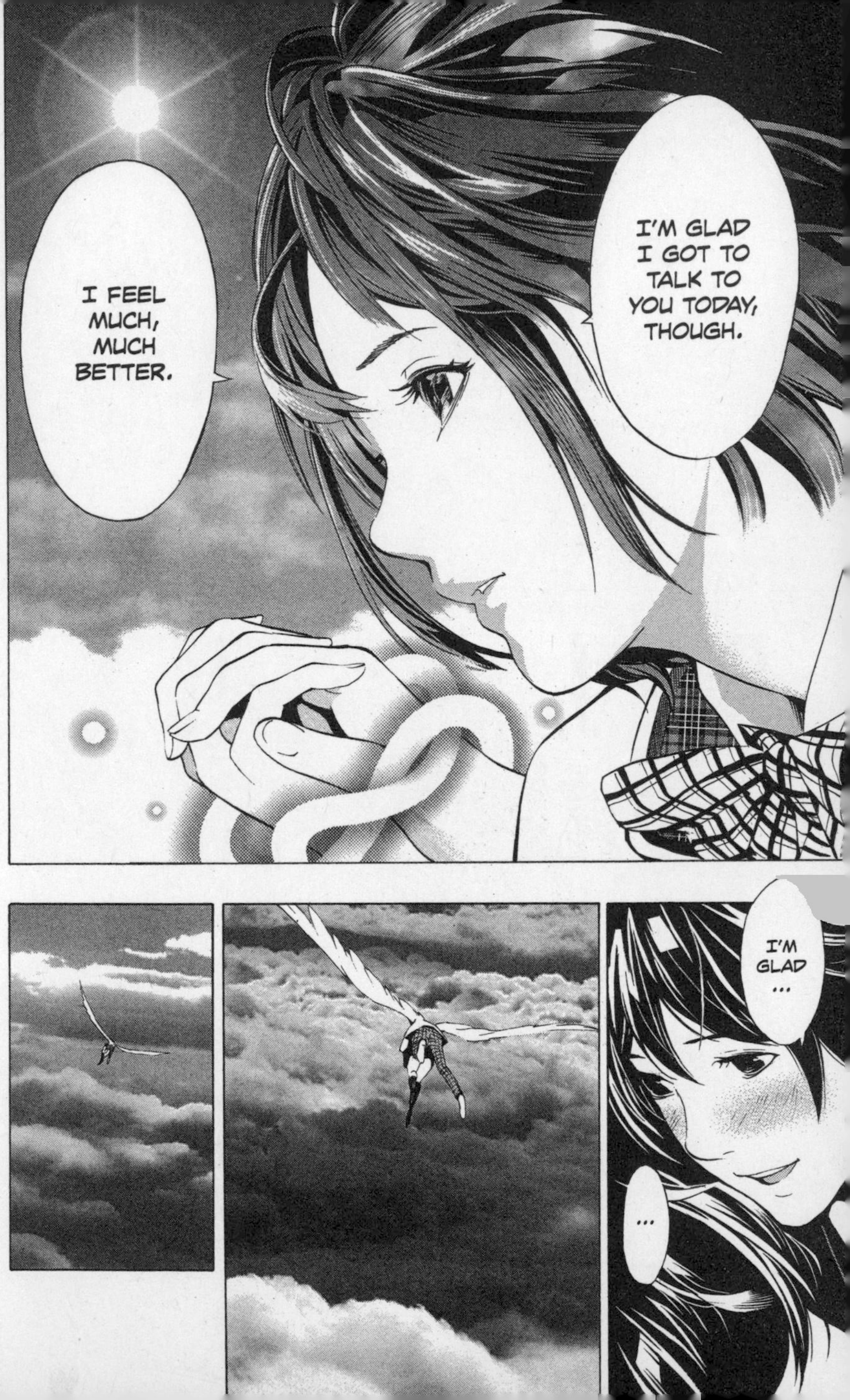
I'M GLAD I GOT TO TALK TO YOU TODAY, THOUGH.
I FEEL MUCH, MUCH BETTER.
I'M GLAD ...
...

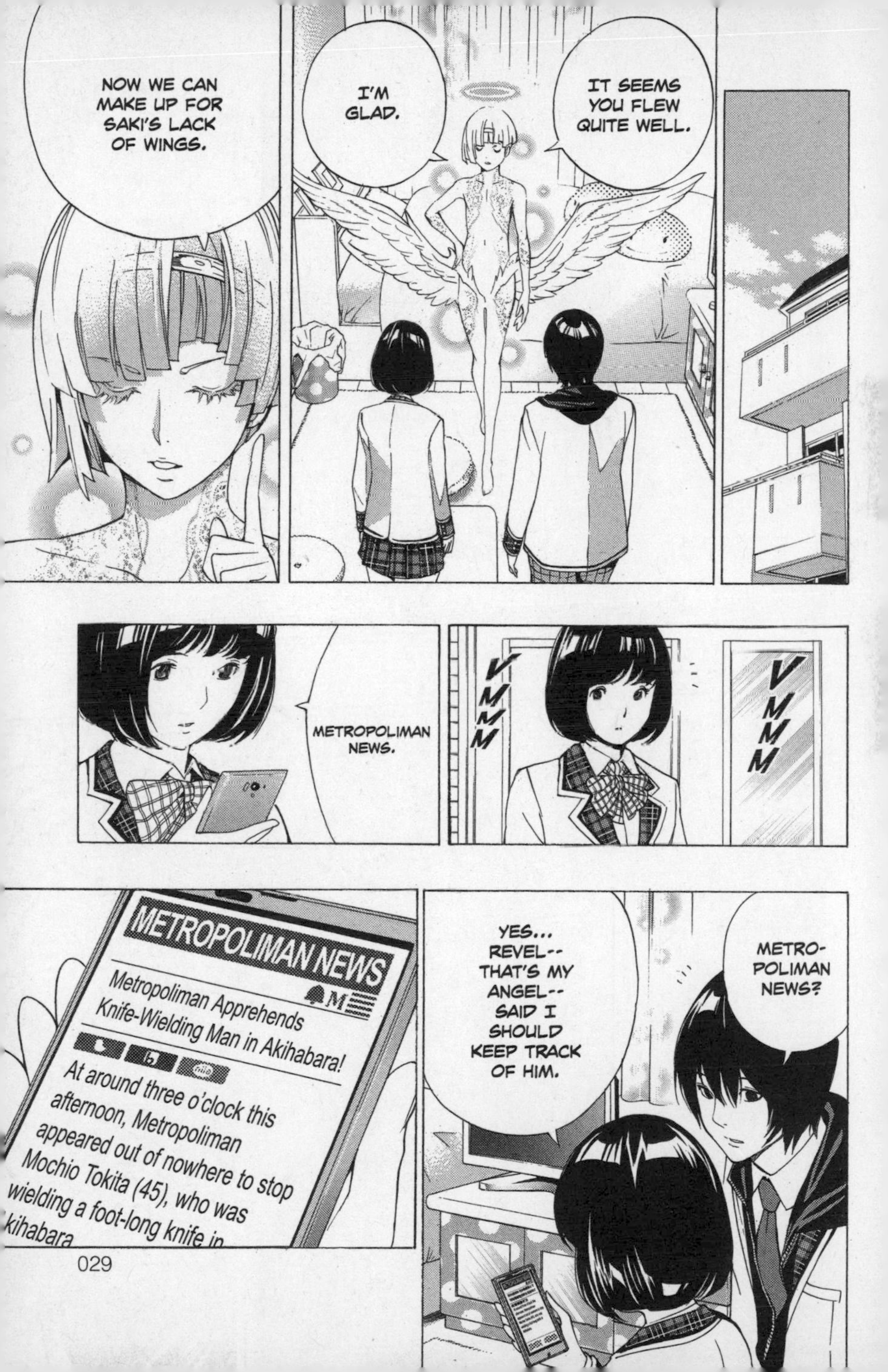
IT SEEMS YOU FLEW QUITE WELL.
I'M GLAD.
NOW WE CAN MAKE UP FOR SAKI'S LACK OF WINGS.
VMMM
VMMM
METROPOLIMAN NEWS.
METRO-POLIMAN NEWS?
YES... REVEL--THAT'S MY ANGEL--SAID I SHOULD KEEP TRACK OF HIM.
METROPOLIMAN NEWS
Metropoliman Apprehends Knife-Wielding Man in Akihabara!
At around three o'clock this afternoon, Metropoliman appeared out of nowhere to stop Mochio Tokita (45), who was wielding a foot-long knife in kihabara

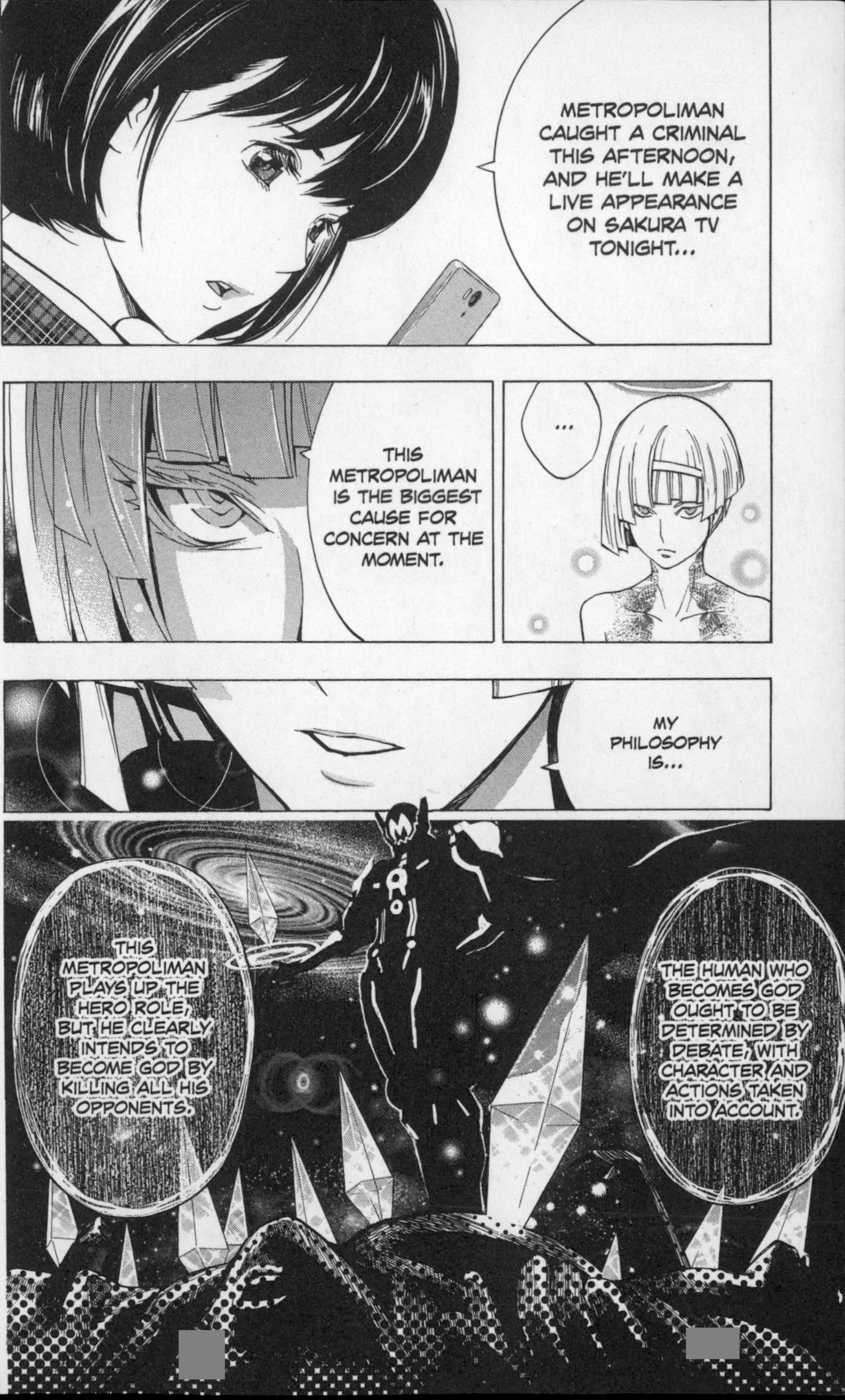
METROPOLIMAN CAUGHT A CRIMINAL THIS AFTERNOON, AND HE'LL MAKE A LIVE APPEARANCE ON SAKURA TV TONIGHT...
...
THIS METROPOLIMAN IS THE BIGGEST CAUSE FOR CONCERN AT THE MOMENT.
MY PHILOSOPHY IS...
THE HUMAN WHO BECOMES GOD OUGHT TO BE DETERMINED BY DEBATE, WITH CHARACTER AND ACTIONS TAKEN INTO ACCOUNT.
THIS METROPOLIMAN PLAYS UP THE HERO ROLE, BUT HE CLEARLY INTENDS TO BECOME GOD BY KILLING ALL HIS OPPONENTS.

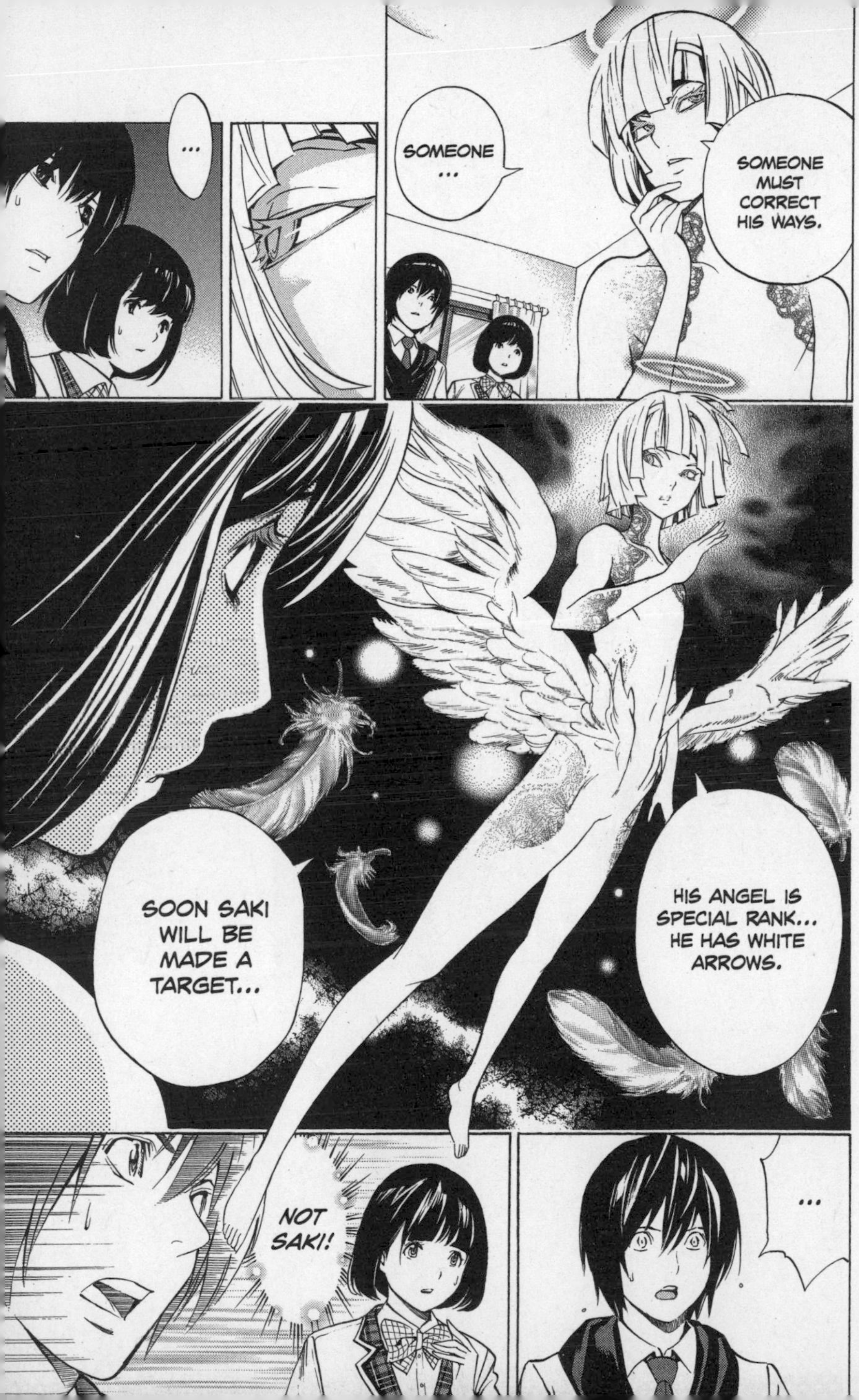
SOMEONE MUST CORRECT HIS WAYS.
SOMEONE ...
...
HIS ANGEL IS SPECIAL RANK... HE HAS WHITE ARROWS.
SOON SAKI WILL BE MADE A TARGET...
...
NOT SAKI!

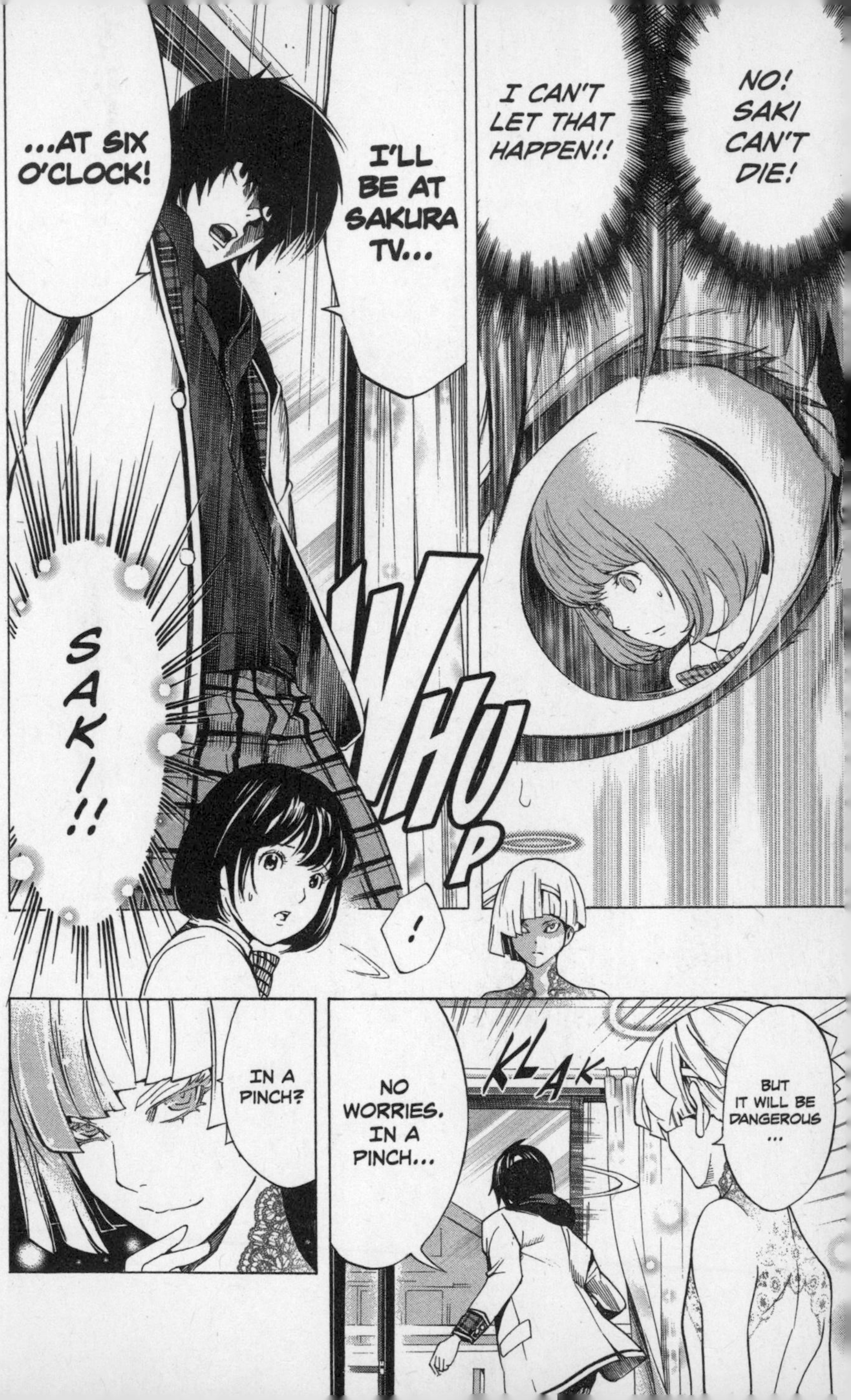
NO! SAKI CAN'T DIE!
I CAN'T LET THAT HAPPEN!!
I'LL BE AT SAKURA TV...
...AT SIX O'CLOCK!
WHUP
SAKI!!
!
BUT IT WILL BE DANGEROUS...
KLAK
NO WORRIES. IN A PINCH...
IN A PINCH?

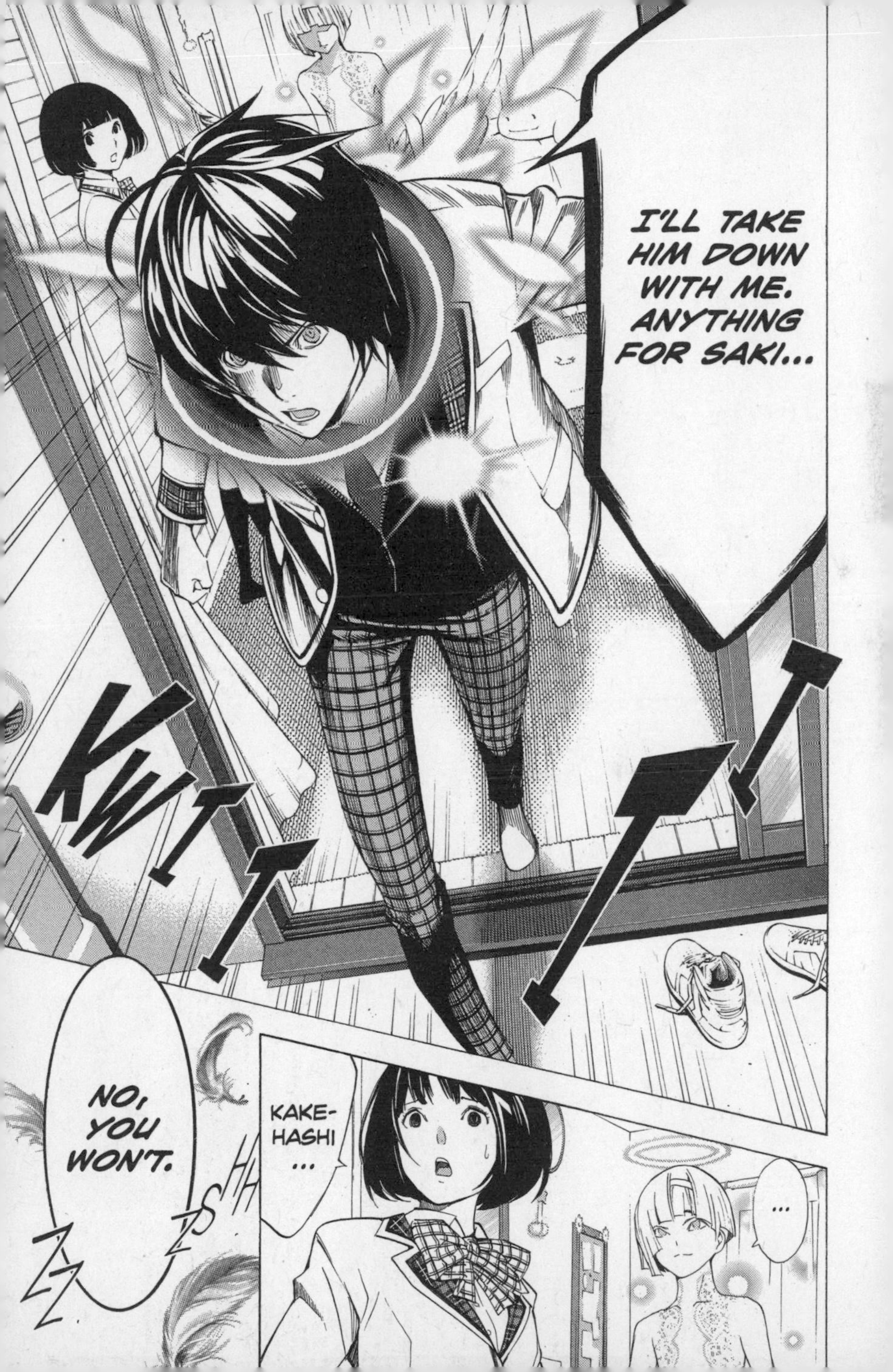
I'LL TAKE HIM DOWN WITH ME. ANYTHING FOR SAKI...
...
KAKE-HASHI ...
NO, YOU WON'T.

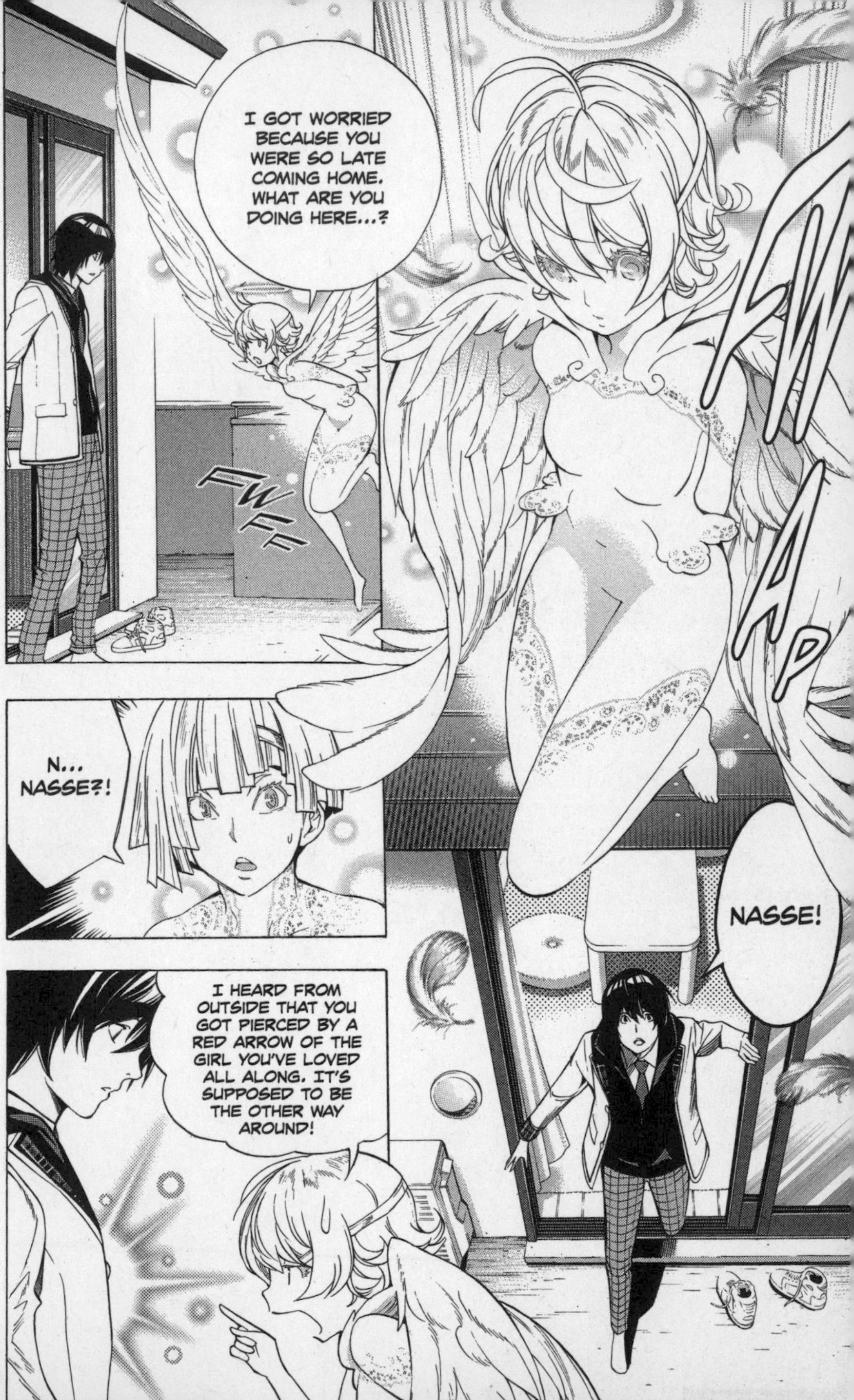
FWAP
NASSE!
I GOT WORRIED BECAUSE YOU WERE SO LATE COMING HOME. WHAT ARE YOU DOING HERE...?
FWFF
N... NASSE?!
I HEARD FROM OUTSIDE THAT YOU GOT PIERCED BY A RED ARROW OF THE GIRL YOU'VE LOVED ALL ALONG. IT'S SUPPOSED TO BE THE OTHER WAY AROUND!

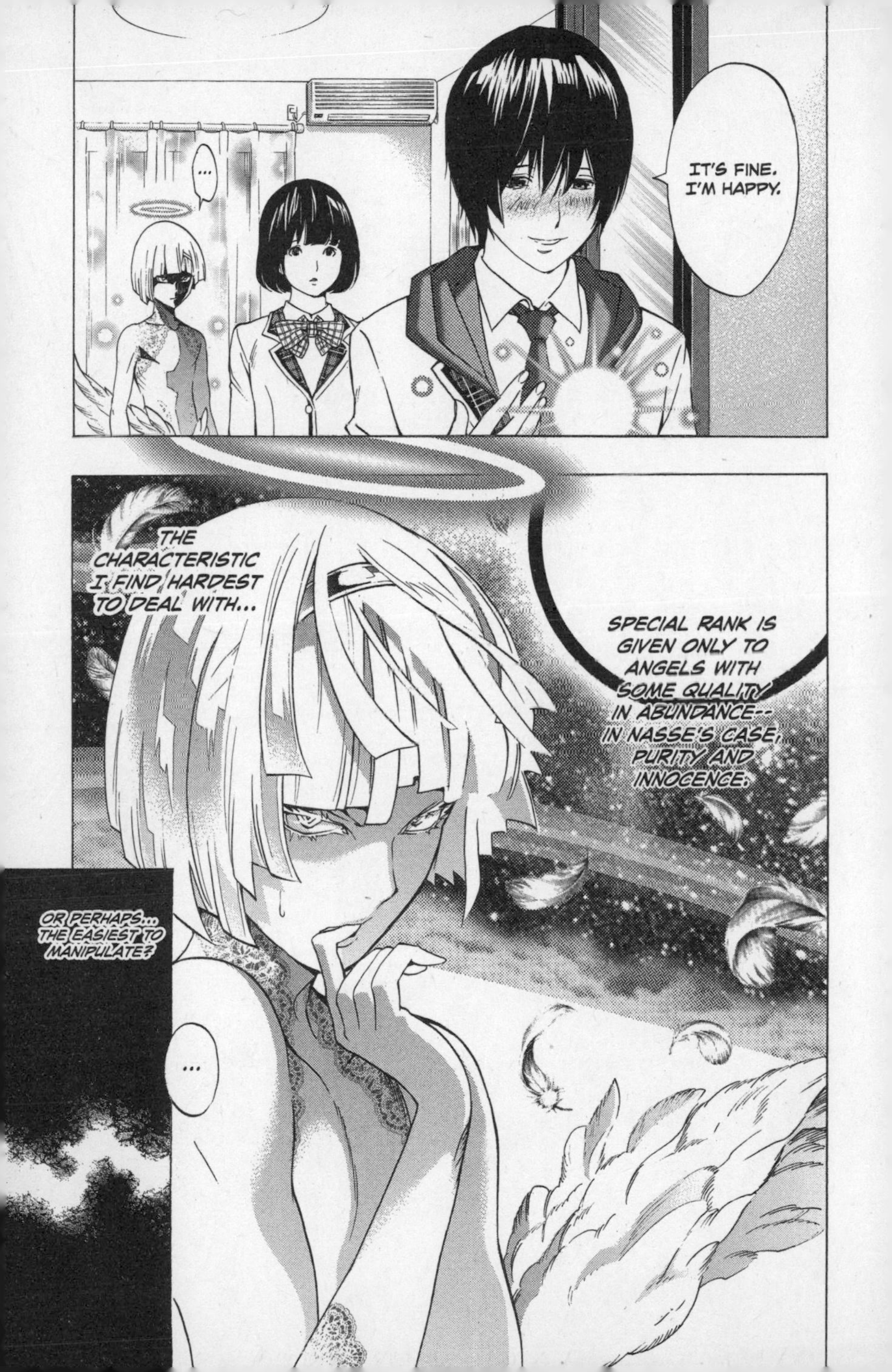
IT'S FINE. I'M HAPPY.
...
SPECIAL RANK IS GIVEN ONLY TO ANGELS WITH SOME QUALITY IN ABUNDANCE-- IN NASSE'S CASE, PURITY AND INNOCENCE.
THE CHARACTERISTIC I FIND HARDEST TO DEAL WITH...
OR PERHAPS... THE EASIEST TO MANIPULATE?
...

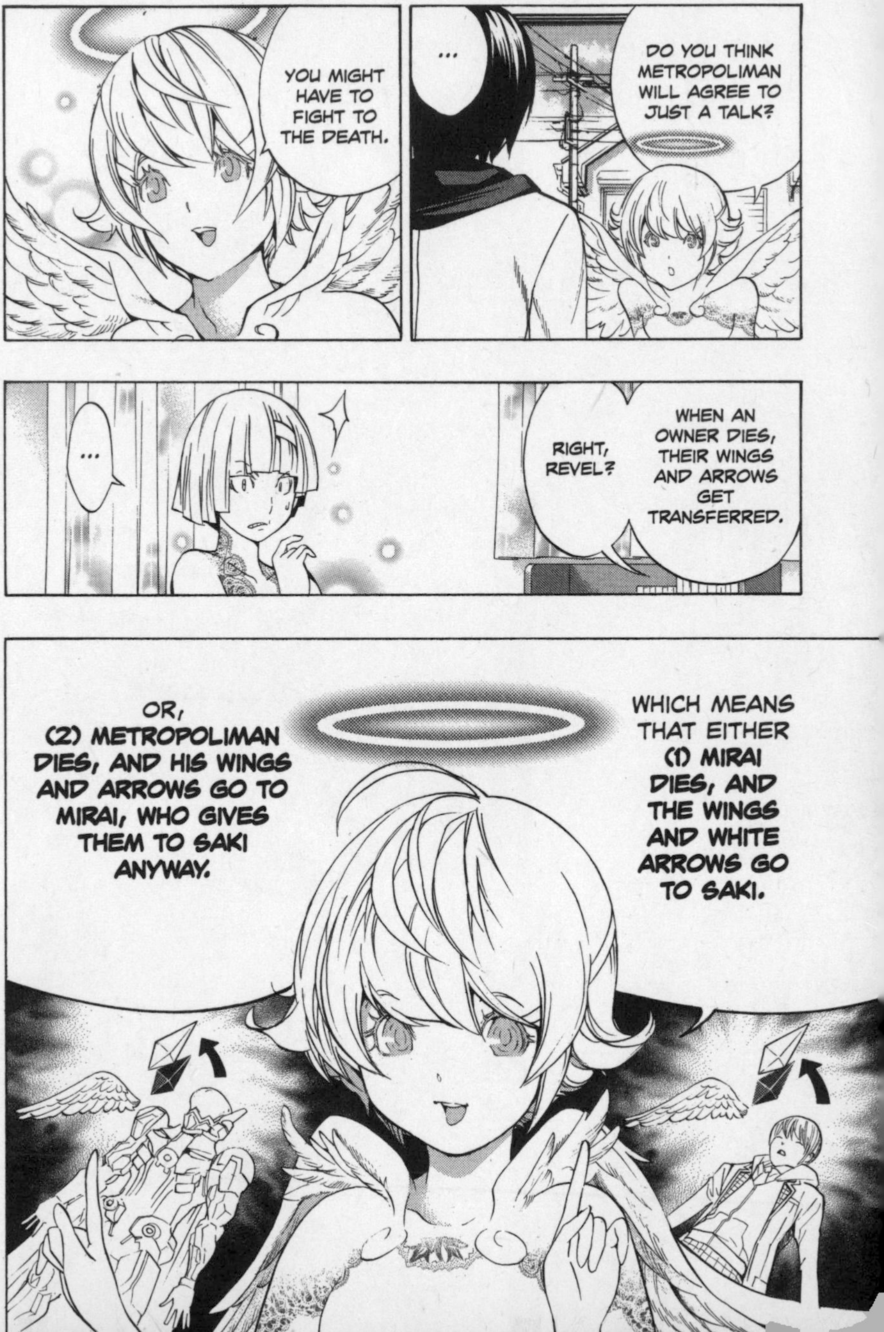
DO YOU THINK METROPOLIMAN WILL AGREE TO JUST A TALK?
...
YOU MIGHT HAVE TO FIGHT TO THE DEATH.
WHEN AN OWNER DIES, THEIR WINGS AND ARROWS GET TRANSFERRED.
RIGHT, REVEL?
...
WHICH MEANS THAT EITHER (1) MIRAI DIES, AND THE WINGS AND WHITE ARROWS GO TO SAKI.
OR, (2) METROPOLIMAN DIES, AND HIS WINGS AND ARROWS GO TO MIRAI, WHO GIVES THEM TO SAKI ANYWAY.

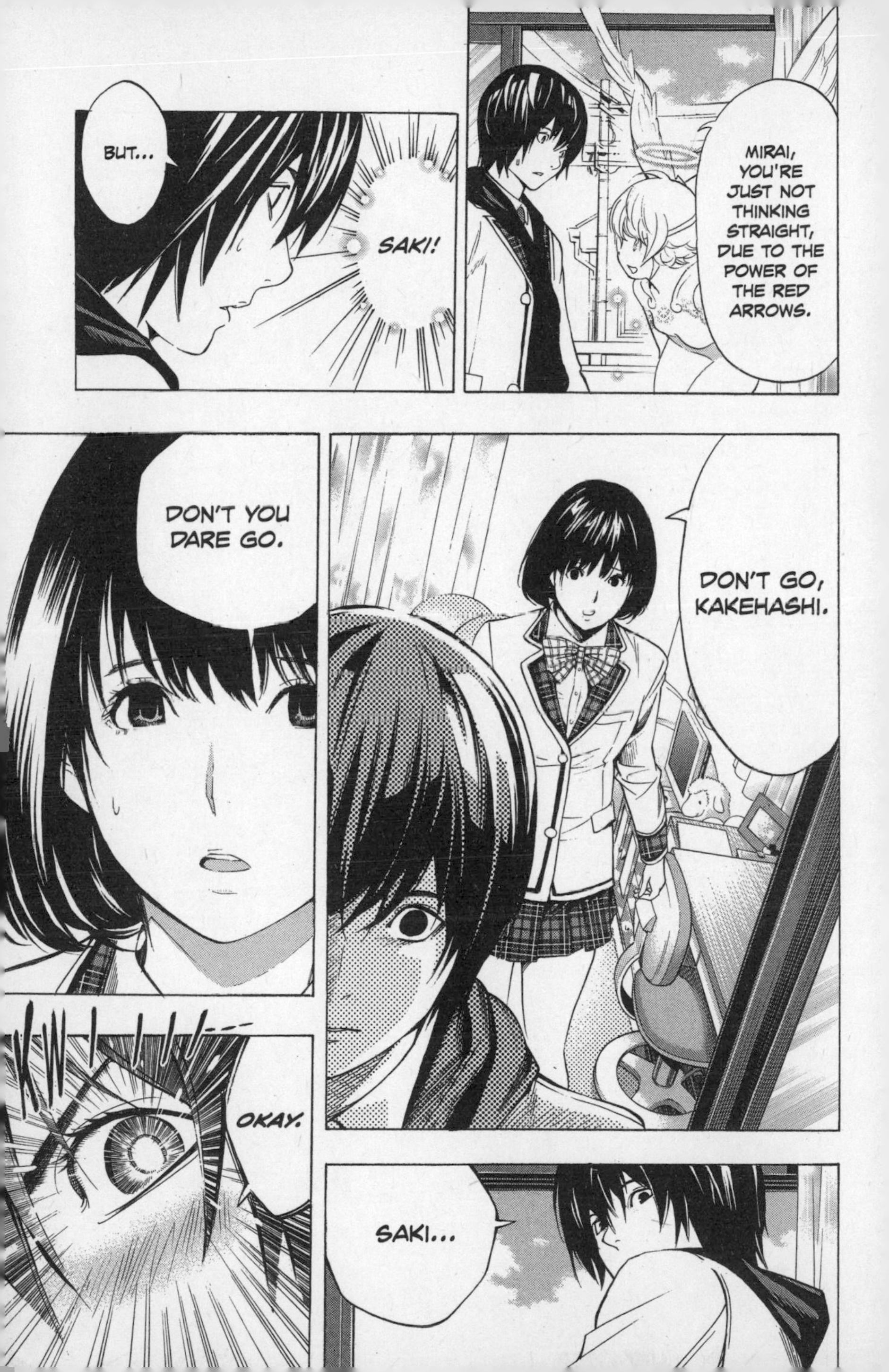
MIRAI, YOU'RE JUST NOT THINKING STRAIGHT, DUE TO THE POWER OF THE RED ARROWS.
SAKI!
BUT...
DON'T GO, KAKEHASHI.
DON'T YOU DARE GO.
SAKI...
OKAY.

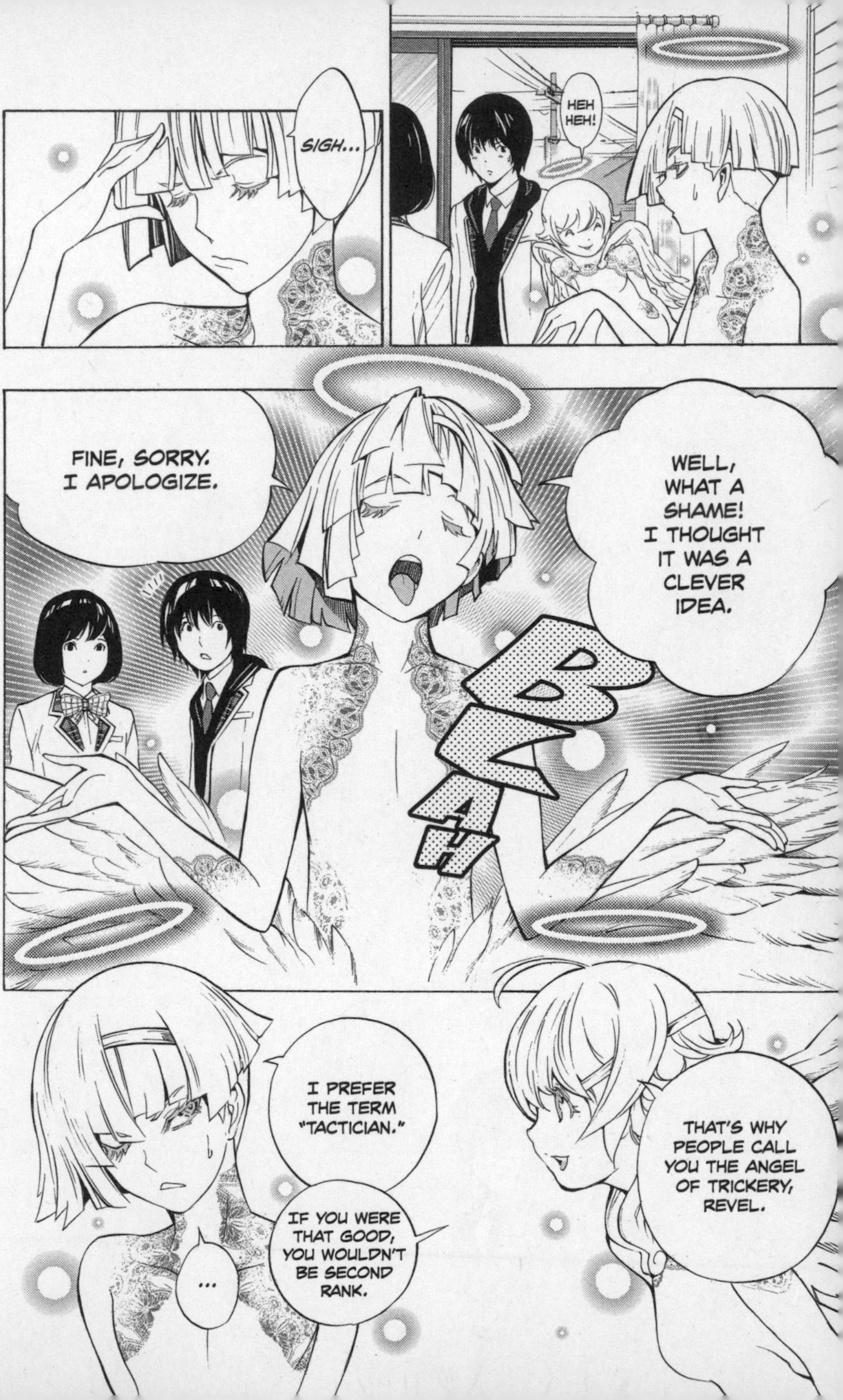
HEH HEH!
SIGH...
WELL, WHAT A SHAME! I THOUGHT IT WAS A CLEVER IDEA.
BAH!!
FINE, SORRY. I APOLOGIZE.
THAT'S WHY PEOPLE CALL YOU THE ANGEL OF TRICKERY, REVEL.
I PREFER THE TERM "TACTICIAN."
IF YOU WERE THAT GOOD, YOU WOULDN'T BE SECOND RANK.
...

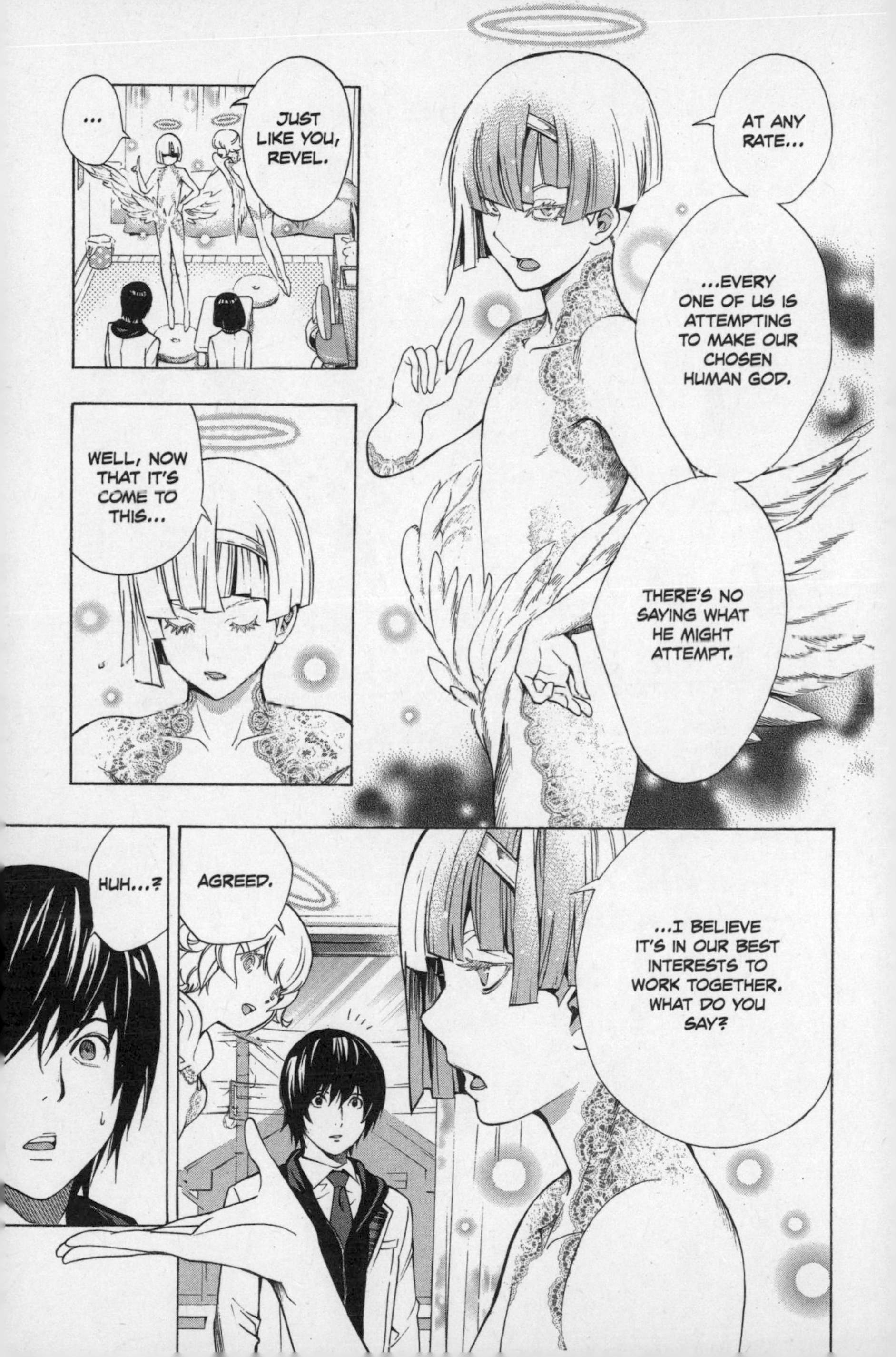
AT ANY RATE...
...EVERY ONE OF US IS ATTEMPTING TO MAKE OUR CHOSEN HUMAN GOD.
THERE'S NO SAYING WHAT HE MIGHT ATTEMPT.
JUST LIKE YOU, REVEL.
...
WELL, NOW THAT IT'S COME TO THIS...
...I BELIEVE IT'S IN OUR BEST INTERESTS TO WORK TOGETHER. WHAT DO YOU SAY?
AGREED.
HUH...?

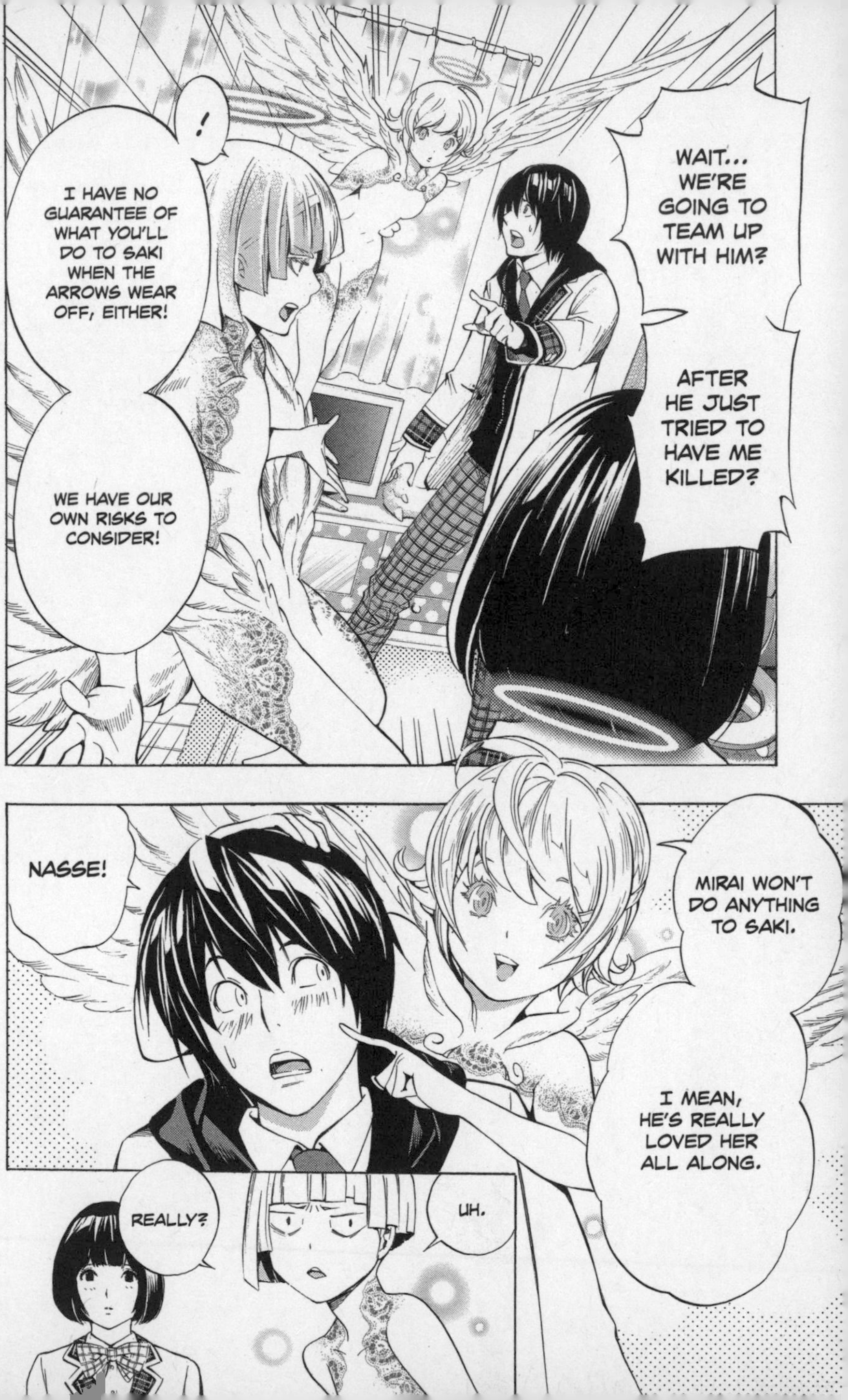
WAIT... WE'RE GOING TO TEAM UP WITH HIM?
AFTER HE JUST TRIED TO HAVE ME KILLED?
!
I HAVE NO GUARANTEE OF WHAT YOU'LL DO TO SAKI WHEN THE ARROWS WEAR OFF, EITHER!
WE HAVE OUR OWN RISKS TO CONSIDER!
MIRAI WON'T DO ANYTHING TO SAKI.
NASSE!
I MEAN, HE'S REALLY LOVED HER ALL ALONG.
UH.
REALLY?

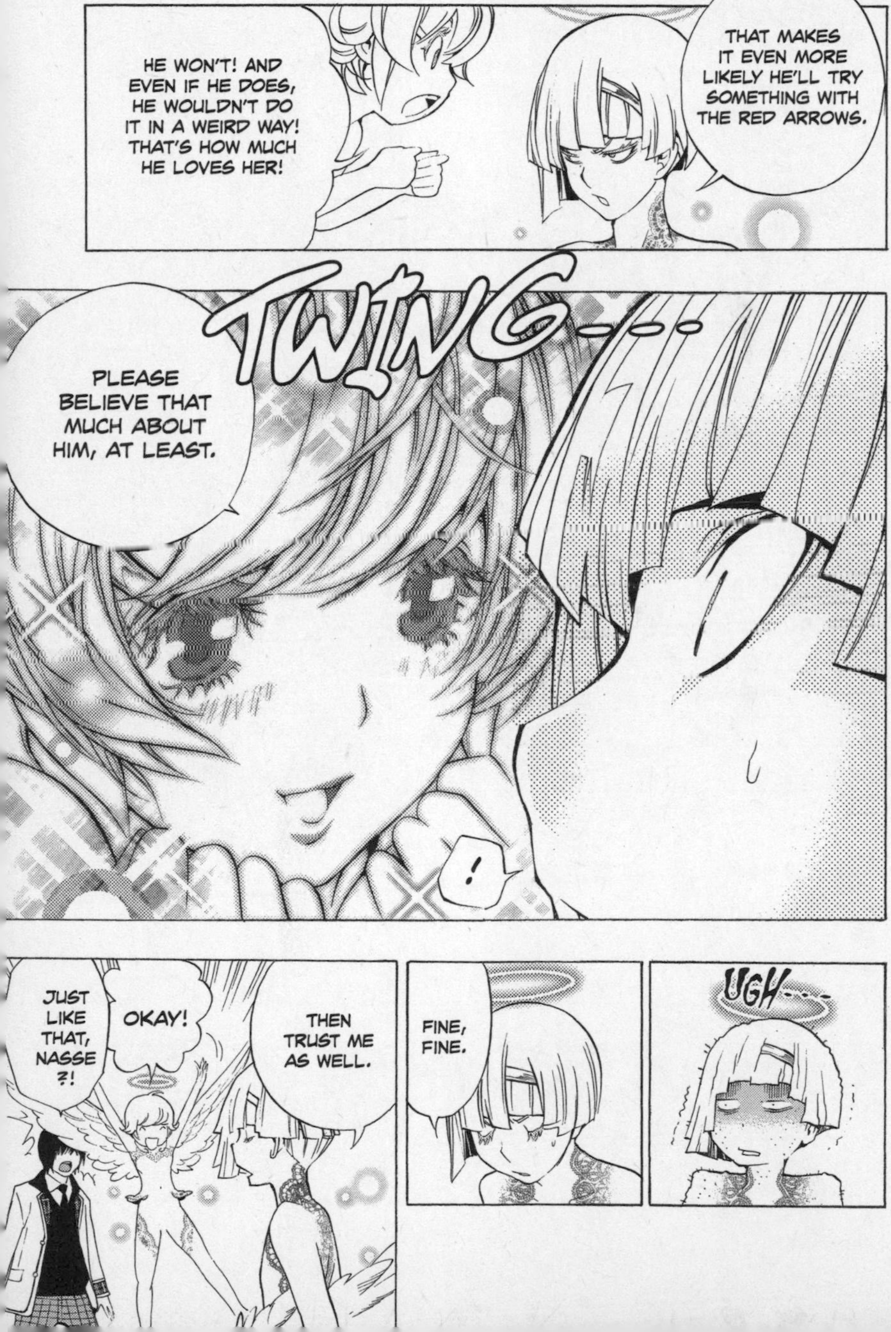
THAT MAKES IT EVEN MORE LIKELY HE'LL TRY SOMETHING WITH THE RED ARROWS.
HE WON'T! AND EVEN IF HE DOES, HE WOULDN'T DO IT IN A WEIRD WAY! THAT'S HOW MUCH HE LOVES HER!
TWING...
PLEASE BELIEVE THAT MUCH ABOUT HIM, AT LEAST.
!
UGH...
FINE, FINE.
THEN TRUST ME AS WELL.
OKAY!
JUST LIKE THAT, NASSE?!

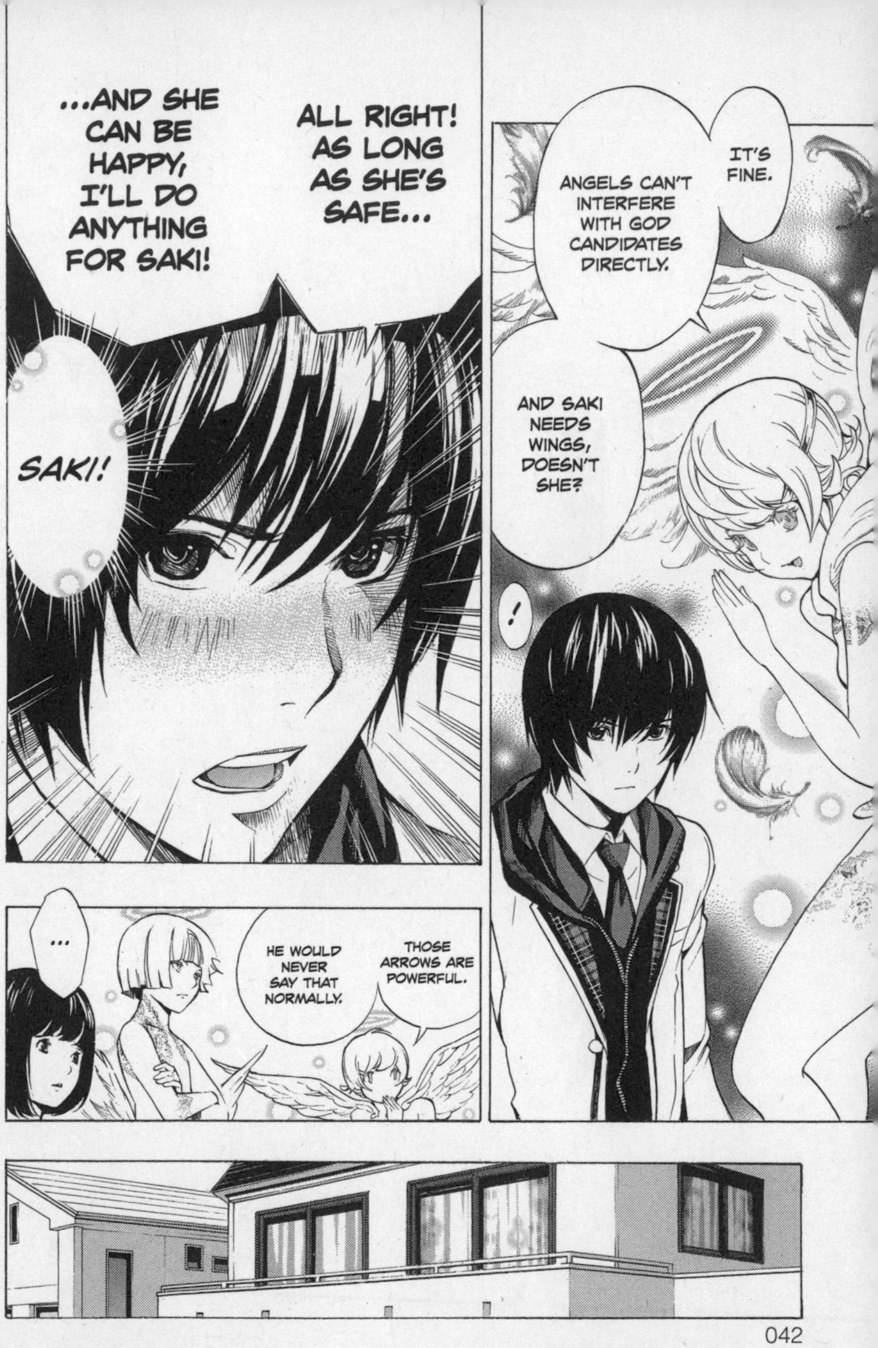
IT'S FINE.
ANGELS CAN'T INTERFERE WITH GOD CANDIDATES DIRECTLY.
AND SAKI NEEDS WINGS, DOESN'T SHE?
!
ALL RIGHT! AS LONG AS SHE'S SAFE...
...AND SHE CAN BE HAPPY, I'LL DO ANYTHING FOR SAKI!
SAKI!
THOSE ARROWS ARE POWERFUL.
HE WOULD NEVER SAY THAT NORMALLY.
...

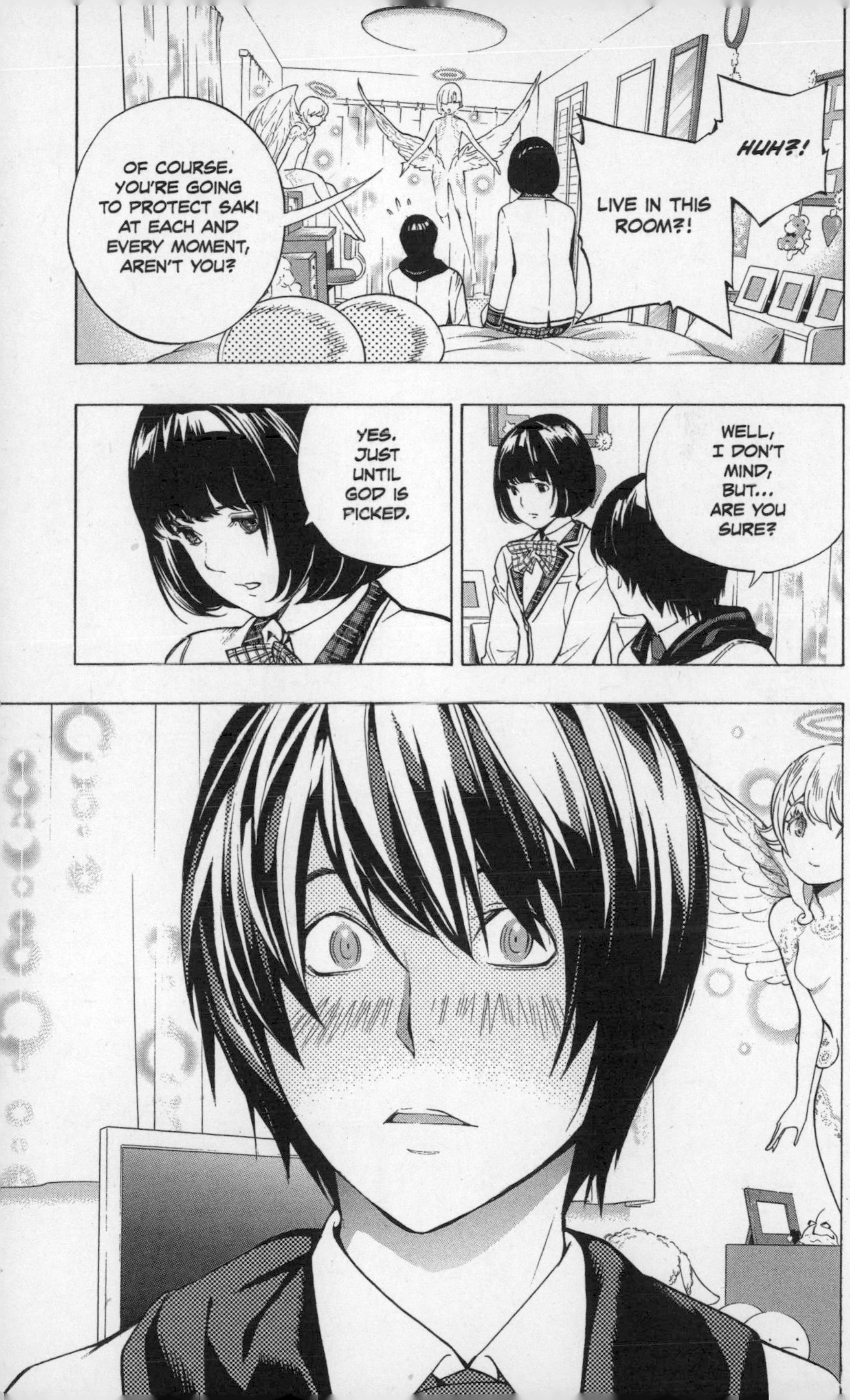
HUH?!
LIVE IN THIS ROOM?!
OF COURSE. YOU'RE GOING TO PROTECT SAKI AT EACH AND EVERY MOMENT, AREN'T YOU?
WELL, I DON'T MIND, BUT... ARE YOU SURE?
YES. JUST UNTIL GOD IS PICKED.

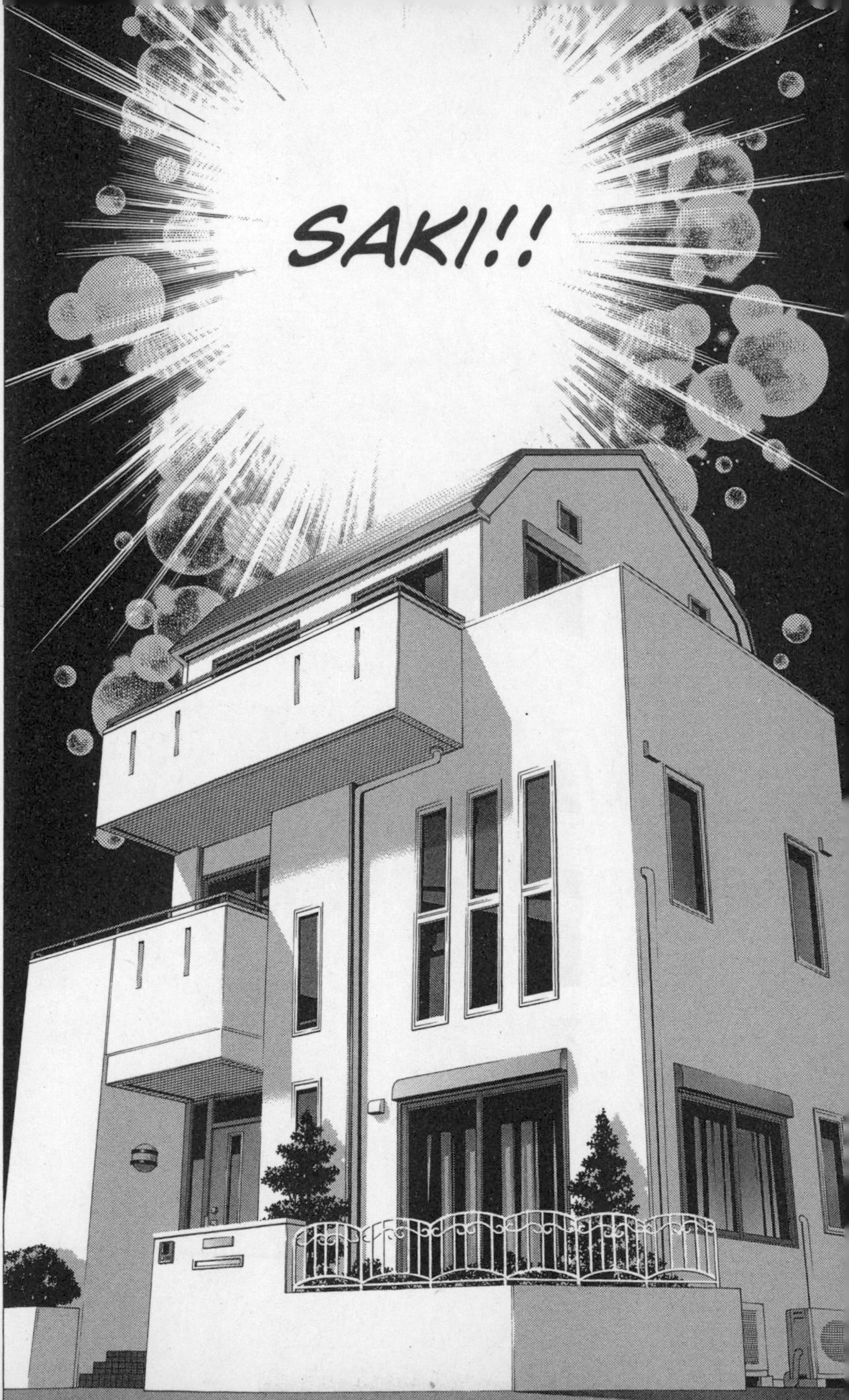
SAKI!!

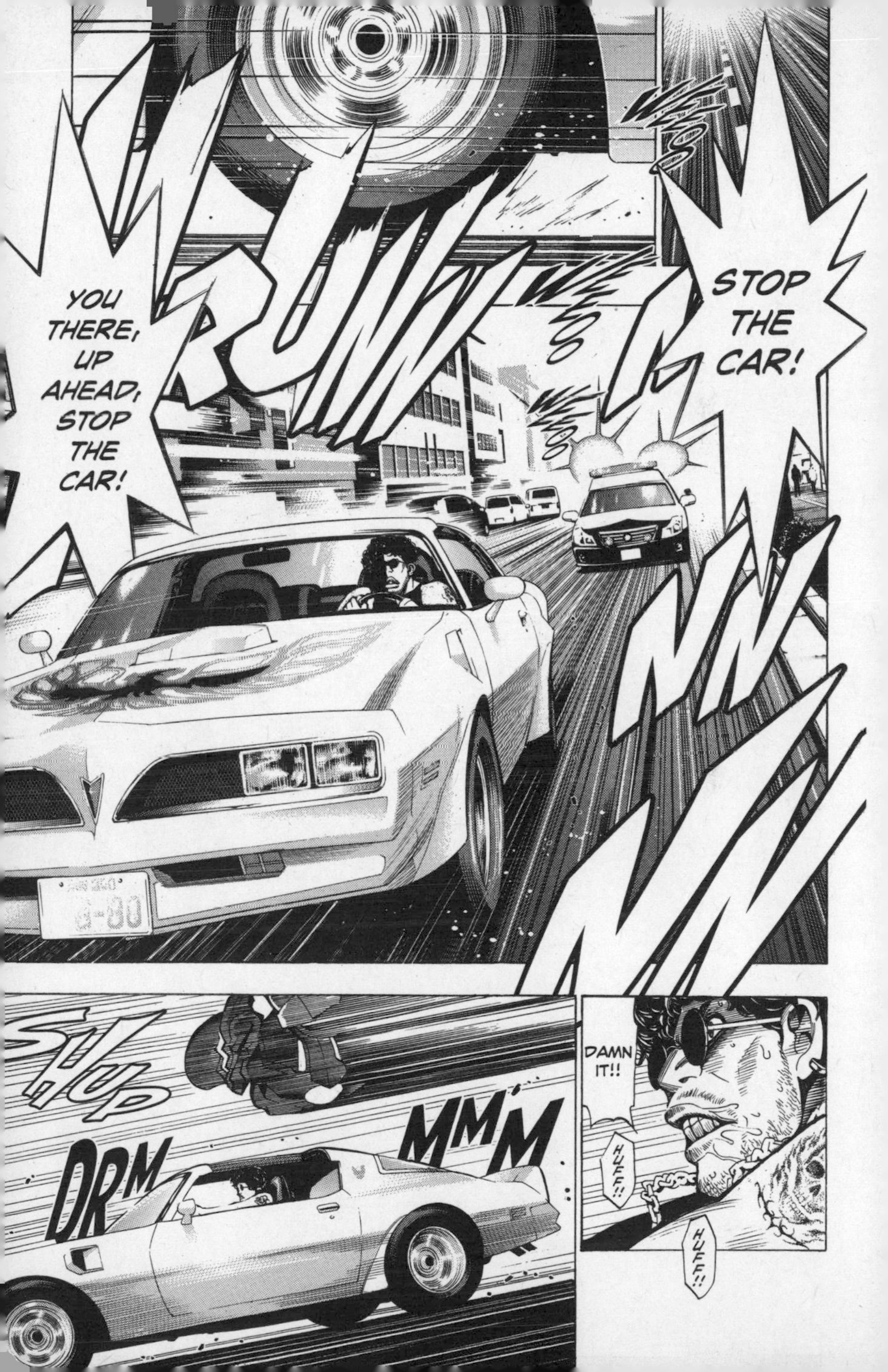
STOP THE CAR!
YOU THERE, UP AHEAD, STOP THE CAR!
DAMN IT!!
HUFF!!
HUFF!!
SHUP
DRM
MMM

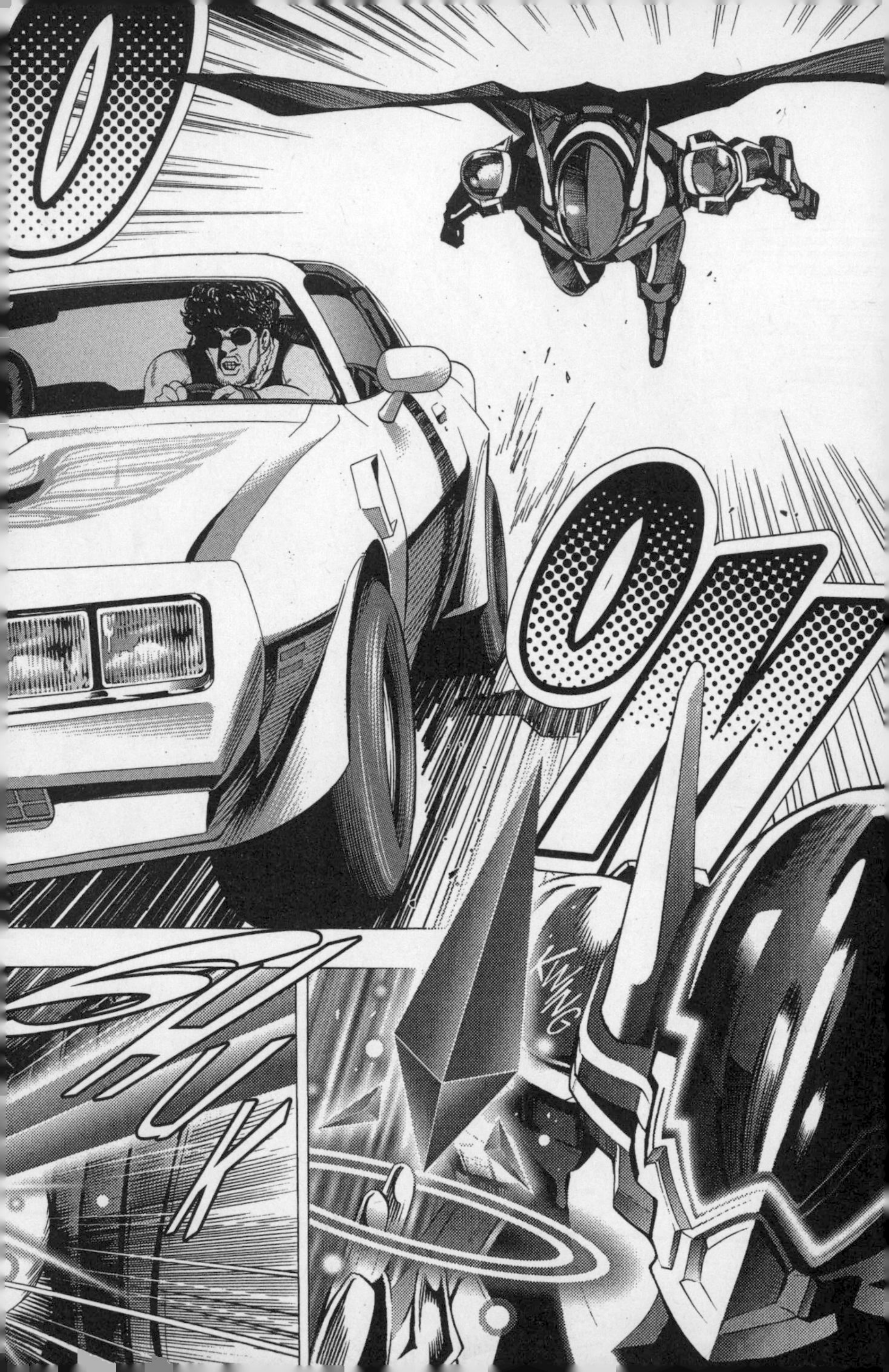
KWING
SHUK

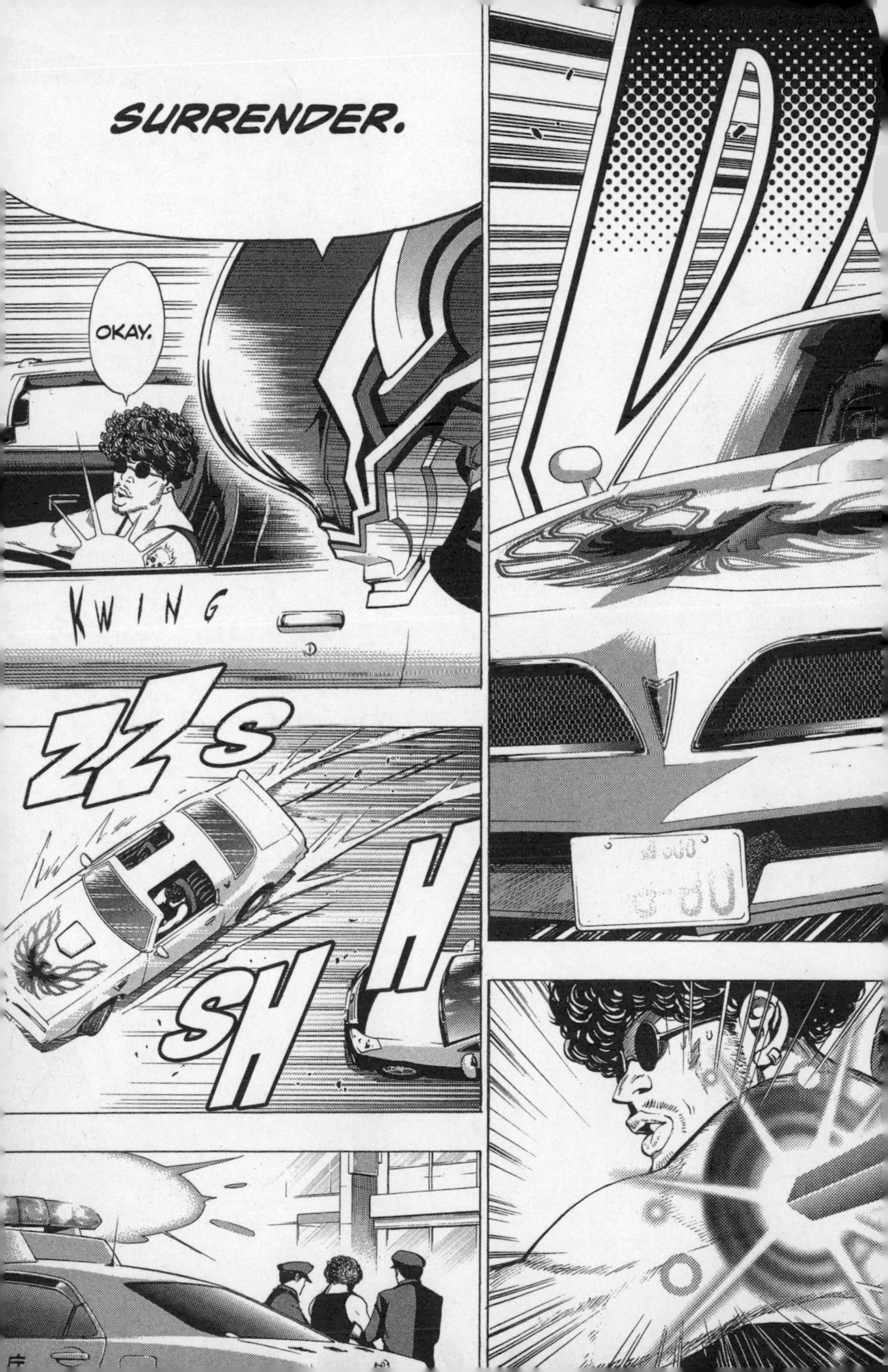
SURRENDER.
OKAY.
KWING
ZZSH
SHH

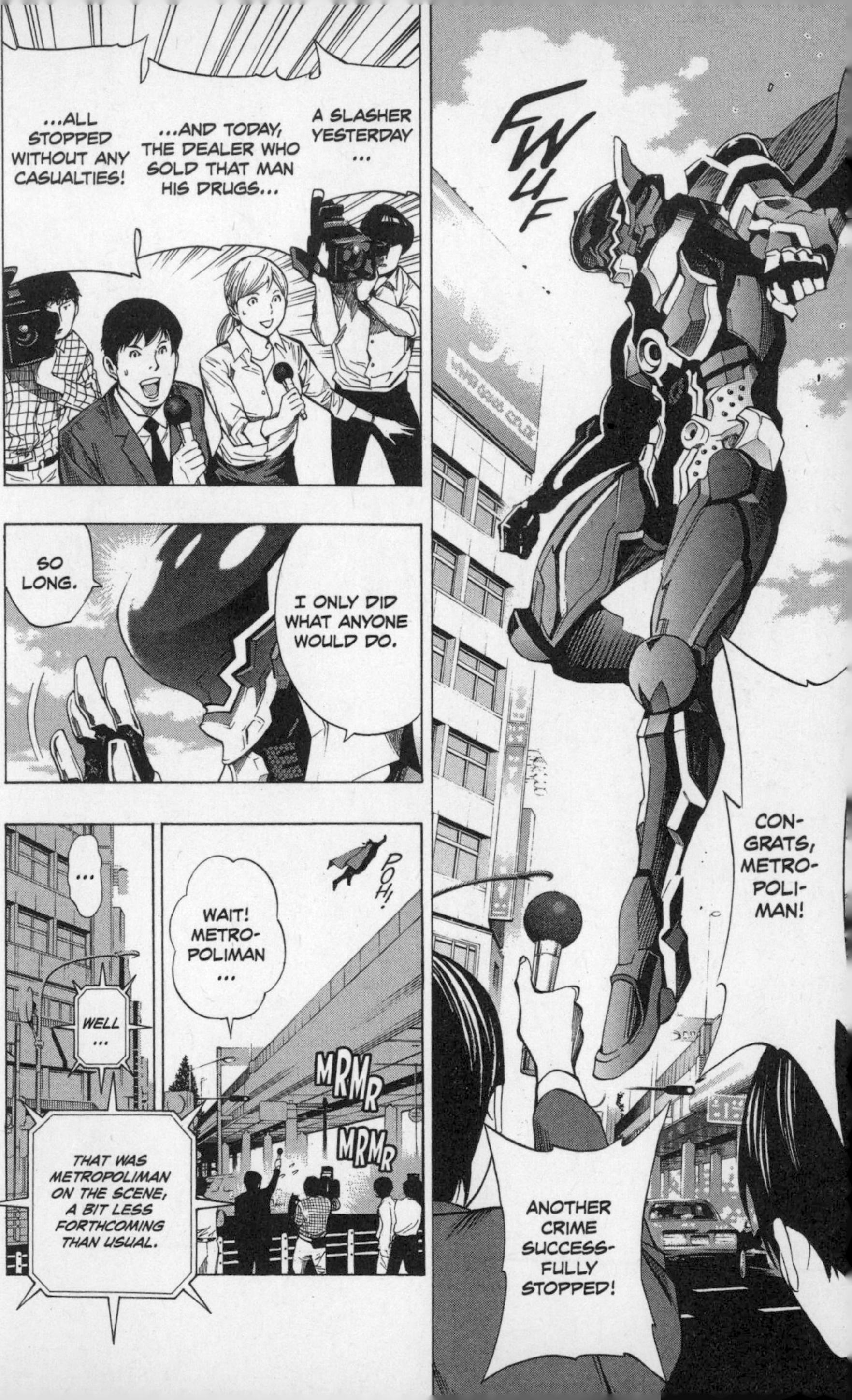
FWUF
CONGRATS, METROPOLIMAN!
ANOTHER CRIME SUCCESSFULLY STOPPED!
A SLASHER YESTERDAY...
...AND TODAY, THE DEALER WHO SOLD THAT MAN HIS DRUGS...
...ALL STOPPED WITHOUT ANY CASUALTIES!
I ONLY DID WHAT ANYONE WOULD DO.
SO LONG.
POH!
WAIT! METROPOLIMAN...
MRMR
MRMR
...
WELL...
THAT WAS METROPOLIMAN ON THE SCENE, A BIT LESS FORTHCOMING THAN USUAL.

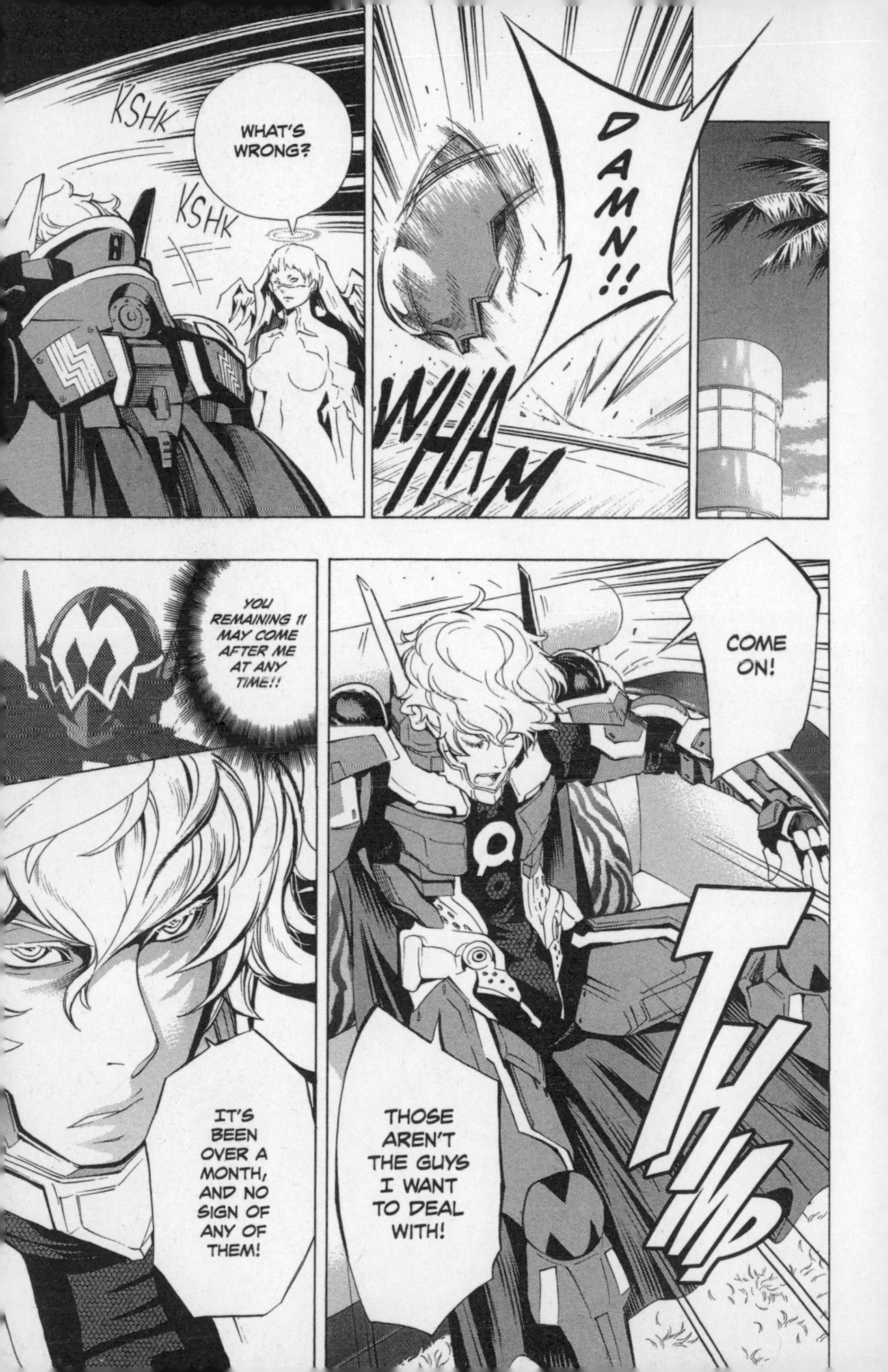
DAMN!!
WHAM
KSHK
WHAT'S WRONG?
KSHK
COME ON!
THOSE AREN'T THE GUYS I WANT TO DEAL WITH!
THUMP
YOU REMAINING 11 MAY COME AFTER ME AT ANY TIME!!
IT'S BEEN OVER A MONTH, AND NO SIGN OF ANY OF THEM!

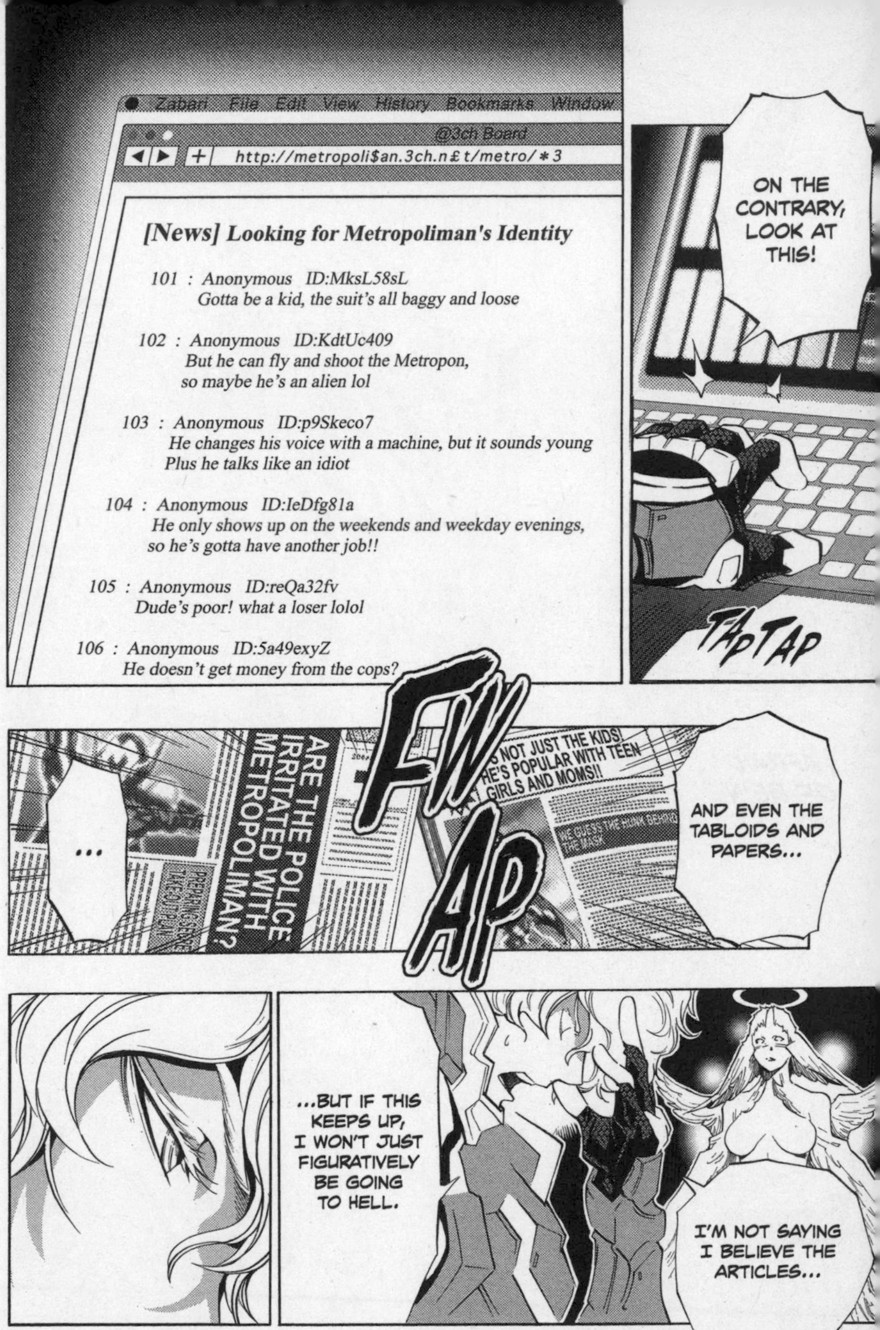
ON THE CONTRARY, LOOK AT THIS!
TAP TAP
Zabari File Edit View History Bookmarks Window
@3ch Board
http://metropoli$an.3ch.n£t/metro/*3
[News] Looking for Metropoliman's Identity
101 : Anonymous ID:MksL58sL
Gotta be a kid, the suit's all baggy and loose
102 : Anonymous ID:KdtUc409
But he can fly and shoot the Metropon, so maybe he's an alien lol
103 : Anonymous ID:p9Skeco7
He changes his voice with a machine, but it sounds young
Plus he talks like an idiot
104 : Anonymous ID:IeDfg81a
He only shows up on the weekends and weekday evenings, so he's gotta have another job!!
105 : Anonymous ID:reQa32fv
Dude's poor! what a loser lolol
106 : Anonymous ID:5a49exyZ
He doesn't get money from the cops?
AND EVEN THE TABLOIDS AND PAPERS...
S NOT JUST THE KIDS! HE'S POPULAR WITH TEEN GIRLS AND MOMS!!
FWAP
ARE THE POLICE IRRITATED WITH METROPOLIMAN?
...
I'M NOT SAYING I BELIEVE THE ARTICLES...
...BUT IF THIS KEEPS UP, I WON'T JUST FIGURATIVELY BE GOING TO HELL.

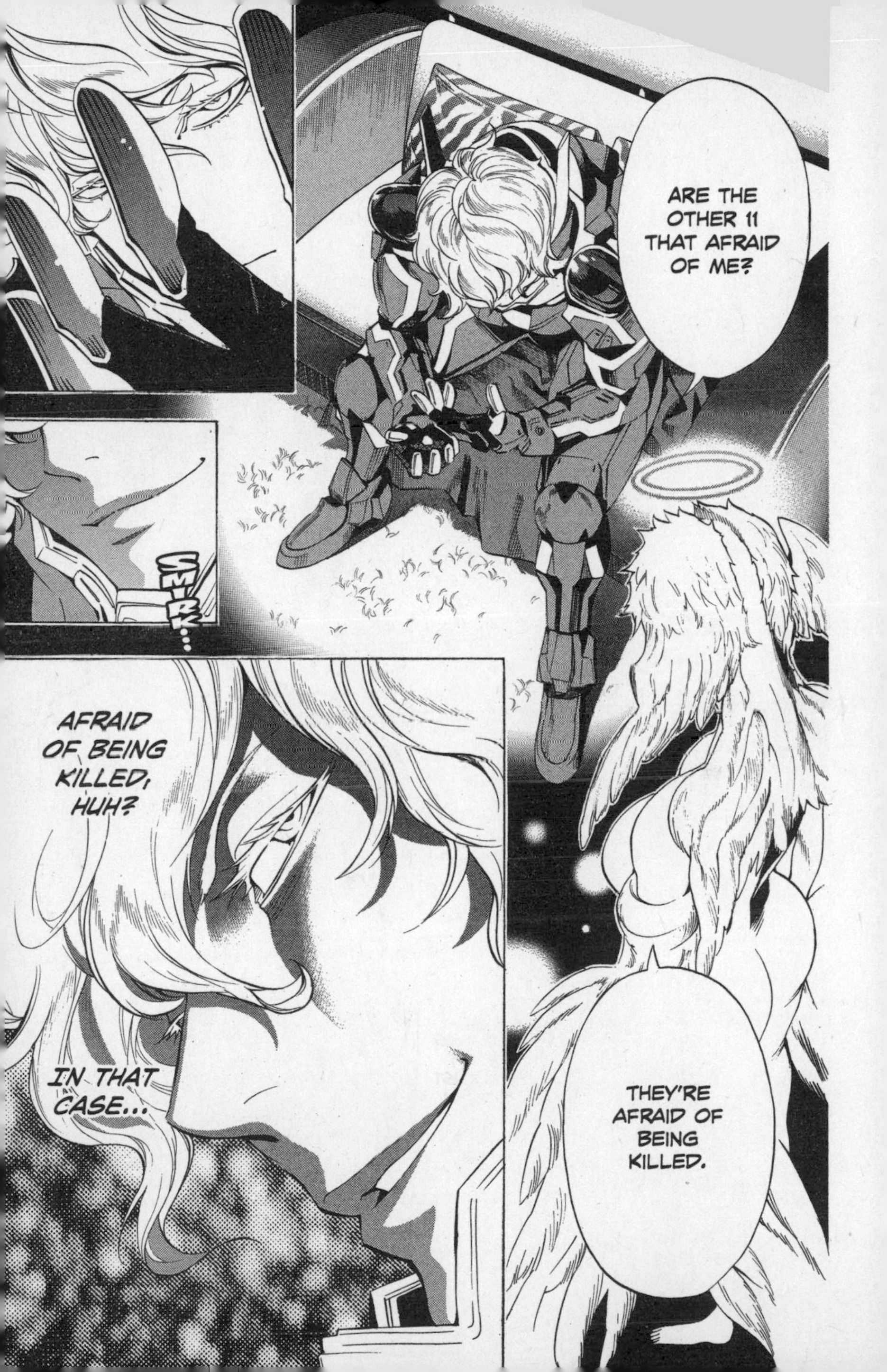
ARE THE OTHER 11 THAT AFRAID OF ME?
THEY'RE AFRAID OF BEING KILLED.
SMIRK...
AFRAID OF BEING KILLED, HUH?
IN THAT CASE...

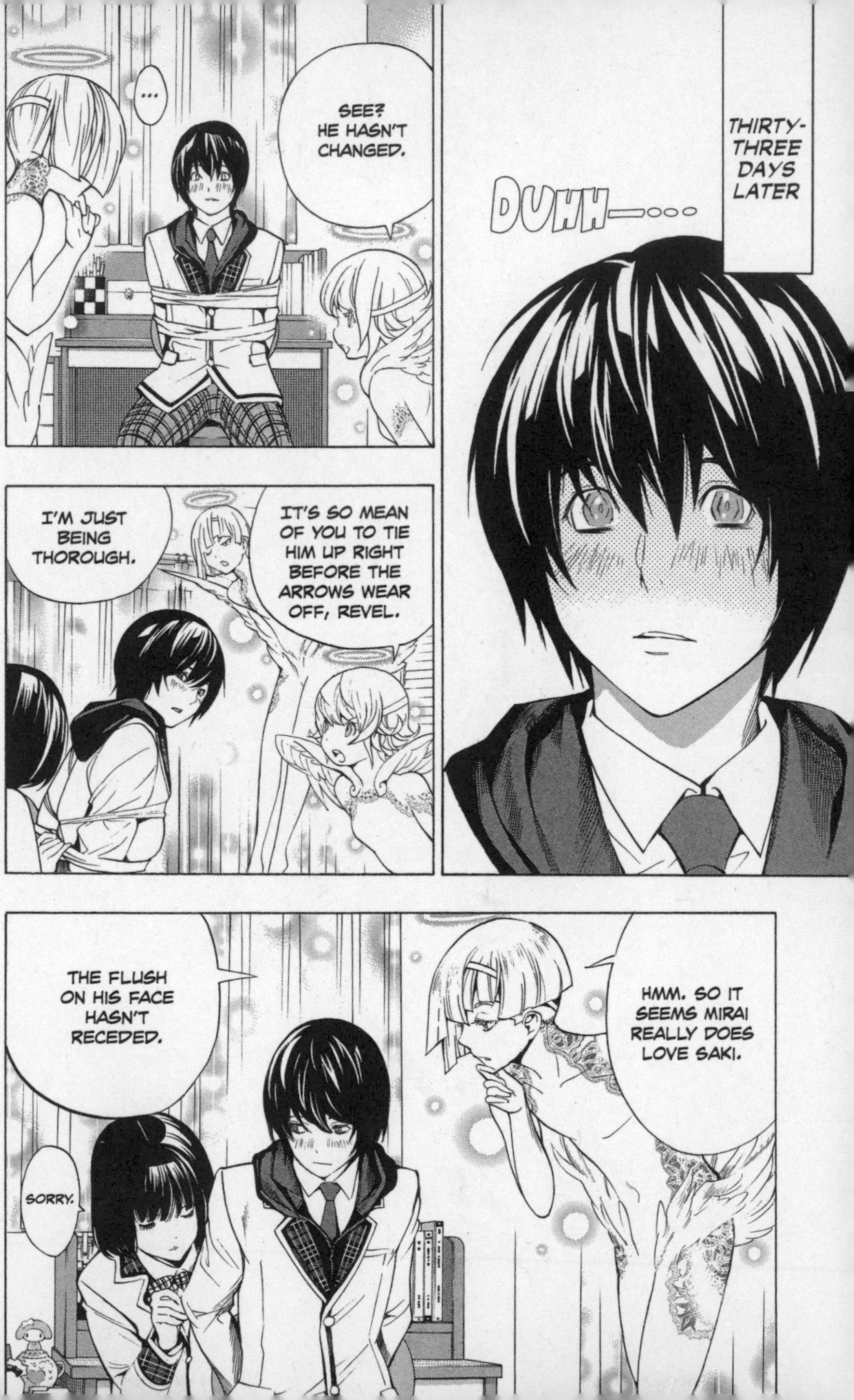
THIRTY-THREE DAYS LATER
DUHH—...
SEE? HE HASN'T CHANGED.
...
IT'S SO MEAN OF YOU TO TIE HIM UP RIGHT BEFORE THE ARROWS WEAR OFF, REVEL.
I'M JUST BEING THOROUGH.
HMM. SO IT SEEMS MIRAI REALLY DOES LOVE SAKI.
THE FLUSH ON HIS FACE HASN'T RECEDED.
SORRY.

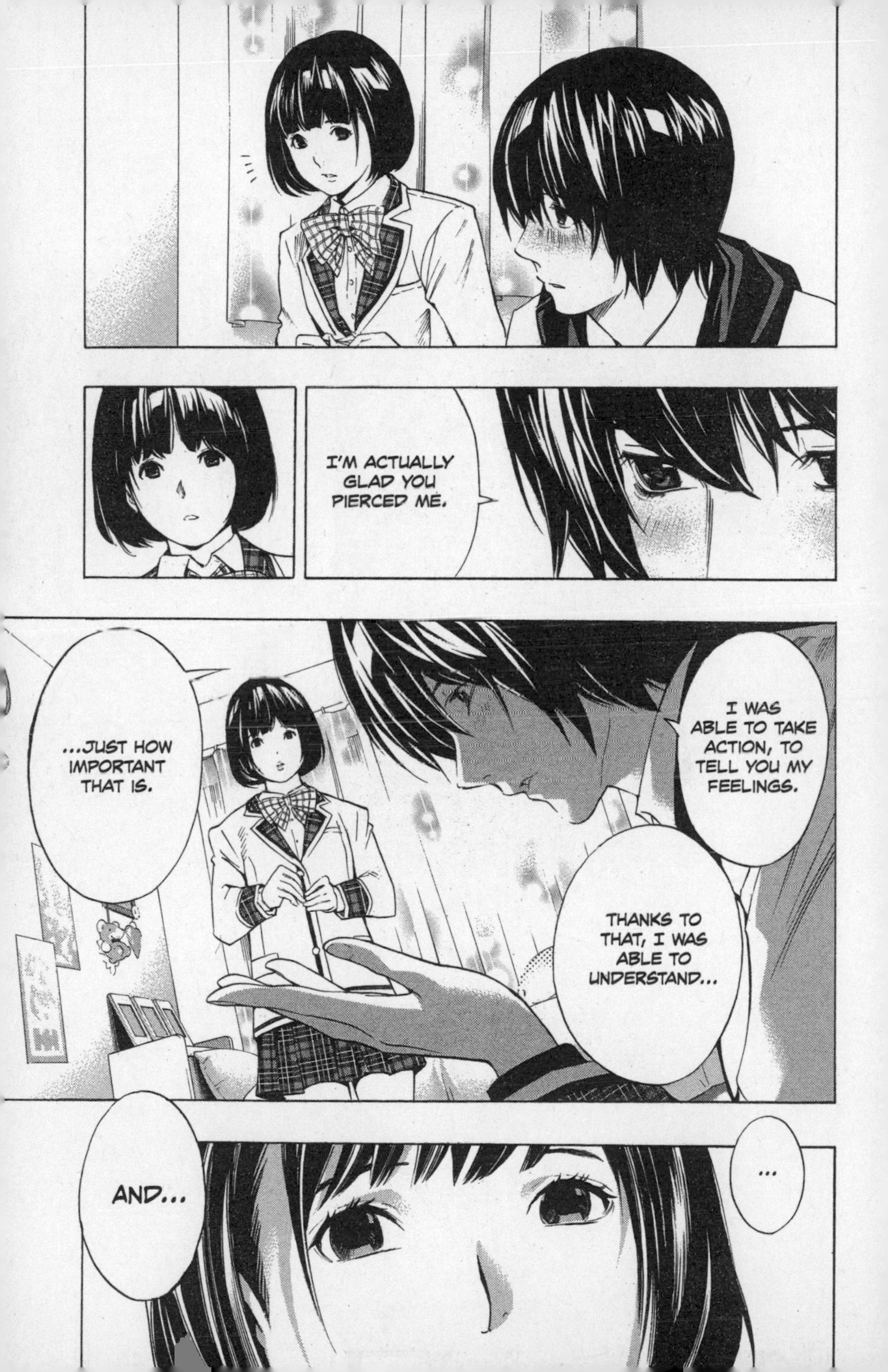
I'M ACTUALLY GLAD YOU PIERCED ME.
I WAS ABLE TO TAKE ACTION, TO TELL YOU MY FEELINGS.
THANKS TO THAT, I WAS ABLE TO UNDERSTAND...
...JUST HOW IMPORTANT THAT IS.
...
AND...

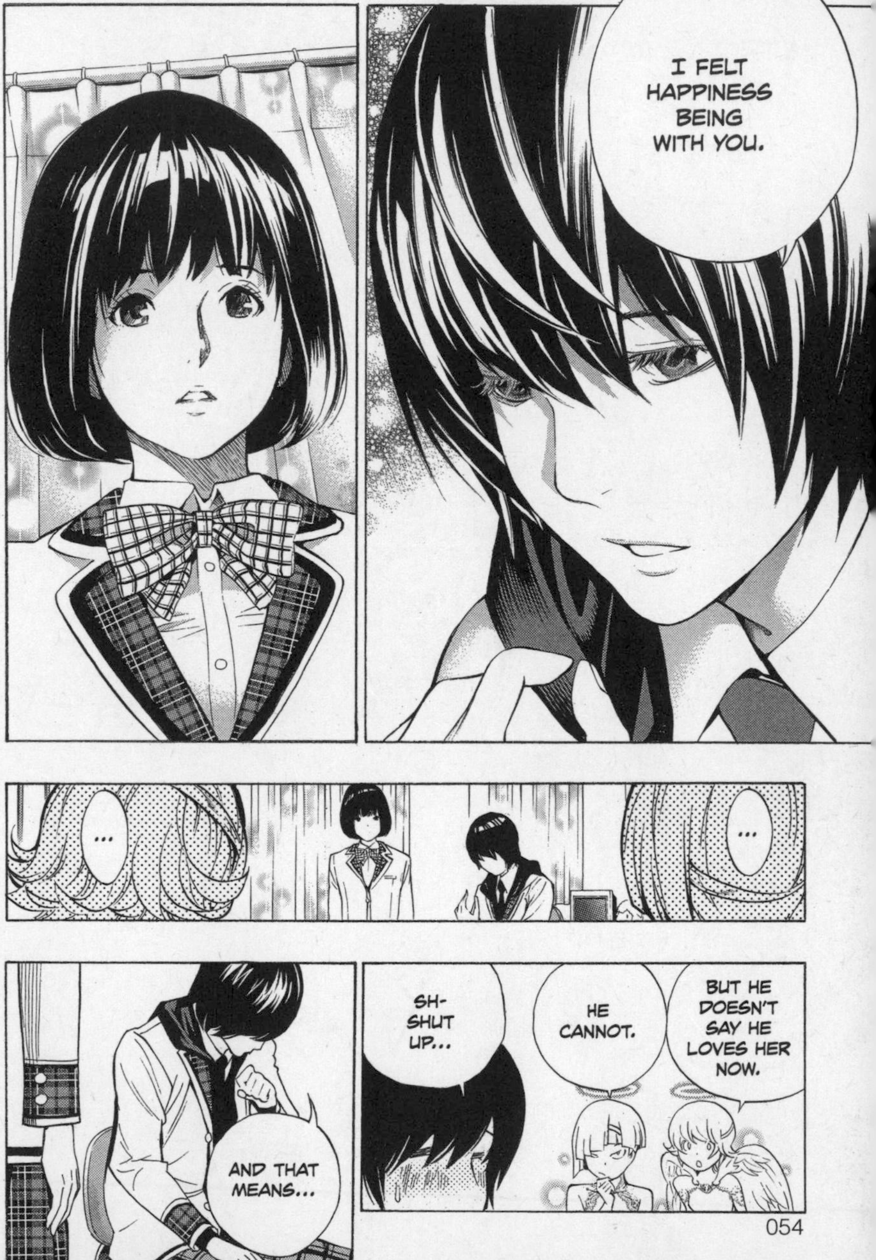
I FELT HAPPINESS BEING WITH YOU.
...
...
BUT HE DOESN'T SAY HE LOVES HER NOW.
HE CANNOT.
SH-SHUT UP...
AND THAT MEANS...

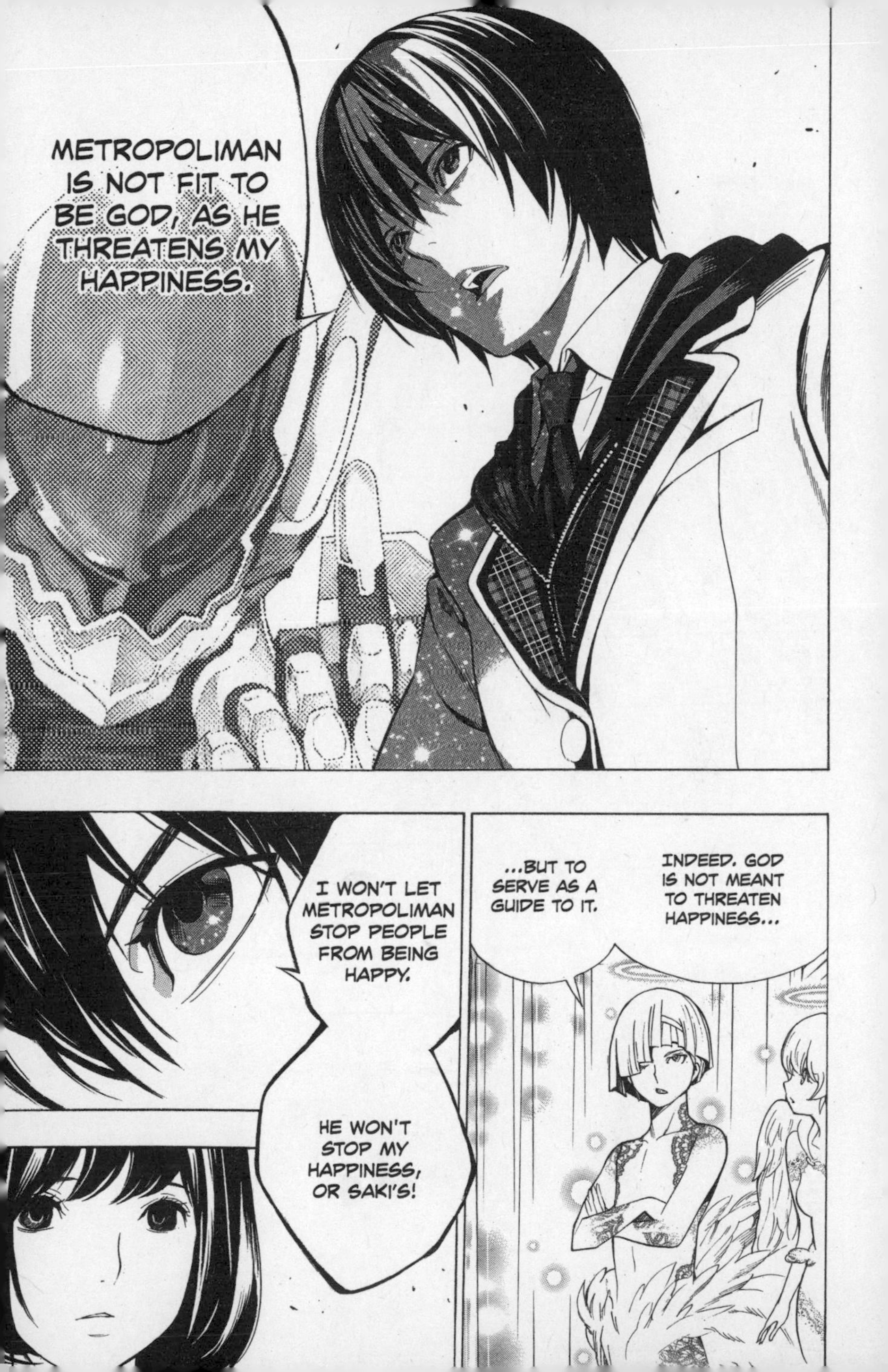
METROPOLIMAN IS NOT FIT TO BE GOD, AS HE THREATENS MY HAPPINESS.
INDEED. GOD IS NOT MEANT TO THREATEN HAPPINESS...
...BUT TO SERVE AS A GUIDE TO IT.
I WON'T LET METROPOLIMAN STOP PEOPLE FROM BEING HAPPY.
HE WON'T STOP MY HAPPINESS, OR SAKI'S!

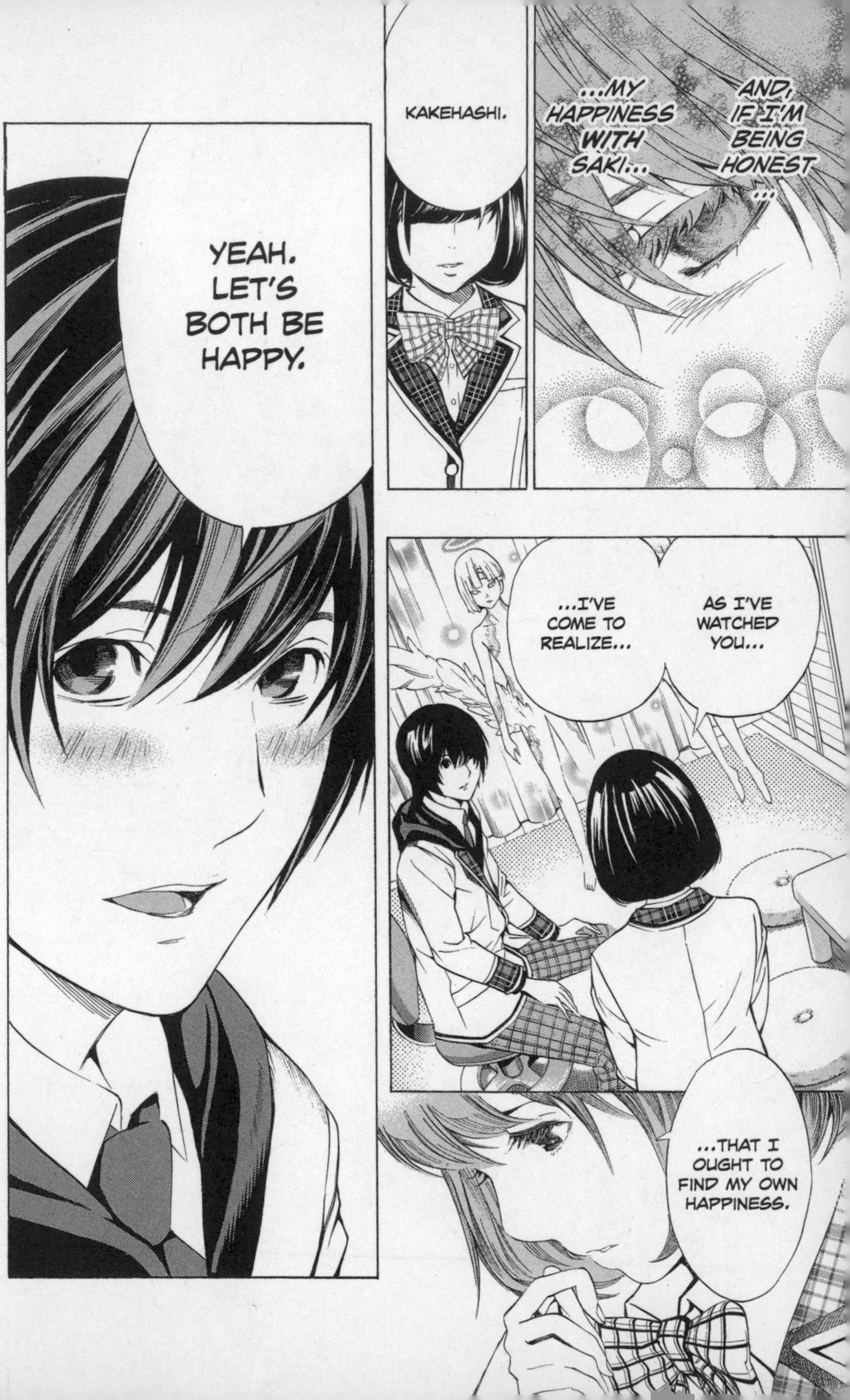
AND, IF I'M BEING HONEST...
...MY HAPPINESS WITH SAKI...
KAKEHASHI.
AS I'VE WATCHED YOU...
...I'VE COME TO REALIZE...
...THAT I OUGHT TO FIND MY OWN HAPPINESS.
YEAH. LET'S BOTH BE HAPPY.

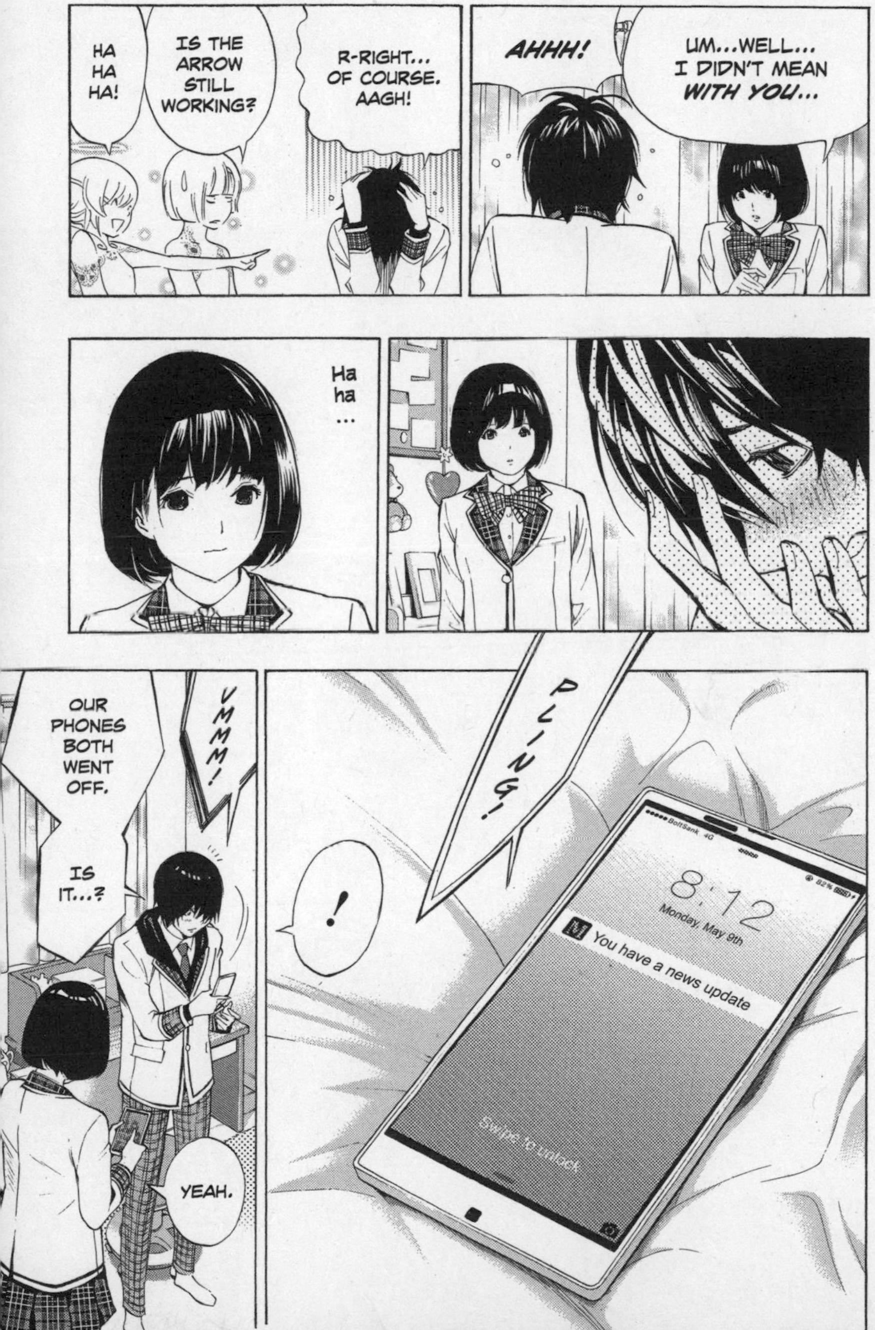
UM...WELL... I DIDN'T MEAN *WITH YOU*...
AHHH!
R-RIGHT... OF COURSE. AAGH!
IS THE ARROW STILL WORKING?
HA HA HA!
Ha ha ...
PLING!
!
8:12
Monday, May 9th
You have a news update
Swipe to unlock
UMMM!
OUR PHONES BOTH WENT OFF.
IS IT...?
YEAH.

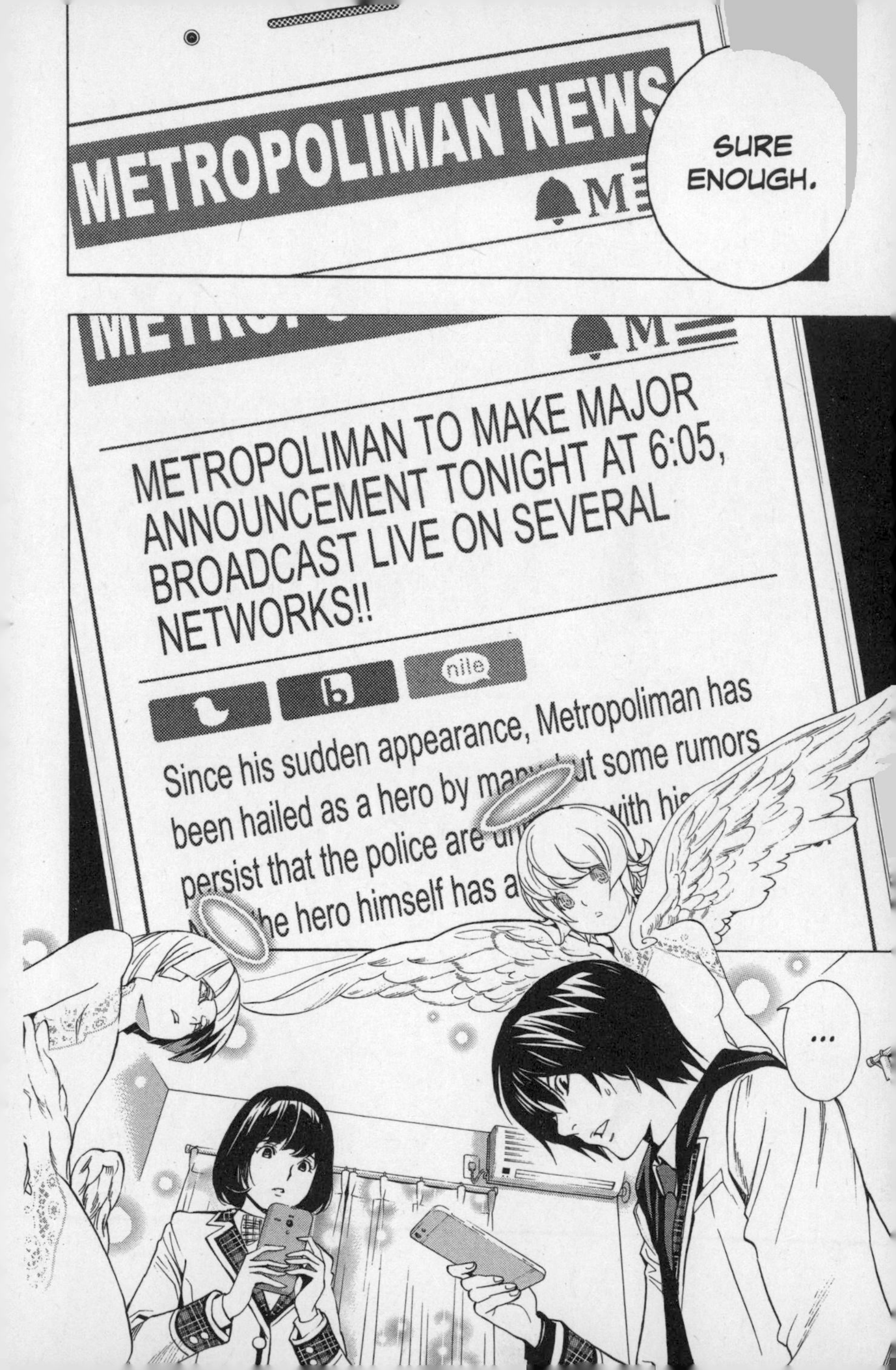
METROPOLIMAN NEWS
SURE ENOUGH.
METROPOLIMAN TO MAKE MAJOR ANNOUNCEMENT TONIGHT AT 6:05, BROADCAST LIVE ON SEVERAL NETWORKS!!
nile
Since his sudden appearance, Metropoliman has
been hailed as a hero by man
ut some rumors
persist that the police are
with his
he hero himself has a
...

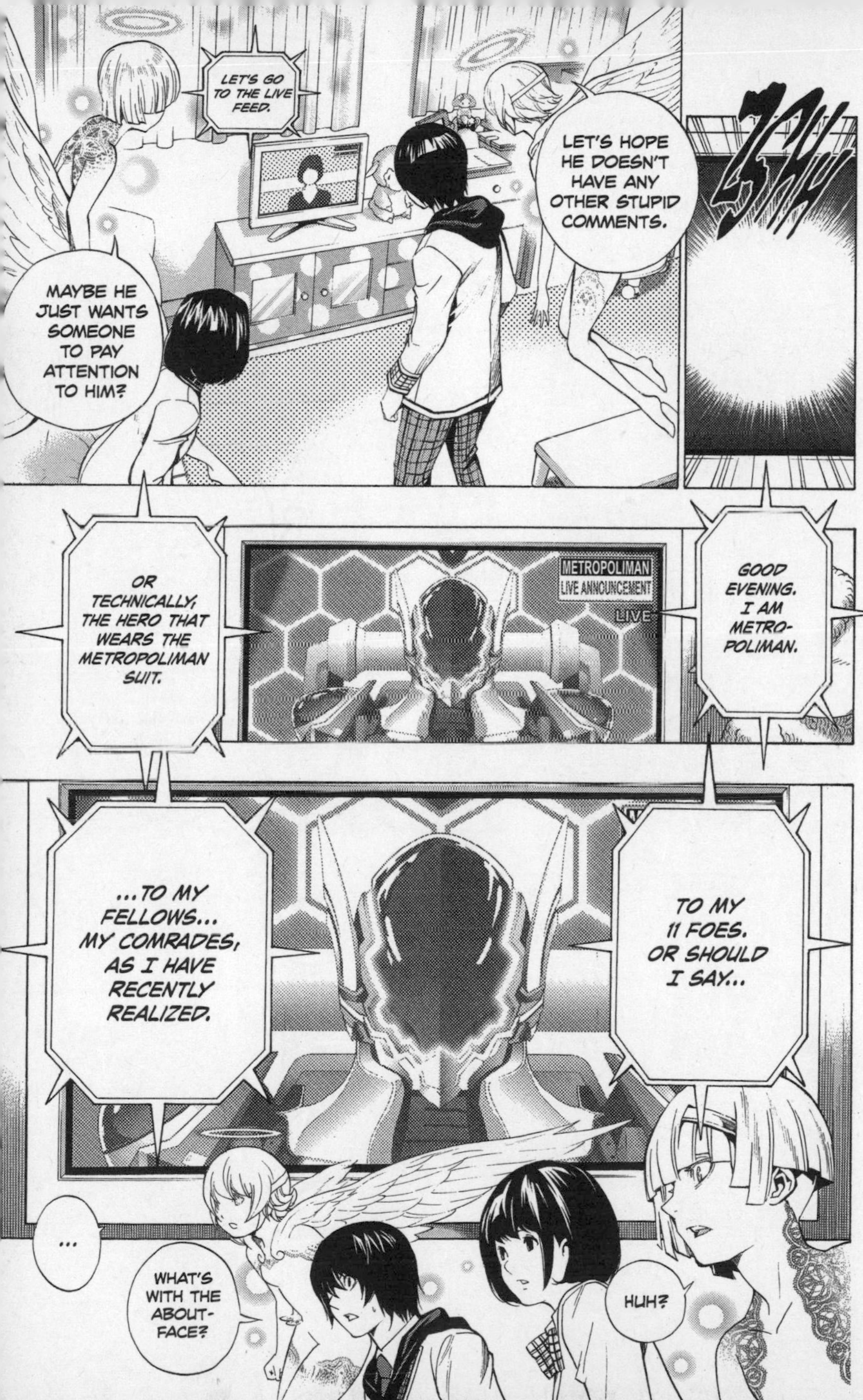
ZSHH
LET'S HOPE HE DOESN'T HAVE ANY OTHER STUPID COMMENTS.
LET'S GO TO THE LIVE FEED.
MAYBE HE JUST WANTS SOMEONE TO PAY ATTENTION TO HIM?
METROPOLIMAN LIVE ANNOUNCEMENT
LIVE
GOOD EVENING. I AM METROPOLIMAN.
OR TECHNICALLY, THE HERO THAT WEARS THE METROPOLIMAN SUIT.
TO MY 11 FOES. OR SHOULD I SAY...
...TO MY FELLOWS... MY COMRADES, AS I HAVE RECENTLY REALIZED.
HUH?
WHAT'S WITH THE ABOUT-FACE?
...

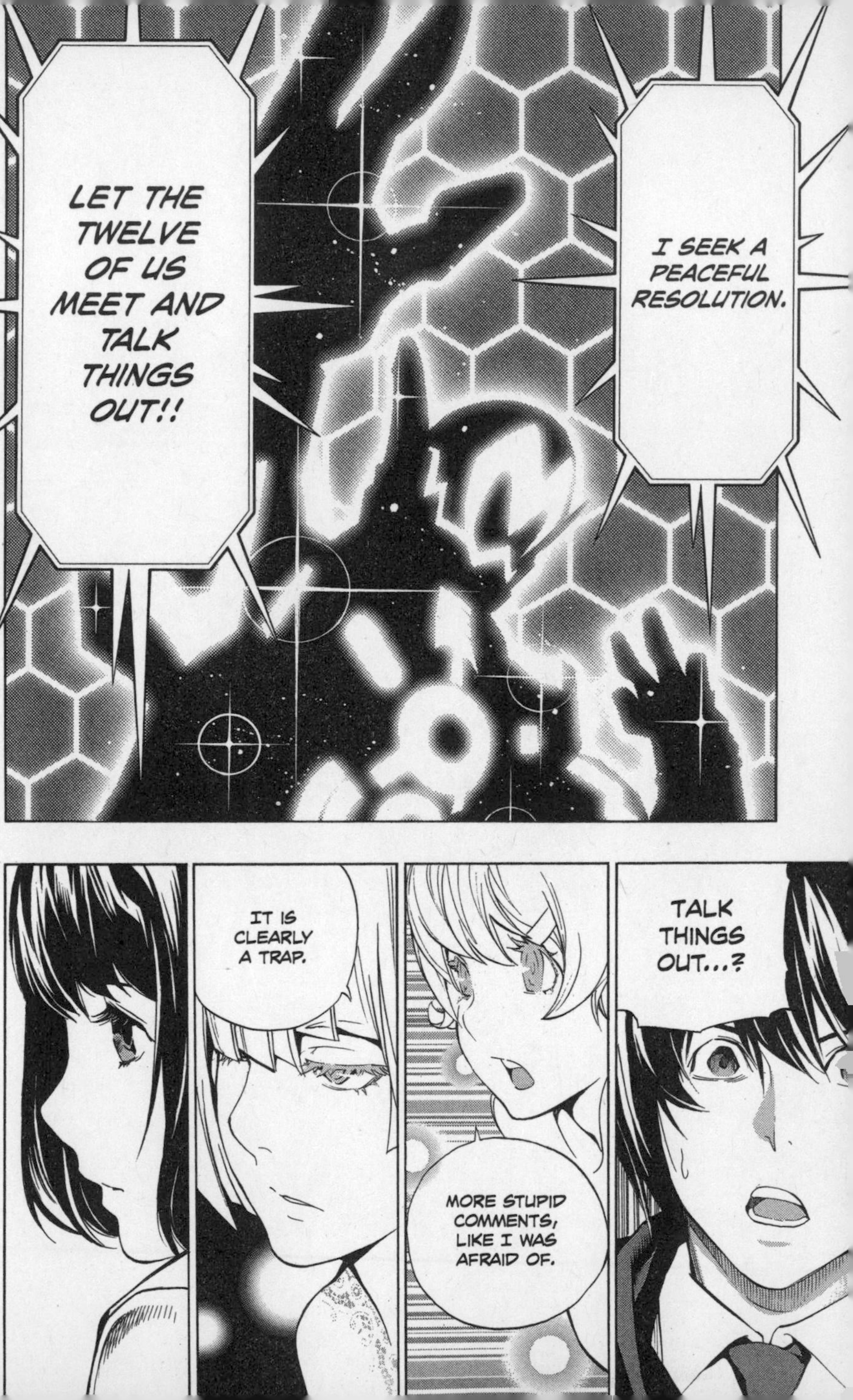
I SEEK A PEACEFUL RESOLUTION.
LET THE TWELVE OF US MEET AND TALK THINGS OUT!!
TALK THINGS OUT...?
MORE STUPID COMMENTS, LIKE I WAS AFRAID OF.
IT IS CLEARLY A TRAP.

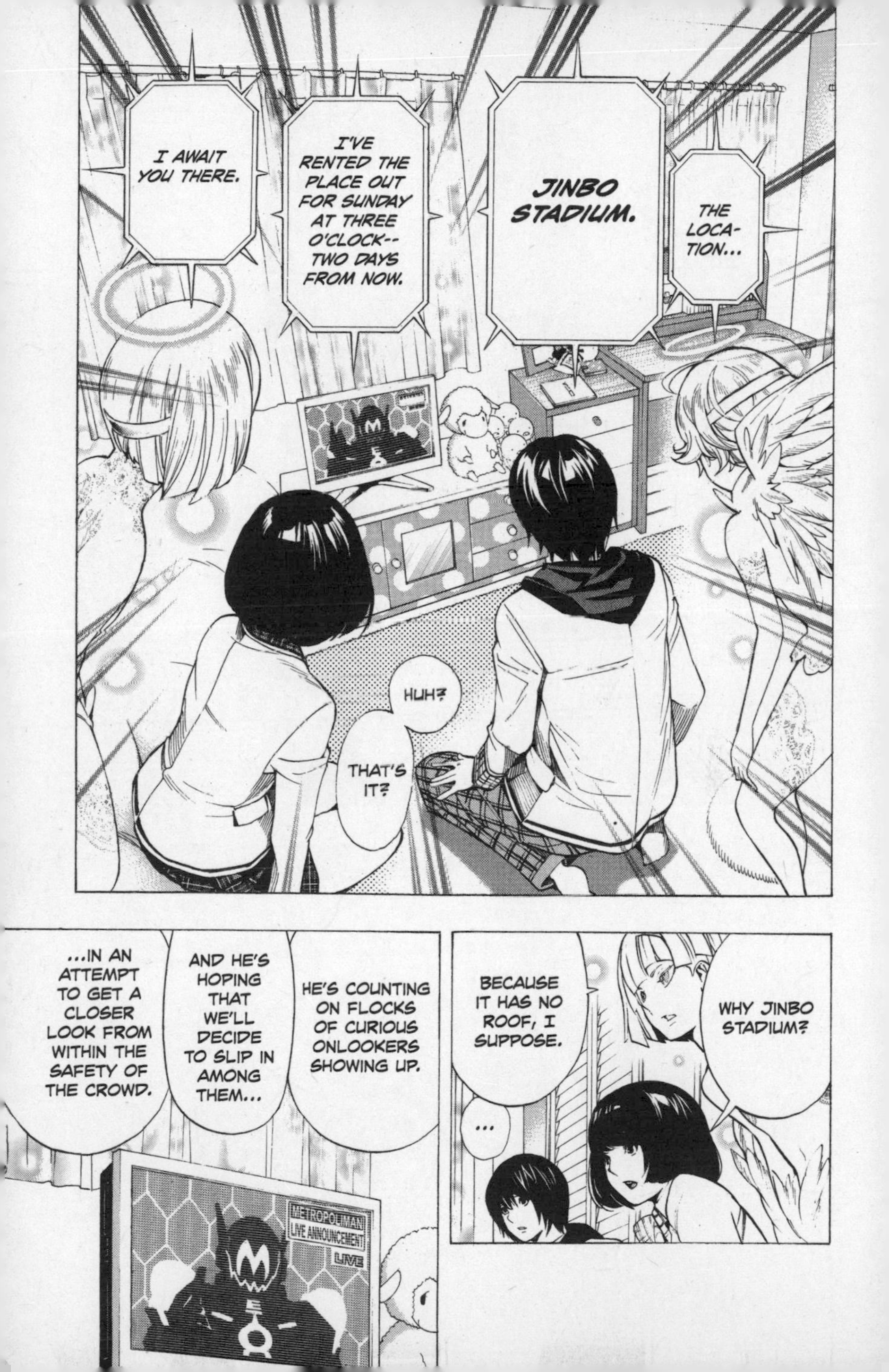
THE LOCATION...
JINBO STADIUM.
I'VE RENTED THE PLACE OUT FOR SUNDAY AT THREE O'CLOCK--TWO DAYS FROM NOW.
I AWAIT YOU THERE.
HUH?
THAT'S IT?
WHY JINBO STADIUM?
BECAUSE IT HAS NO ROOF, I SUPPOSE.
...
METROPOLIMAN
LIVE ANNOUNCEMENT
LIVE
HE'S COUNTING ON FLOCKS OF CURIOUS ONLOOKERS SHOWING UP.
AND HE'S HOPING THAT WE'LL DECIDE TO SLIP IN AMONG THEM...
...IN AN ATTEMPT TO GET A CLOSER LOOK FROM WITHIN THE SAFETY OF THE CROWD.

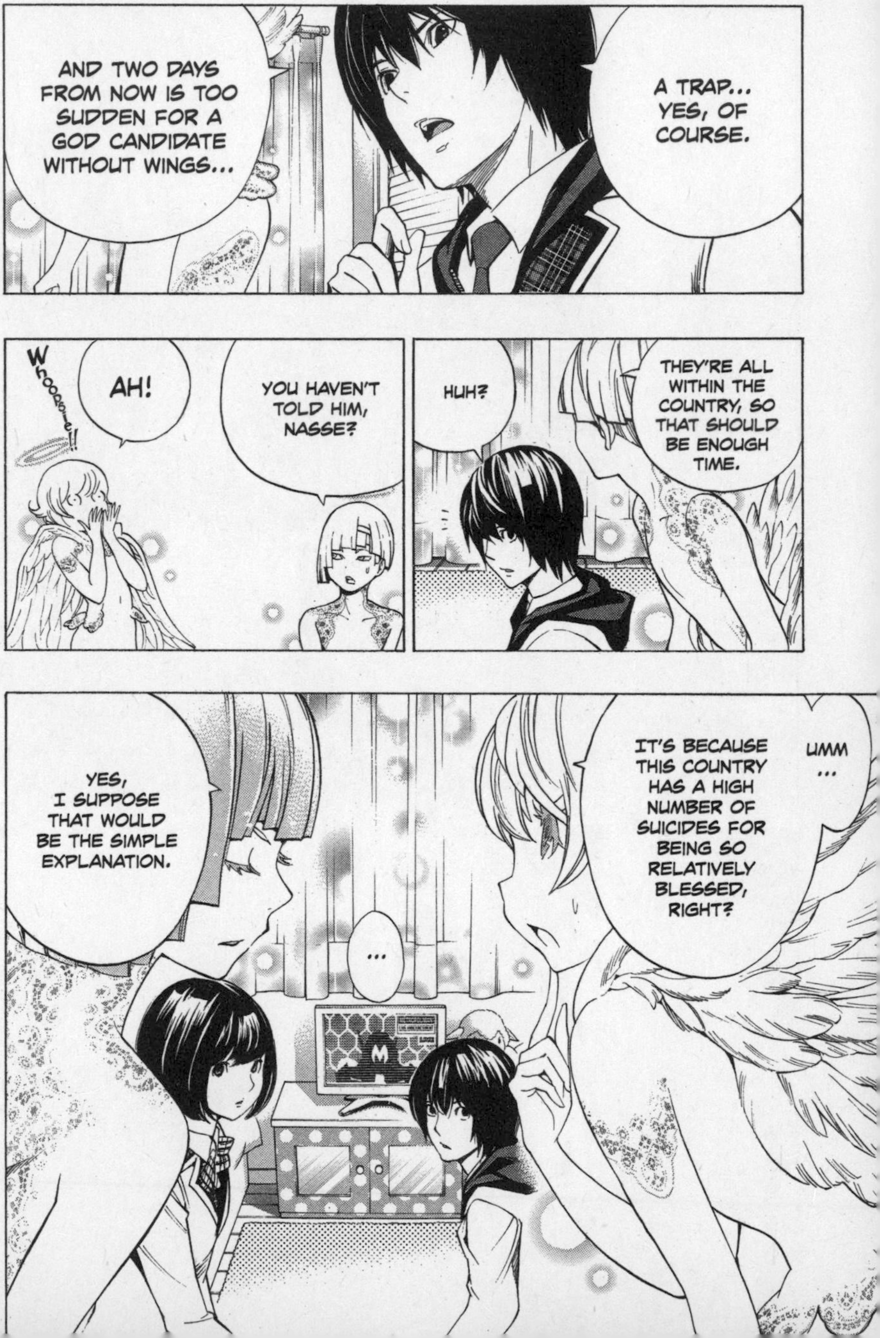
A TRAP... YES, OF COURSE.
AND TWO DAYS FROM NOW IS TOO SUDDEN FOR A GOD CANDIDATE WITHOUT WINGS...
THEY'RE ALL WITHIN THE COUNTRY, SO THAT SHOULD BE ENOUGH TIME.
HUH?
YOU HAVEN'T TOLD HIM, NASSE?
AH!
Whoopsie!!
UMM ...
IT'S BECAUSE THIS COUNTRY HAS A HIGH NUMBER OF SUICIDES FOR BEING SO RELATIVELY BLESSED, RIGHT?
YES, I SUPPOSE THAT WOULD BE THE SIMPLE EXPLANATION.
...

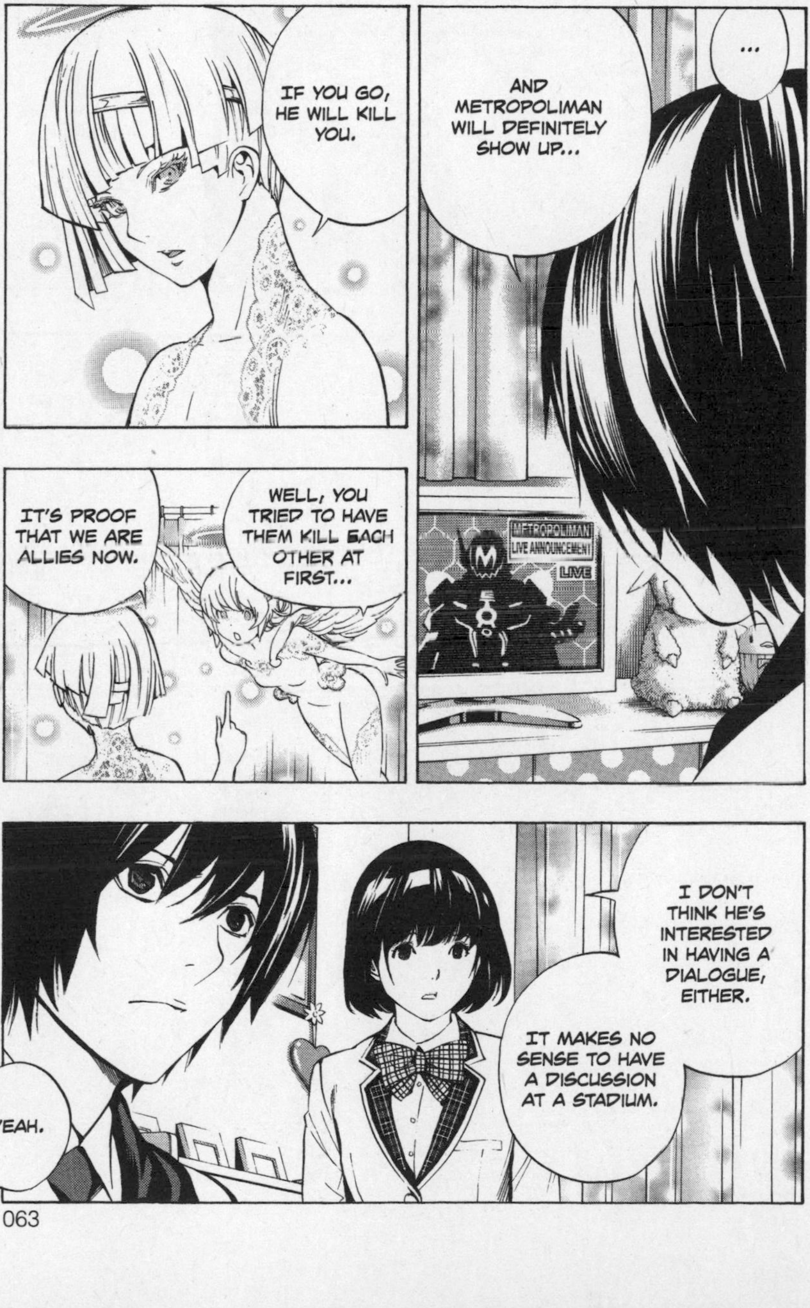
...
AND METROPOLIMAN WILL DEFINITELY SHOW UP...
METROPOLIMAN LIVE ANNOUNCEMENT
LIVE
IF YOU GO, HE WILL KILL YOU.
WELL, YOU TRIED TO HAVE THEM KILL EACH OTHER AT FIRST...
IT'S PROOF THAT WE ARE ALLIES NOW.
I DON'T THINK HE'S INTERESTED IN HAVING A DIALOGUE, EITHER.
IT MAKES NO SENSE TO HAVE A DISCUSSION AT A STADIUM.
YEAH.

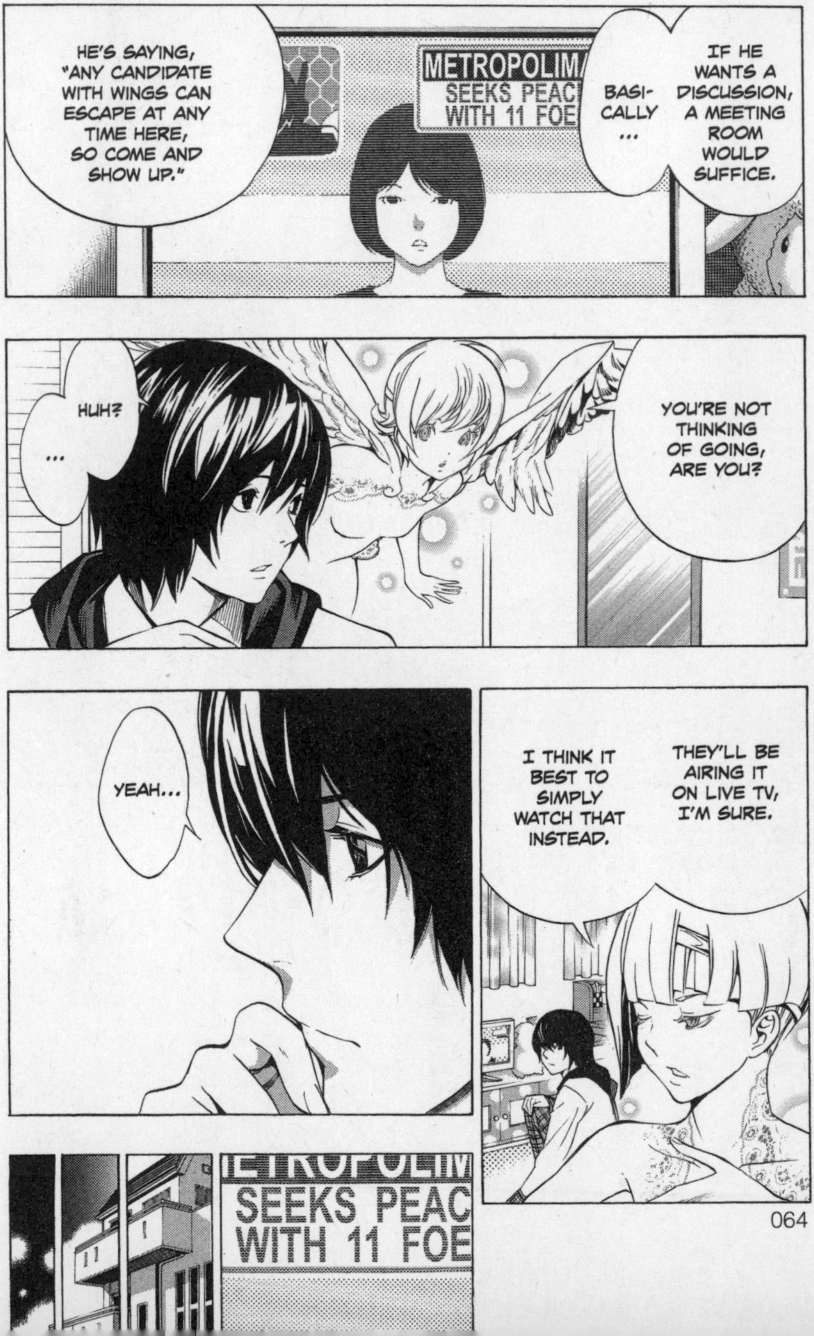
IF HE WANTS A DISCUSSION, A MEETING ROOM WOULD SUFFICE.
BASI-CALLY ...
METROPOLIM
SEEKS PEAC
WITH 11 FOE
HE'S SAYING, "ANY CANDIDATE WITH WINGS CAN ESCAPE AT ANY TIME HERE, SO COME AND SHOW UP."
YOU'RE NOT THINKING OF GOING, ARE YOU?
HUH?
...
THEY'LL BE AIRING IT ON LIVE TV, I'M SURE.
I THINK IT BEST TO SIMPLY WATCH THAT INSTEAD.
YEAH...
SEEKS PEAC
WITH 11 FOE

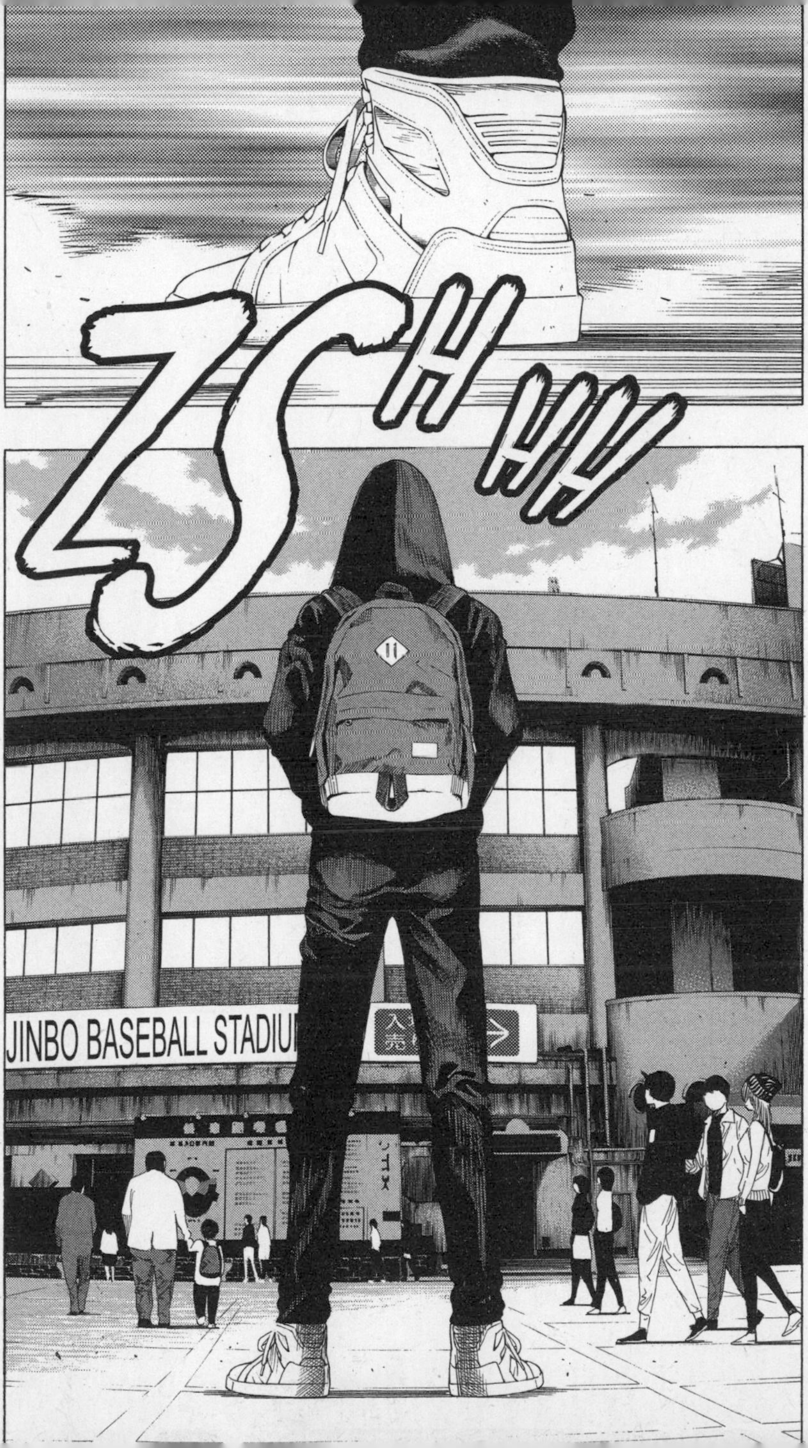
ZSH
JINBO BASEBALL STADIU

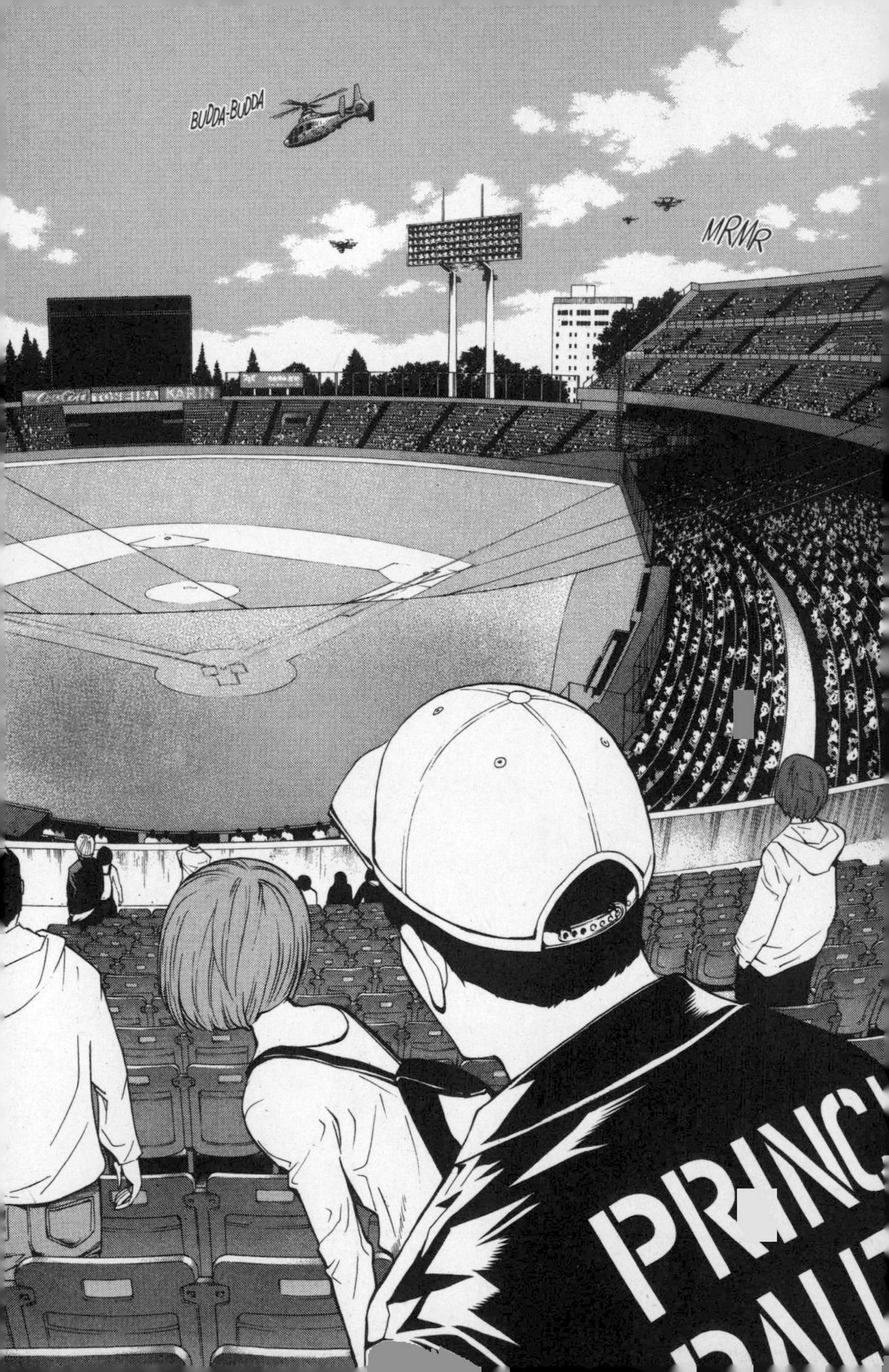
BUDDA-BUDDA
MRMR
KARIN

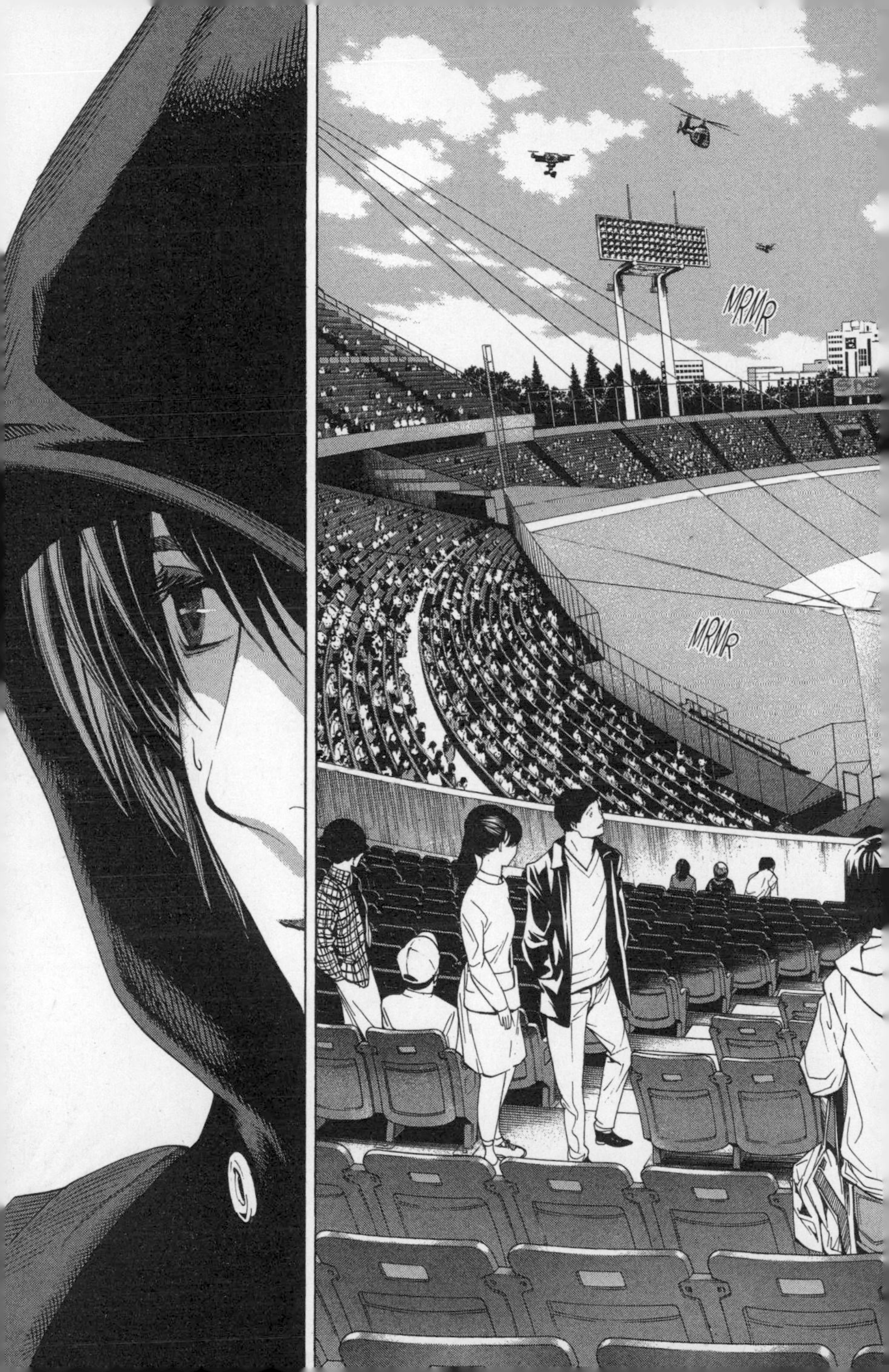
MRMR
MRMR

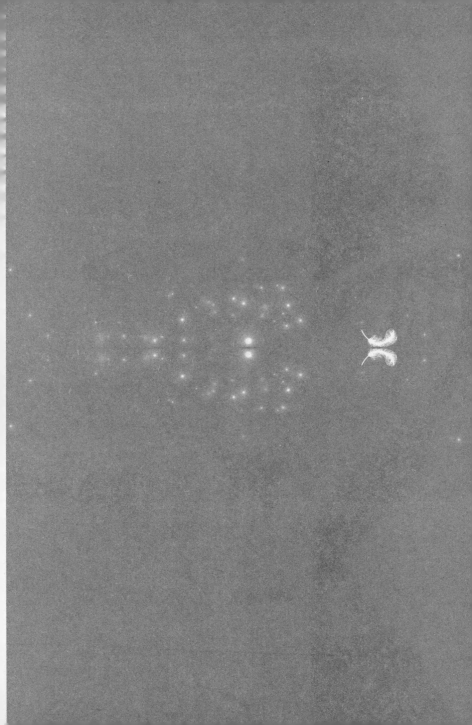

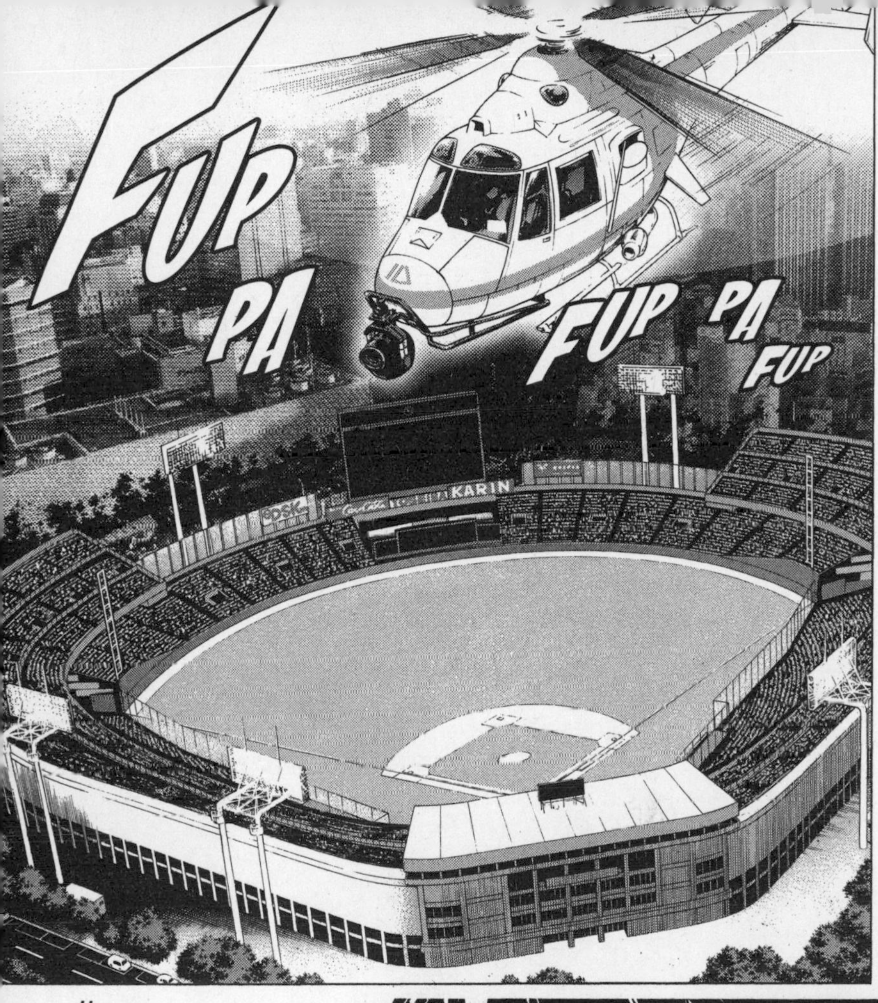
FUP
PA
FUP
FUP
PA
KARIN

5 The Big Reveal

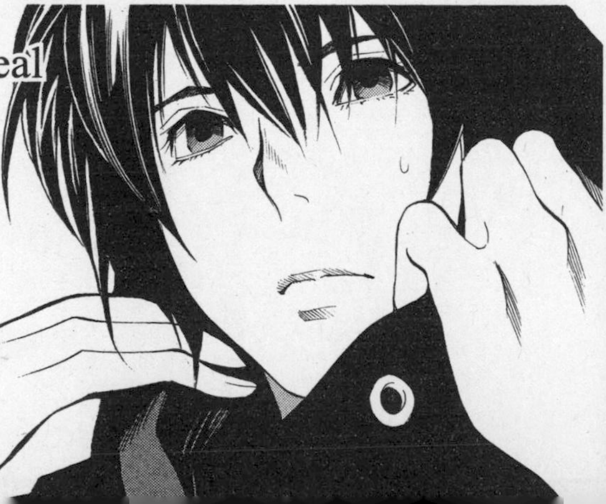

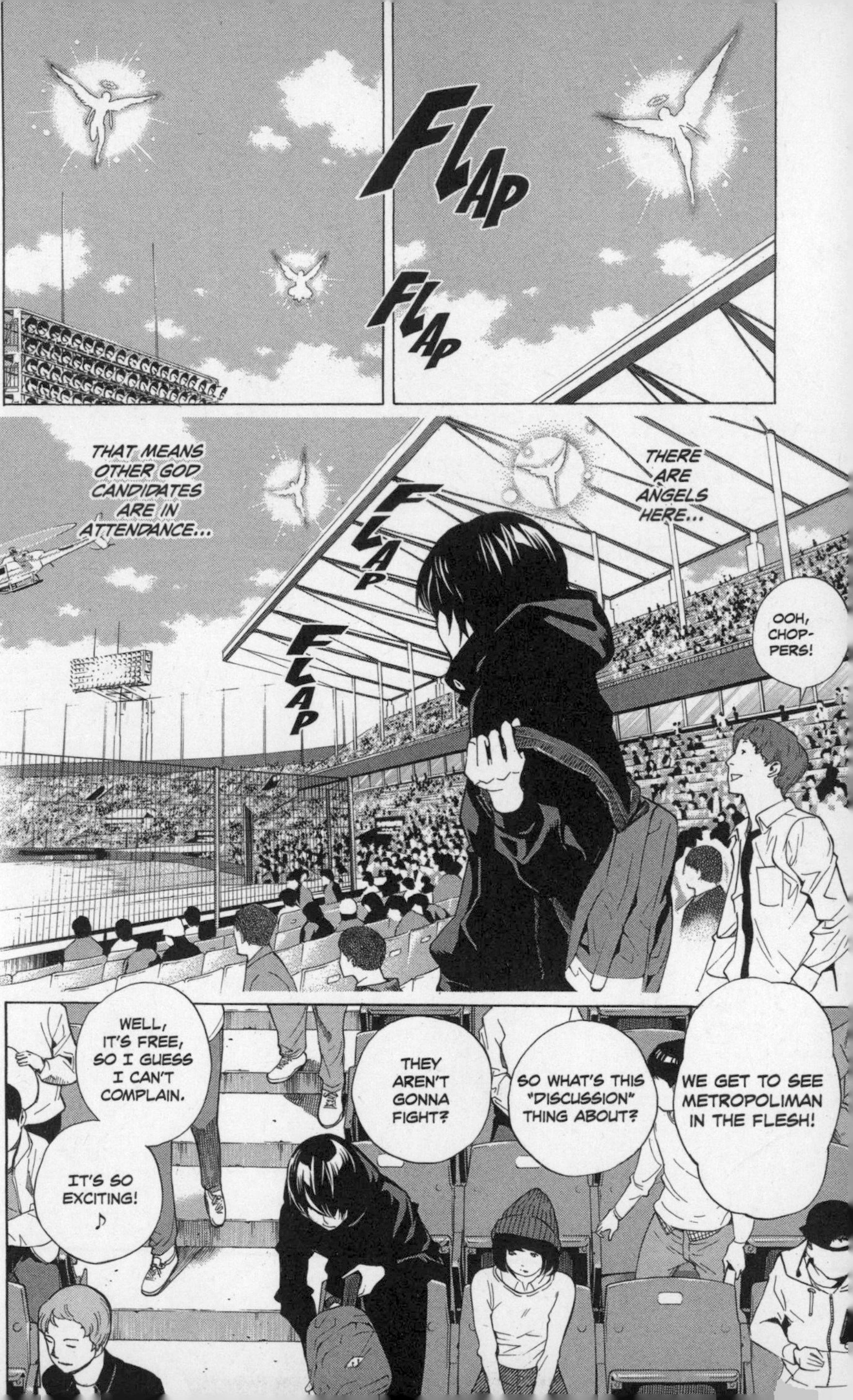
FLAP
FLAP
THERE ARE ANGELS HERE...
THAT MEANS OTHER GOD CANDIDATES ARE IN ATTENDANCE...
FLAP
FLAP
OOH, CHOP-PERS!
WE GET TO SEE METROPOLIMAN IN THE FLESH!
SO WHAT'S THIS "DISCUSSION" THING ABOUT?
THEY AREN'T GONNA FIGHT?
WELL, IT'S FREE, SO I GUESS I CAN'T COMPLAIN.
IT'S SO EXCITING! ♪

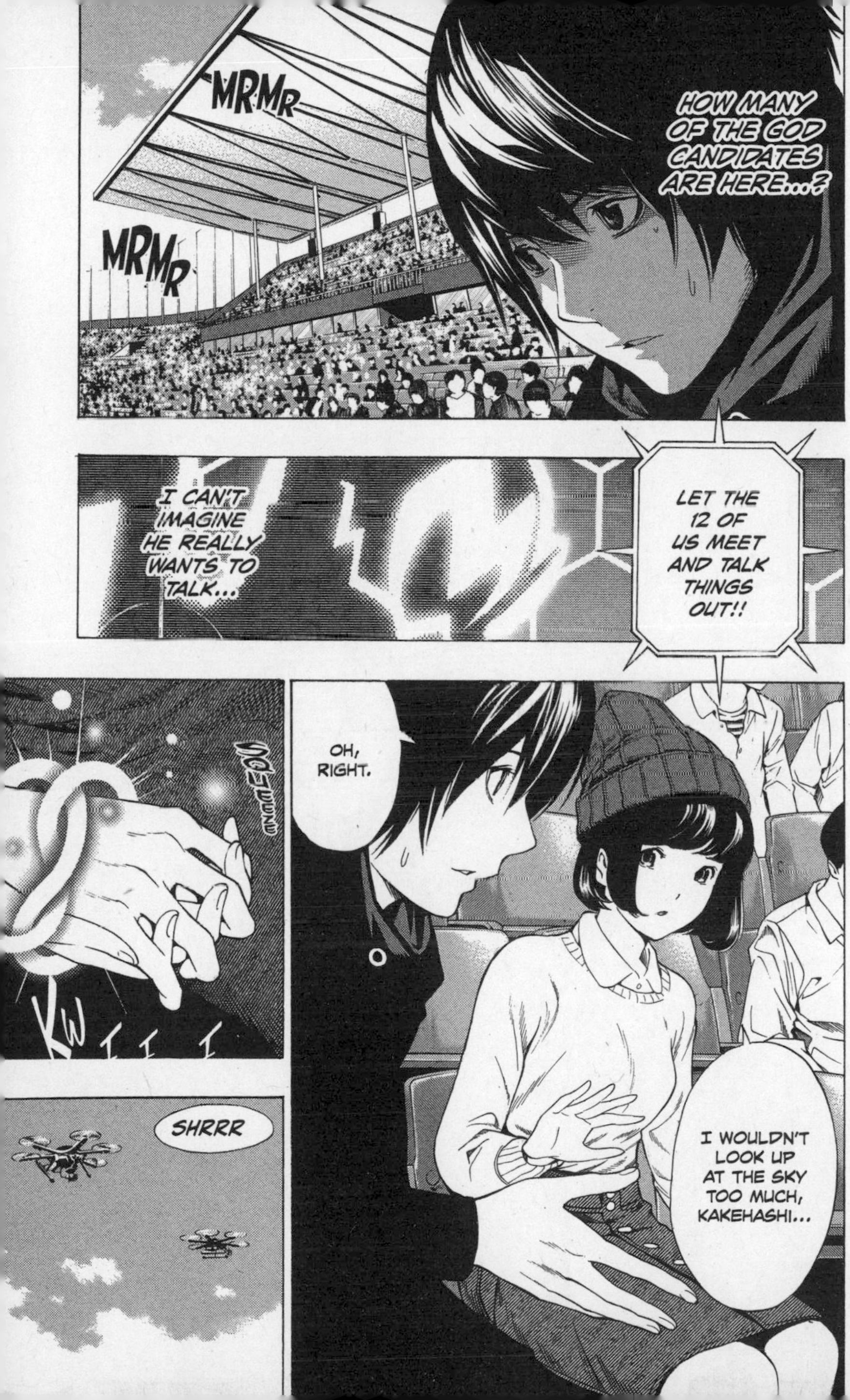
HOW MANY OF THE GOD CANDIDATES ARE HERE...?
MRMR
MRMR
LET THE 12 OF US MEET AND TALK THINGS OUT!!
I CAN'T IMAGINE HE REALLY WANTS TO TALK...
OH, RIGHT.
I WOULDN'T LOOK UP AT THE SKY TOO MUCH, KAKEHASHI...
SQUEEZE
KWIII
SHRRR

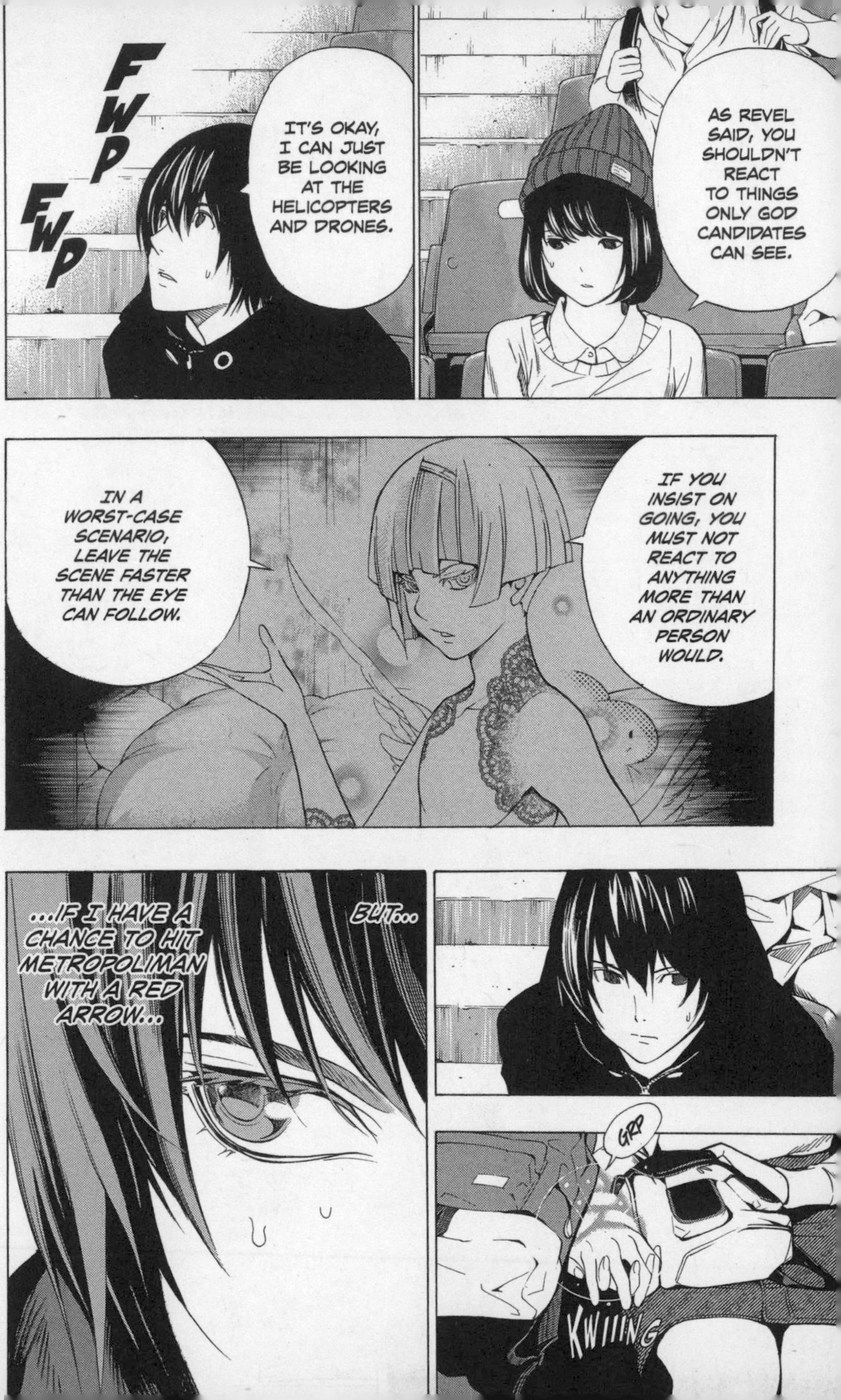
AS REVEL SAID, YOU SHOULDN'T REACT TO THINGS ONLY GOD CANDIDATES CAN SEE.
IT'S OKAY, I CAN JUST BE LOOKING AT THE HELICOPTERS AND DRONES.
FWP
FWP
IF YOU INSIST ON GOING, YOU MUST NOT REACT TO ANYTHING MORE THAN AN ORDINARY PERSON WOULD.
IN A WORST-CASE SCENARIO, LEAVE THE SCENE FASTER THAN THE EYE CAN FOLLOW.
GRP
KWIIING
BUT...
...IF I HAVE A CHANCE TO HIT METROPOLIMAN WITH A RED ARROW...

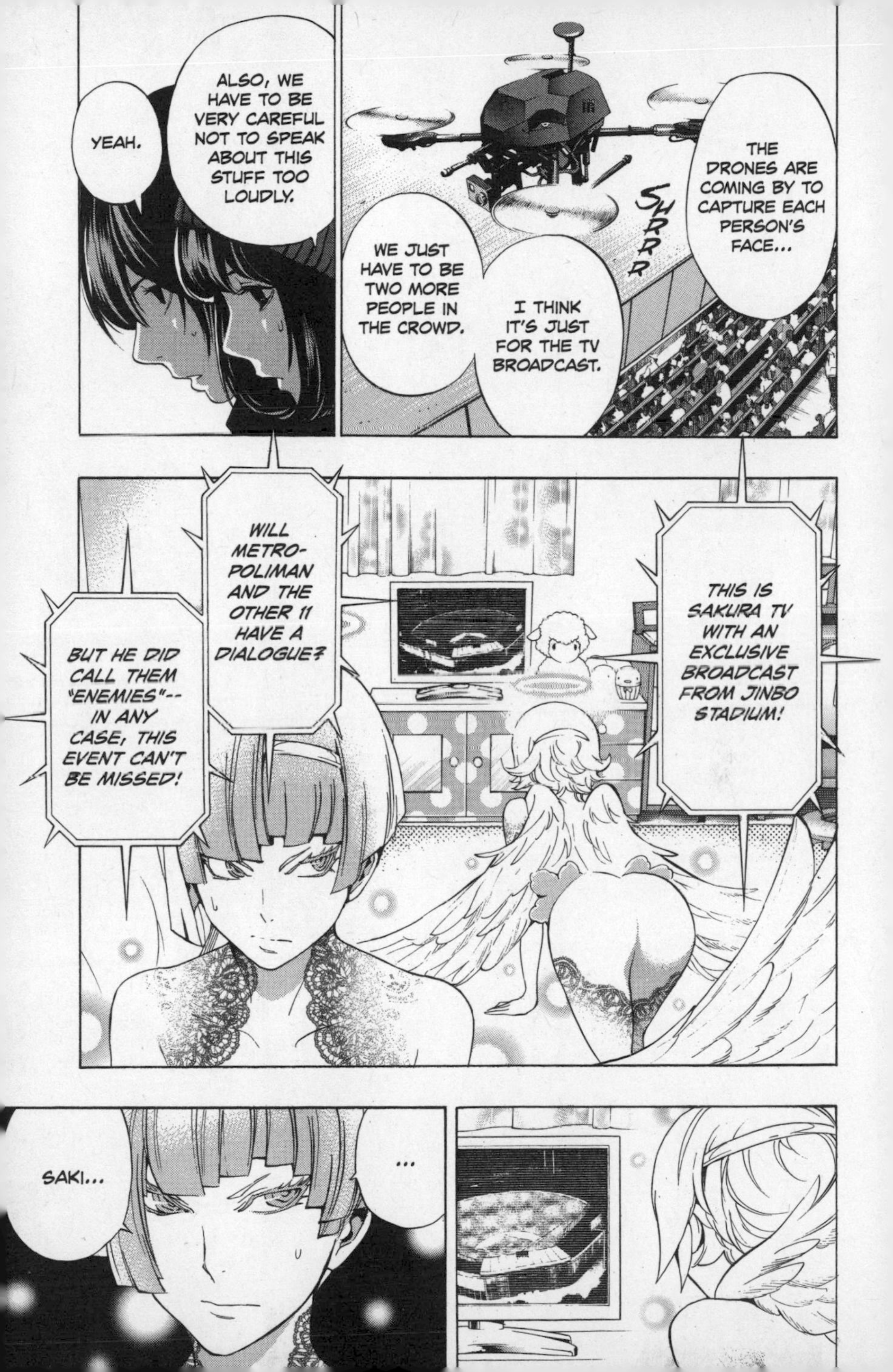
THE DRONES ARE COMING BY TO CAPTURE EACH PERSON'S FACE...
SHRRR
I THINK IT'S JUST FOR THE TV BROADCAST.
WE JUST HAVE TO BE TWO MORE PEOPLE IN THE CROWD.
ALSO, WE HAVE TO BE VERY CAREFUL NOT TO SPEAK ABOUT THIS STUFF TOO LOUDLY.
YEAH.
THIS IS SAKURA TV WITH AN EXCLUSIVE BROADCAST FROM JINBO STADIUM!
WILL METRO-POLIMAN AND THE OTHER 11 HAVE A DIALOGUE?
BUT HE DID CALL THEM "ENEMIES"-- IN ANY CASE, THIS EVENT CAN'T BE MISSED!
...
SAKI...

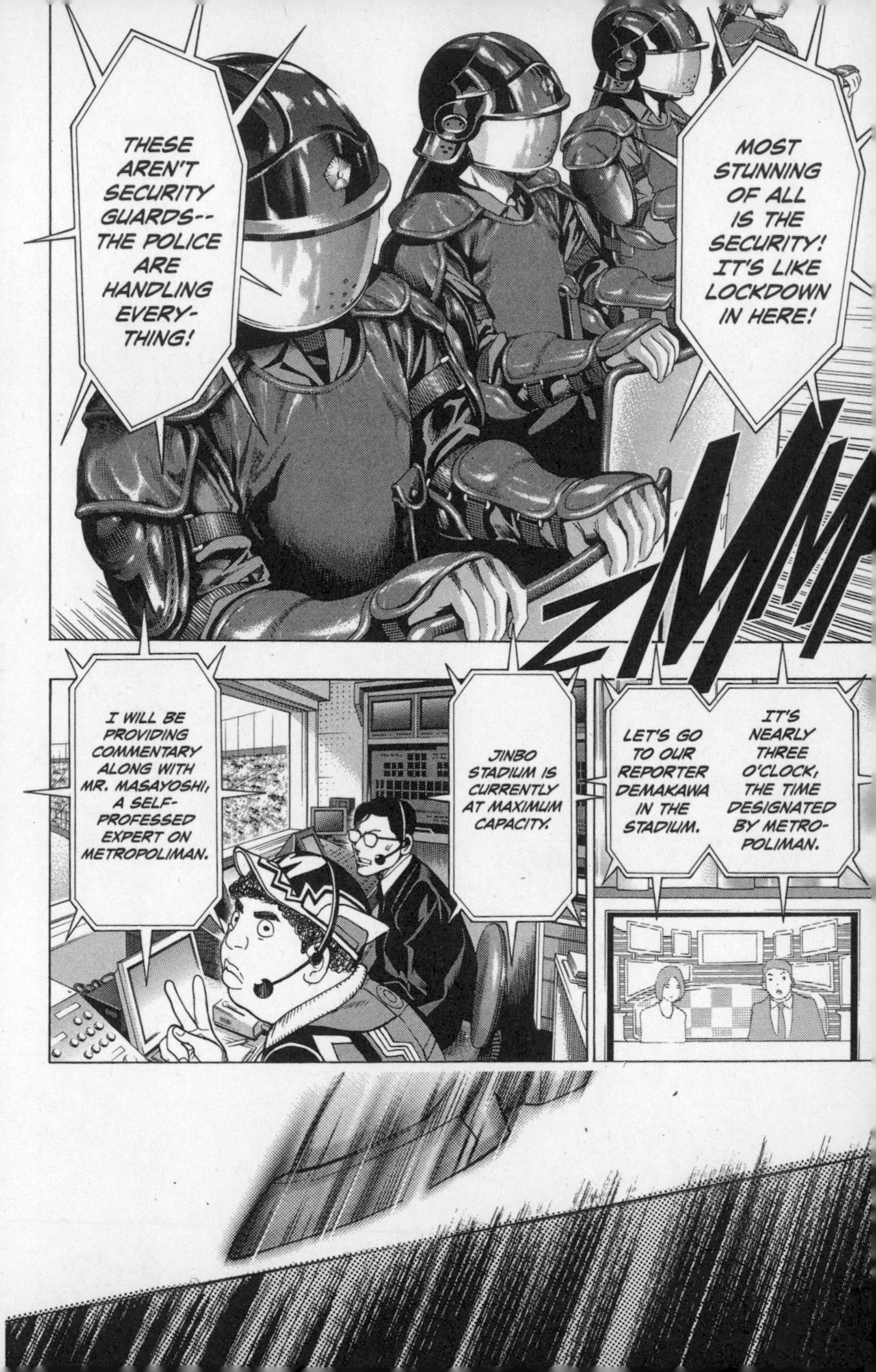
MOST STUNNING OF ALL IS THE SECURITY! IT'S LIKE LOCKDOWN IN HERE!
THESE AREN'T SECURITY GUARDS-- THE POLICE ARE HANDLING EVERY-THING!
ZMMM
IT'S NEARLY THREE O'CLOCK, THE TIME DESIGNATED BY METRO-POLIMAN.
LET'S GO TO OUR REPORTER DEMAKAWA IN THE STADIUM.
JINBO STADIUM IS CURRENTLY AT MAXIMUM CAPACITY.
I WILL BE PROVIDING COMMENTARY ALONG WITH MR. MASAYOSHI, A SELF-PROFESSED EXPERT ON METROPOLIMAN.

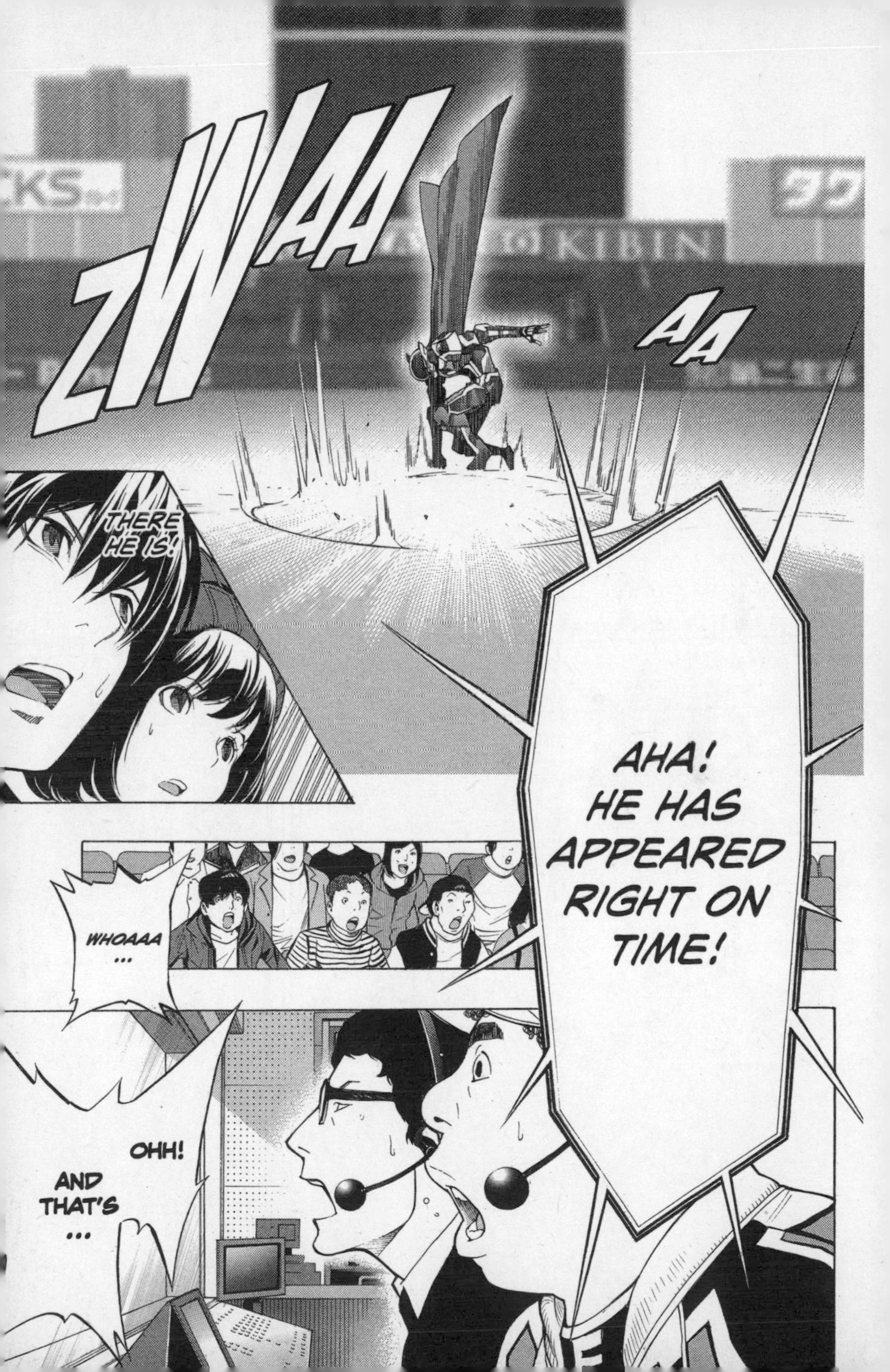
ZWAAAA
AA
THERE HE IS!
WHOAAA...
AHA! HE HAS APPEARED RIGHT ON TIME!
OHH!
AND THAT'S...

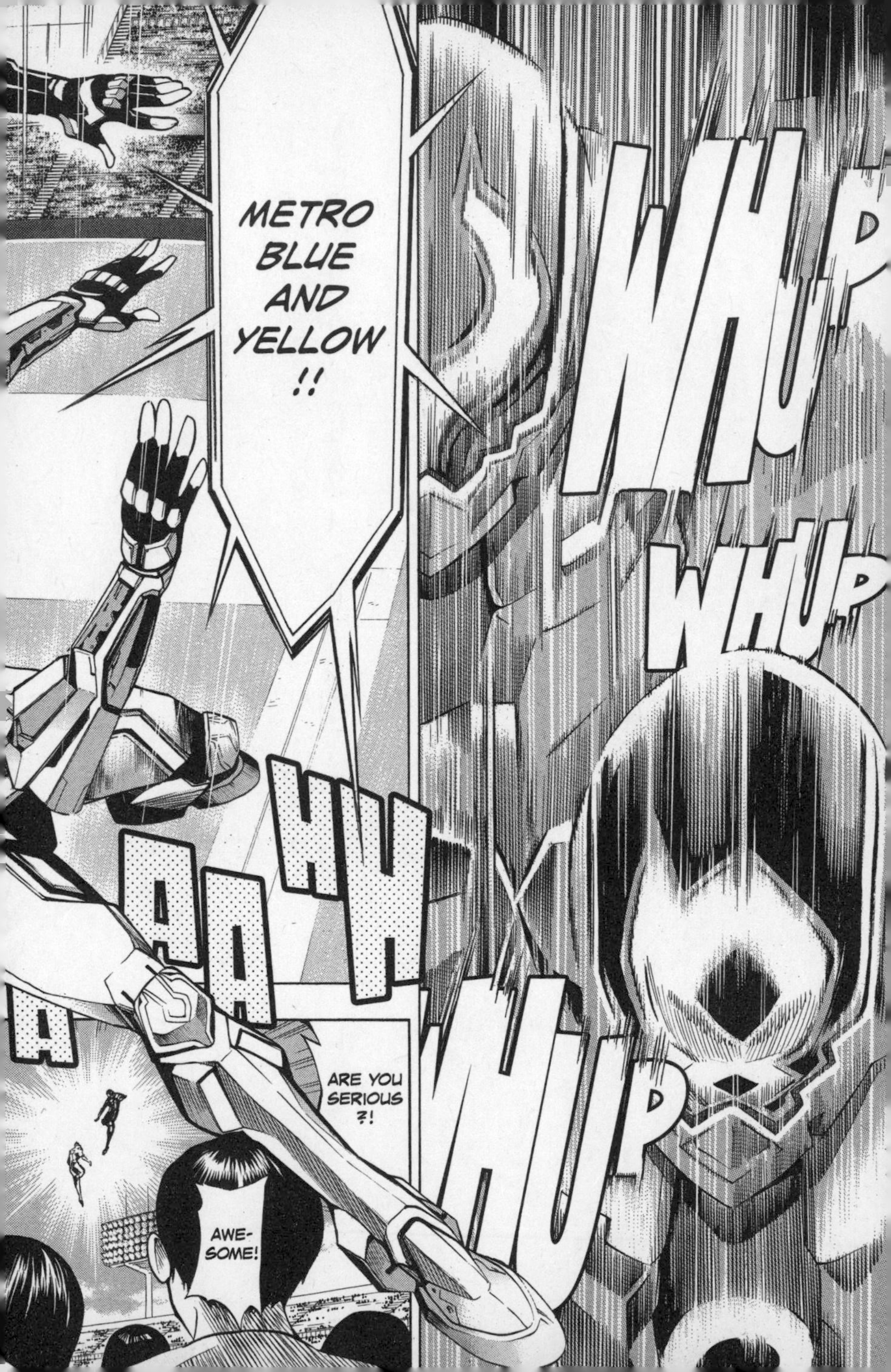
WHUP
WHUP
WHUP
METRO BLUE AND YELLOW !!
AAAHH
ARE YOU SERIOUS ?!
AWE-SOME!

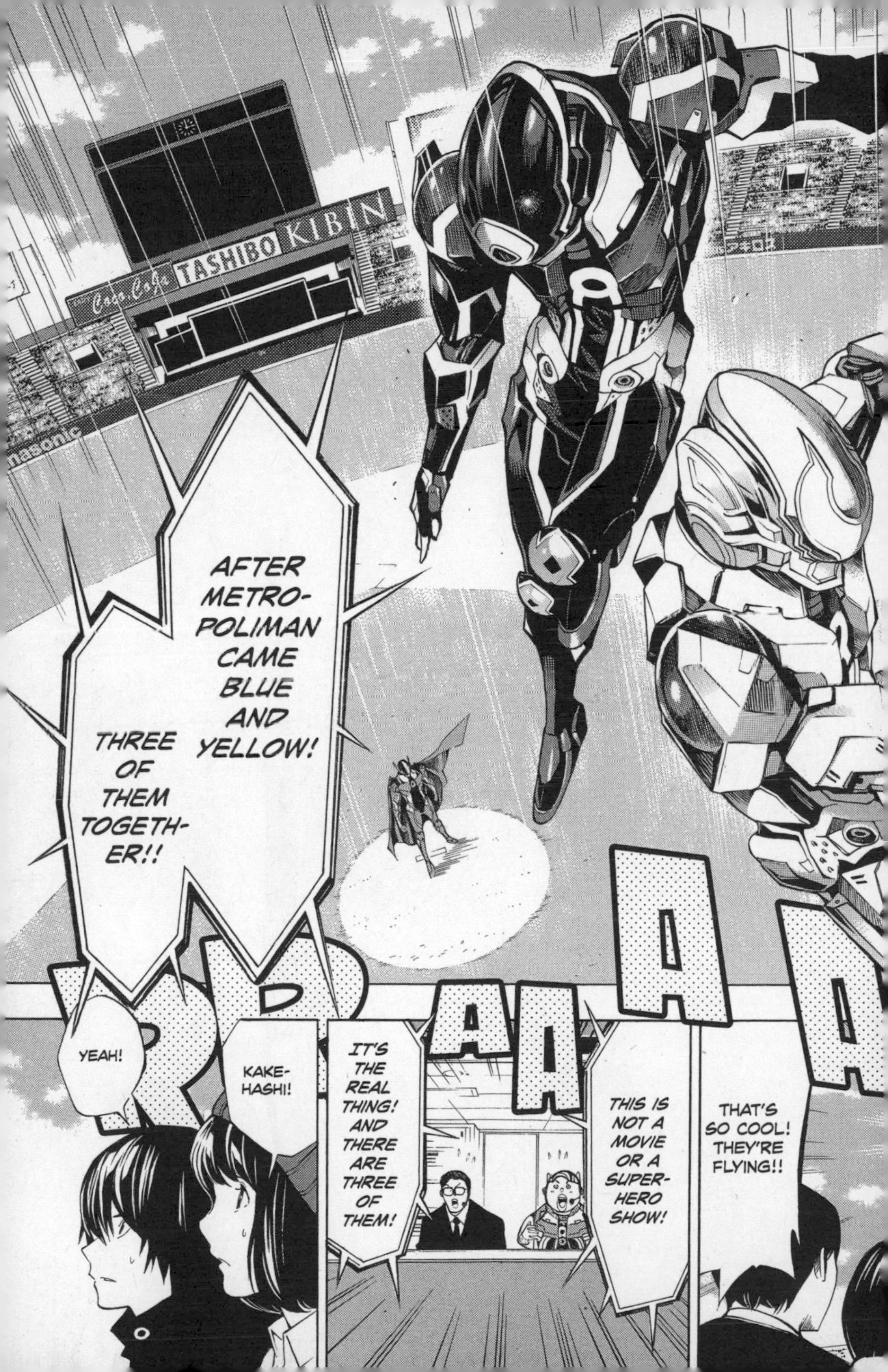
TASHIBO
KIBIN
AFTER METROPOLIMAN CAME BLUE AND YELLOW!
THREE OF THEM TOGETHER!!
THAT'S SO COOL! THEY'RE FLYING!!
THIS IS NOT A MOVIE OR A SUPERHERO SHOW!
IT'S THE REAL THING! AND THERE ARE THREE OF THEM!
KAKEHASHI!
YEAH!

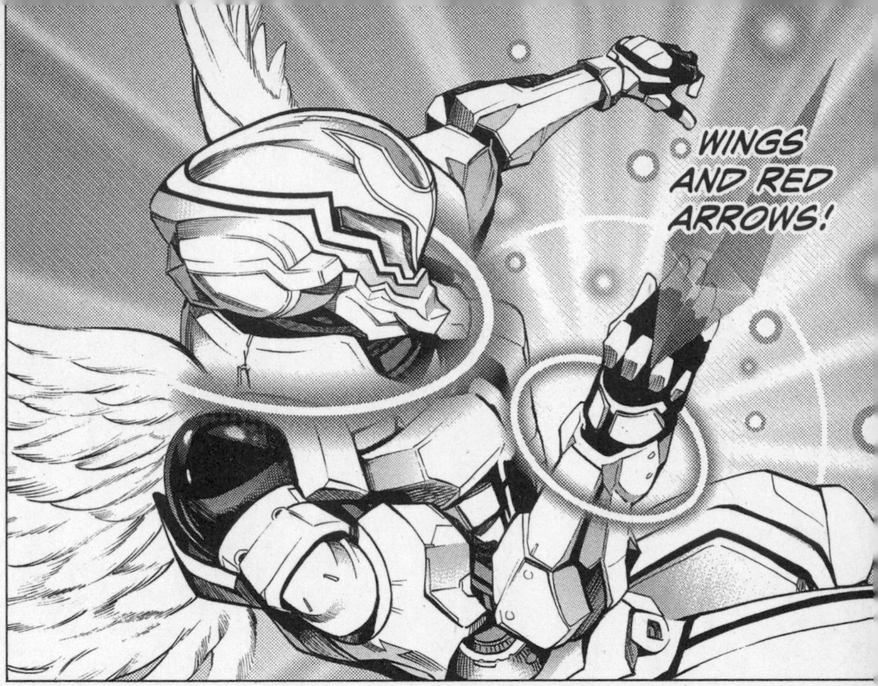
WINGS AND RED ARROWS!
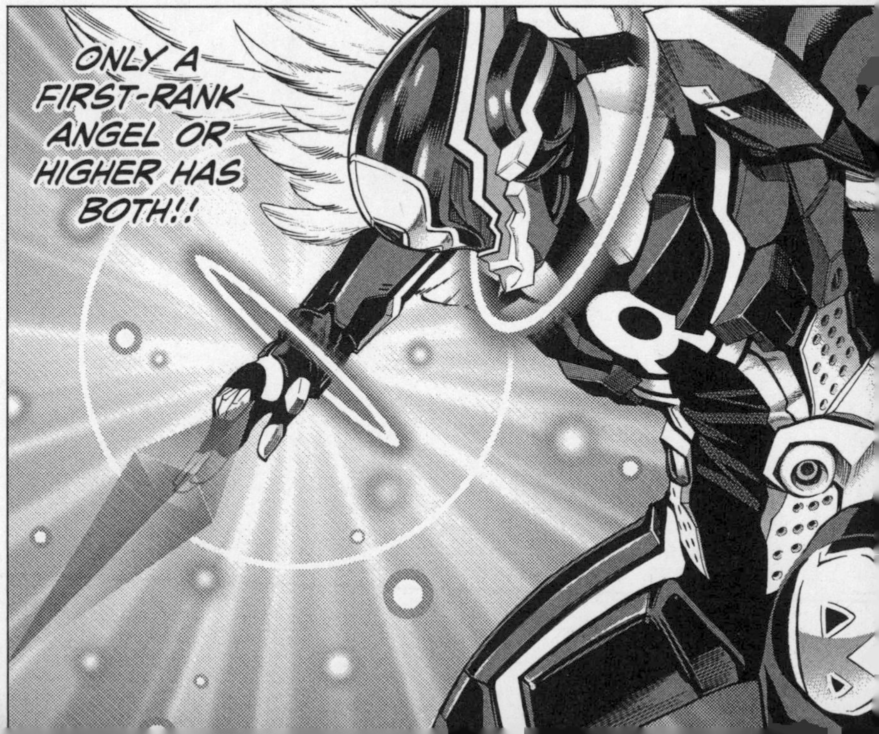
ONLY A FIRST-RANK ANGEL OR HIGHER HAS BOTH!!

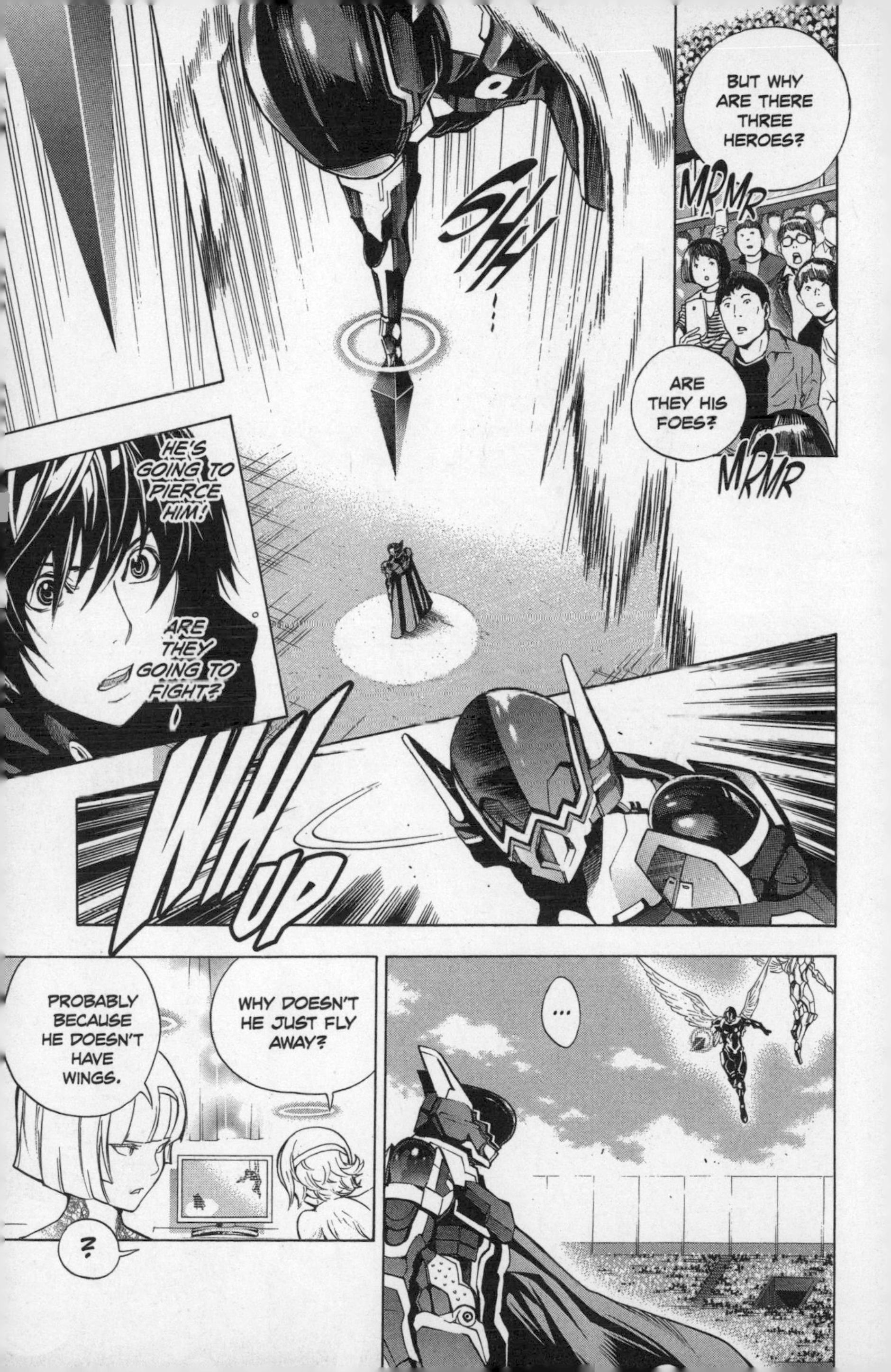
BUT WHY ARE THERE THREE HEROES?
MRMR
ARE THEY HIS FOES?
MRMR
SHH
HE'S GOING TO PIERCE HIM!
ARE THEY GOING TO FIGHT?
WHUP
...
WHY DOESN'T HE JUST FLY AWAY?
PROBABLY BECAUSE HE DOESN'T HAVE WINGS.
?

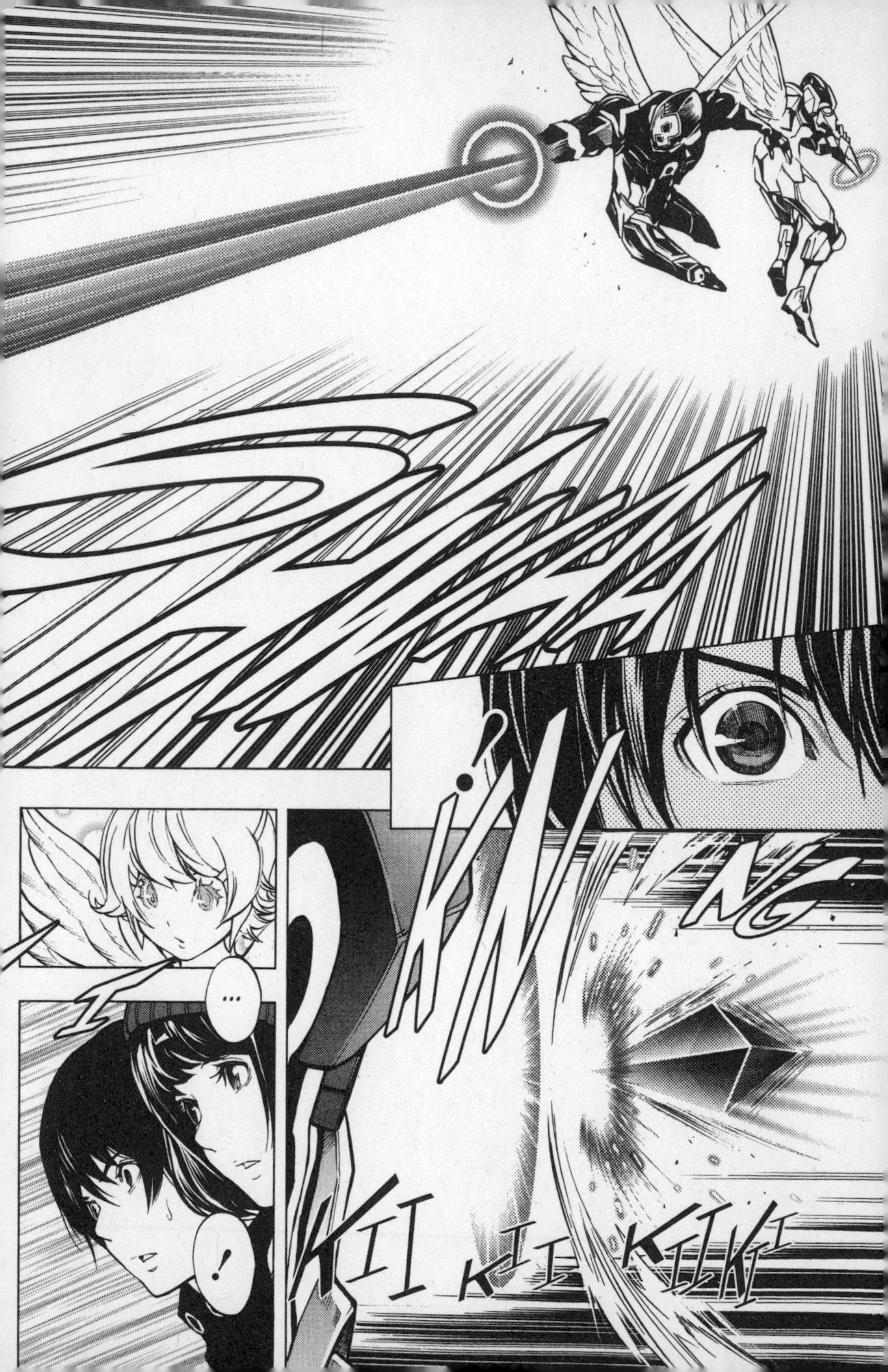
KII KII KIKI
...
!

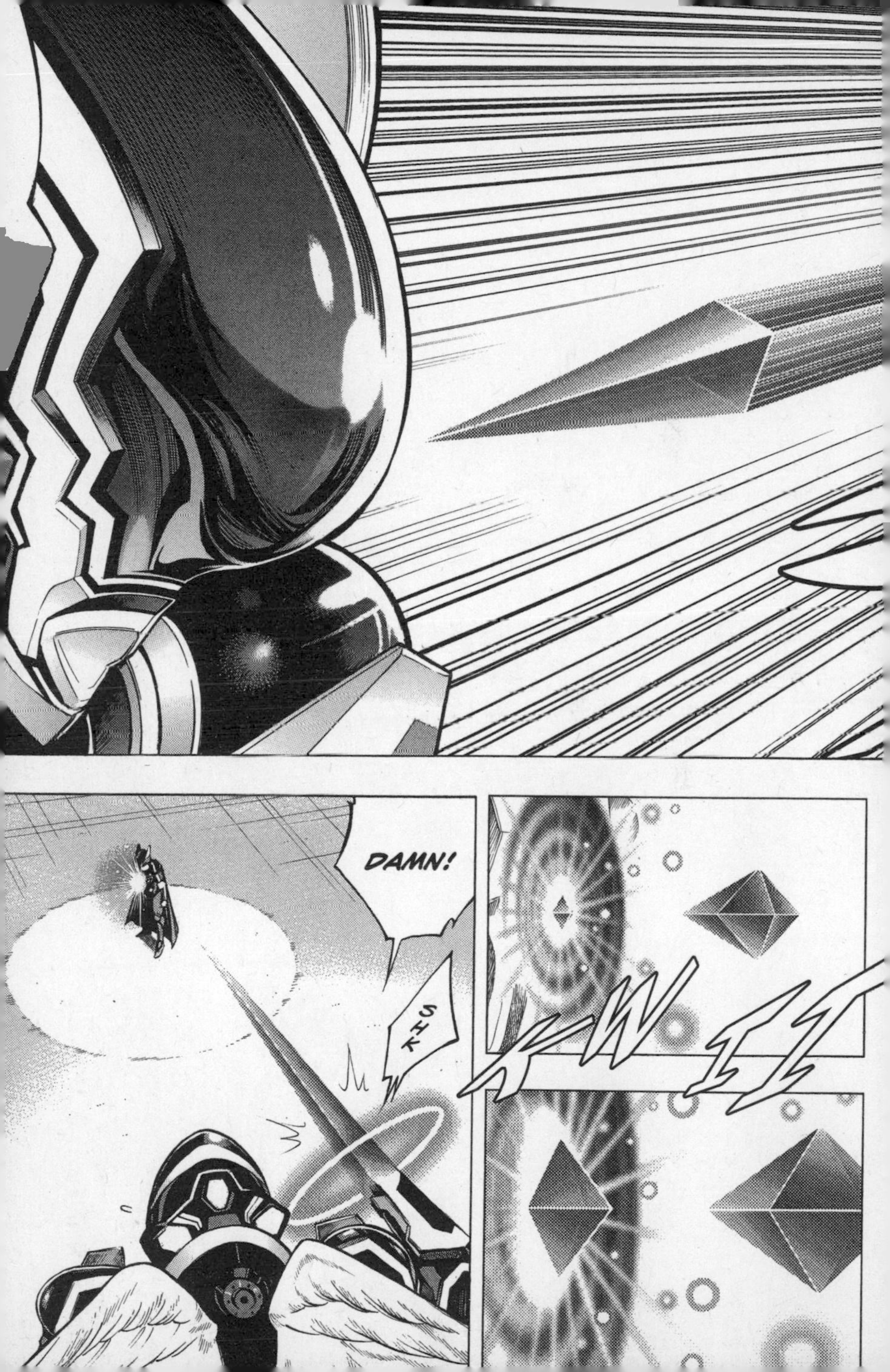
KWII
DAMN!
SHK

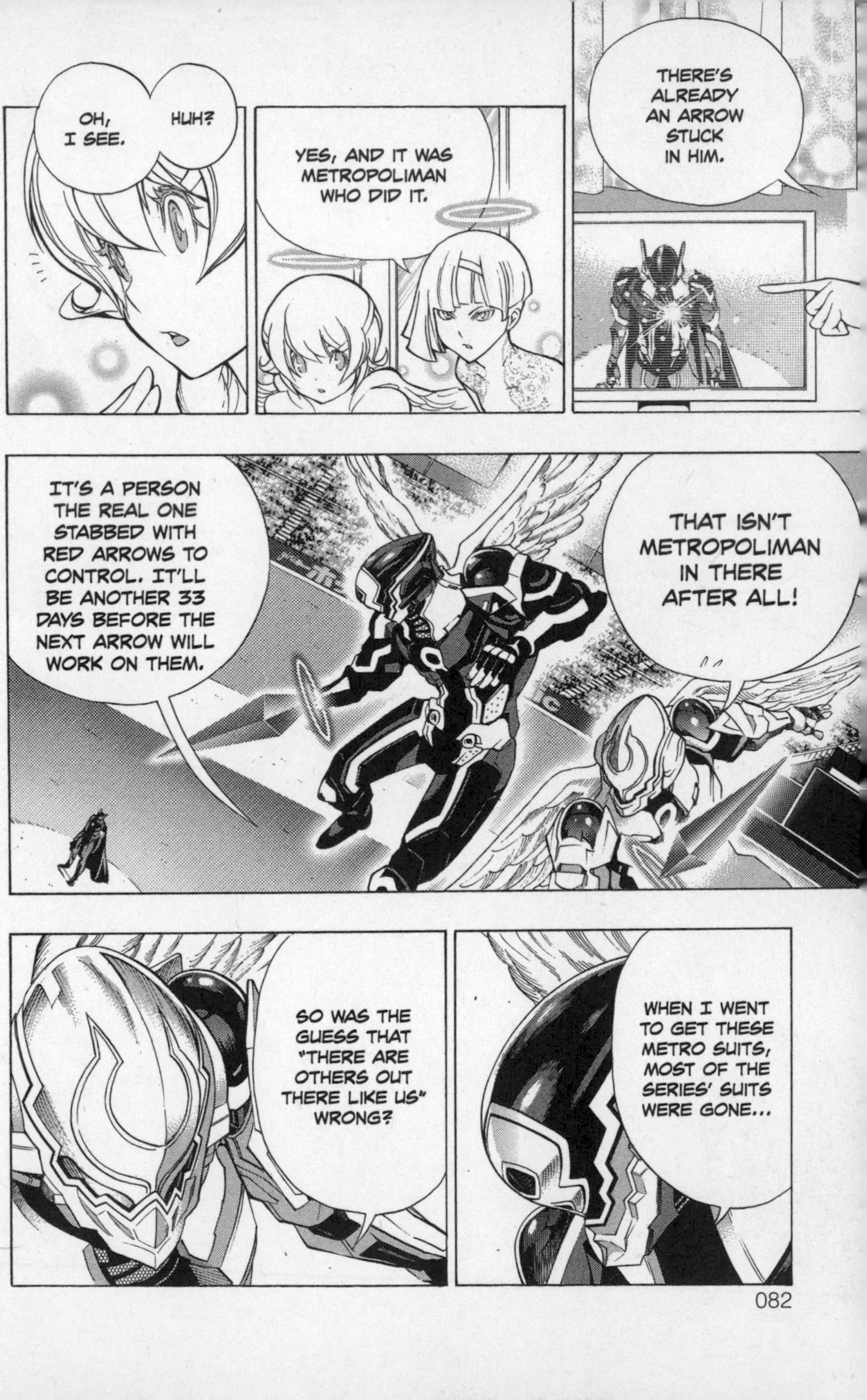
THERE'S ALREADY AN ARROW STUCK IN HIM.
YES, AND IT WAS METROPOLIMAN WHO DID IT.
HUH?
OH, I SEE.
THAT ISN'T METROPOLIMAN IN THERE AFTER ALL!
IT'S A PERSON THE REAL ONE STABBED WITH RED ARROWS TO CONTROL. IT'LL BE ANOTHER 33 DAYS BEFORE THE NEXT ARROW WILL WORK ON THEM.
WHEN I WENT TO GET THESE METRO SUITS, MOST OF THE SERIES' SUITS WERE GONE...
SO WAS THE GUESS THAT "THERE ARE OTHERS OUT THERE LIKE US" WRONG?

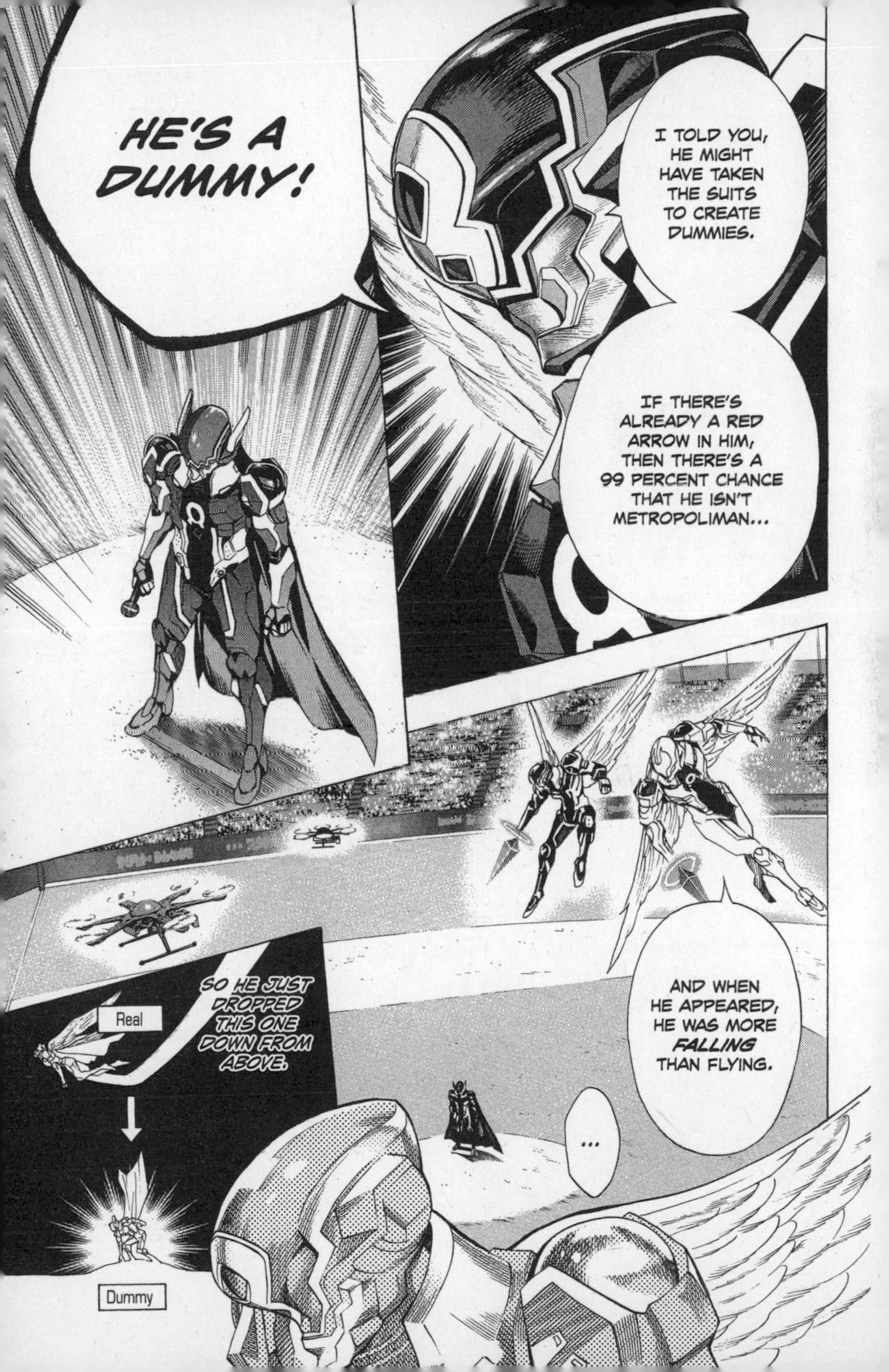
I TOLD YOU, HE MIGHT HAVE TAKEN THE SUITS TO CREATE DUMMIES.
IF THERE'S ALREADY A RED ARROW IN HIM, THEN THERE'S A 99 PERCENT CHANCE THAT HE ISN'T METROPOLIMAN...
HE'S A DUMMY!
AND WHEN HE APPEARED, HE WAS MORE FALLING THAN FLYING.
SO HE JUST DROPPED THIS ONE DOWN FROM ABOVE.
Real
Dummy
...

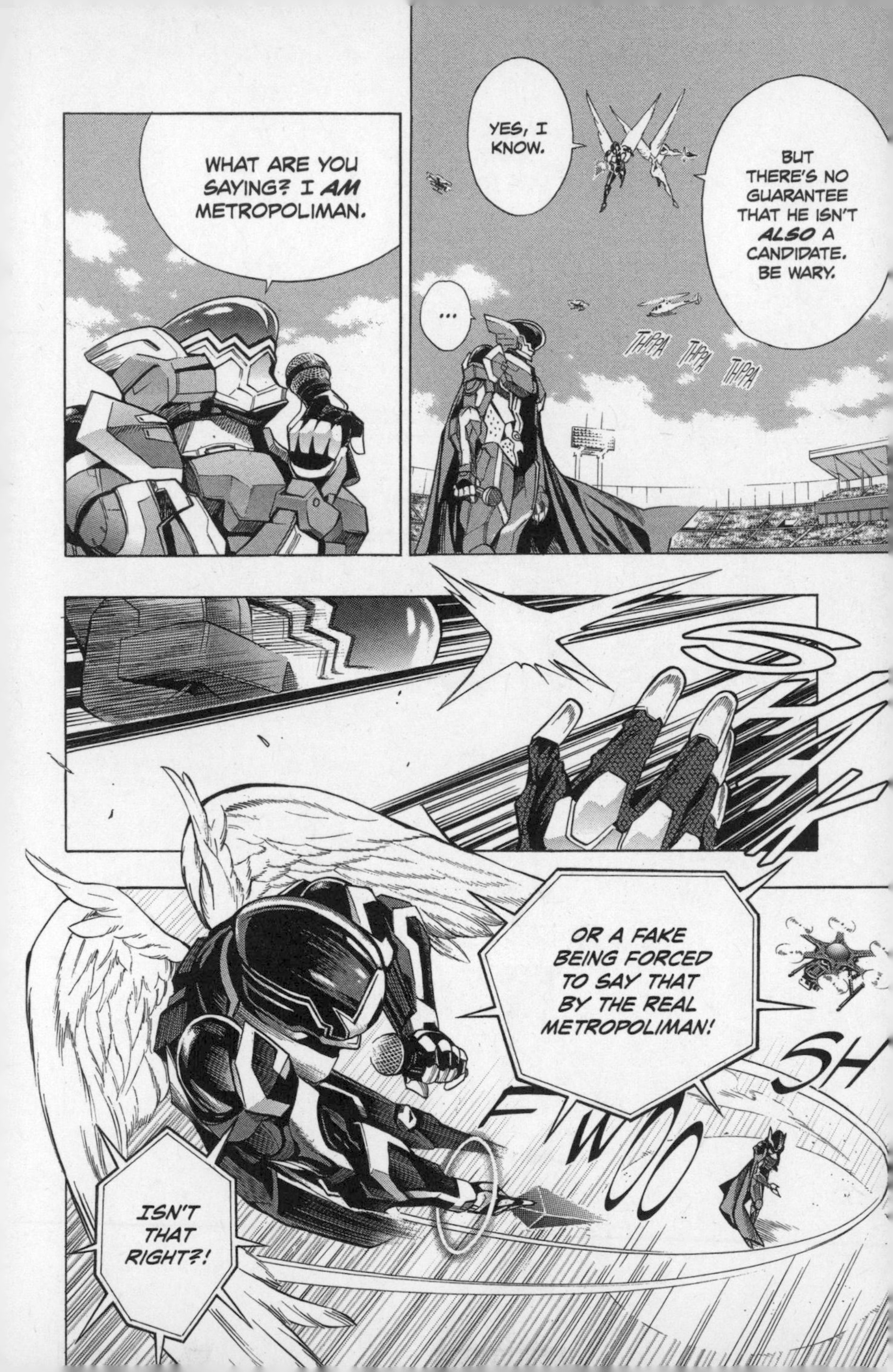
YES, I KNOW.
BUT THERE'S NO GUARANTEE THAT HE ISN'T *ALSO* A CANDIDATE. BE WARY.
...
THPPA THPPA THPPA
WHAT ARE YOU SAYING? I *AM* METROPOLIMAN.
OR A FAKE BEING FORCED TO SAY THAT BY THE REAL METROPOLIMAN!
SH
FWOO
ISN'T THAT RIGHT?!

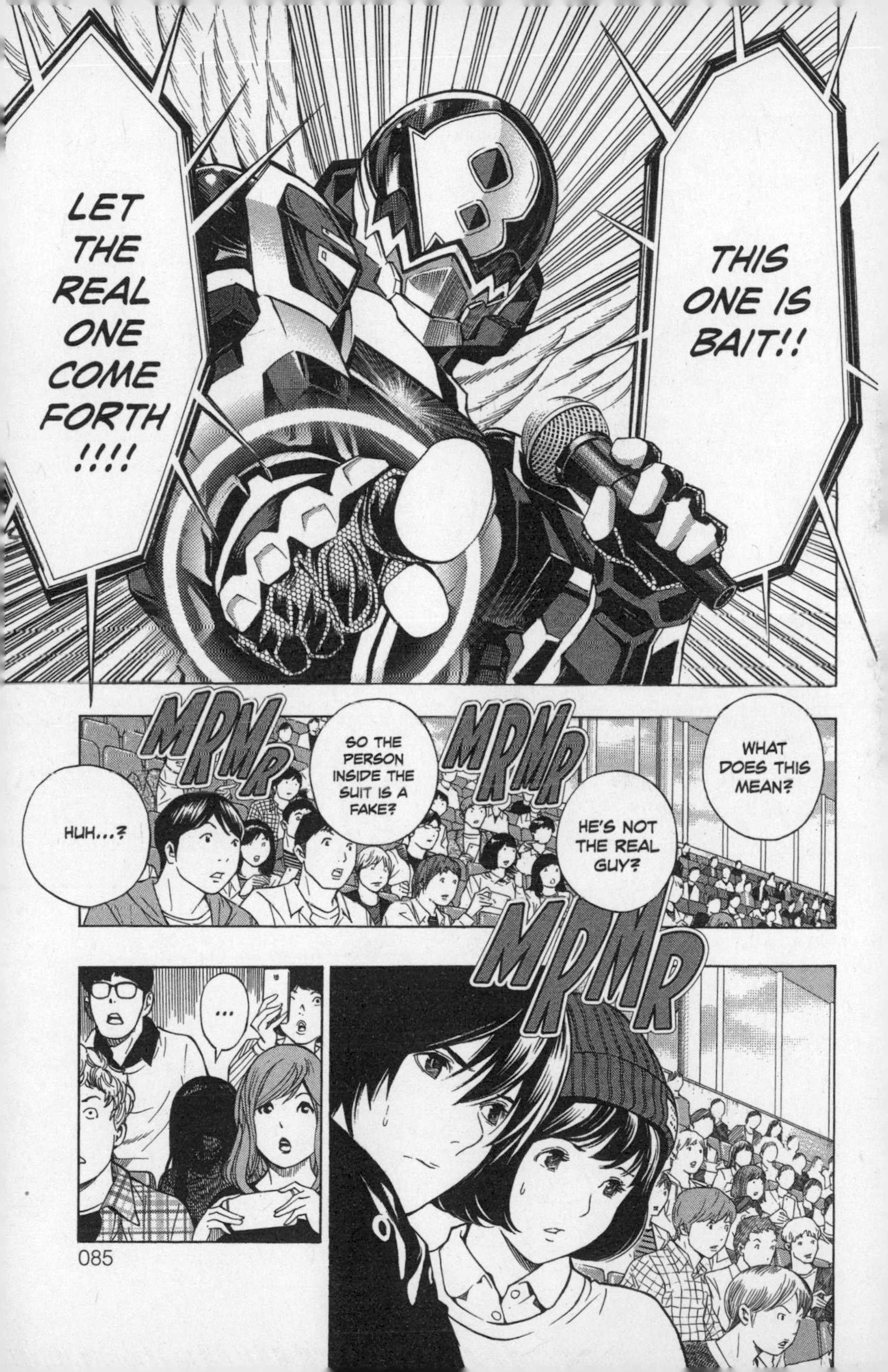
THIS ONE IS BAIT!!
LET THE REAL ONE COME FORTH!!!!
MRMR
WHAT DOES THIS MEAN?
HE'S NOT THE REAL GUY?
MRMR
SO THE PERSON INSIDE THE SUIT IS A FAKE?
MRMR
HUH...?
MRMR
...

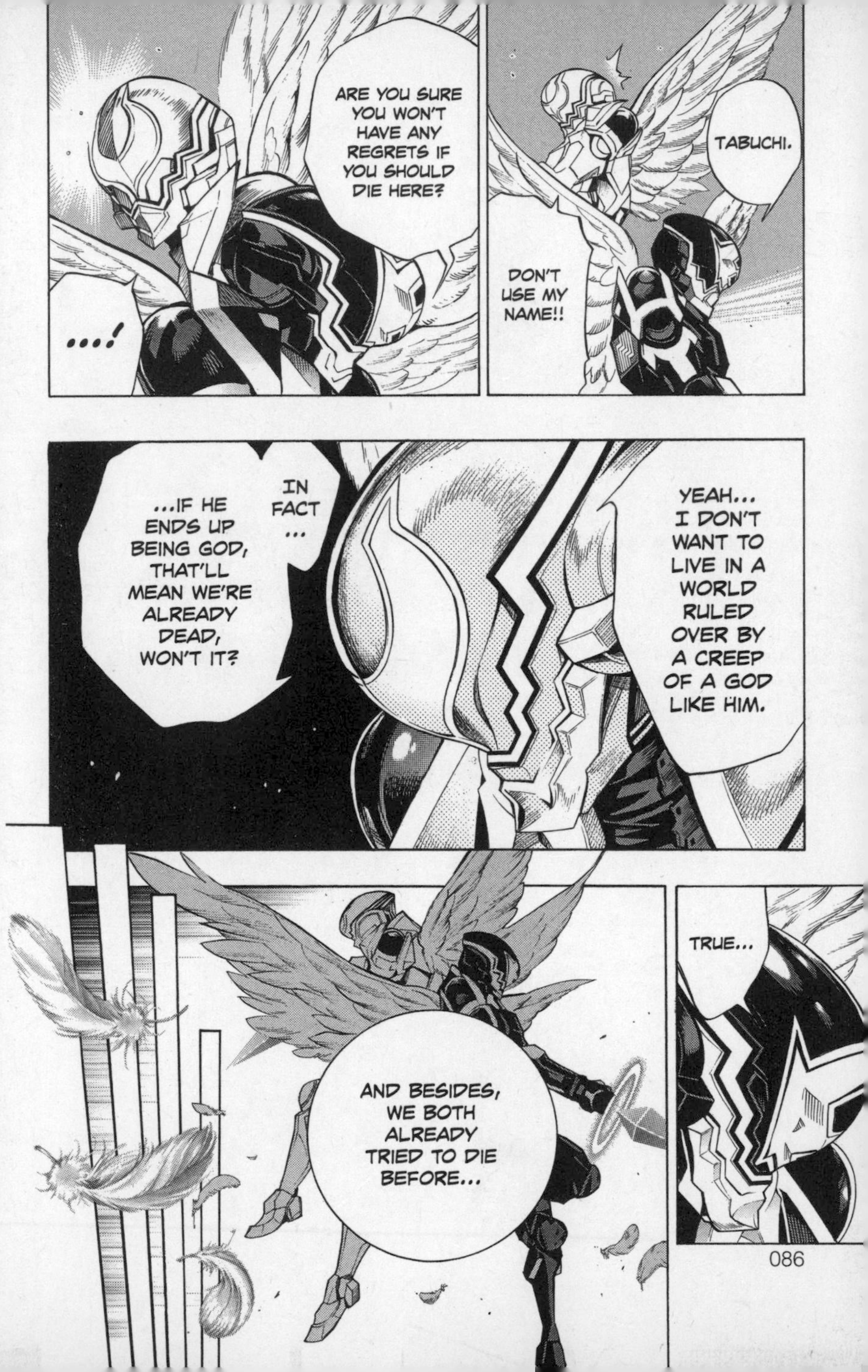

TABUCHI.
DON'T USE MY NAME!!
ARE YOU SURE YOU WON'T HAVE ANY REGRETS IF YOU SHOULD DIE HERE?
...!
YEAH... I DON'T WANT TO LIVE IN A WORLD RULED OVER BY A CREEP OF A GOD LIKE HIM.
IN FACT...
...IF HE ENDS UP BEING GOD, THAT'LL MEAN WE'RE ALREADY DEAD, WON'T IT?
TRUE...
AND BESIDES, WE BOTH ALREADY TRIED TO DIE BEFORE...

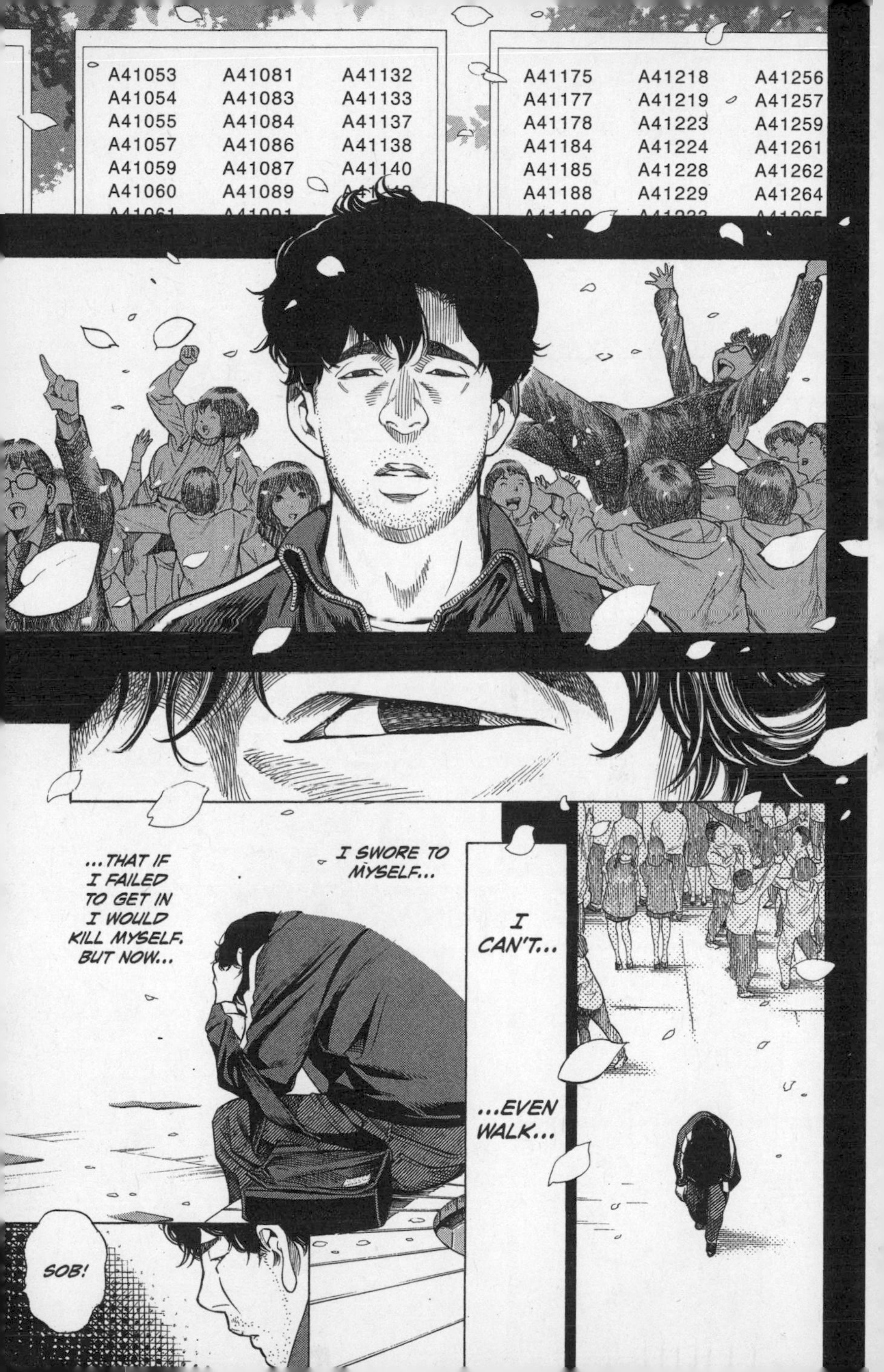
A41175 A41218 A41256
A41177 A41219 A41257
A41178 A41223 A41259
A41184 A41224 A41261
A41185 A41228 A41262
A41188 A41229 A41264
A41053 A41081 A41132
A41054 A41083 A41133
A41055 A41084 A41137
A41057 A41086 A41138
A41059 A41087 A41140
A41060 A41089
I SWORE TO MYSELF...
...THAT IF I FAILED TO GET IN I WOULD KILL MYSELF. BUT NOW...
I CAN'T...
...EVEN WALK...
SOB!

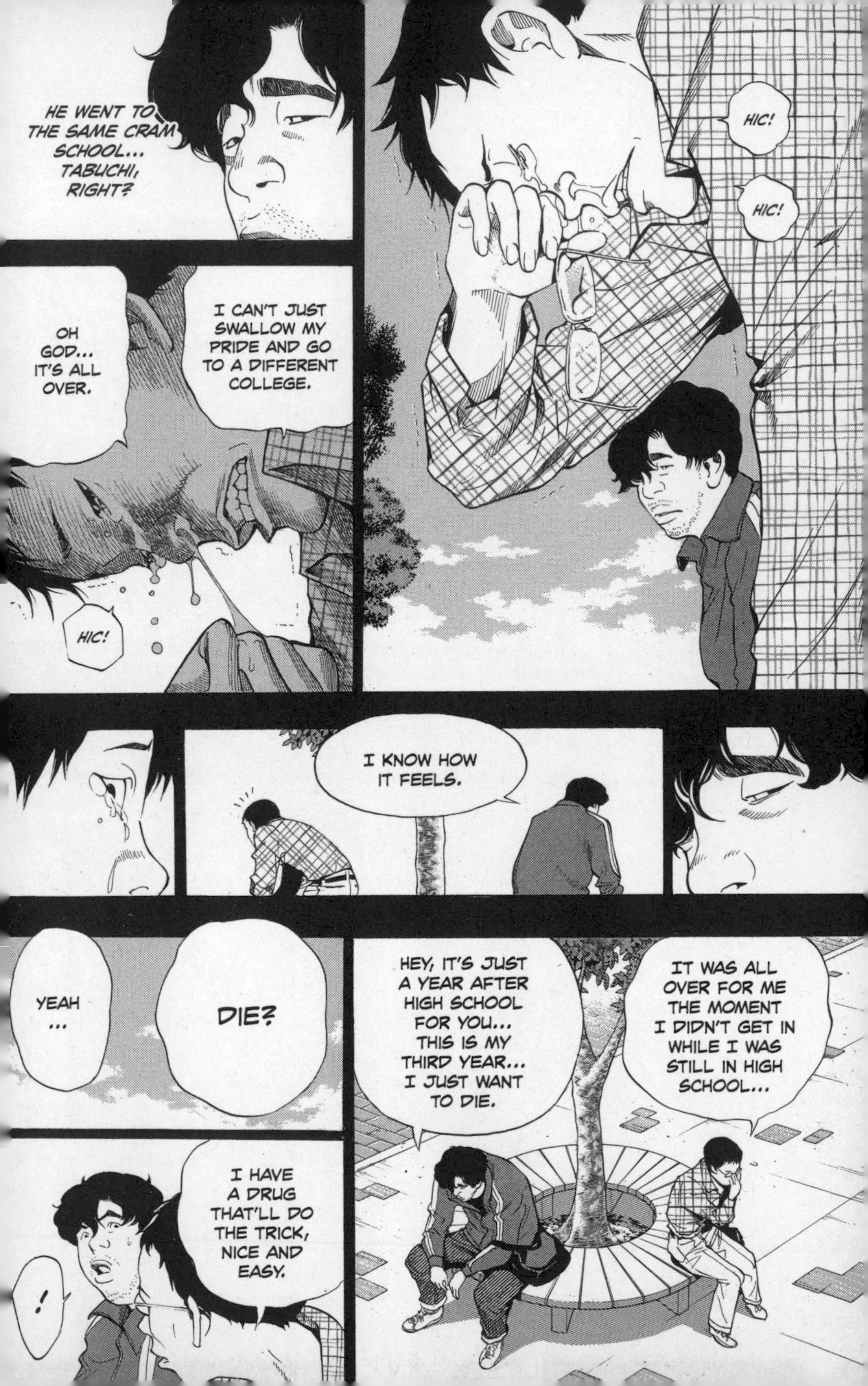
HIC!
HIC!
HE WENT TO THE SAME CRAM SCHOOL... TABUCHI, RIGHT?
I CAN'T JUST SWALLOW MY PRIDE AND GO TO A DIFFERENT COLLEGE.
OH GOD... IT'S ALL OVER.
HIC!
I KNOW HOW IT FEELS.
IT WAS ALL OVER FOR ME THE MOMENT I DIDN'T GET IN WHILE I WAS STILL IN HIGH SCHOOL...
HEY, IT'S JUST A YEAR AFTER HIGH SCHOOL FOR YOU... THIS IS MY THIRD YEAR... I JUST WANT TO DIE.
DIE?
YEAH ...
I HAVE A DRUG THAT'LL DO THE TRICK, NICE AND EASY.
!

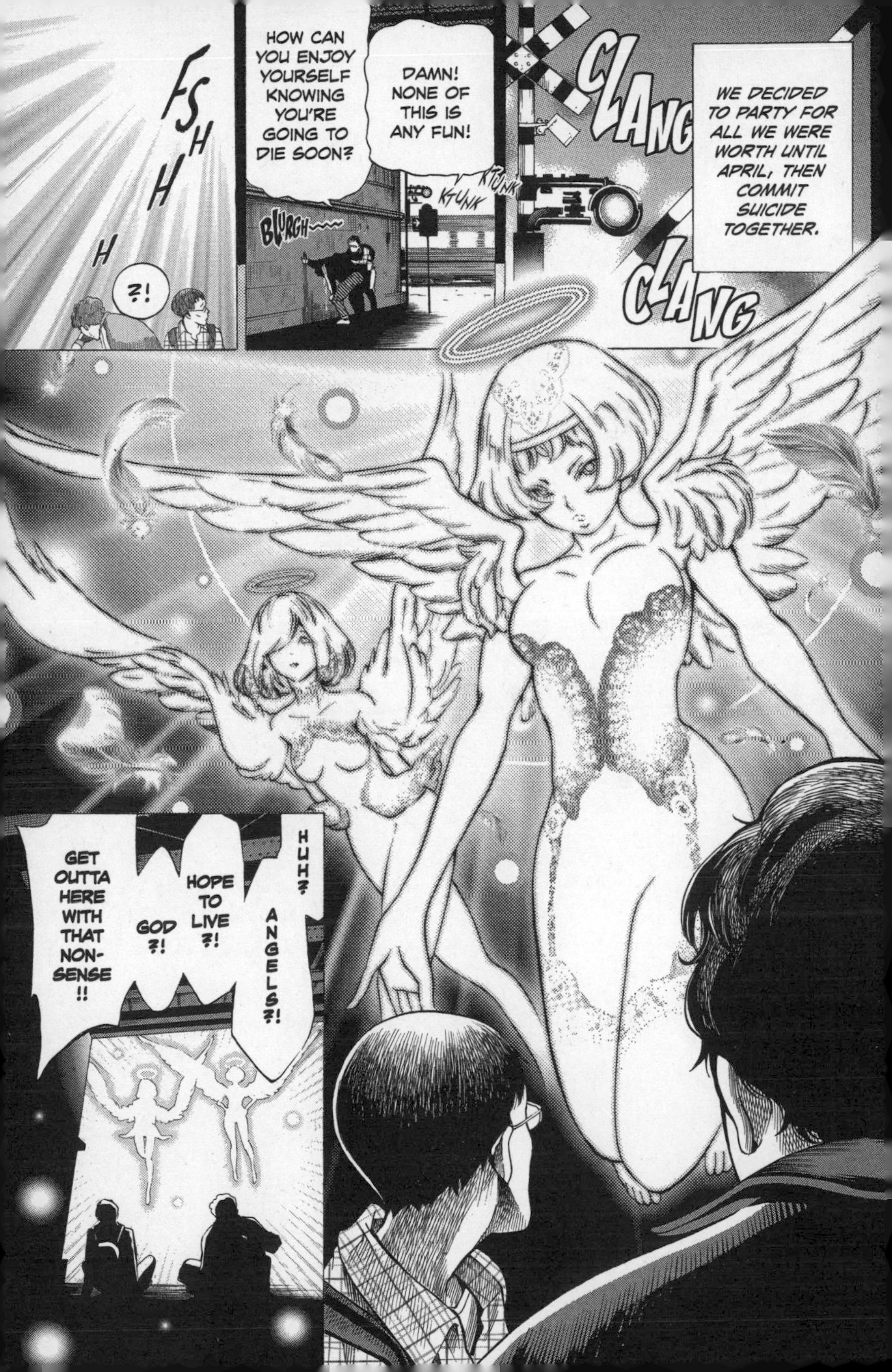
WE DECIDED TO PARTY FOR ALL WE WERE WORTH UNTIL APRIL, THEN COMMIT SUICIDE TOGETHER.
CLANG
CLANG
KTUNK
KTUNK
DAMN! NONE OF THIS IS ANY FUN!
HOW CAN YOU ENJOY YOURSELF KNOWING YOU'RE GOING TO DIE SOON?
BLURGH~~~
FSHHH
?!
HUH? ANGELS?!
HOPE TO LIVE?!
GOD?!
GET OUTTA HERE WITH THAT NON-SENSE!!

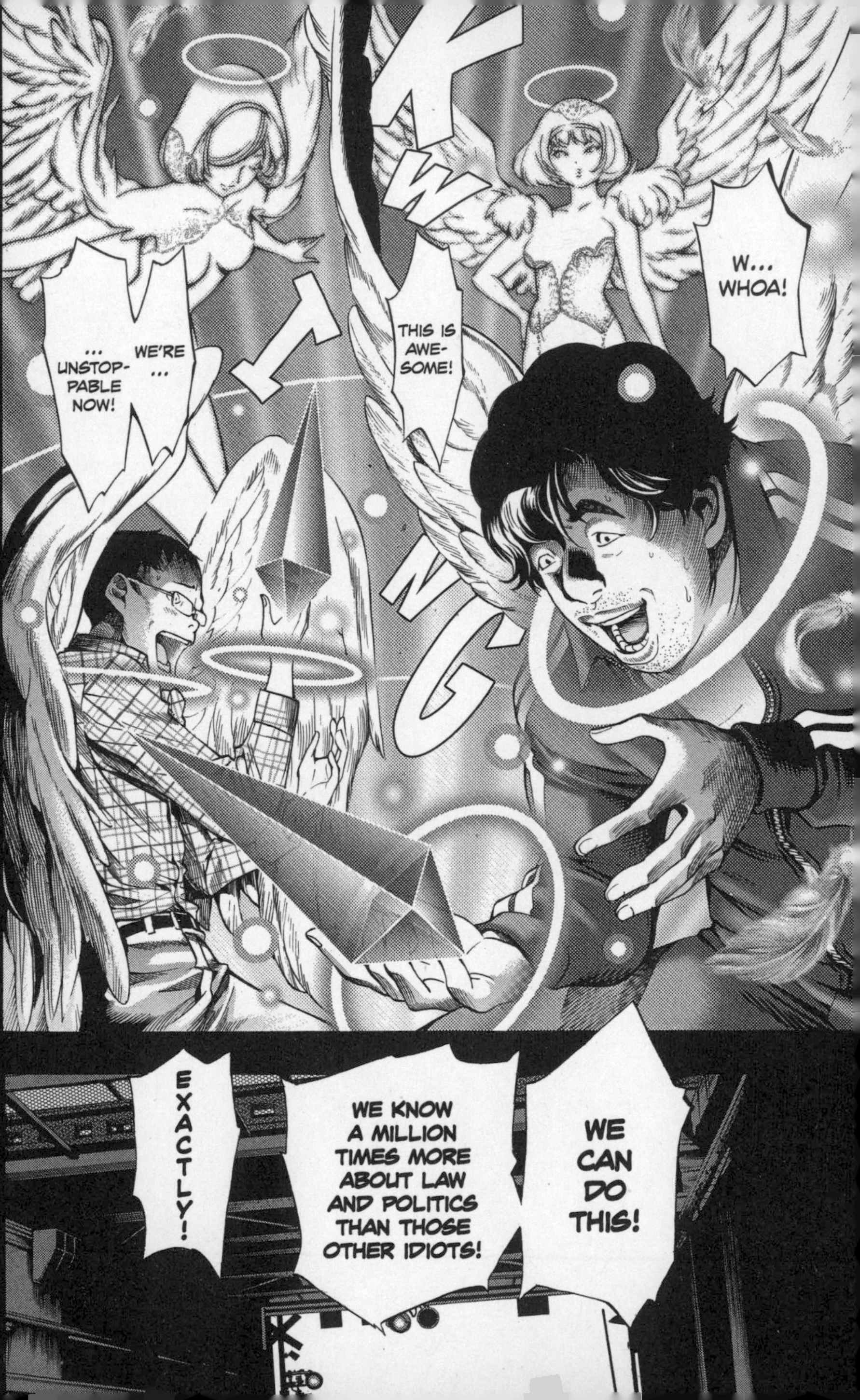
W... WHOA!
THIS IS AWE-SOME!
... WE'RE ... UNSTOP-PABLE NOW!
WE CAN DO THIS!
WE KNOW A MILLION TIMES MORE ABOUT LAW AND POLITICS THAN THOSE OTHER IDIOTS!
EXACTLY!

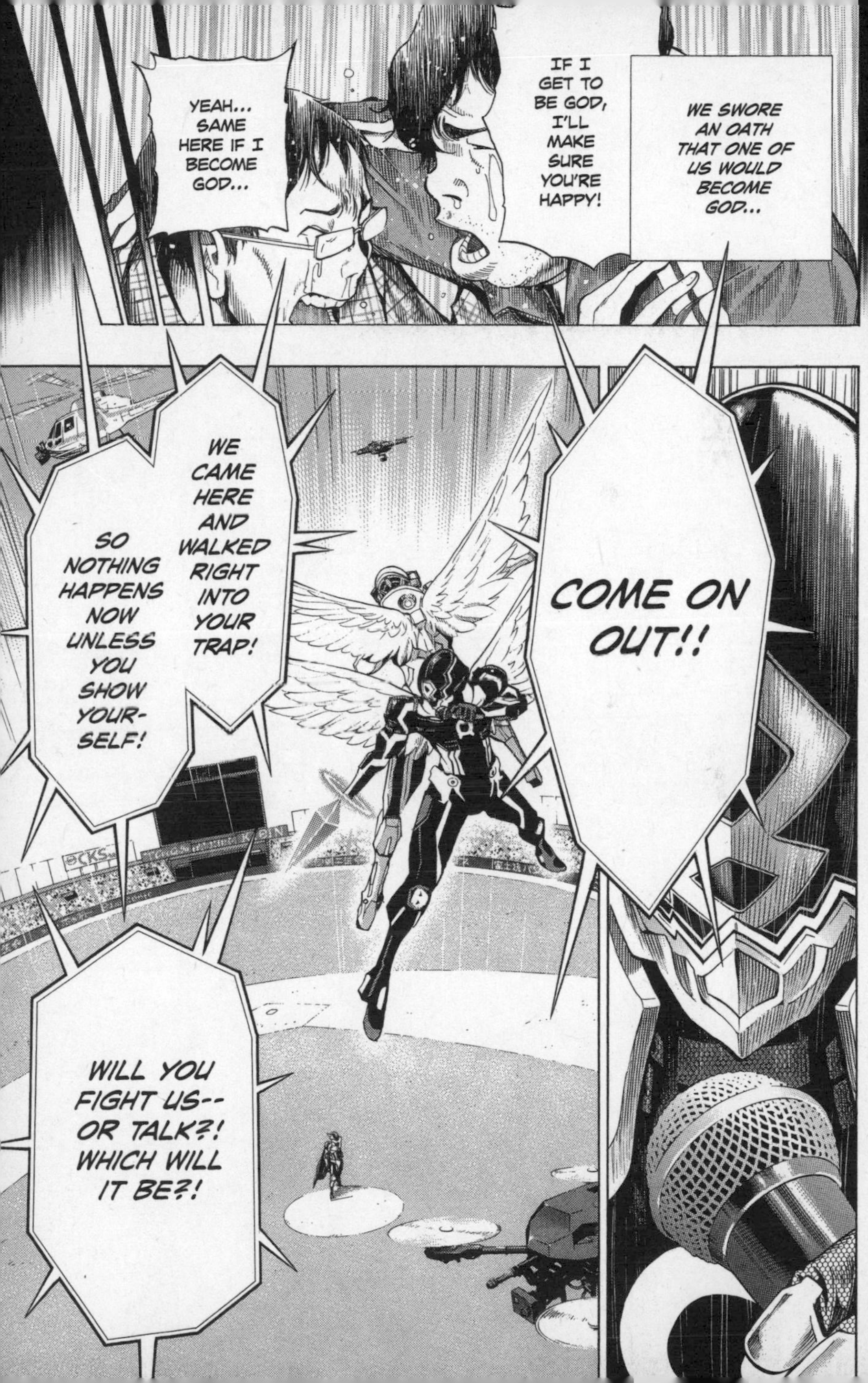
WE SWORE AN OATH THAT ONE OF US WOULD BECOME GOD...
IF I GET TO BE GOD, I'LL MAKE SURE YOU'RE HAPPY!
YEAH... SAME HERE IF I BECOME GOD...
COME ON OUT!!
WE CAME HERE AND WALKED RIGHT INTO YOUR TRAP!
SO NOTHING HAPPENS NOW UNLESS YOU SHOW YOUR-SELF!
WILL YOU FIGHT US-- OR TALK?! WHICH WILL IT BE?!

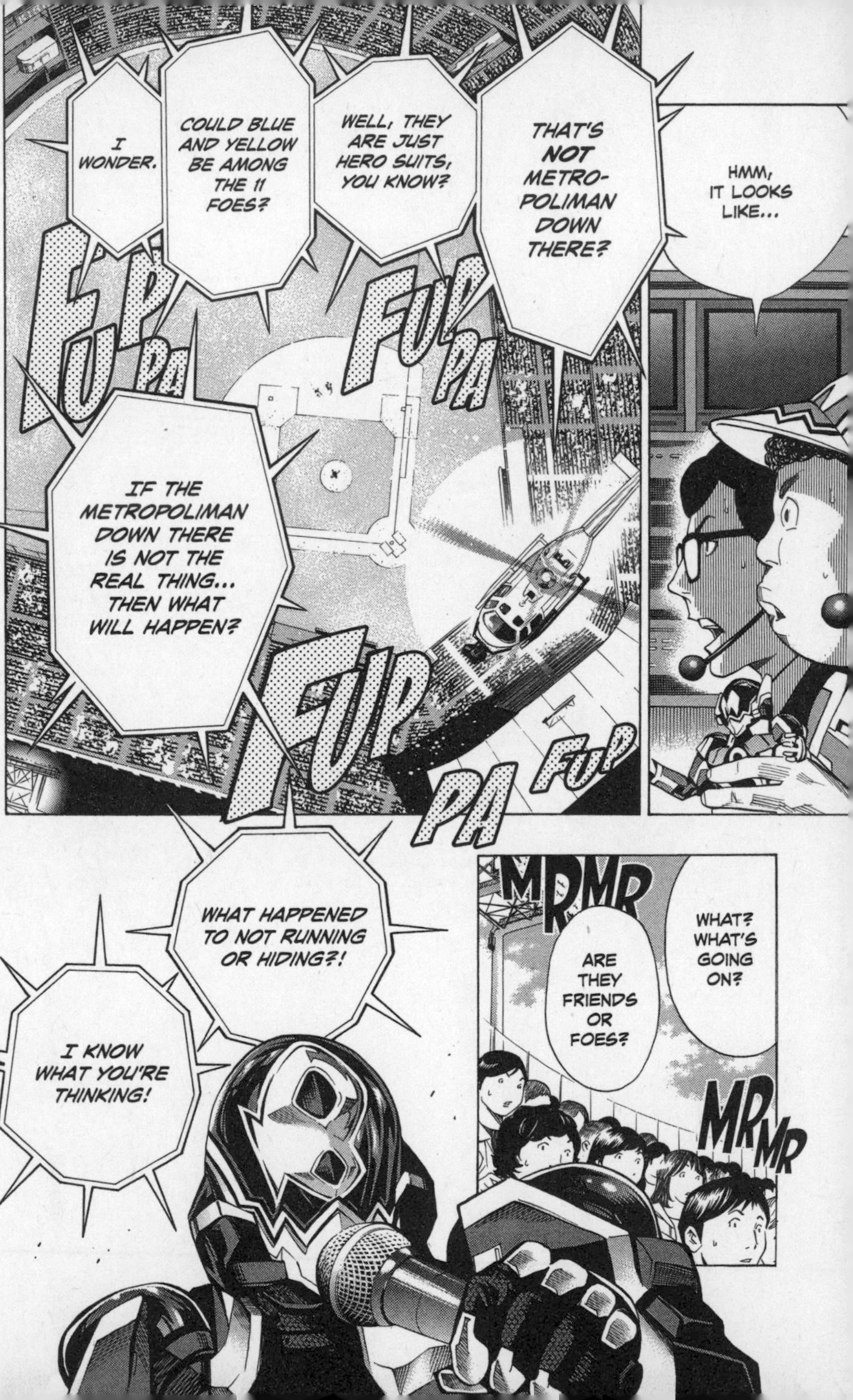
HMM, IT LOOKS LIKE...
THAT'S NOT METROPOLIMAN DOWN THERE?
WELL, THEY ARE JUST HERO SUITS, YOU KNOW?
COULD BLUE AND YELLOW BE AMONG THE 11 FOES?
I WONDER.
FUPA
FUPA
IF THE METROPOLIMAN DOWN THERE IS NOT THE REAL THING... THEN WHAT WILL HAPPEN?
FUPA
FUPA
MRMR
WHAT? WHAT'S GOING ON?
ARE THEY FRIENDS OR FOES?
MRMR
WHAT HAPPENED TO NOT RUNNING OR HIDING?!
I KNOW WHAT YOU'RE THINKING!

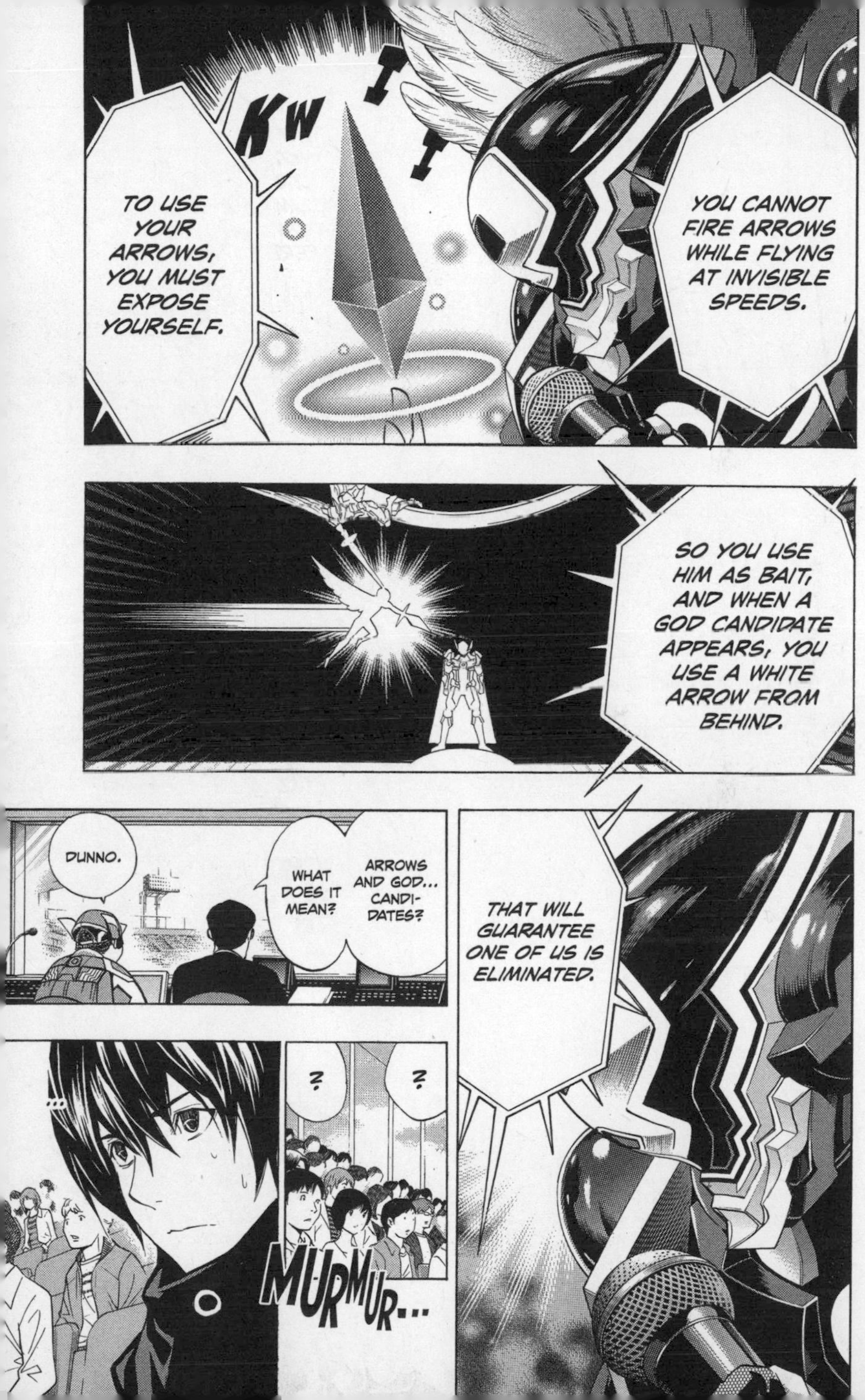
YOU CANNOT FIRE ARROWS WHILE FLYING AT INVISIBLE SPEEDS.
KWII
TO USE YOUR ARROWS, YOU MUST EXPOSE YOURSELF.
SO YOU USE HIM AS BAIT, AND WHEN A GOD CANDIDATE APPEARS, YOU USE A WHITE ARROW FROM BEHIND.
THAT WILL GUARANTEE ONE OF US IS ELIMINATED.
ARROWS AND GOD... CANDI-DATES?
WHAT DOES IT MEAN?
DUNNO.
?
?
MURMUR...
...

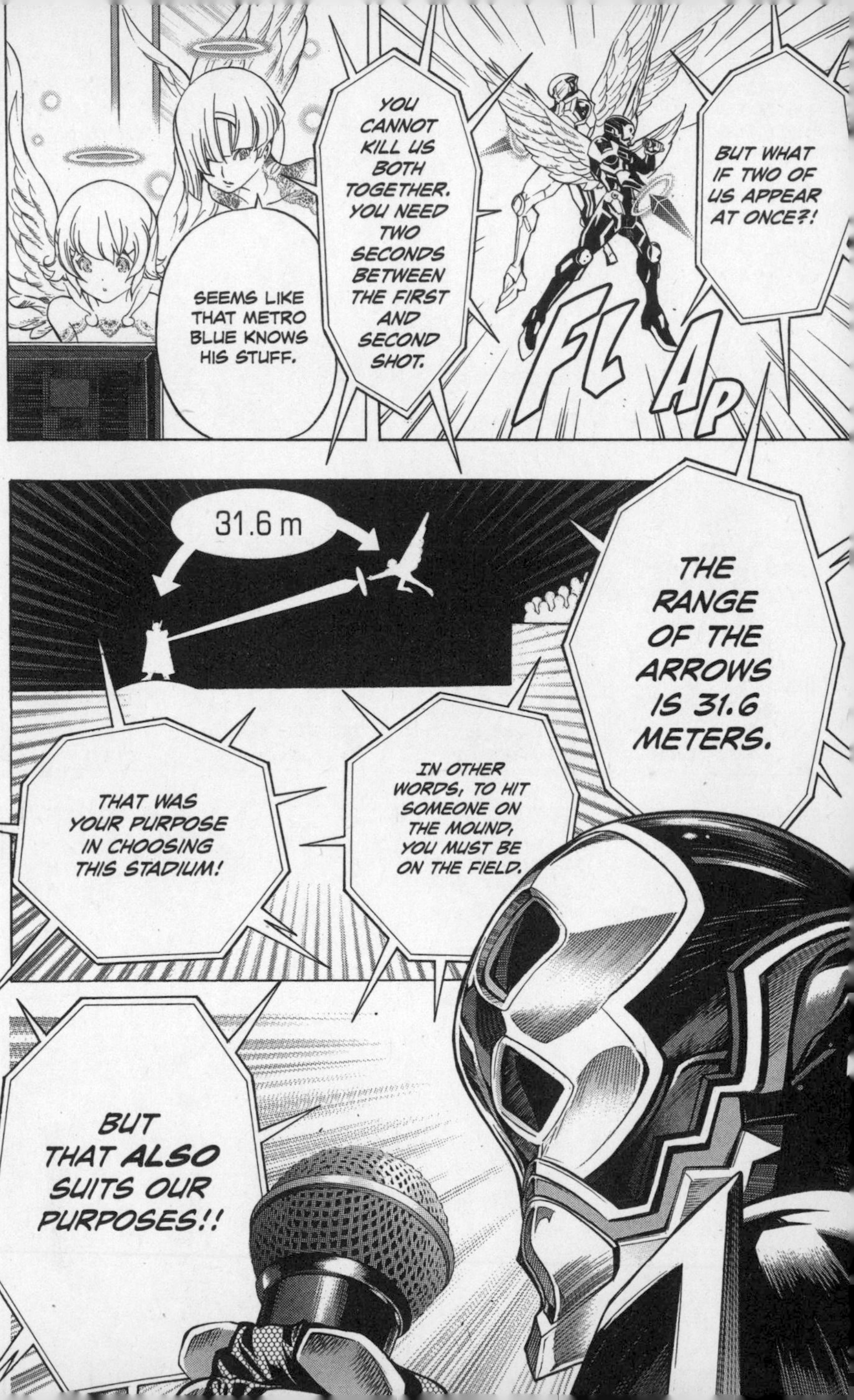
BUT WHAT IF TWO OF US APPEAR AT ONCE?!
FLAP
YOU CANNOT KILL US BOTH TOGETHER. YOU NEED TWO SECONDS BETWEEN THE FIRST AND SECOND SHOT.
SEEMS LIKE THAT METRO BLUE KNOWS HIS STUFF.
THE RANGE OF THE ARROWS IS 31.6 METERS.
31.6 m
IN OTHER WORDS, TO HIT SOMEONE ON THE MOUND, YOU MUST BE ON THE FIELD.
THAT WAS YOUR PURPOSE IN CHOOSING THIS STADIUM!
BUT THAT ALSO SUITS OUR PURPOSES!!

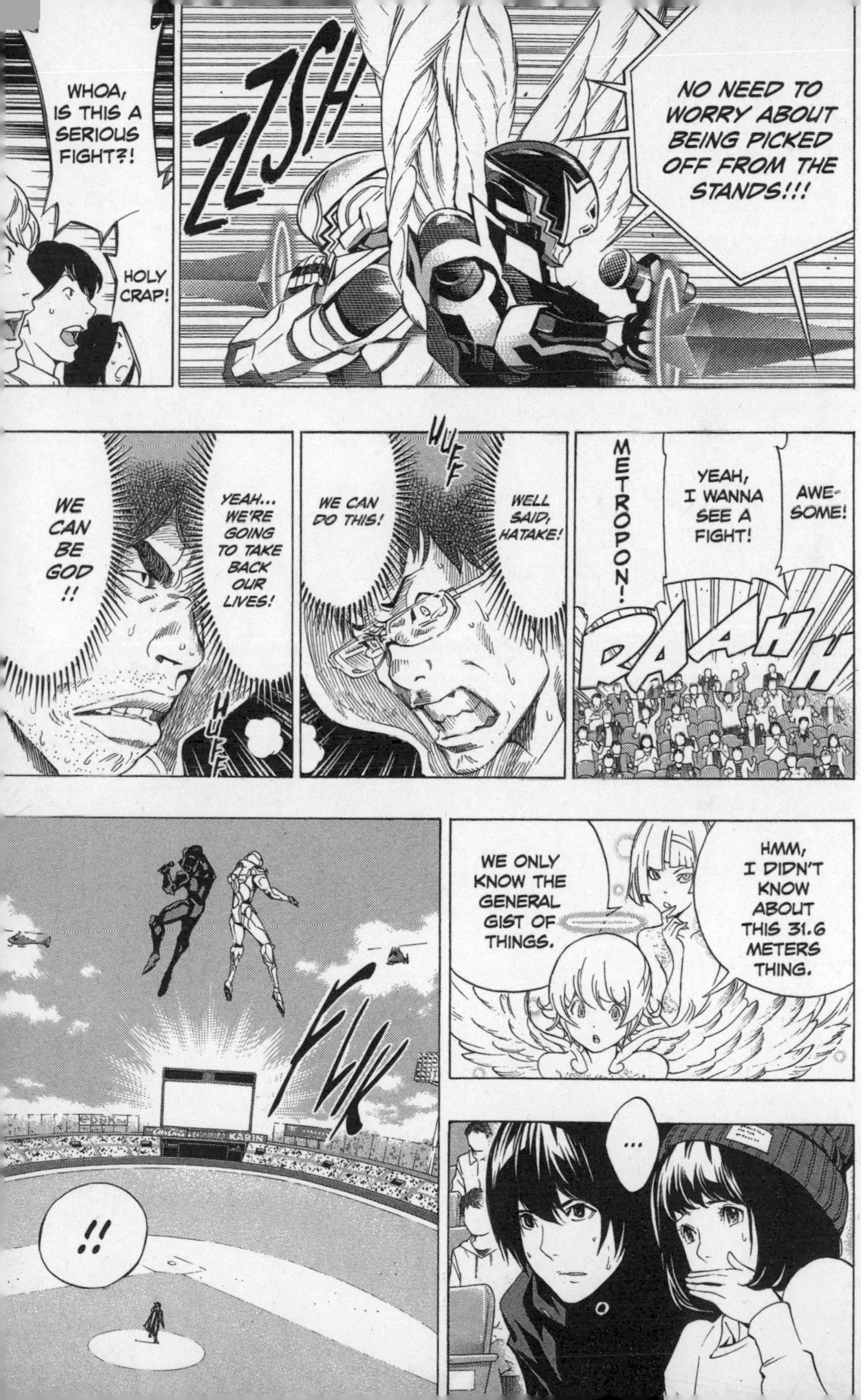

ZZSH
NO NEED TO WORRY ABOUT BEING PICKED OFF FROM THE STANDS!!!
WHOA, IS THIS A SERIOUS FIGHT?!
HOLY CRAP!
AWE-SOME!
YEAH, I WANNA SEE A FIGHT!
METROPON!
RAAHH
WELL SAID, HATAKE!
HUFF
WE CAN DO THIS!
YEAH... WE'RE GOING TO TAKE BACK OUR LIVES!
WE CAN BE GOD!!
HUFF
HMM, I DIDN'T KNOW ABOUT THIS 31.6 METERS THING.
WE ONLY KNOW THE GENERAL GIST OF THINGS.
...
FWK
!!

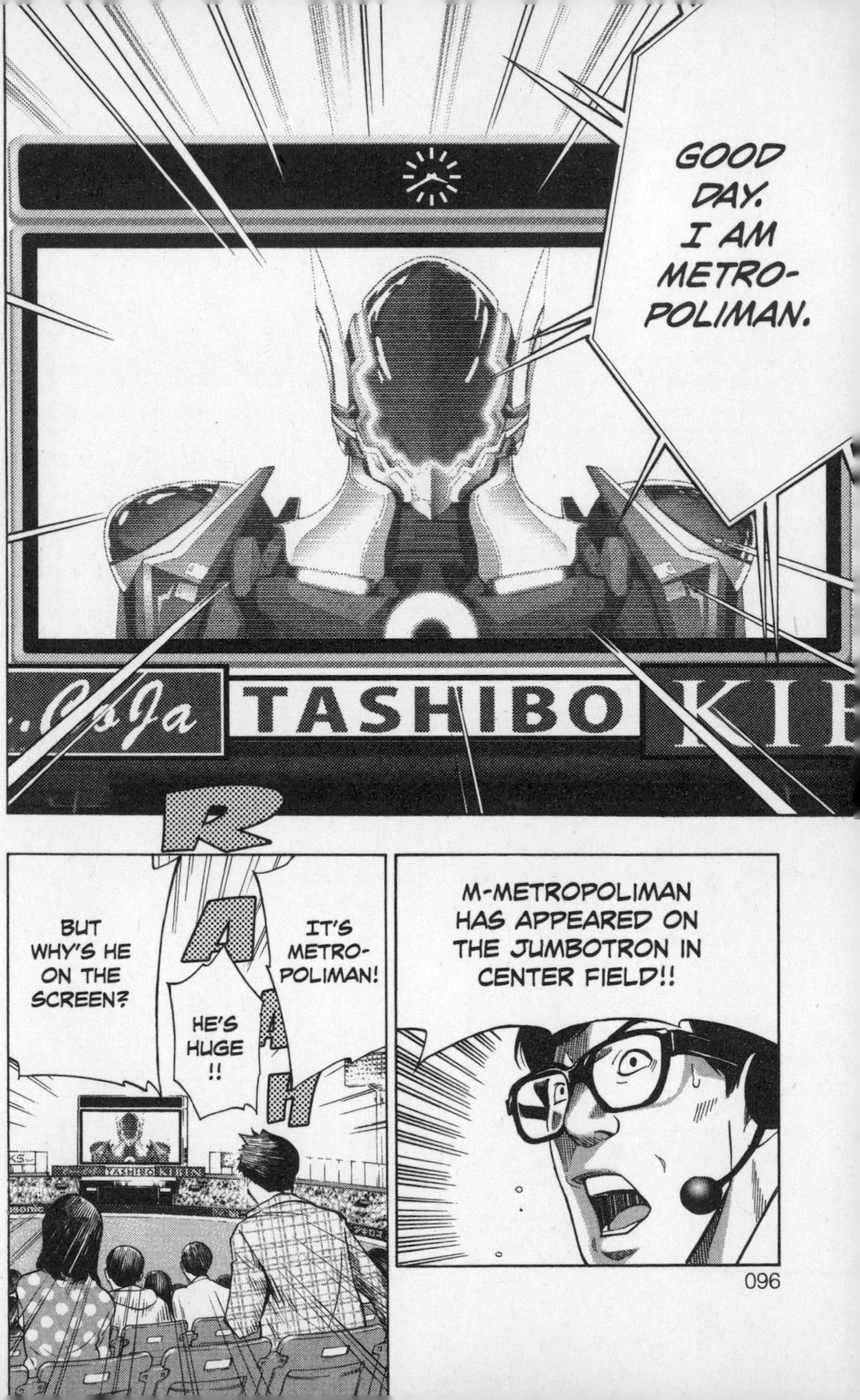
GOOD DAY. I AM METRO-POLIMAN.
TASHIBO
M-METROPOLIMAN HAS APPEARED ON THE JUMBOTRON IN CENTER FIELD!!
IT'S METRO-POLIMAN!
BUT WHY'S HE ON THE SCREEN?
RAAH
HE'S HUGE!!

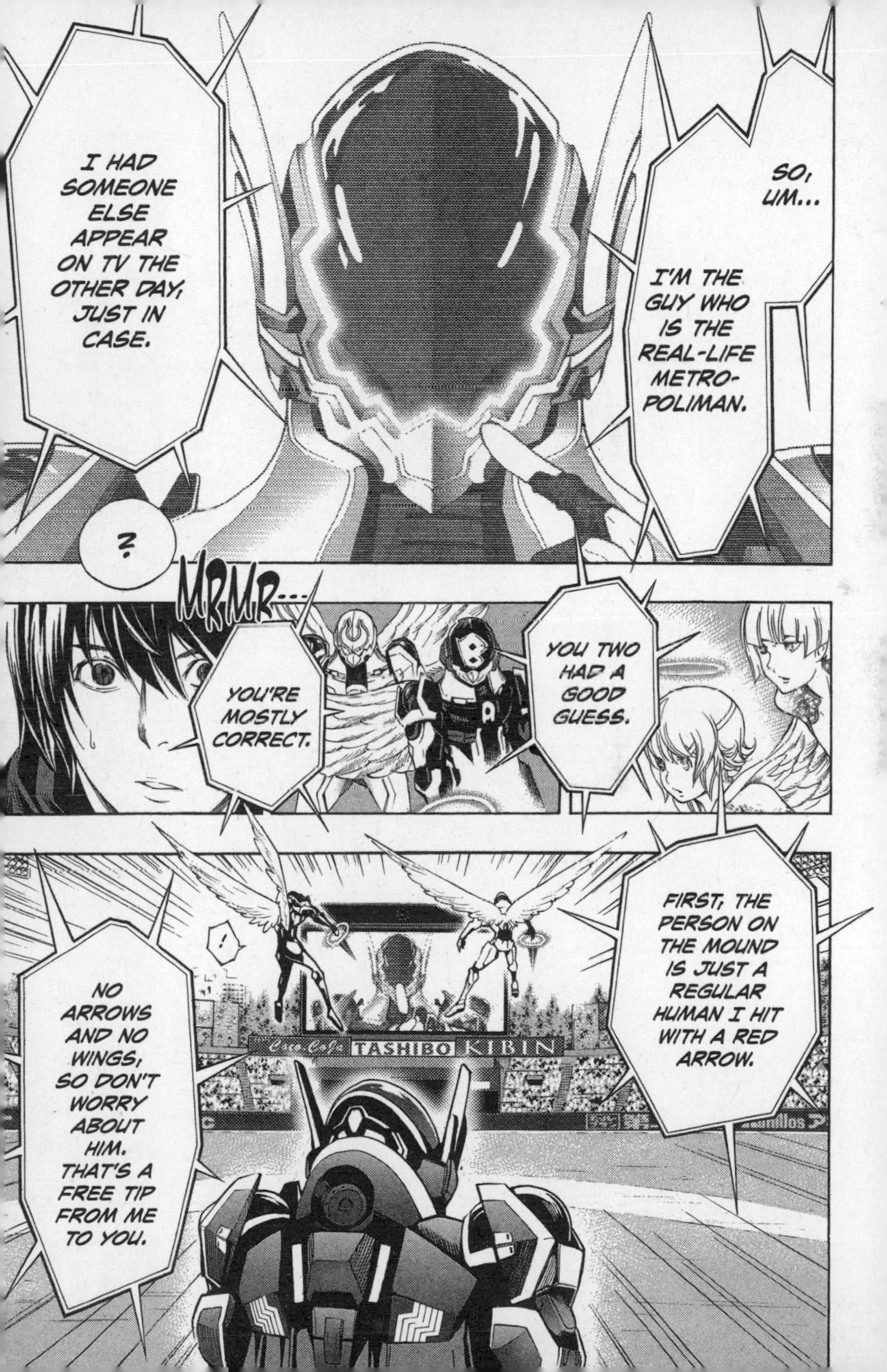
SO, UM...
I'M THE GUY WHO IS THE REAL-LIFE METRO-POLIMAN.
I HAD SOMEONE ELSE APPEAR ON TV THE OTHER DAY, JUST IN CASE.
?
MRMR...
YOU TWO HAD A GOOD GUESS.
YOU'RE MOSTLY CORRECT.
FIRST, THE PERSON ON THE MOUND IS JUST A REGULAR HUMAN I HIT WITH A RED ARROW.
TASHIBO KIBIN
!
NO ARROWS AND NO WINGS, SO DON'T WORRY ABOUT HIM. THAT'S A FREE TIP FROM ME TO YOU.

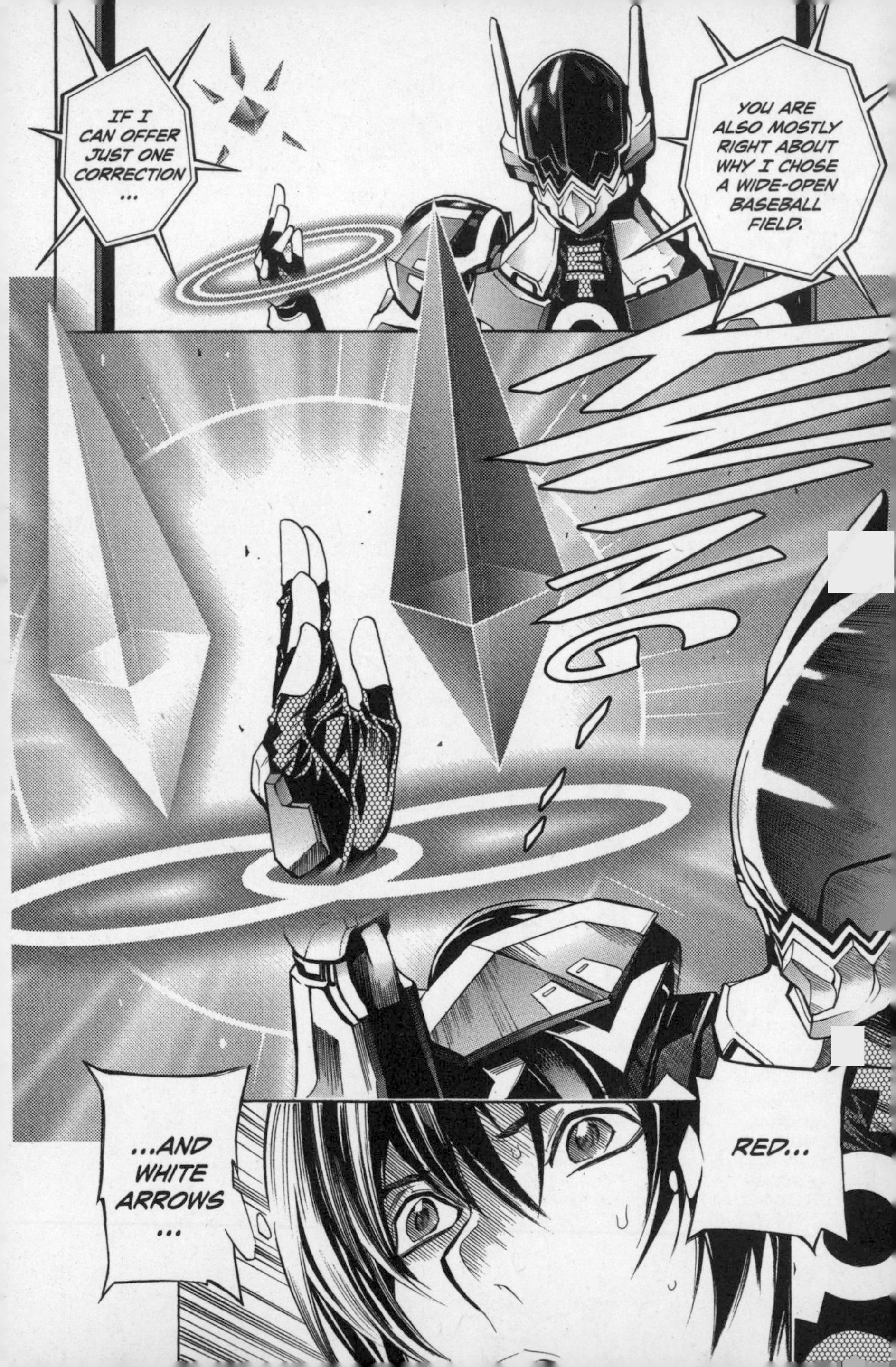
YOU ARE ALSO MOSTLY RIGHT ABOUT WHY I CHOSE A WIDE-OPEN BASEBALL FIELD.
IF I CAN OFFER JUST ONE CORRECTION ...
RED...
...AND WHITE ARROWS ...

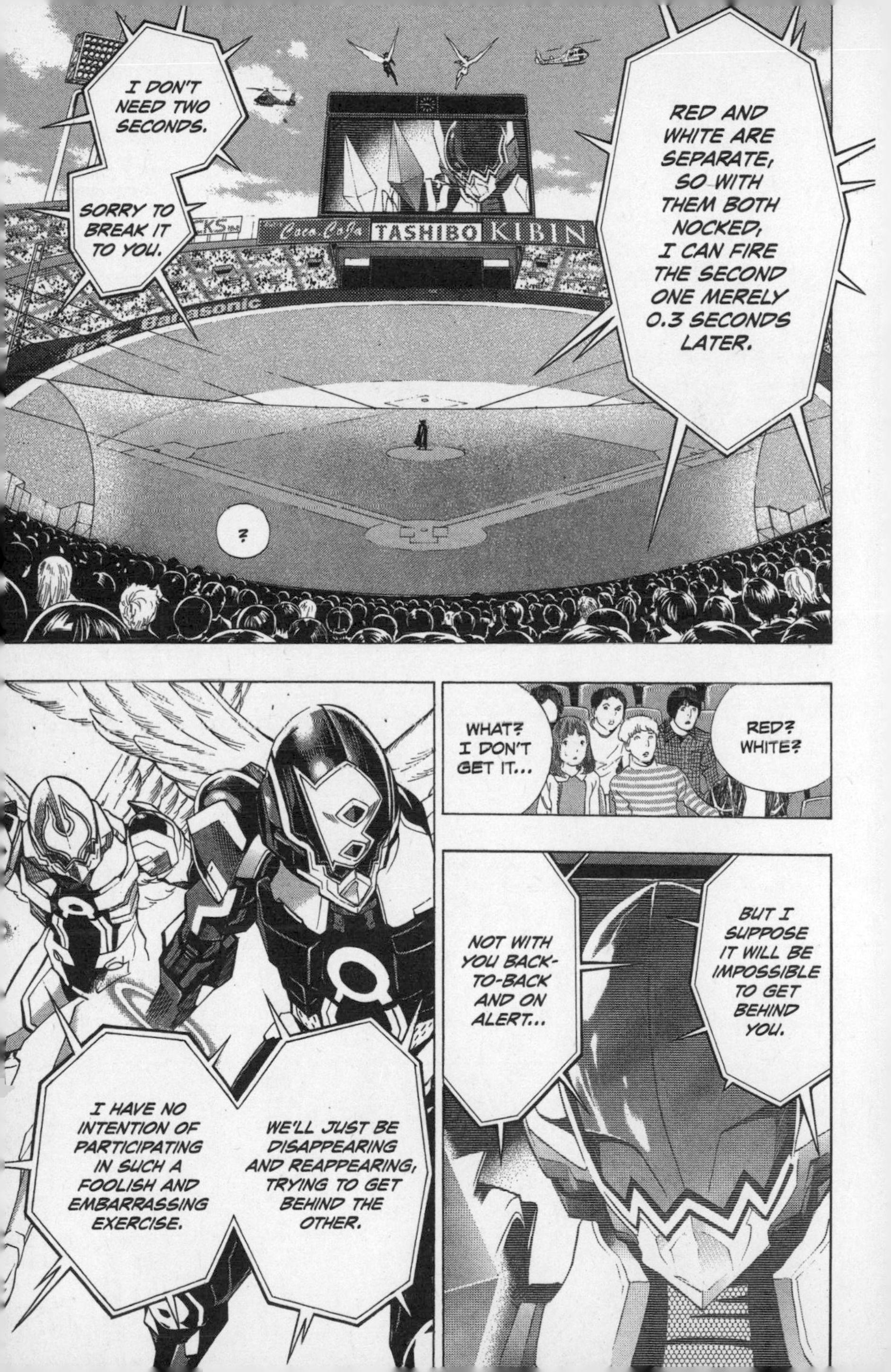
RED AND WHITE ARE SEPARATE, SO WITH THEM BOTH NOCKED, I CAN FIRE THE SECOND ONE MERELY 0.3 SECONDS LATER.
TASHIBO
KIBIN
I DON'T NEED TWO SECONDS.
SORRY TO BREAK IT TO YOU.
?
RED? WHITE?
WHAT? I DON'T GET IT...
BUT I SUPPOSE IT WILL BE IMPOSSIBLE TO GET BEHIND YOU.
NOT WITH YOU BACK-TO-BACK AND ON ALERT...
WE'LL JUST BE DISAPPEARING AND REAPPEARING, TRYING TO GET BEHIND THE OTHER.
I HAVE NO INTENTION OF PARTICIPATING IN SUCH A FOOLISH AND EMBARRASSING EXERCISE.

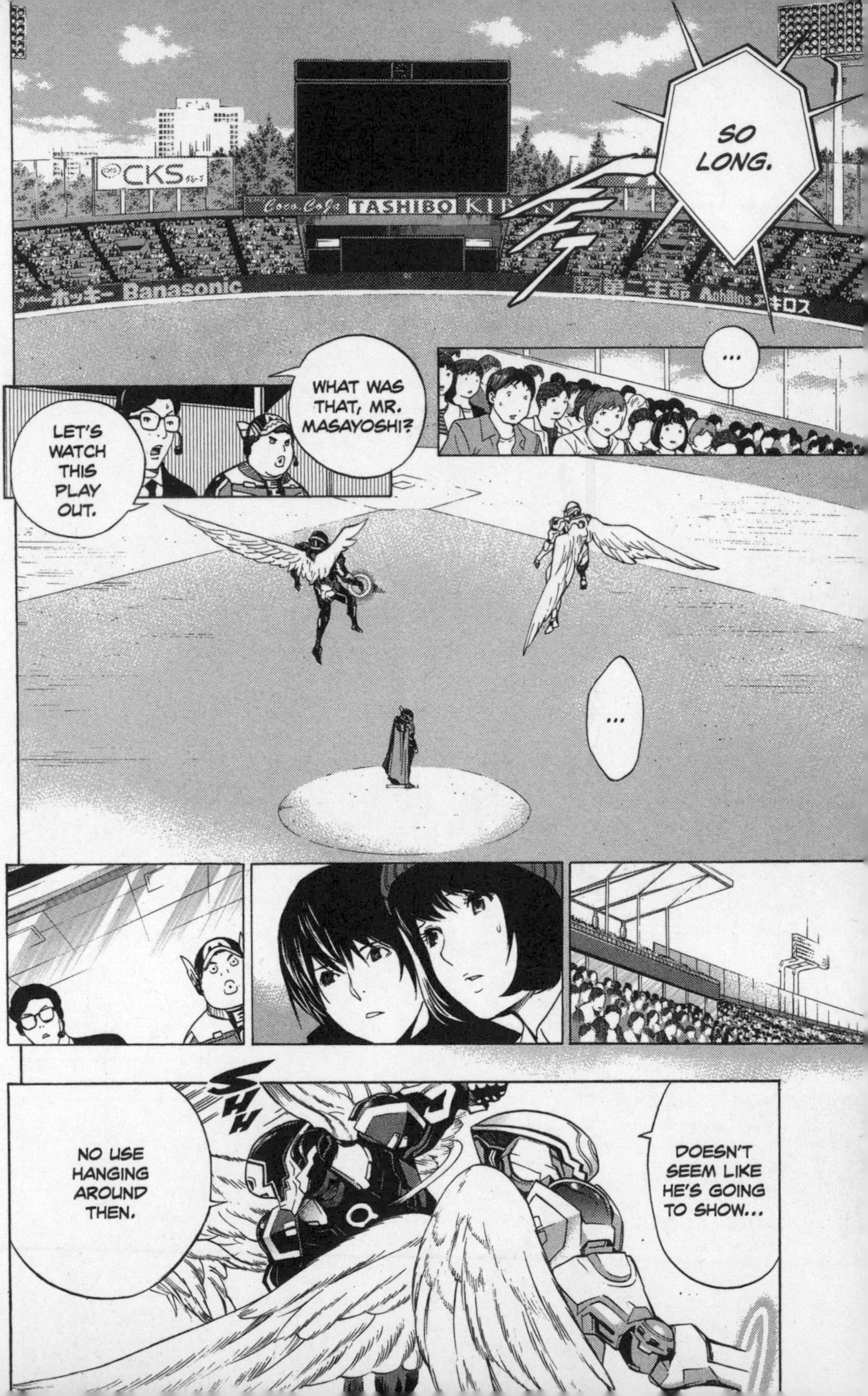
SO LONG.
CKS
TASHIBO
Banasonic
...
WHAT WAS THAT, MR. MASAYOSHI?
LET'S WATCH THIS PLAY OUT.
...
DOESN'T SEEM LIKE HE'S GOING TO SHOW...
NO USE HANGING AROUND THEN.

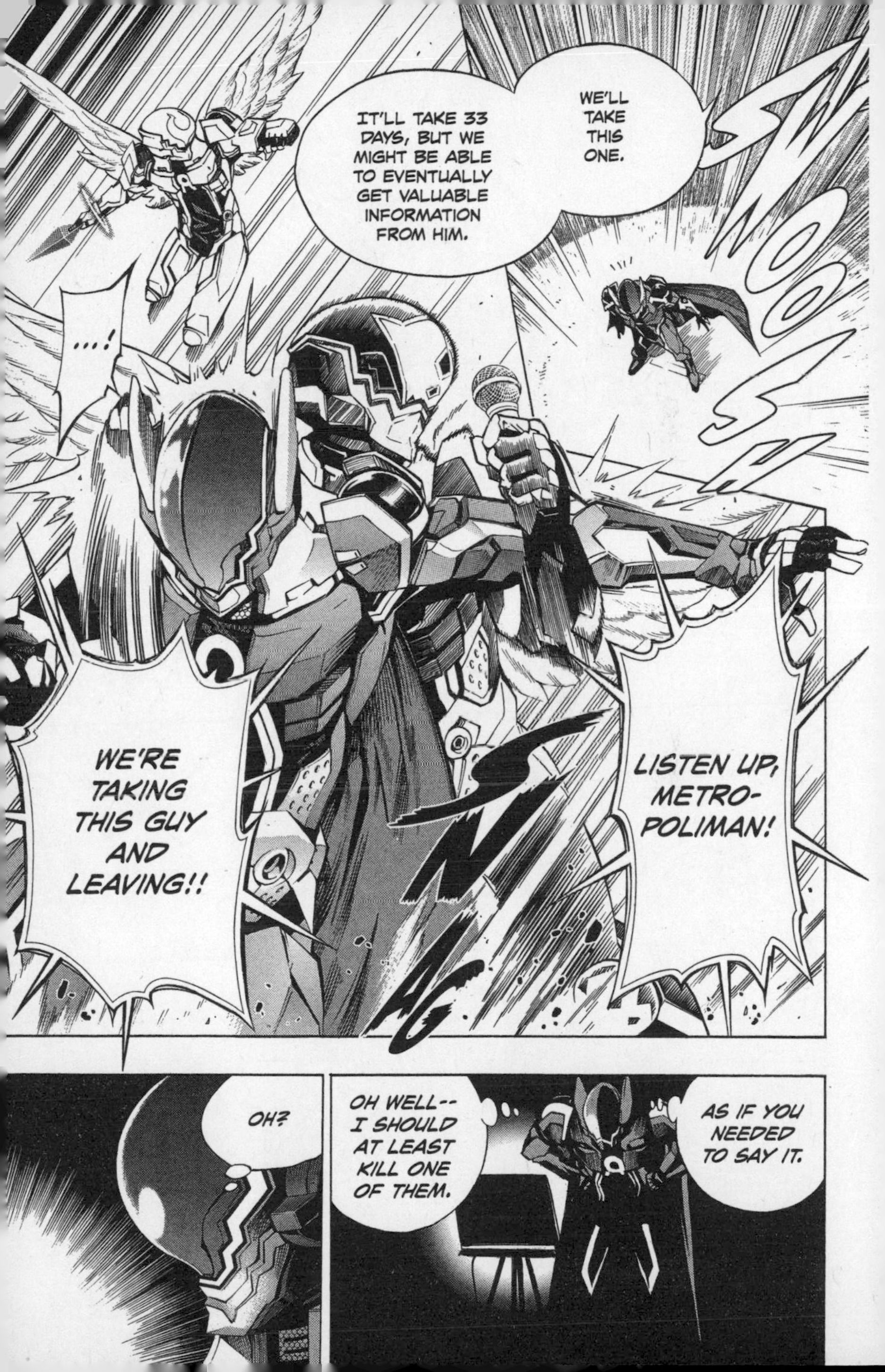
WE'LL TAKE THIS ONE.
IT'LL TAKE 33 DAYS, BUT WE MIGHT BE ABLE TO EVENTUALLY GET VALUABLE INFORMATION FROM HIM.
...!
LISTEN UP, METROPOLIMAN!
WE'RE TAKING THIS GUY AND LEAVING!!
SNAG
AS IF YOU NEEDED TO SAY IT.
OH WELL-- I SHOULD AT LEAST KILL ONE OF THEM.
OH?

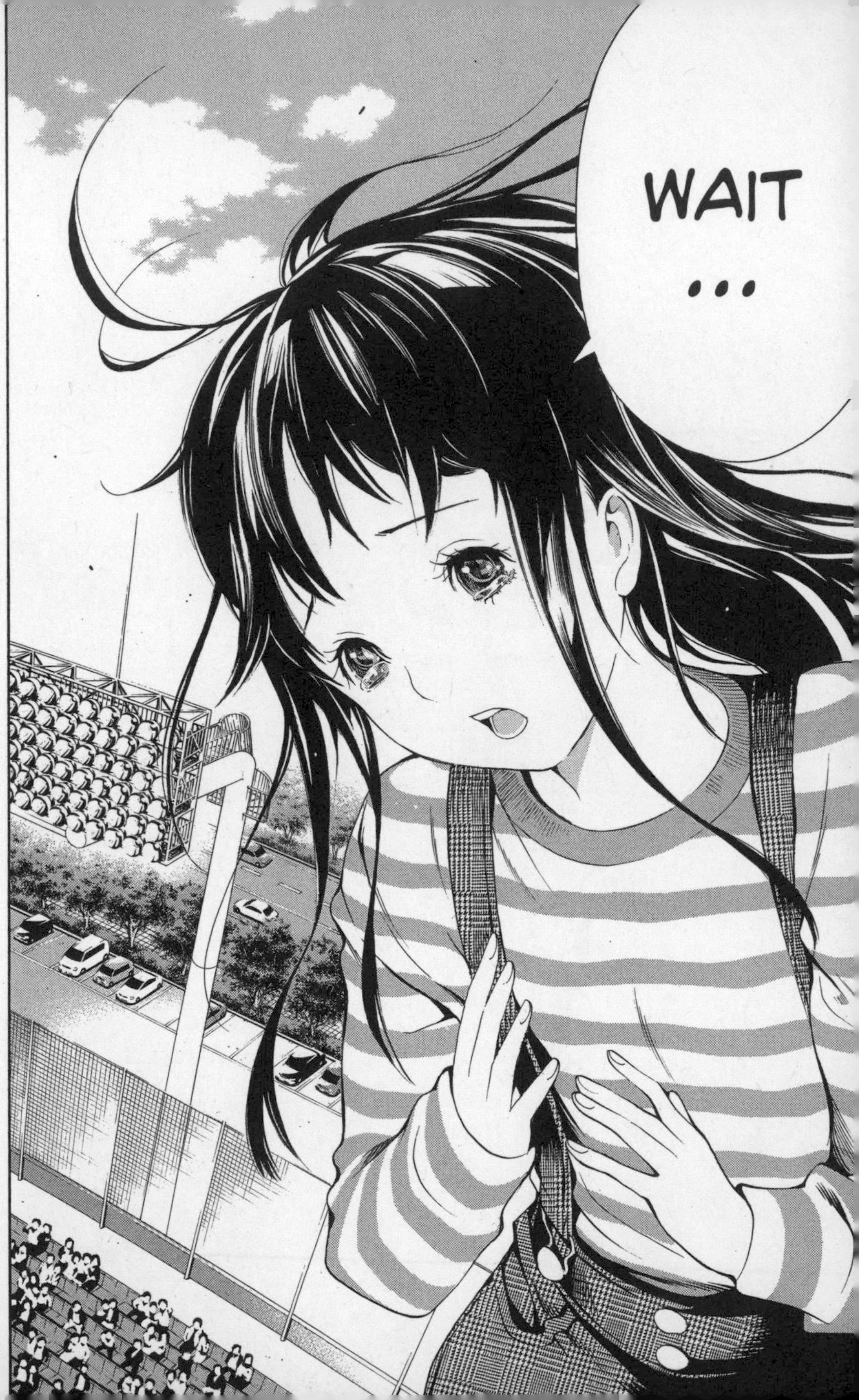
WAIT ...

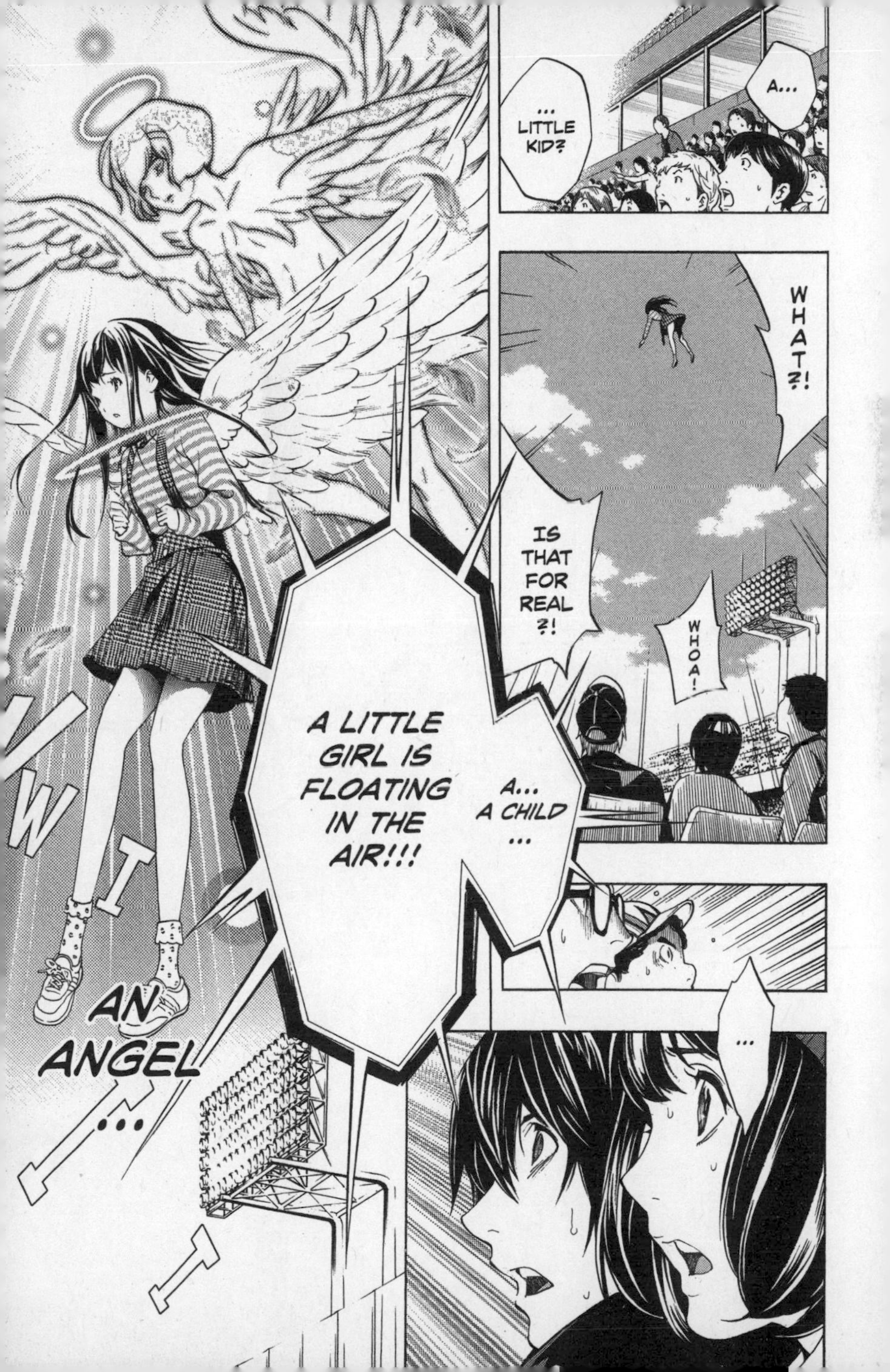
A...
...LITTLE KID?
WHAT?!
WHOA!
IS THAT FOR REAL?!
A... A CHILD...
A LITTLE GIRL IS FLOATING IN THE AIR!!!
...
AN ANGEL...

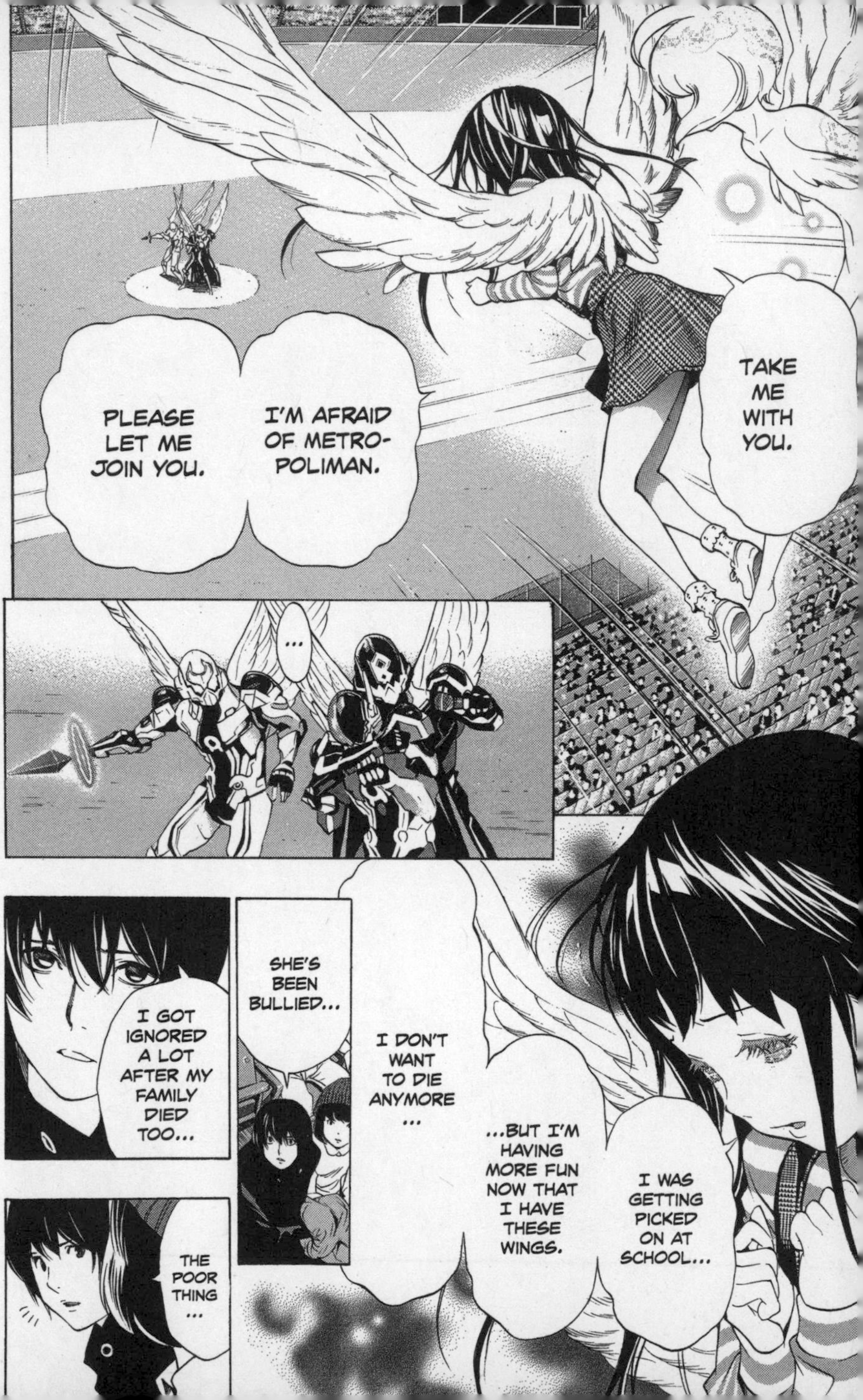
TAKE ME WITH YOU.
I'M AFRAID OF METRO-POLIMAN.
PLEASE LET ME JOIN YOU.
...
I WAS GETTING PICKED ON AT SCHOOL...
...BUT I'M HAVING MORE FUN NOW THAT I HAVE THESE WINGS.
I DON'T WANT TO DIE ANYMORE...
SHE'S BEEN BULLIED...
I GOT IGNORED A LOT AFTER MY FAMILY DIED TOO...
THE POOR THING...

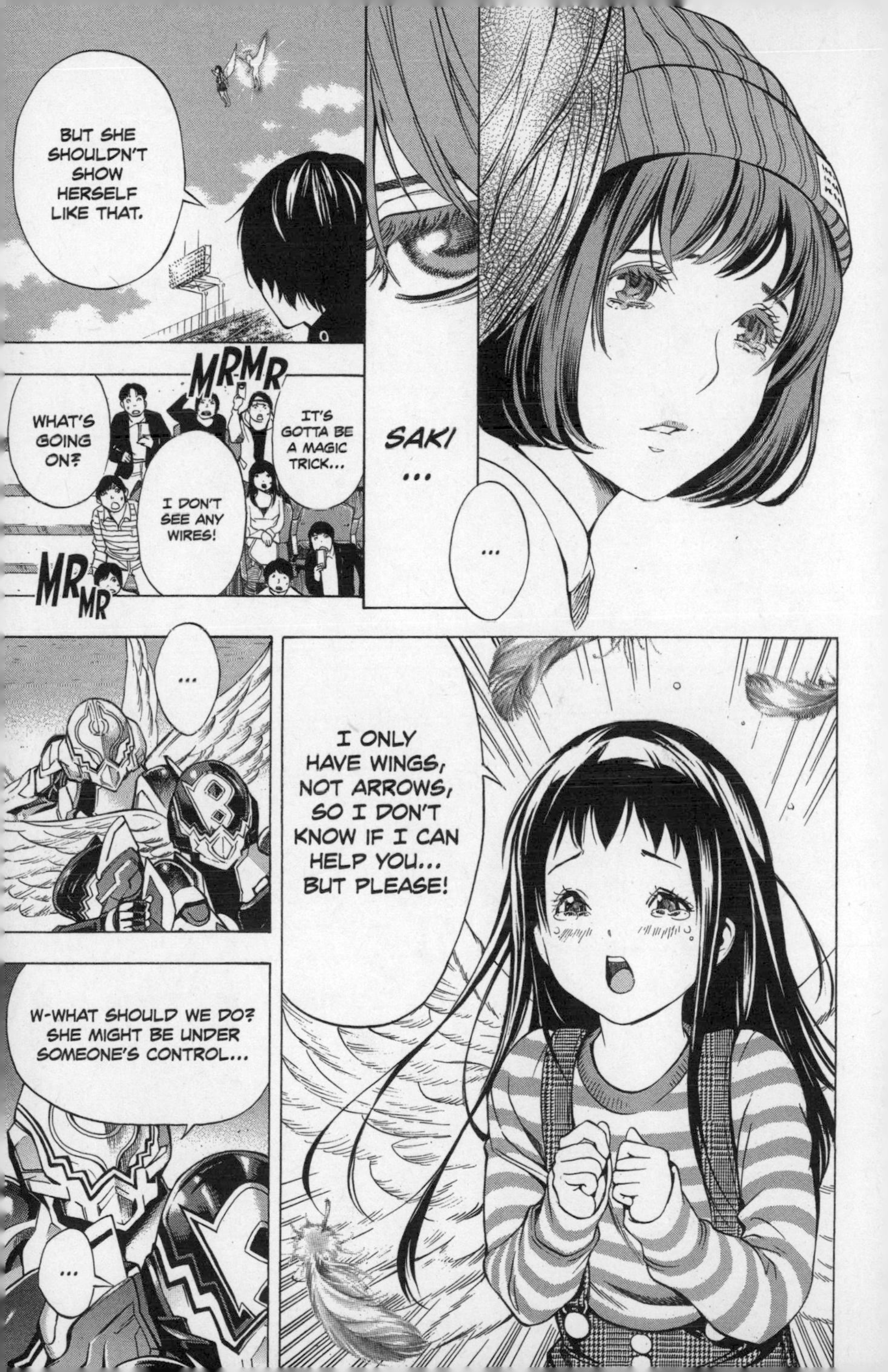
...
SAKI ...
BUT SHE SHOULDN'T SHOW HERSELF LIKE THAT.
MRMR
IT'S GOTTA BE A MAGIC TRICK...
WHAT'S GOING ON?
I DON'T SEE ANY WIRES!
MRMR
I ONLY HAVE WINGS, NOT ARROWS, SO I DON'T KNOW IF I CAN HELP YOU... BUT PLEASE!
...
W-WHAT SHOULD WE DO? SHE MIGHT BE UNDER SOMEONE'S CONTROL...
...

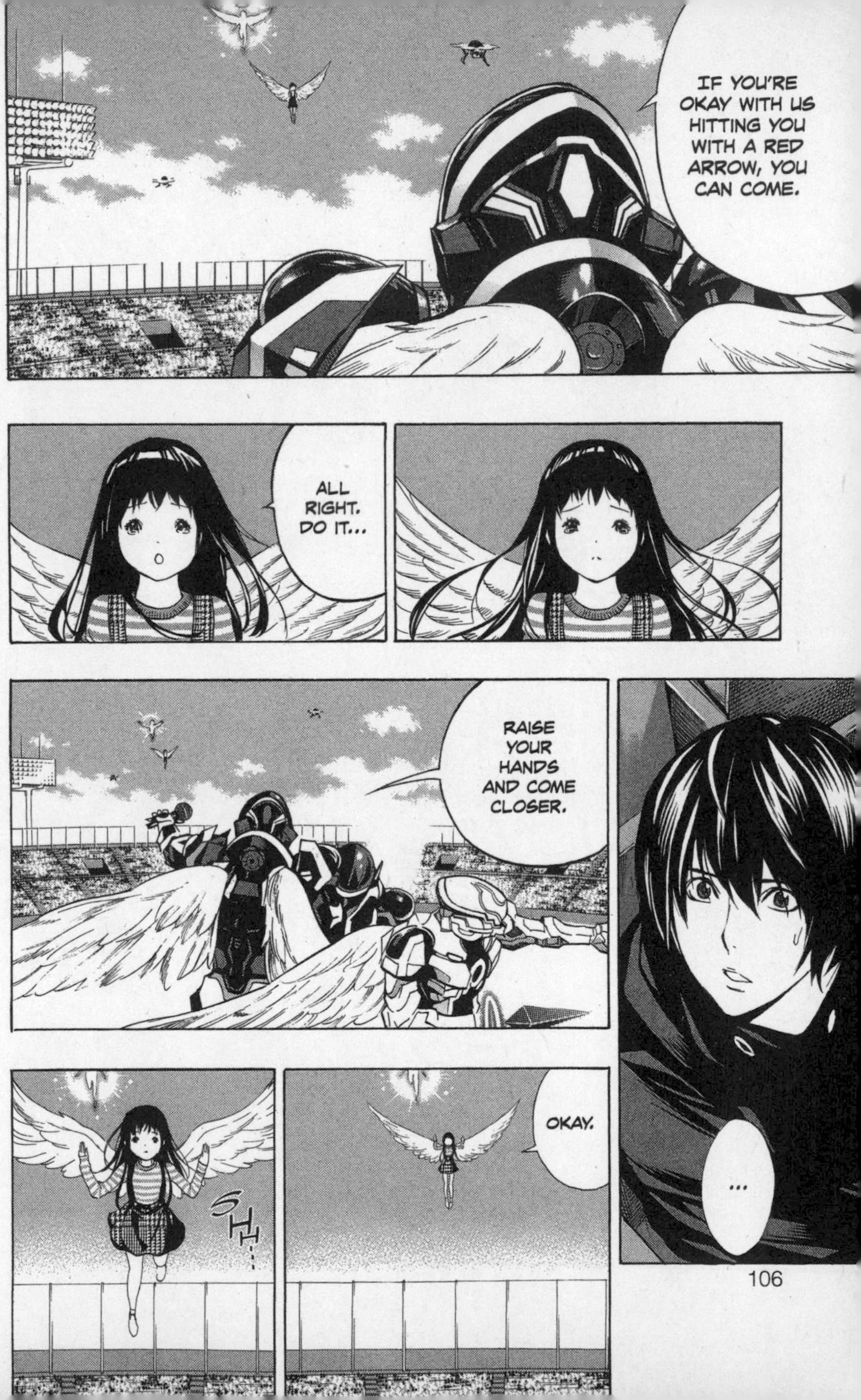
IF YOU'RE OKAY WITH US HITTING YOU WITH A RED ARROW, YOU CAN COME.
ALL RIGHT. DO IT...
...
RAISE YOUR HANDS AND COME CLOSER.
OKAY.
SHH...

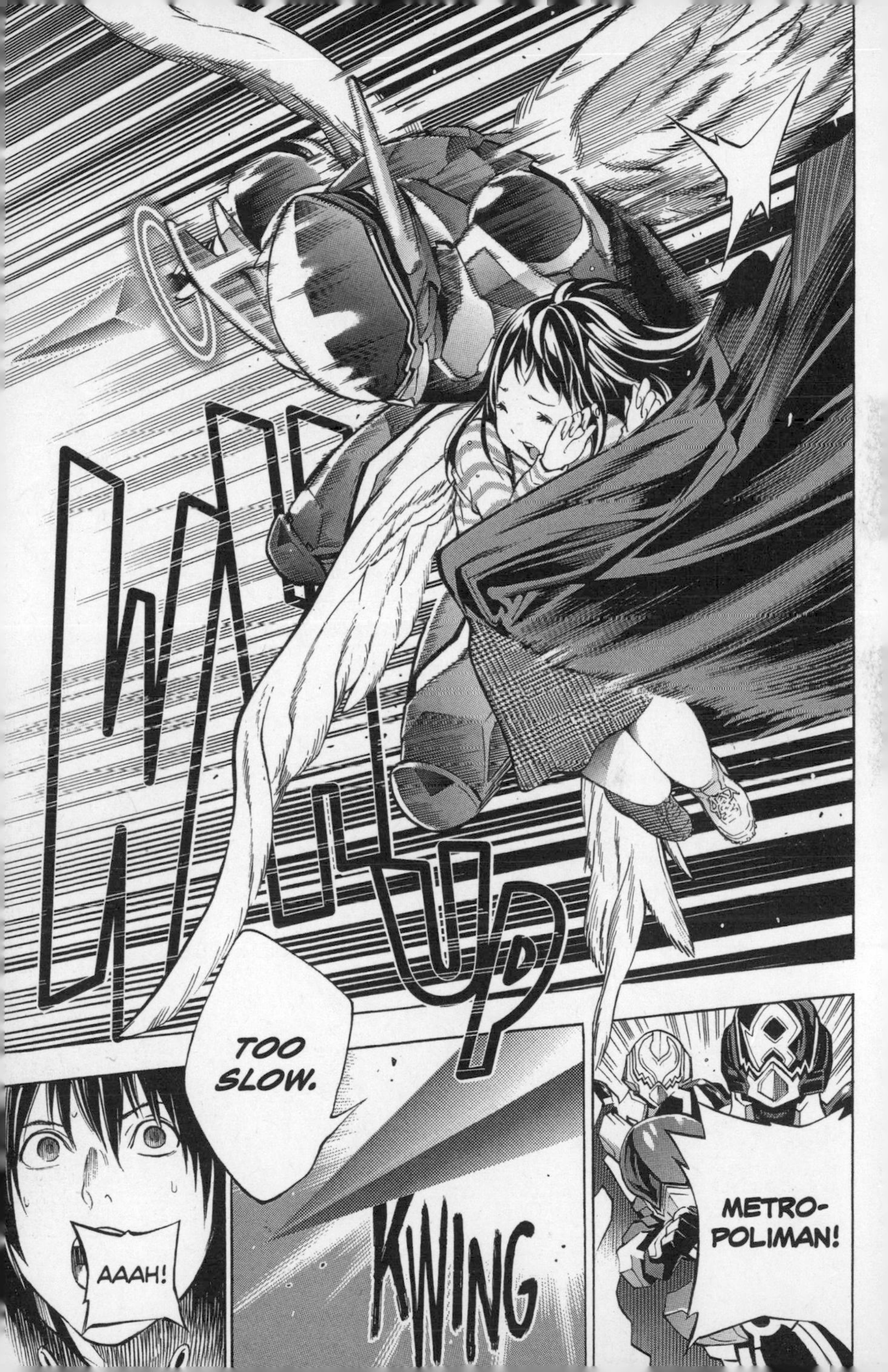
TOO SLOW.
METRO-POLIMAN!
KWING
AAAH!

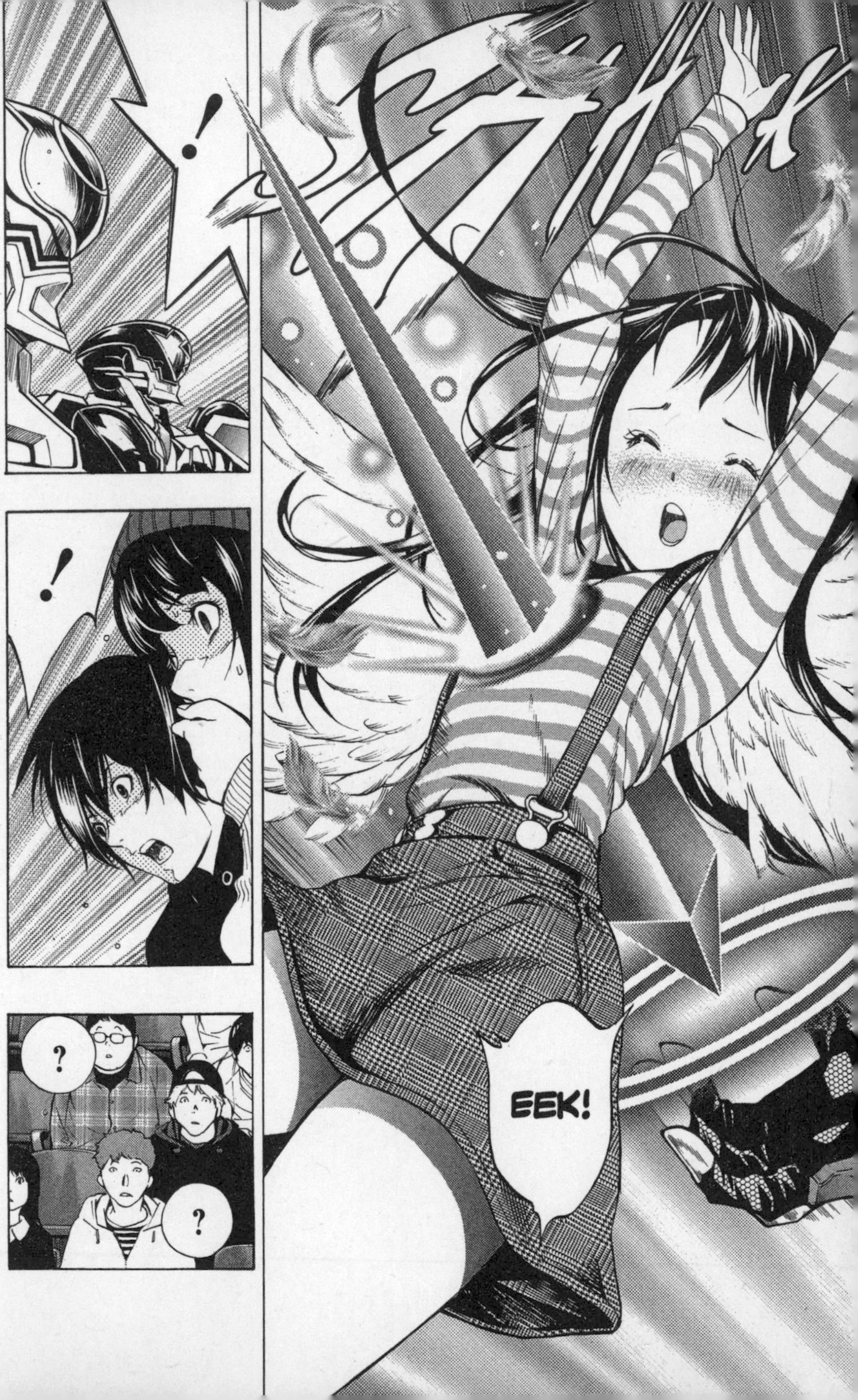
EEK!
!
!
?
?

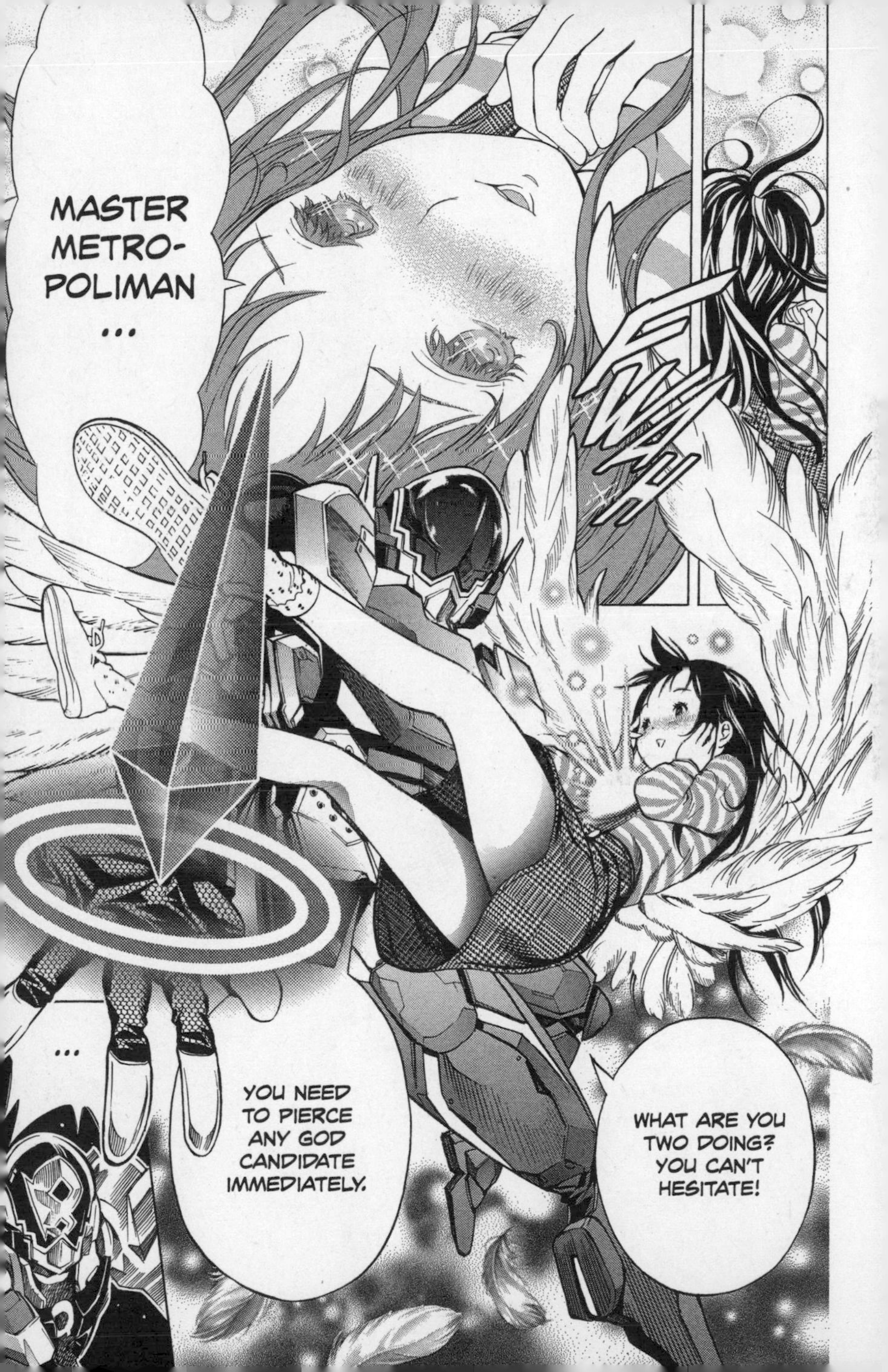
MASTER METRO-POLIMAN ...
WHAT ARE YOU TWO DOING? YOU CAN'T HESITATE!
YOU NEED TO PIERCE ANY GOD CANDIDATE IMMEDIATELY.
...

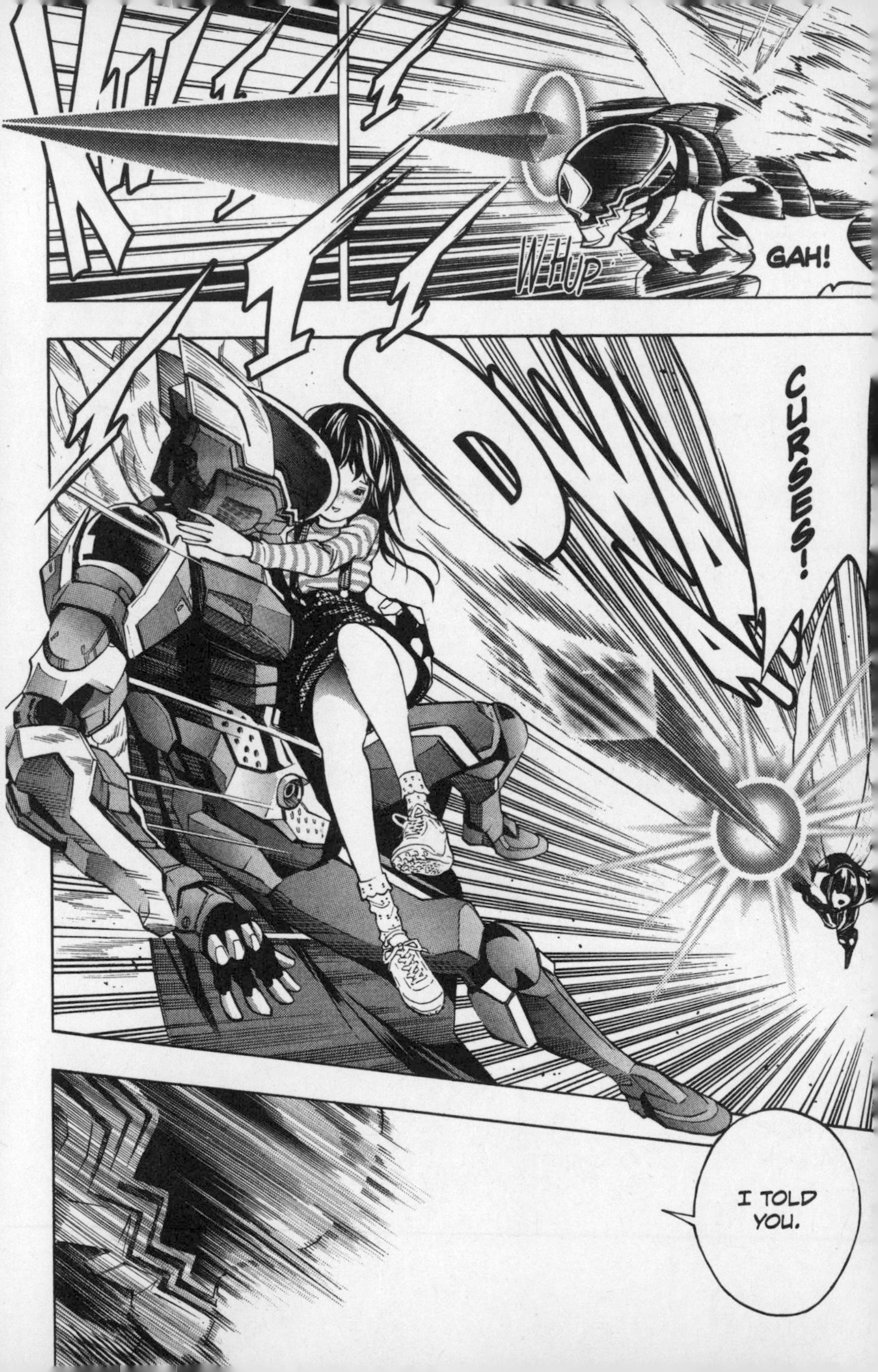
GAH!
WHUP
CURSES!
I TOLD YOU.

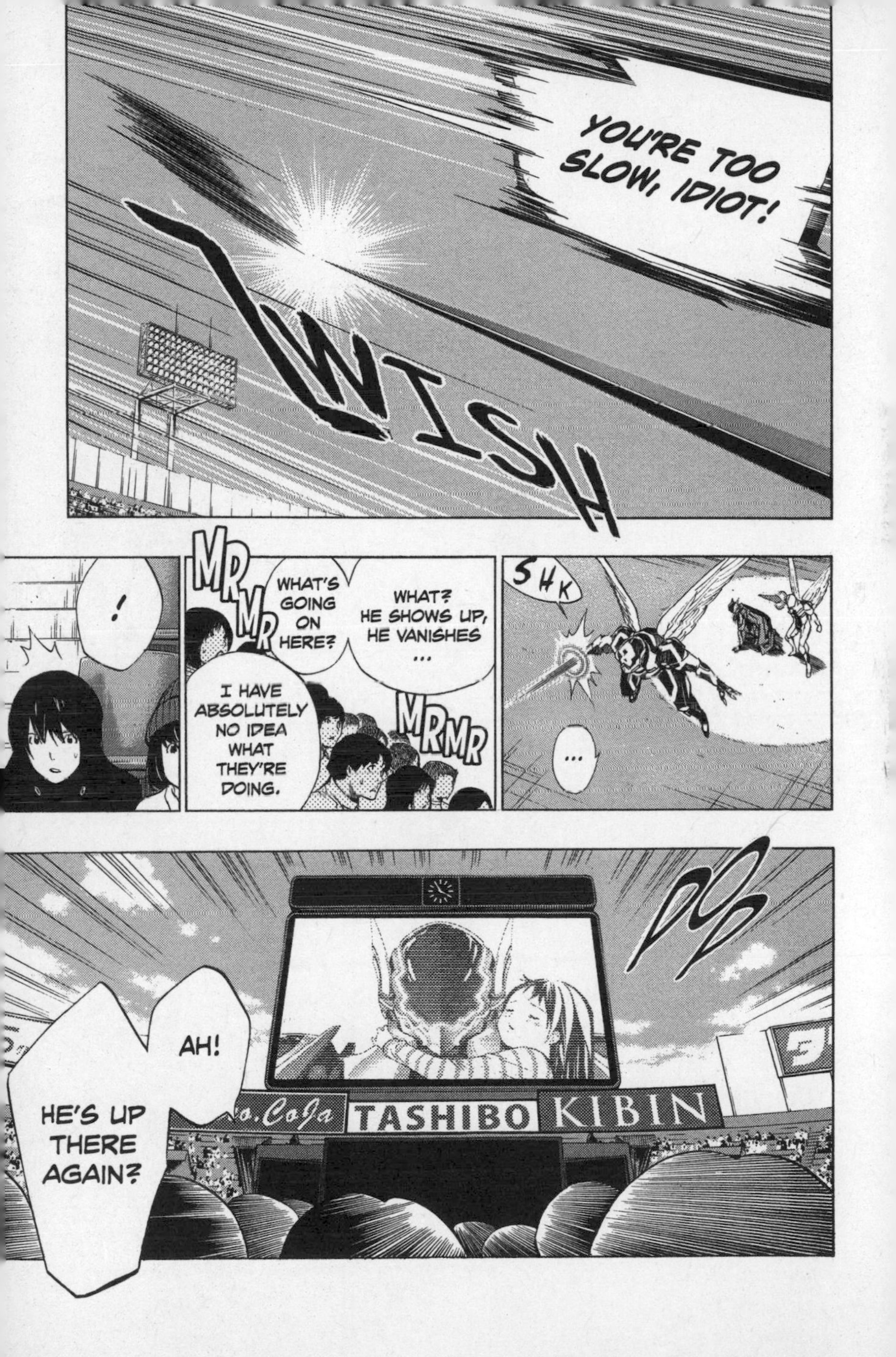
YOU'RE TOO SLOW, IDIOT!
SWISH
SHK
...
WHAT? HE SHOWS UP, HE VANISHES ...
WHAT'S GOING ON HERE?
MRMR
I HAVE ABSOLUTELY NO IDEA WHAT THEY'RE DOING.
MRMR
!
AH!
HE'S UP THERE AGAIN?
TASHIBO
KIBIN

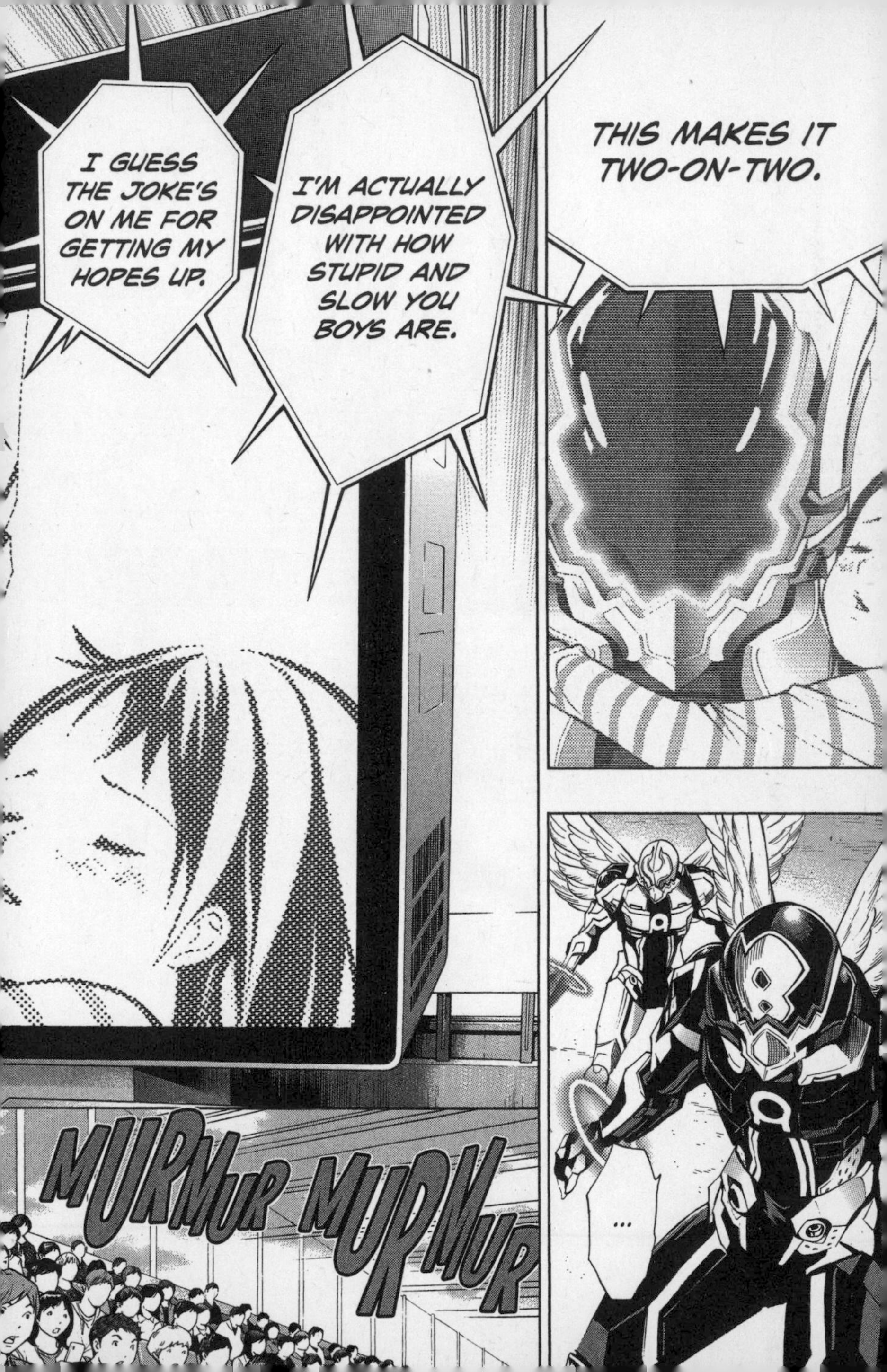
THIS MAKES IT TWO-ON-TWO.
...
I'M ACTUALLY DISAPPOINTED WITH HOW STUPID AND SLOW YOU BOYS ARE.
I GUESS THE JOKE'S ON ME FOR GETTING MY HOPES UP.
MURMUR MURMUR

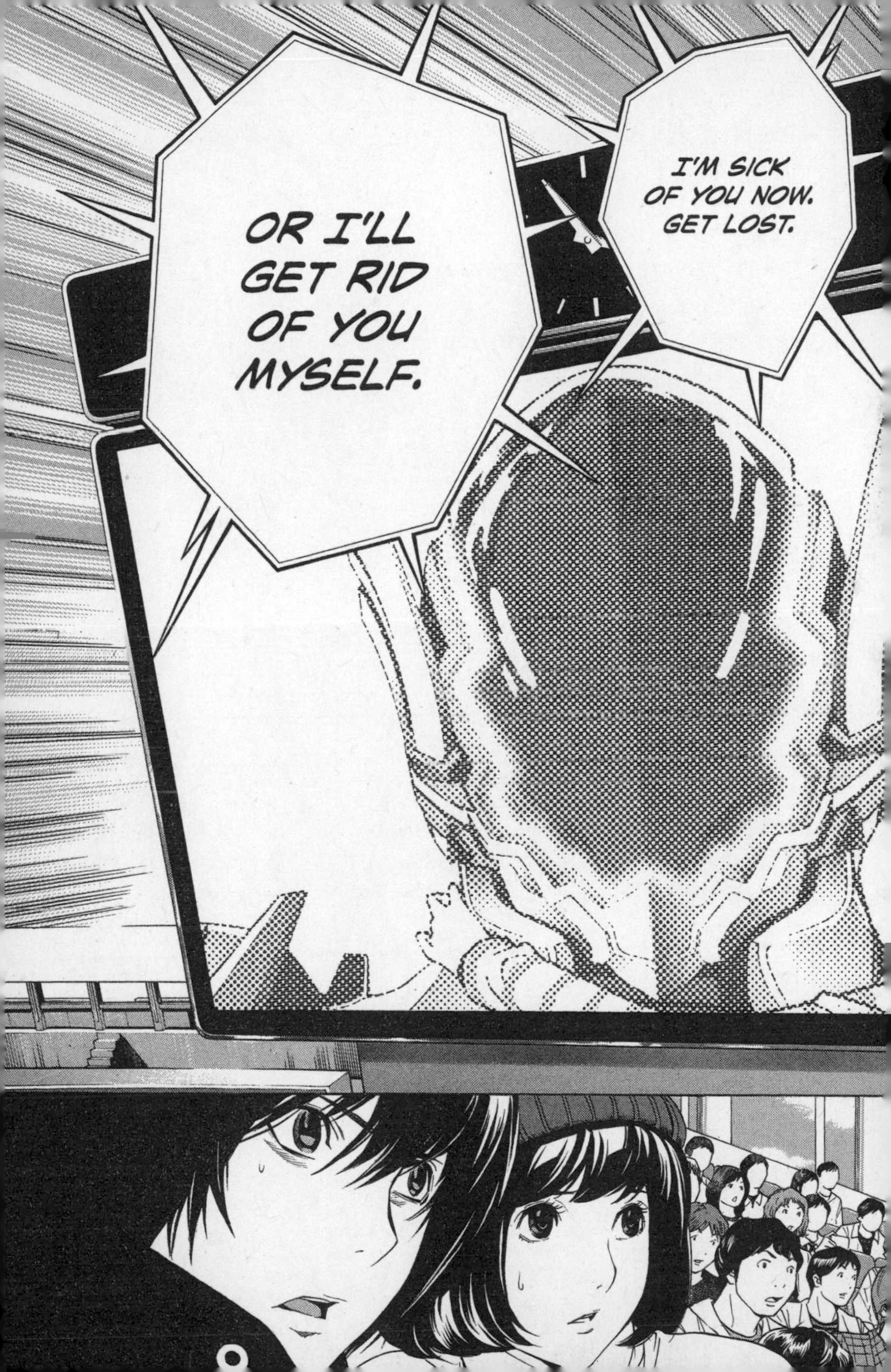
I'M SICK OF YOU NOW. GET LOST.
OR I'LL GET RID OF YOU MYSELF.

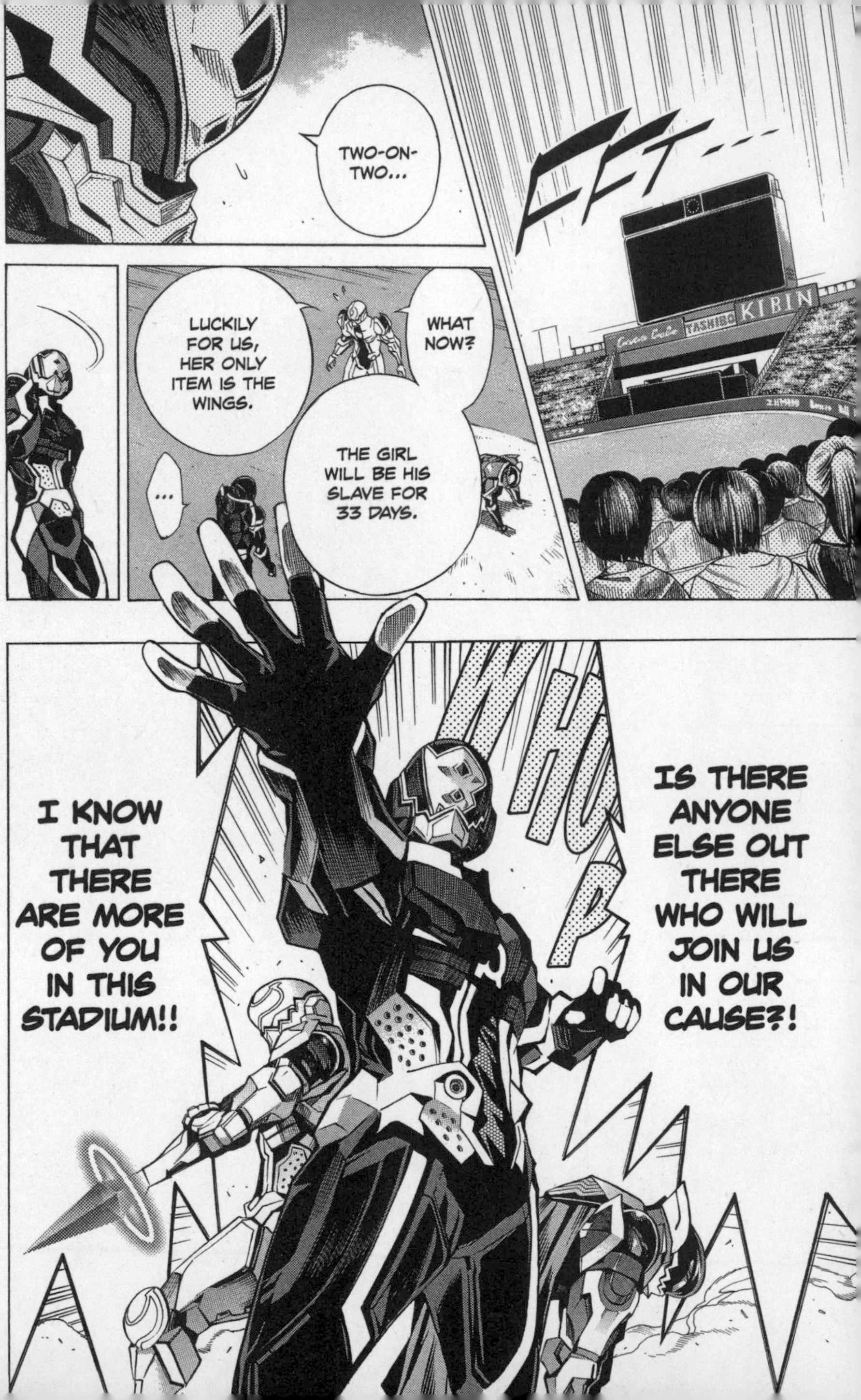
FFT---
KIRIN
TASHIBO
TWO-ON-TWO...
WHAT NOW?
LUCKILY FOR US, HER ONLY ITEM IS THE WINGS.
THE GIRL WILL BE HIS SLAVE FOR 33 DAYS.
...
WHUP
IS THERE ANYONE ELSE OUT THERE WHO WILL JOIN US IN OUR CAUSE?!
I KNOW THAT THERE ARE MORE OF YOU IN THIS STADIUM!!

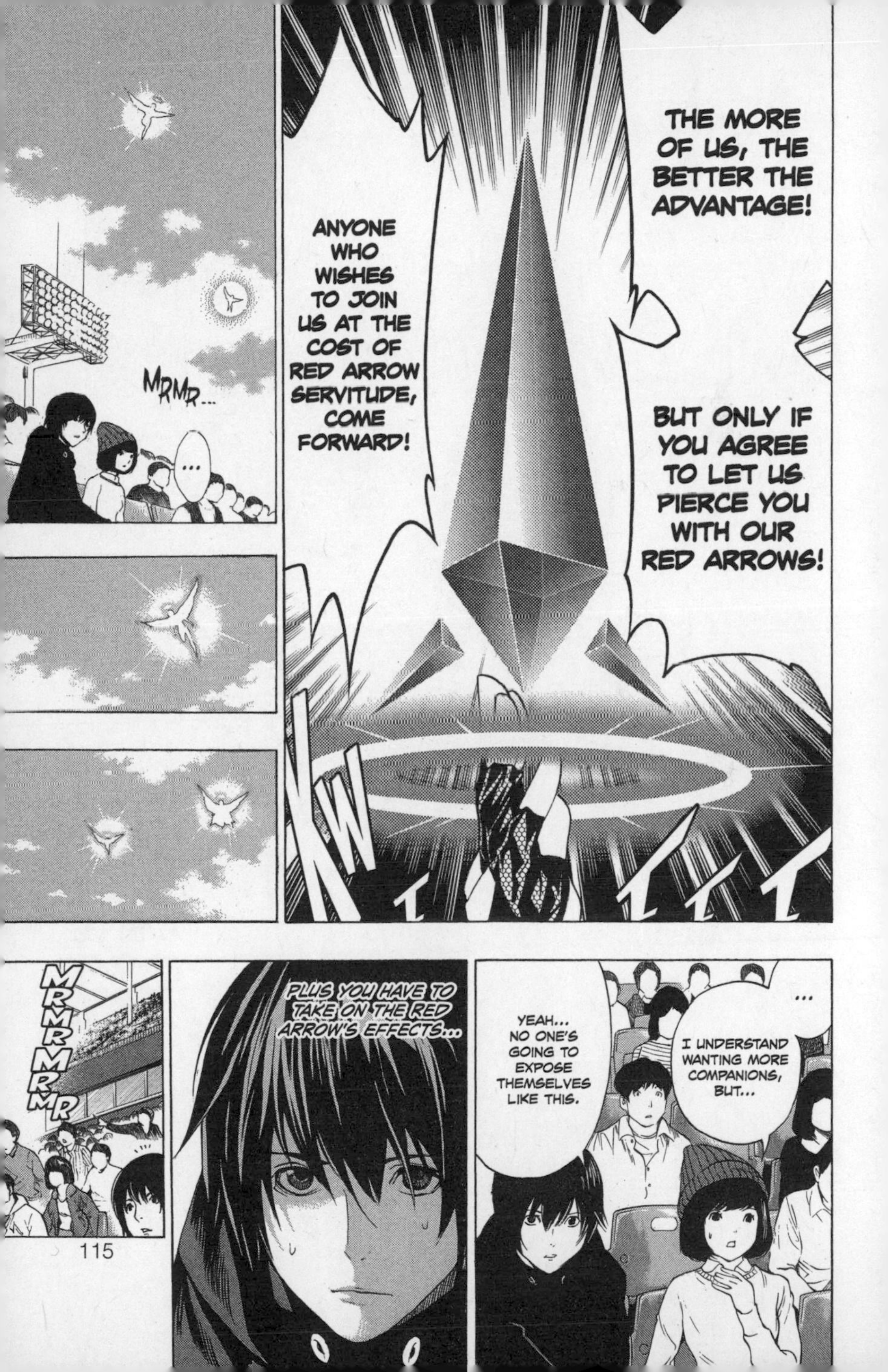
THE MORE OF US, THE BETTER THE ADVANTAGE!
ANYONE WHO WISHES TO JOIN US AT THE COST OF RED ARROW SERVITUDE, COME FORWARD!
BUT ONLY IF YOU AGREE TO LET US PIERCE YOU WITH OUR RED ARROWS!
MRMR...
...
...
I UNDERSTAND WANTING MORE COMPANIONS, BUT...
YEAH... NO ONE'S GOING TO EXPOSE THEMSELVES LIKE THIS.
PLUS YOU HAVE TO TAKE ON THE RED ARROW'S EFFECTS...
MRMRMRMRMR

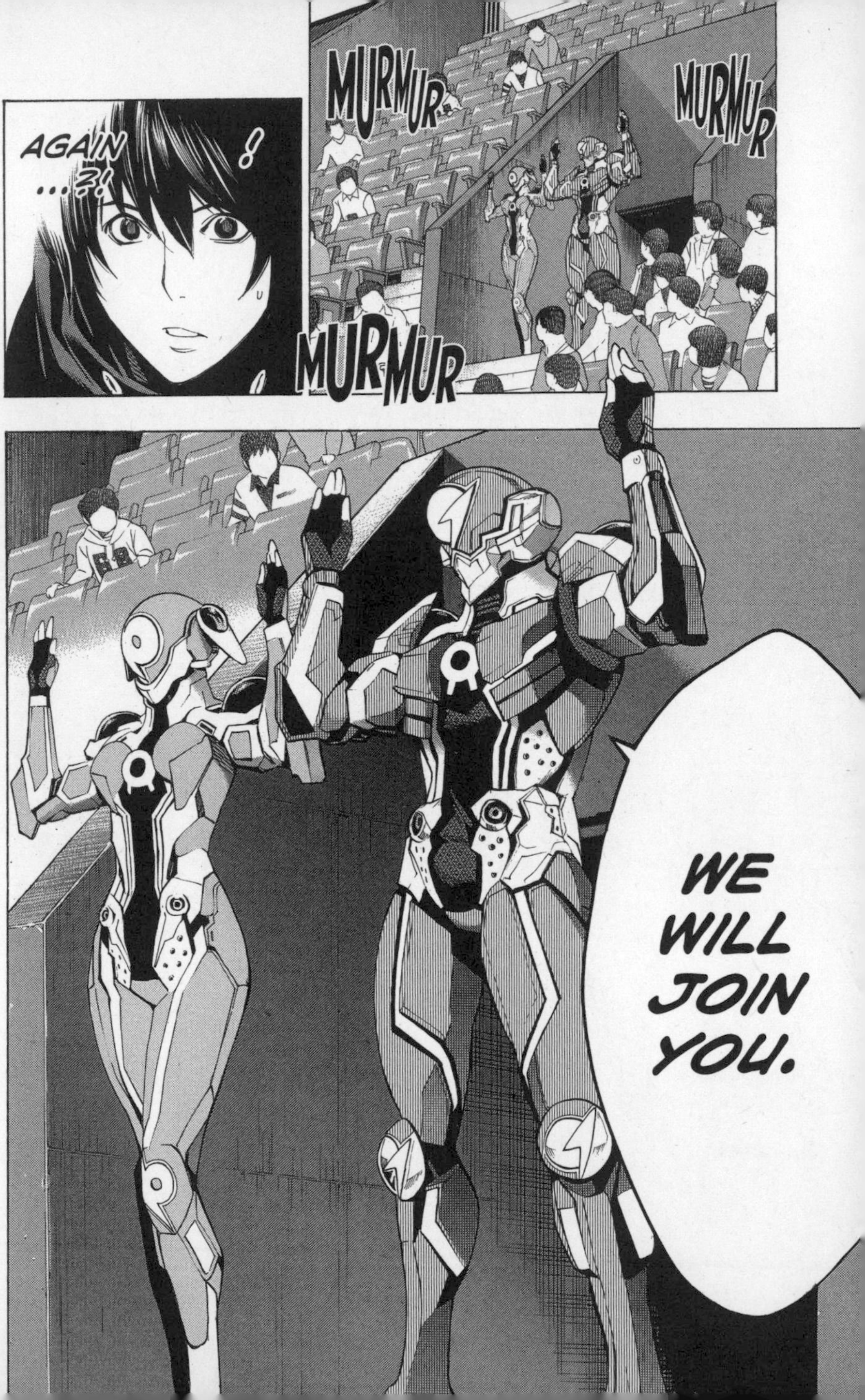
MURMUR
MURMUR
MURMUR
AGAIN ...?!
!
WE WILL JOIN YOU.

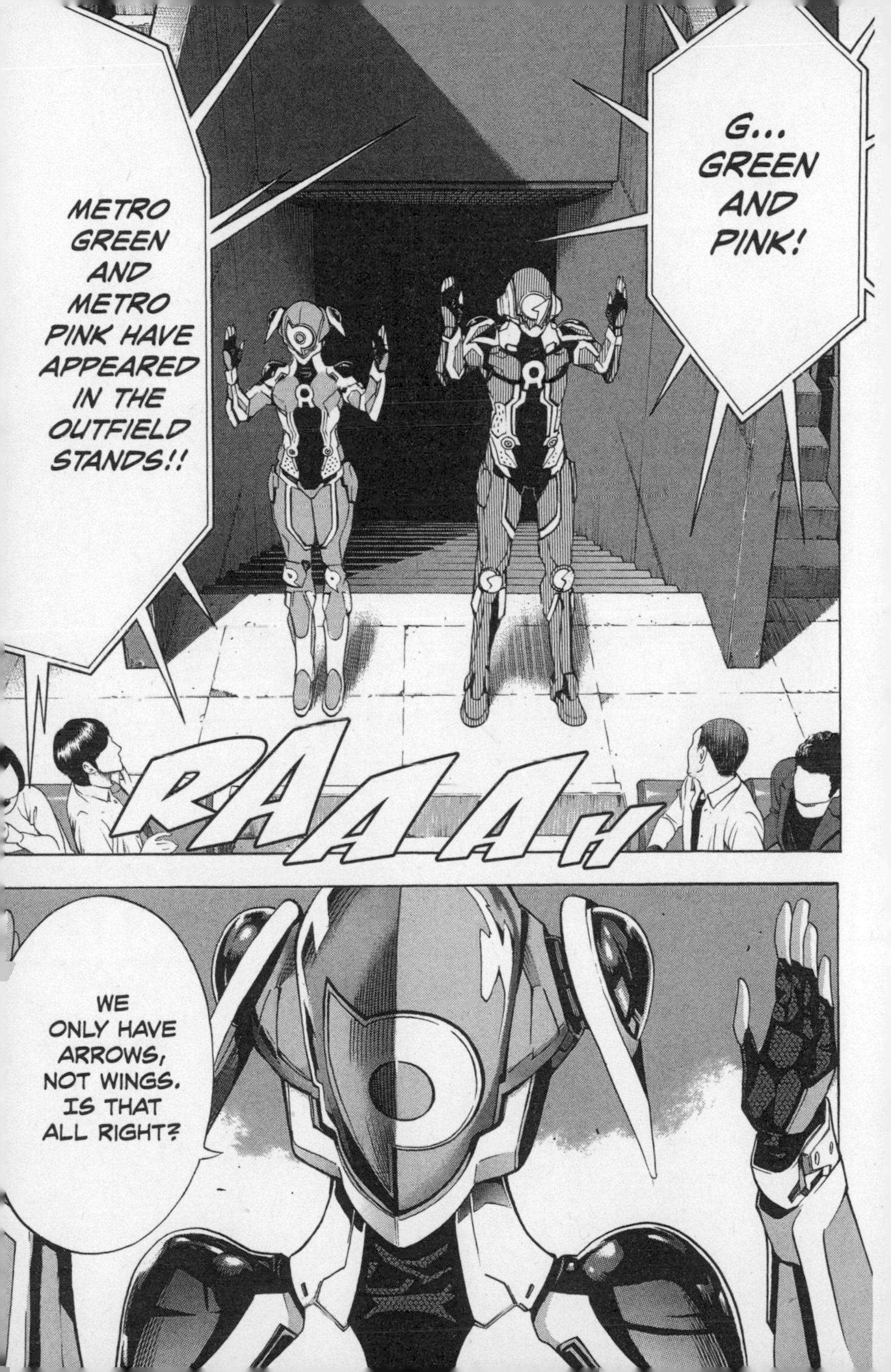
G... GREEN AND PINK!
METRO GREEN AND METRO PINK HAVE APPEARED IN THE OUTFIELD STANDS!!
RAAAAH
WE ONLY HAVE ARROWS, NOT WINGS. IS THAT ALL RIGHT?

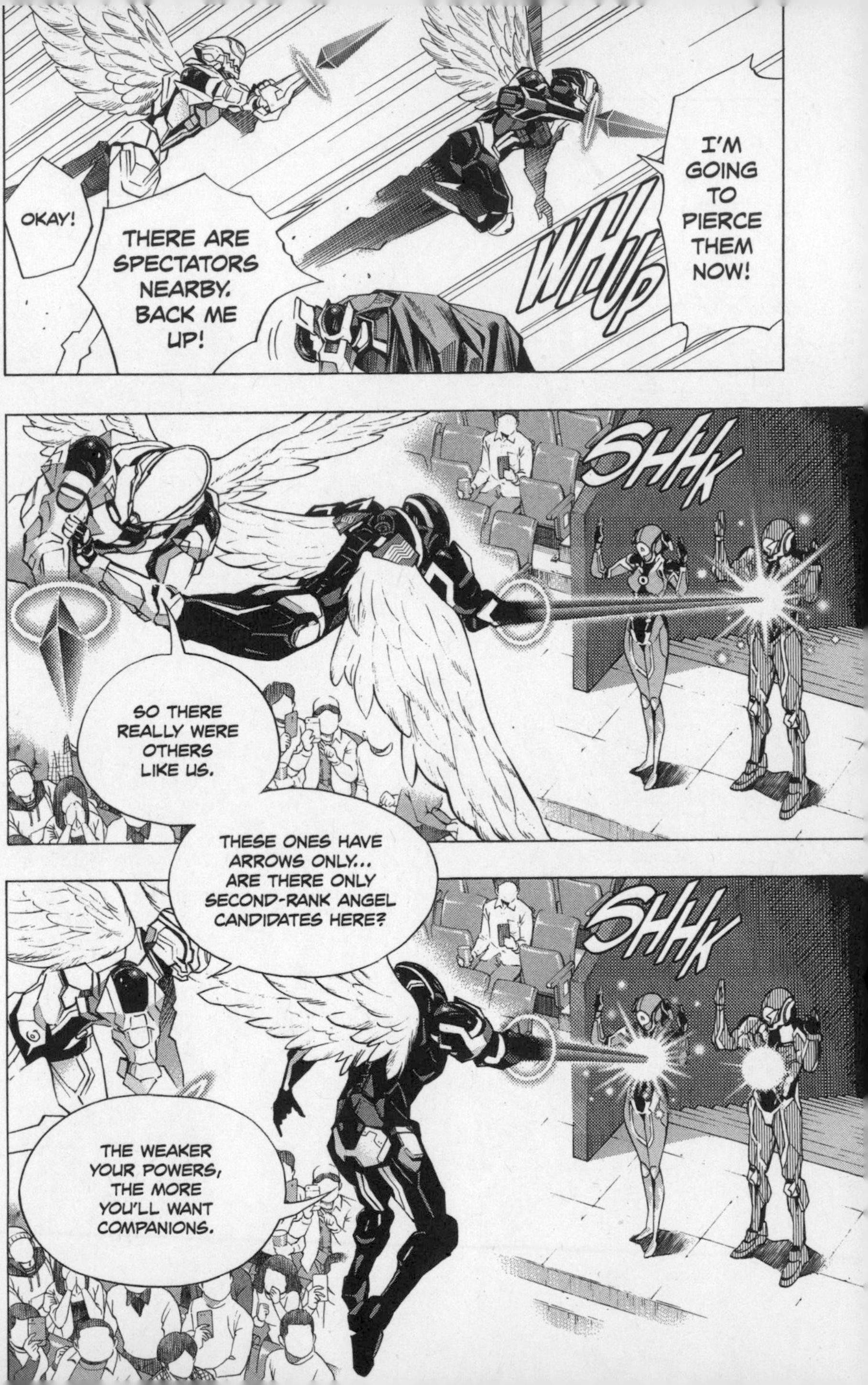
I'M GOING TO PIERCE THEM NOW!
WHUP
THERE ARE SPECTATORS NEARBY. BACK ME UP!
OKAY!
SHHK
SO THERE REALLY WERE OTHERS LIKE US.
SHHK
THESE ONES HAVE ARROWS ONLY... ARE THERE ONLY SECOND-RANK ANGEL CANDIDATES HERE?
THE WEAKER YOUR POWERS, THE MORE YOU'LL WANT COMPANIONS.

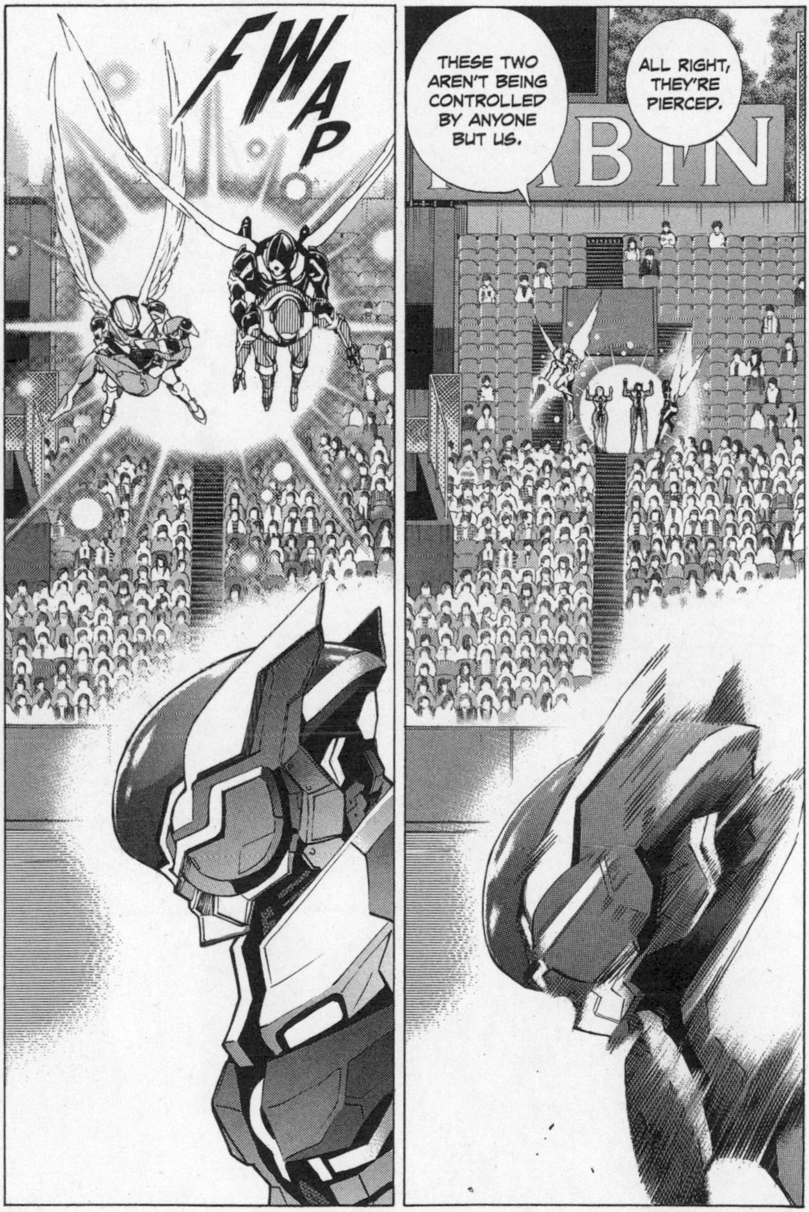
ALL RIGHT, THEY'RE PIERCED.
THESE TWO AREN'T BEING CONTROLLED BY ANYONE BUT US.
FWAP

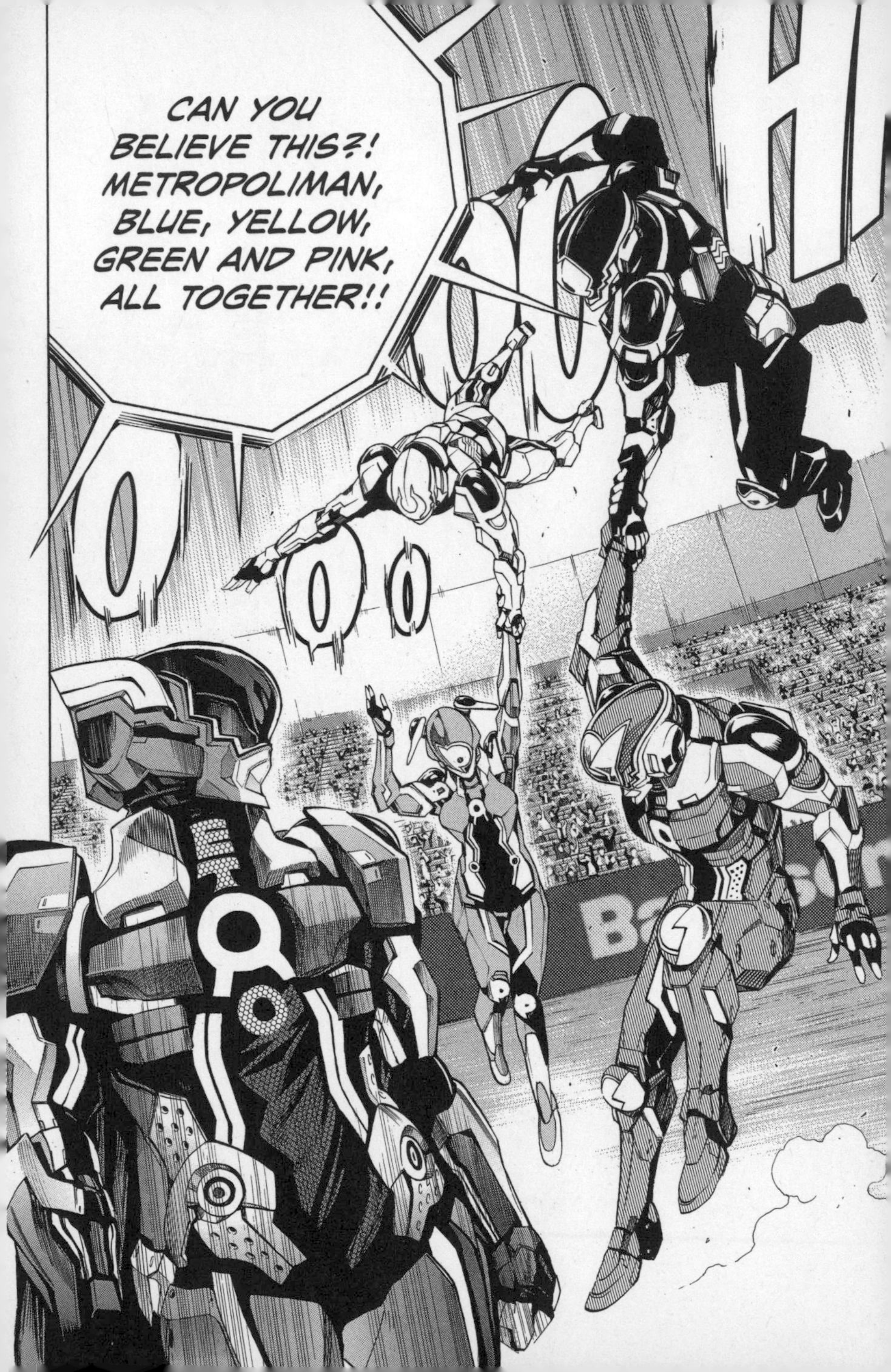
CAN YOU BELIEVE THIS?! METROPOLIMAN, BLUE, YELLOW, GREEN AND PINK, ALL TOGETHER!!

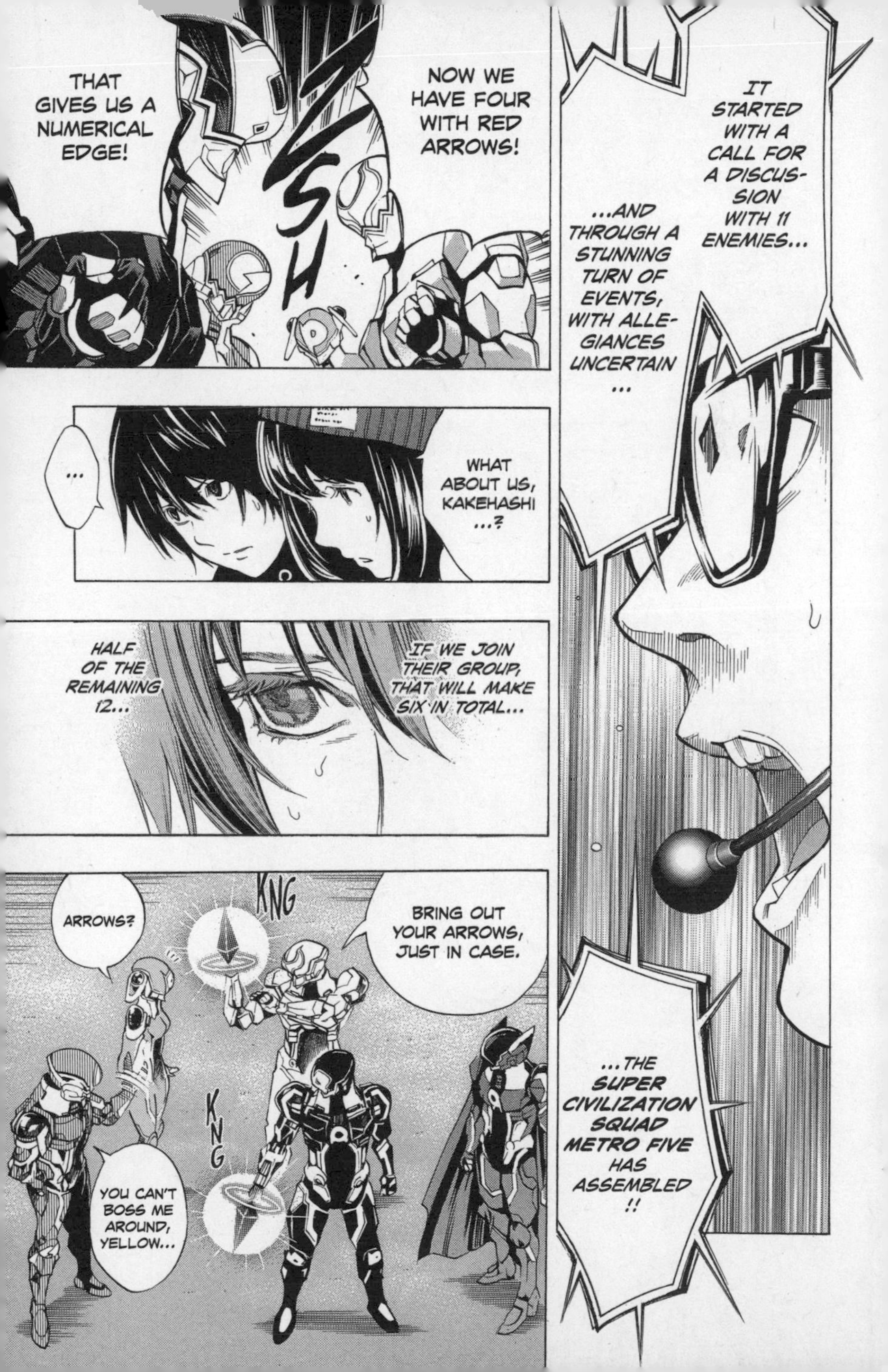
IT STARTED WITH A CALL FOR A DISCUSSION WITH 11 ENEMIES...
...AND THROUGH A STUNNING TURN OF EVENTS, WITH ALLEGIANCES UNCERTAIN...
...THE SUPER CIVILIZATION SQUAD METRO FIVE HAS ASSEMBLED!!
NOW WE HAVE FOUR WITH RED ARROWS!
THAT GIVES US A NUMERICAL EDGE!
WHAT ABOUT US, KAKEHASHI...?
...
IF WE JOIN THEIR GROUP, THAT WILL MAKE SIX IN TOTAL...
HALF OF THE REMAINING 12...
KNG
BRING OUT YOUR ARROWS, JUST IN CASE.
ARROWS?
KNG
YOU CAN'T BOSS ME AROUND, YELLOW...

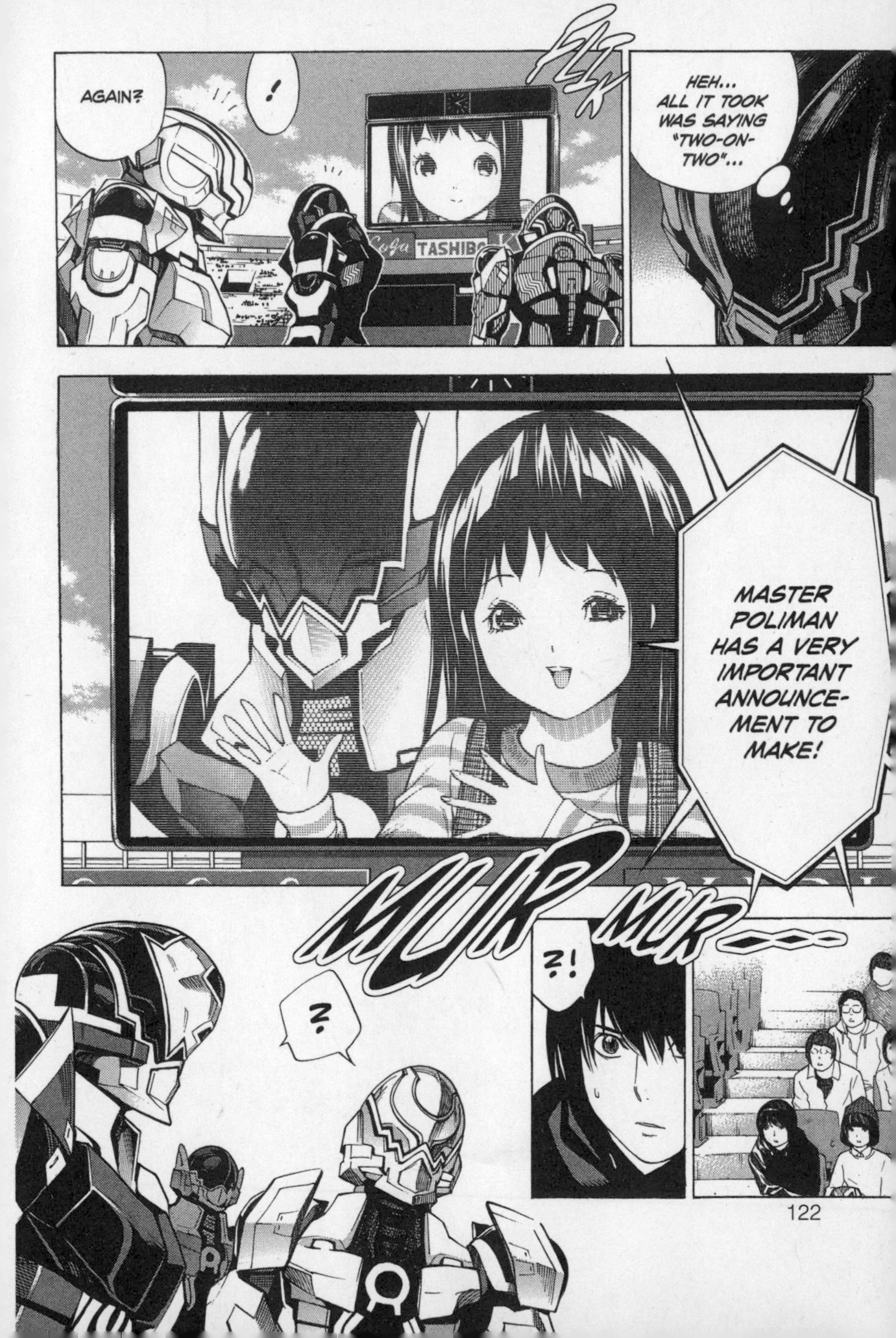

HEH... ALL IT TOOK WAS SAYING "TWO-ON-TWO"...
FLIK
!
AGAIN?
TASHIBO
MASTER POLIMAN HAS A VERY IMPORTANT ANNOUNCE-MENT TO MAKE!
MUR MUR—
?!
?

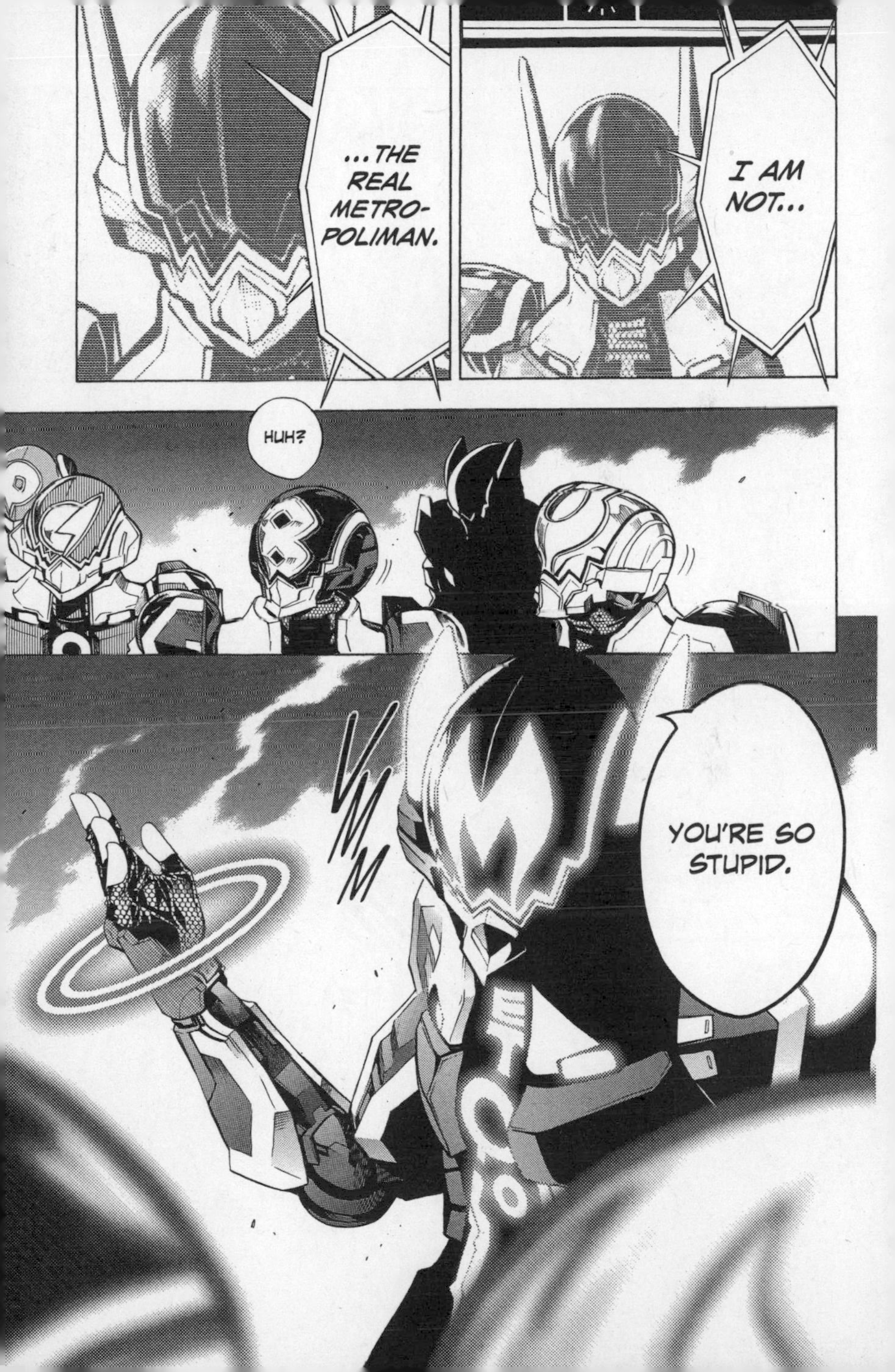
I AM NOT...
...THE REAL METROPOLIMAN.
HUH?
VMM
YOU'RE SO STUPID.

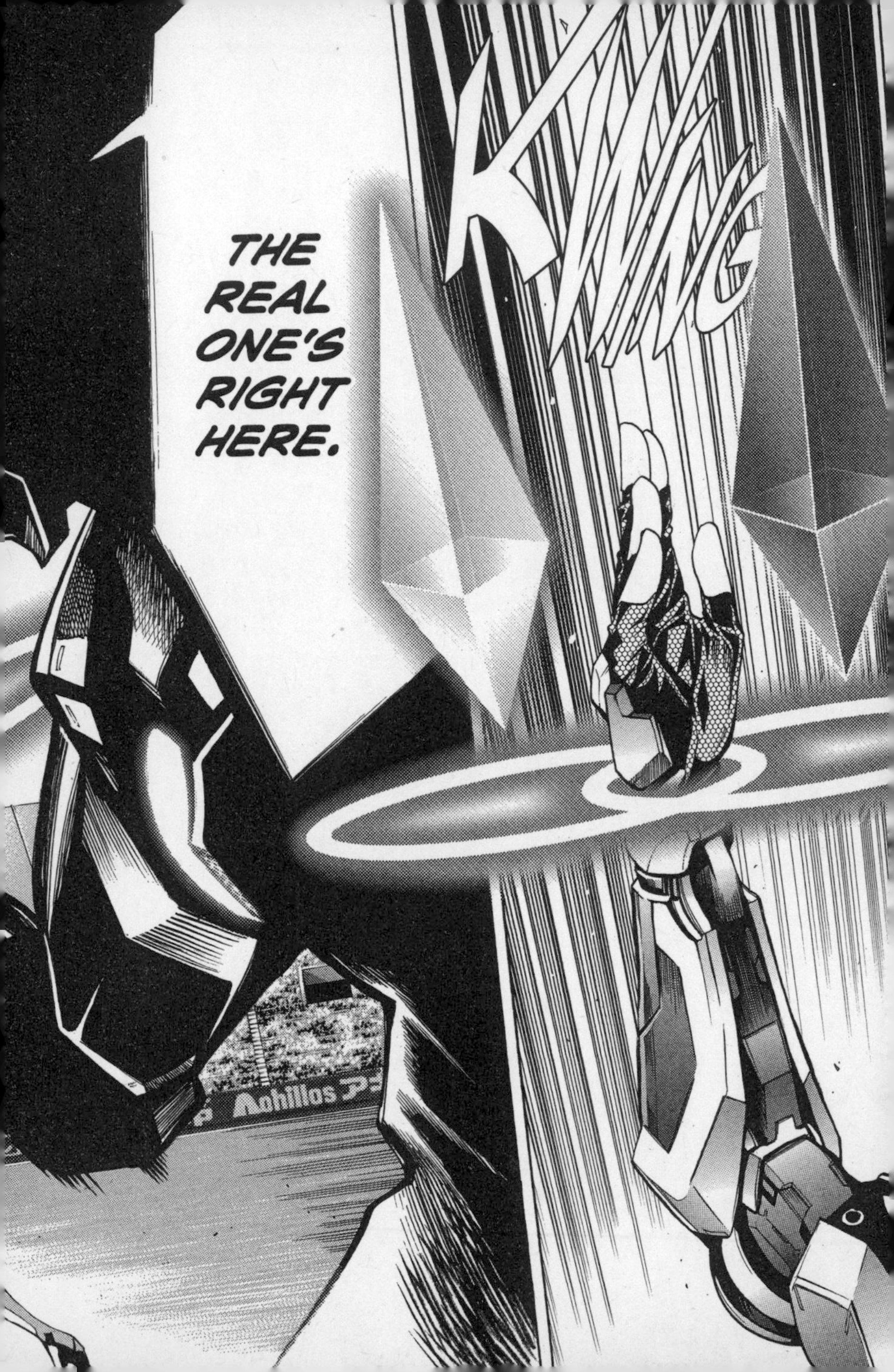
THE REAL ONE'S RIGHT HERE.

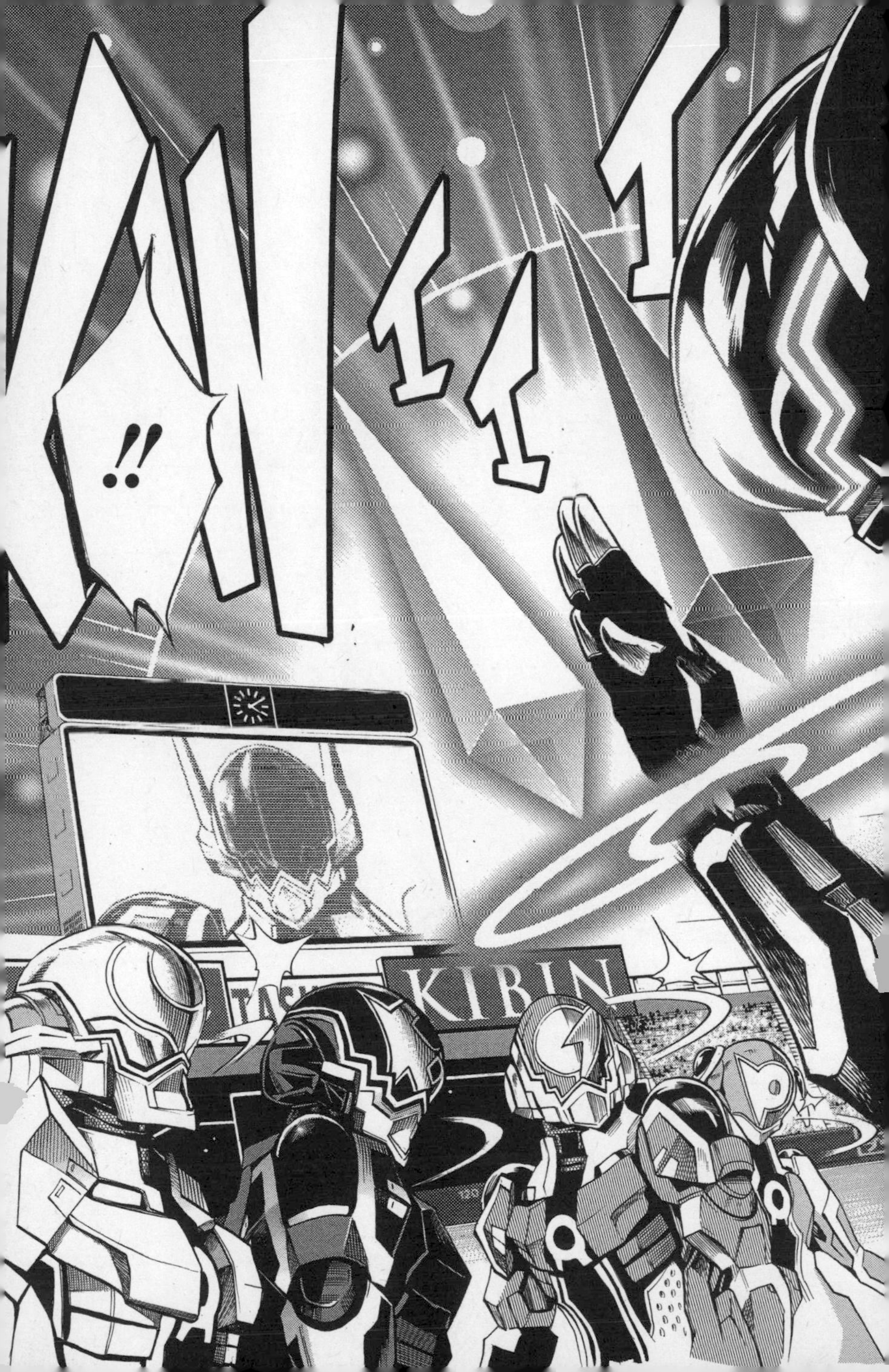
!!
KIBIN

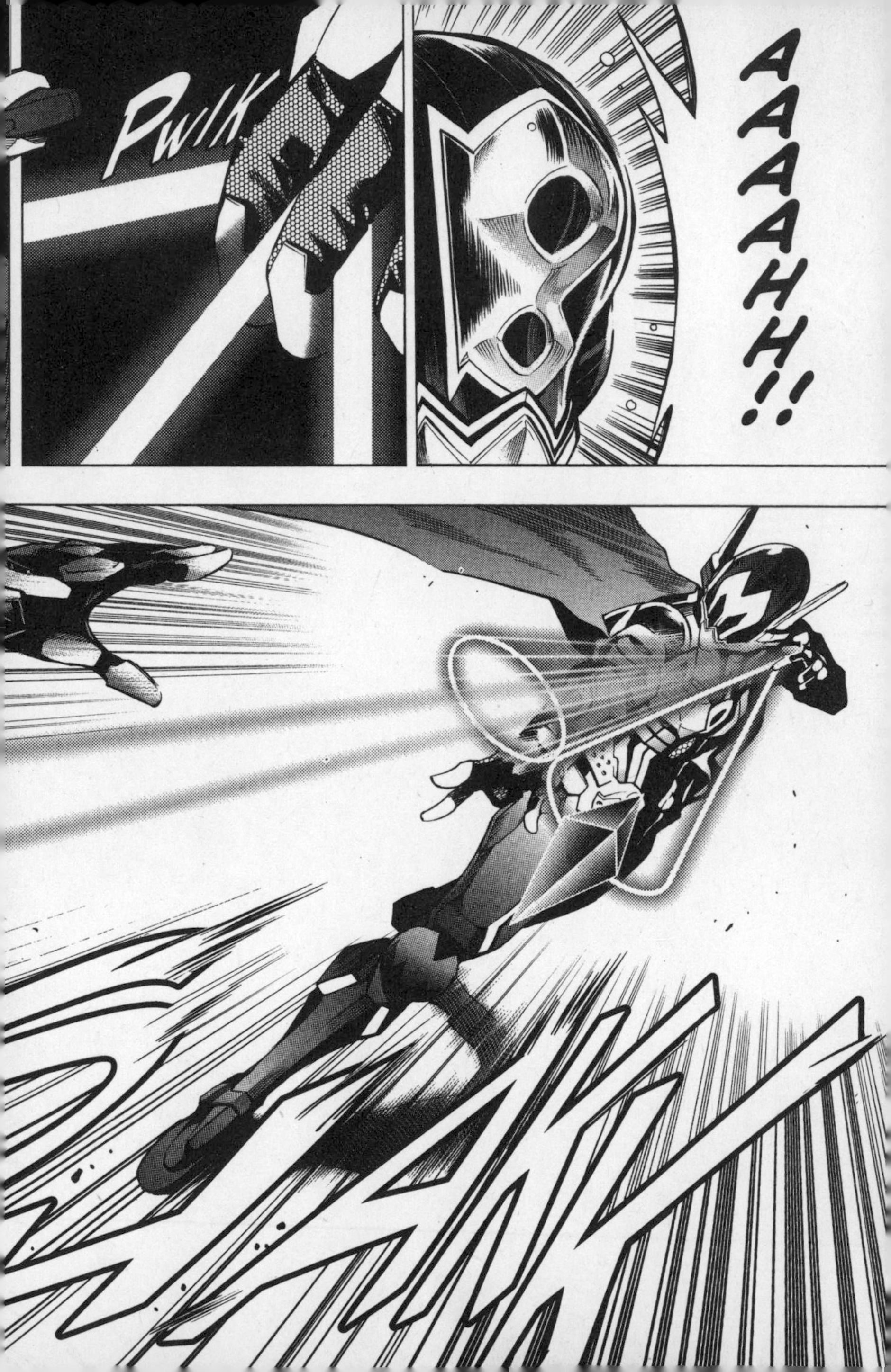
AAAAHH!!
Pwik

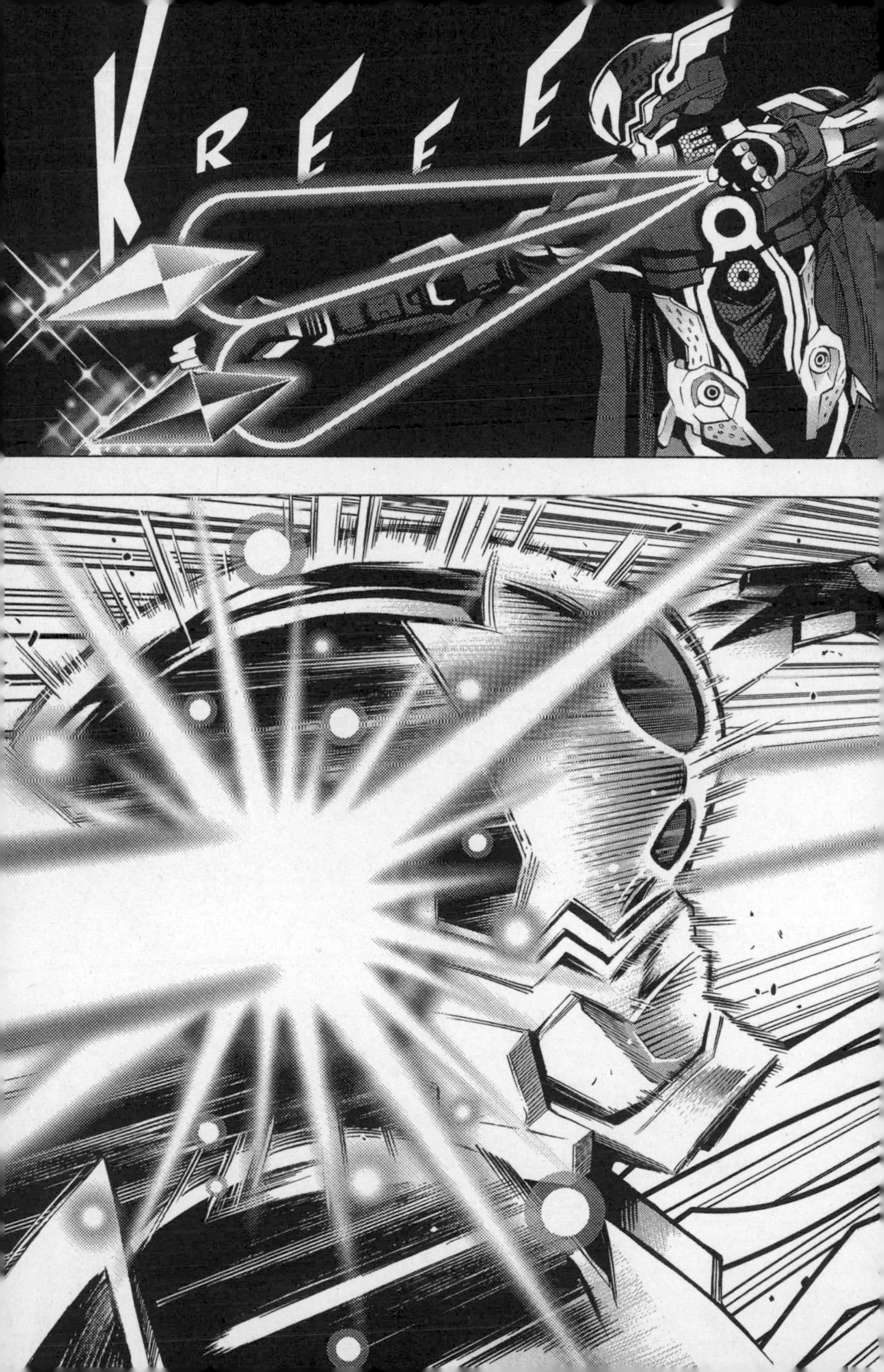
KREEE

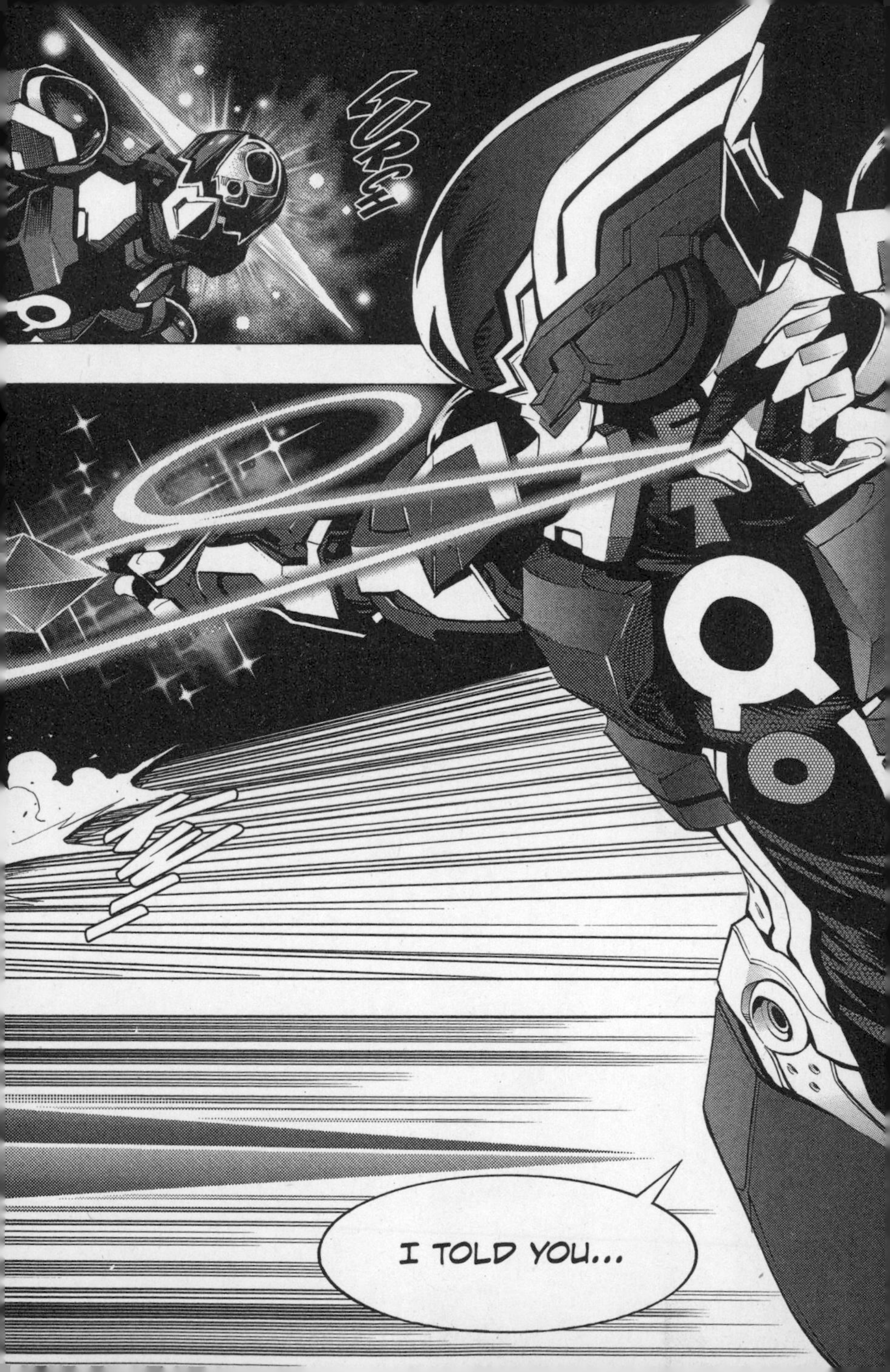
LURCH
I TOLD YOU...

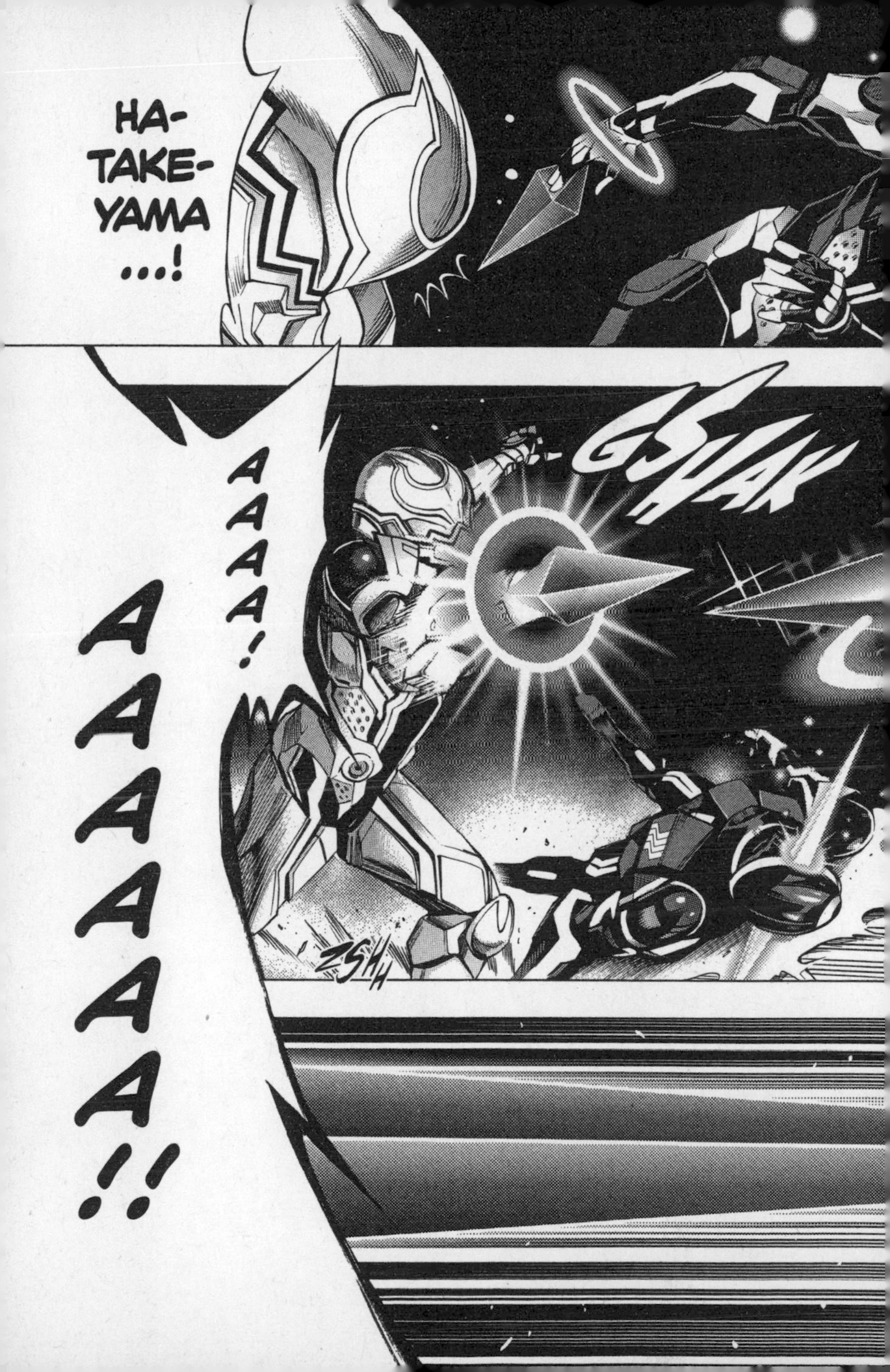
HA-TAKE-YAMA ...!
GSHAK
AAAA!
AAAAAAA!!
ZSHH

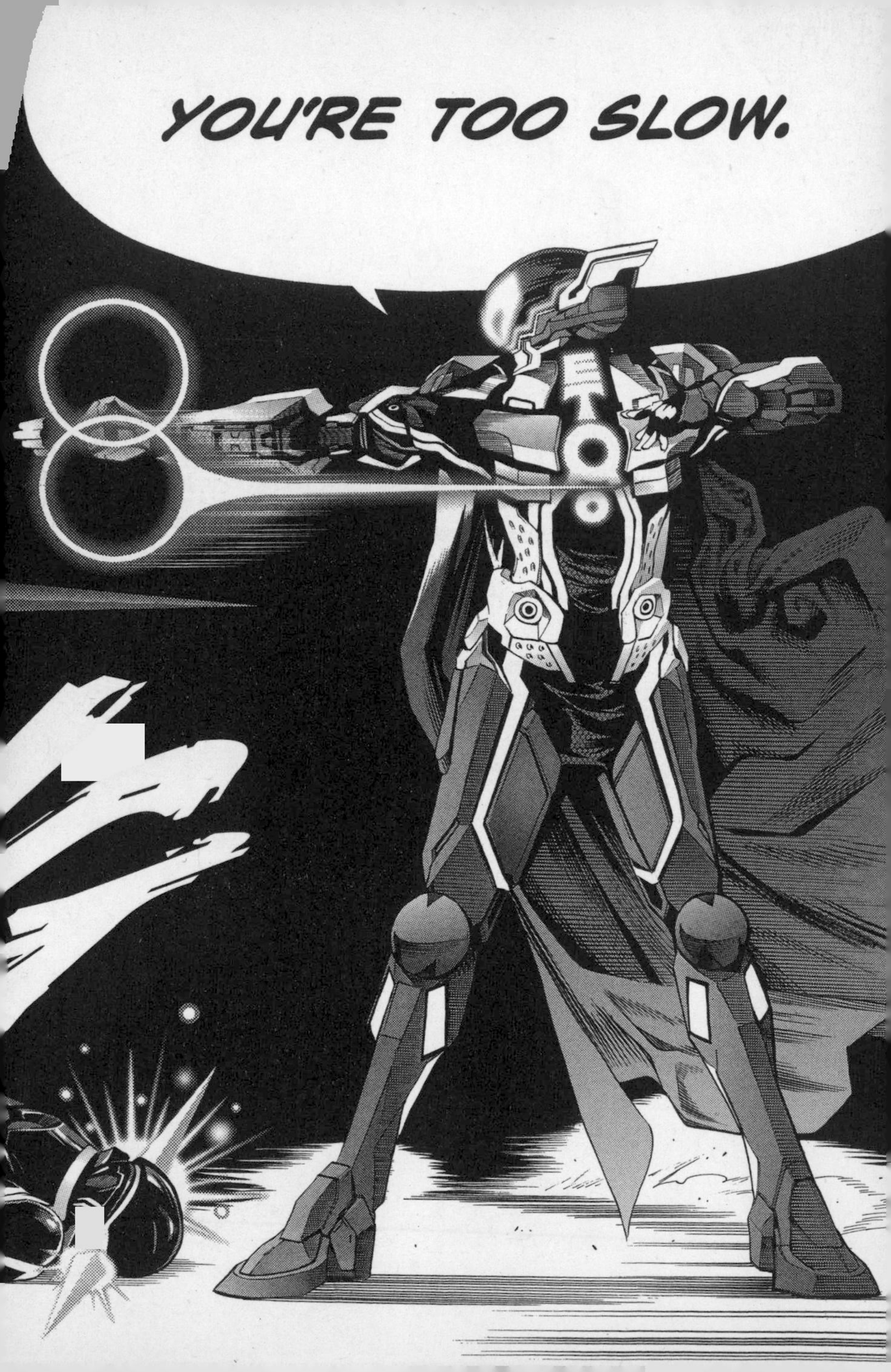
YOU'RE TOO SLOW.

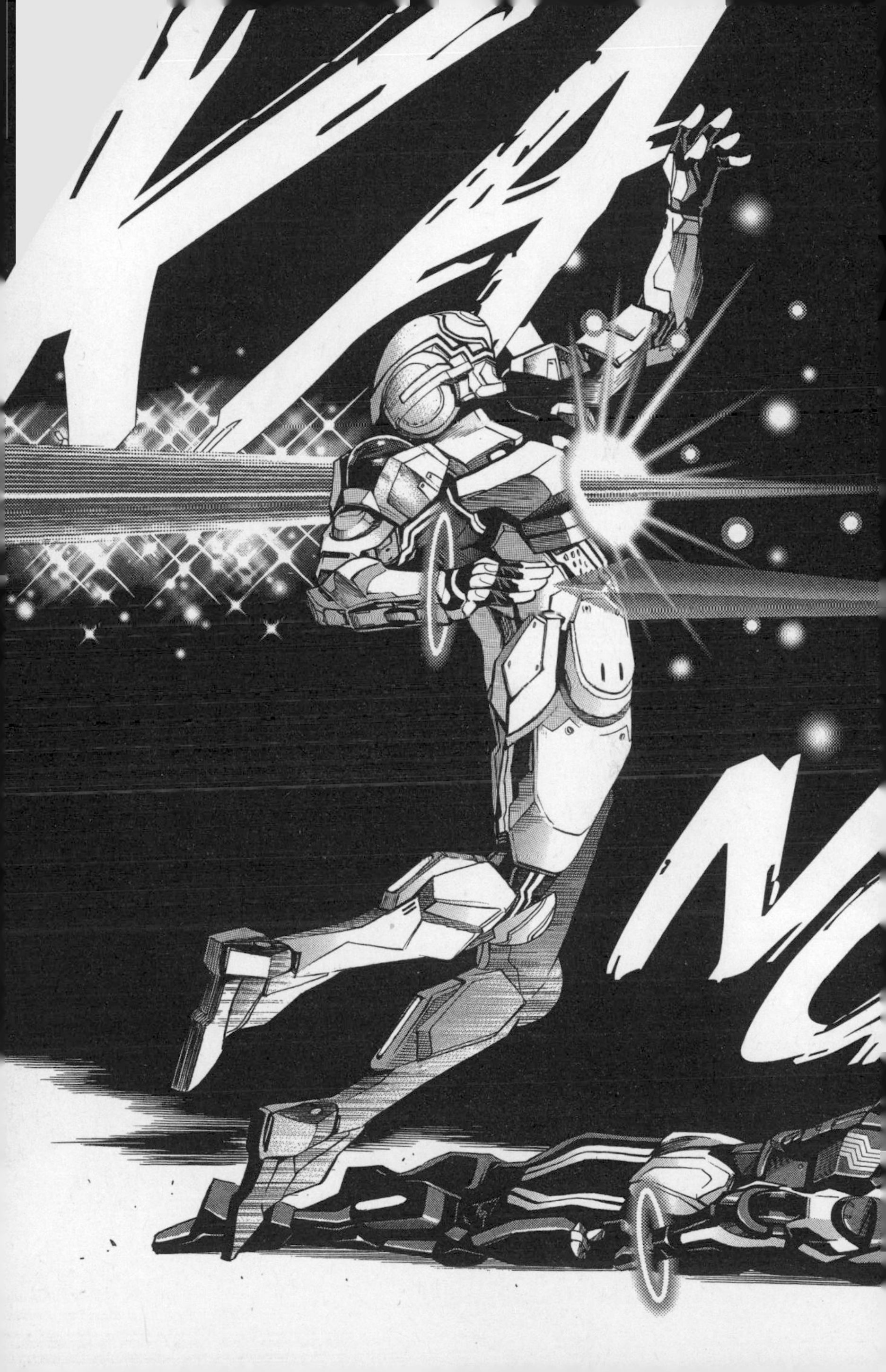

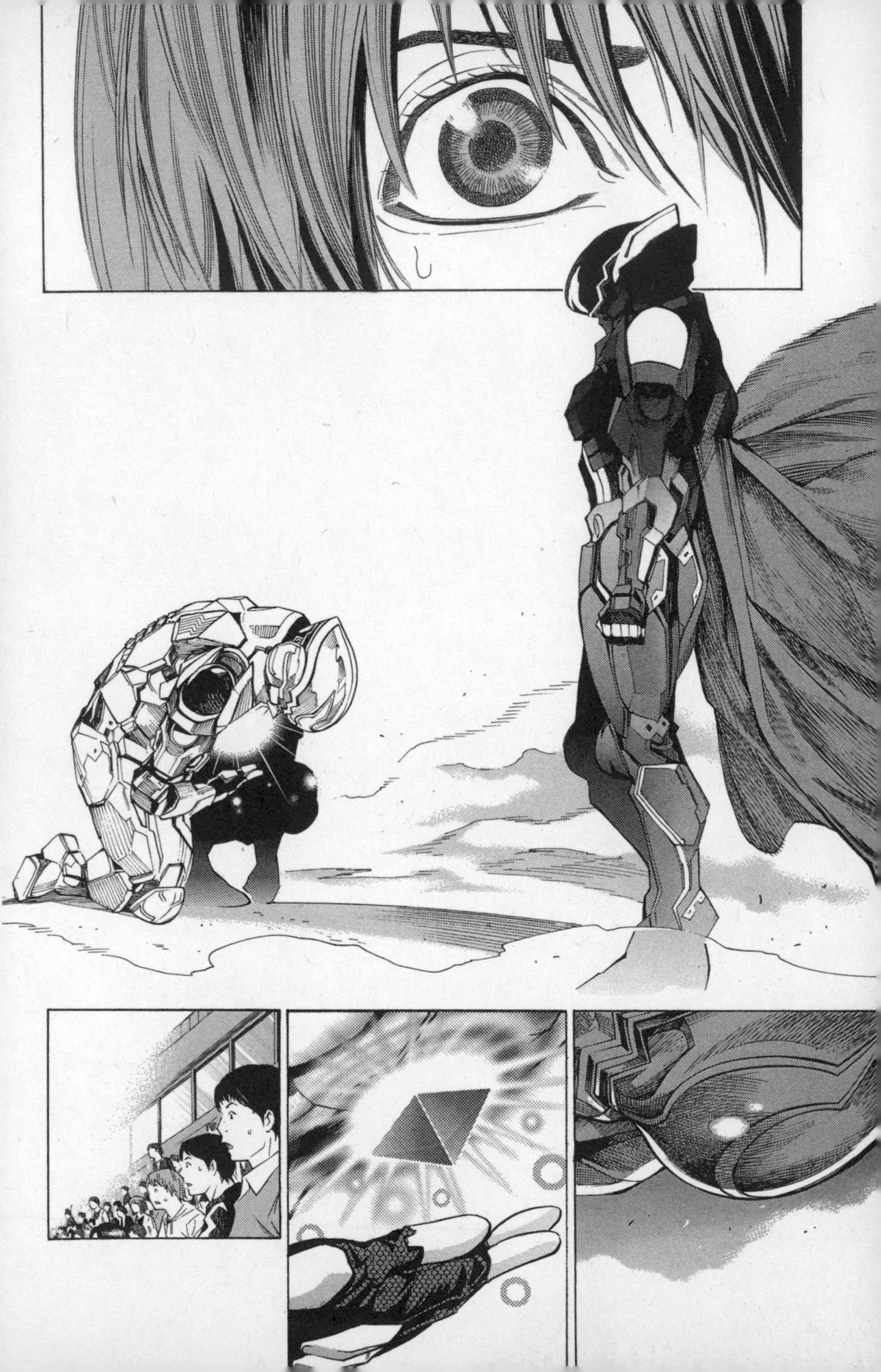

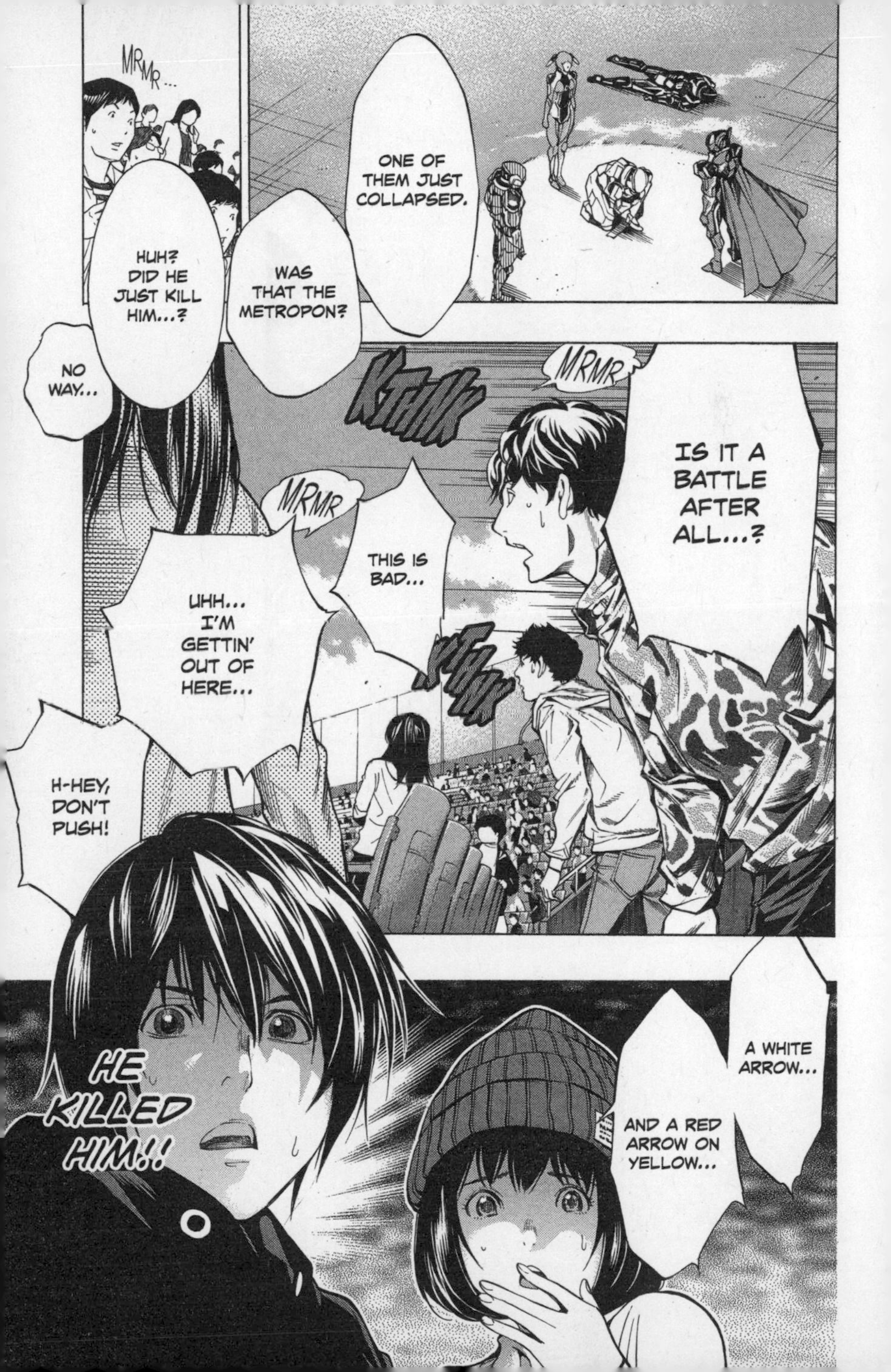
ONE OF THEM JUST COLLAPSED.
WAS THAT THE METROPON?
MRMR...
HUH? DID HE JUST KILL HIM...?
NO WAY...
MRMR
IS IT A BATTLE AFTER ALL...?
MRMR
THIS IS BAD...
UHH... I'M GETTIN' OUT OF HERE...
H-HEY, DON'T PUSH!
A WHITE ARROW...
AND A RED ARROW ON YELLOW...
HE KILLED HIM!!

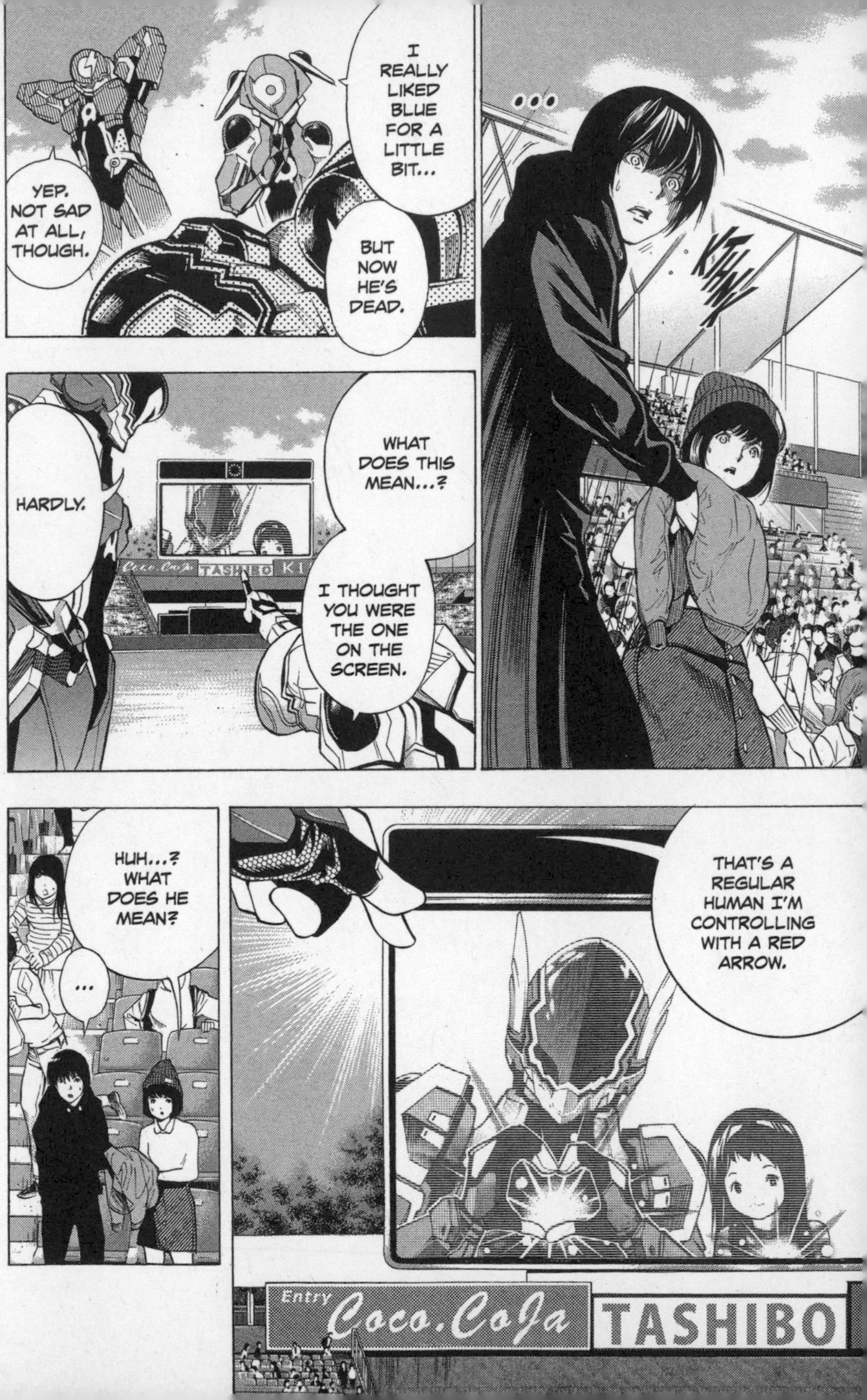
...
KTHNK
I REALLY LIKED BLUE FOR A LITTLE BIT...
BUT NOW HE'S DEAD.
YEP. NOT SAD AT ALL, THOUGH.
WHAT DOES THIS MEAN...?
I THOUGHT YOU WERE THE ONE ON THE SCREEN.
HARDLY.
TASHIBO
THAT'S A REGULAR HUMAN I'M CONTROLLING WITH A RED ARROW.
Entry Coco.CoJa
TASHIBO
HUH...? WHAT DOES HE MEAN?
...

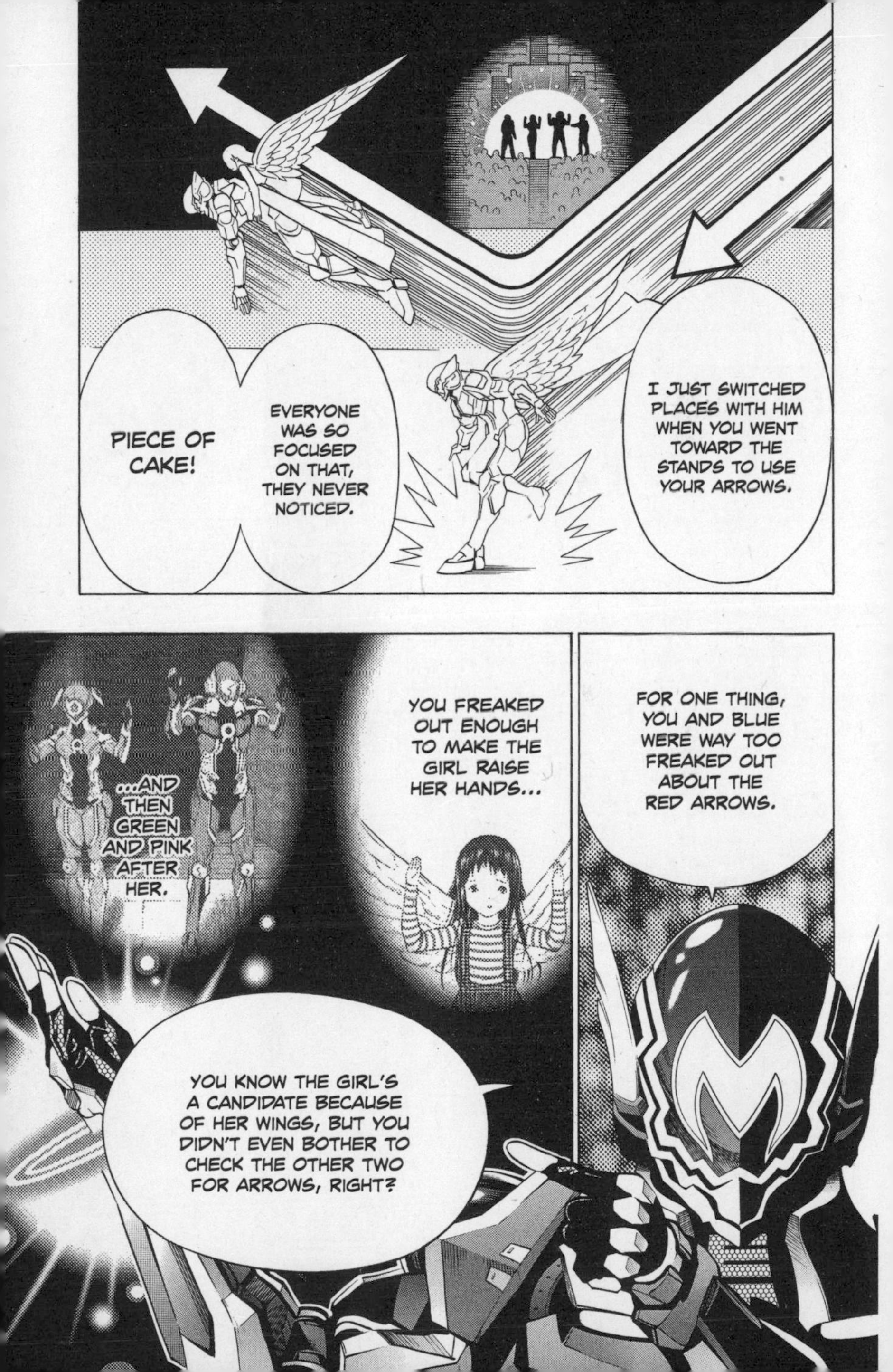
I JUST SWITCHED PLACES WITH HIM WHEN YOU WENT TOWARD THE STANDS TO USE YOUR ARROWS.
EVERYONE WAS SO FOCUSED ON THAT, THEY NEVER NOTICED.
PIECE OF CAKE!
FOR ONE THING, YOU AND BLUE WERE WAY TOO FREAKED OUT ABOUT THE RED ARROWS.
YOU FREAKED OUT ENOUGH TO MAKE THE GIRL RAISE HER HANDS...
...AND THEN GREEN AND PINK AFTER HER.
YOU KNOW THE GIRL'S A CANDIDATE BECAUSE OF HER WINGS, BUT YOU DIDN'T EVEN BOTHER TO CHECK THE OTHER TWO FOR ARROWS, RIGHT?

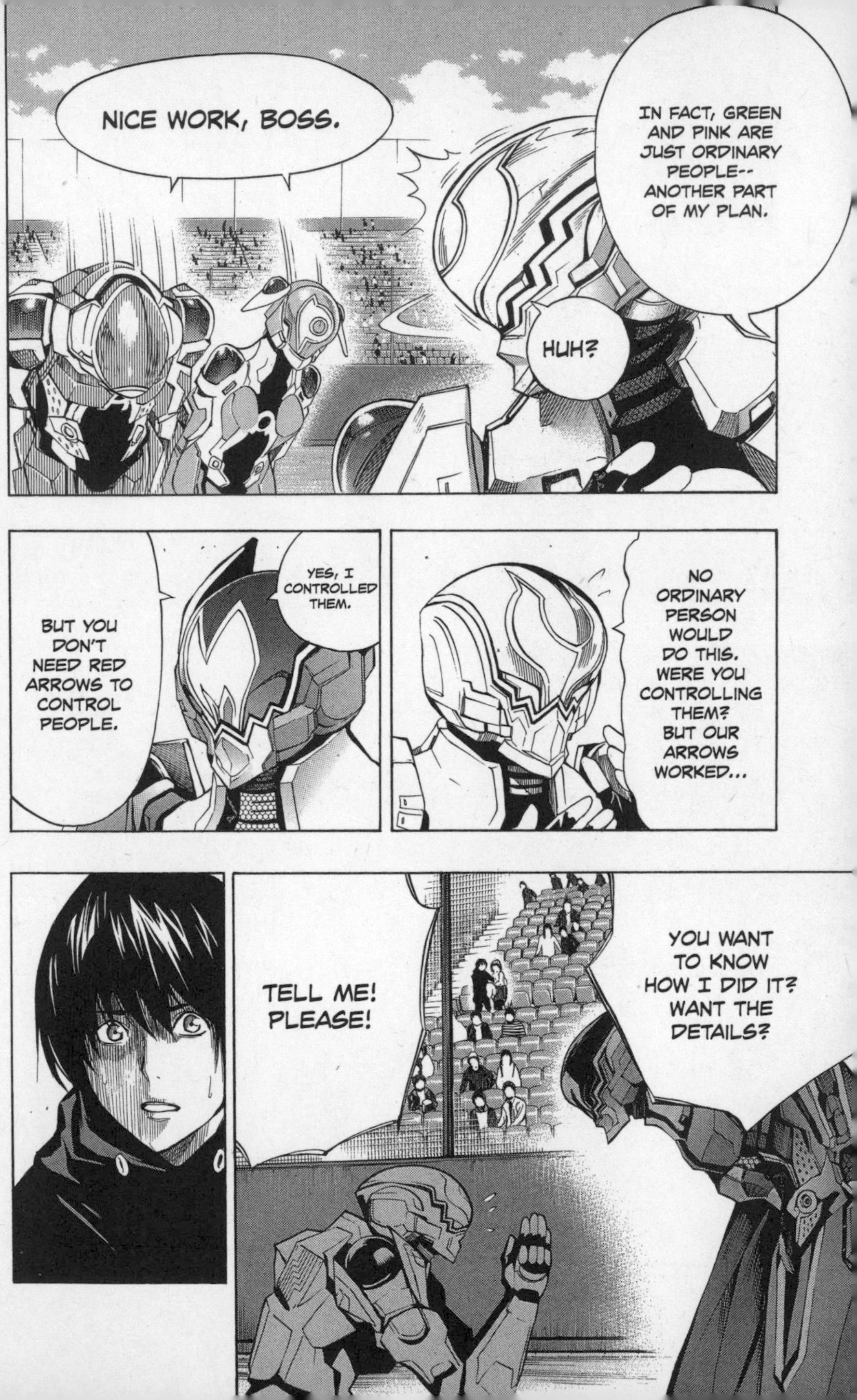
IN FACT, GREEN AND PINK ARE JUST ORDINARY PEOPLE-- ANOTHER PART OF MY PLAN.
HUH?
NICE WORK, BOSS.
NO ORDINARY PERSON WOULD DO THIS. WERE YOU CONTROLLING THEM? BUT OUR ARROWS WORKED...
YES, I CONTROLLED THEM.
BUT YOU DON'T NEED RED ARROWS TO CONTROL PEOPLE.
YOU WANT TO KNOW HOW I DID IT? WANT THE DETAILS?
TELL ME! PLEASE!

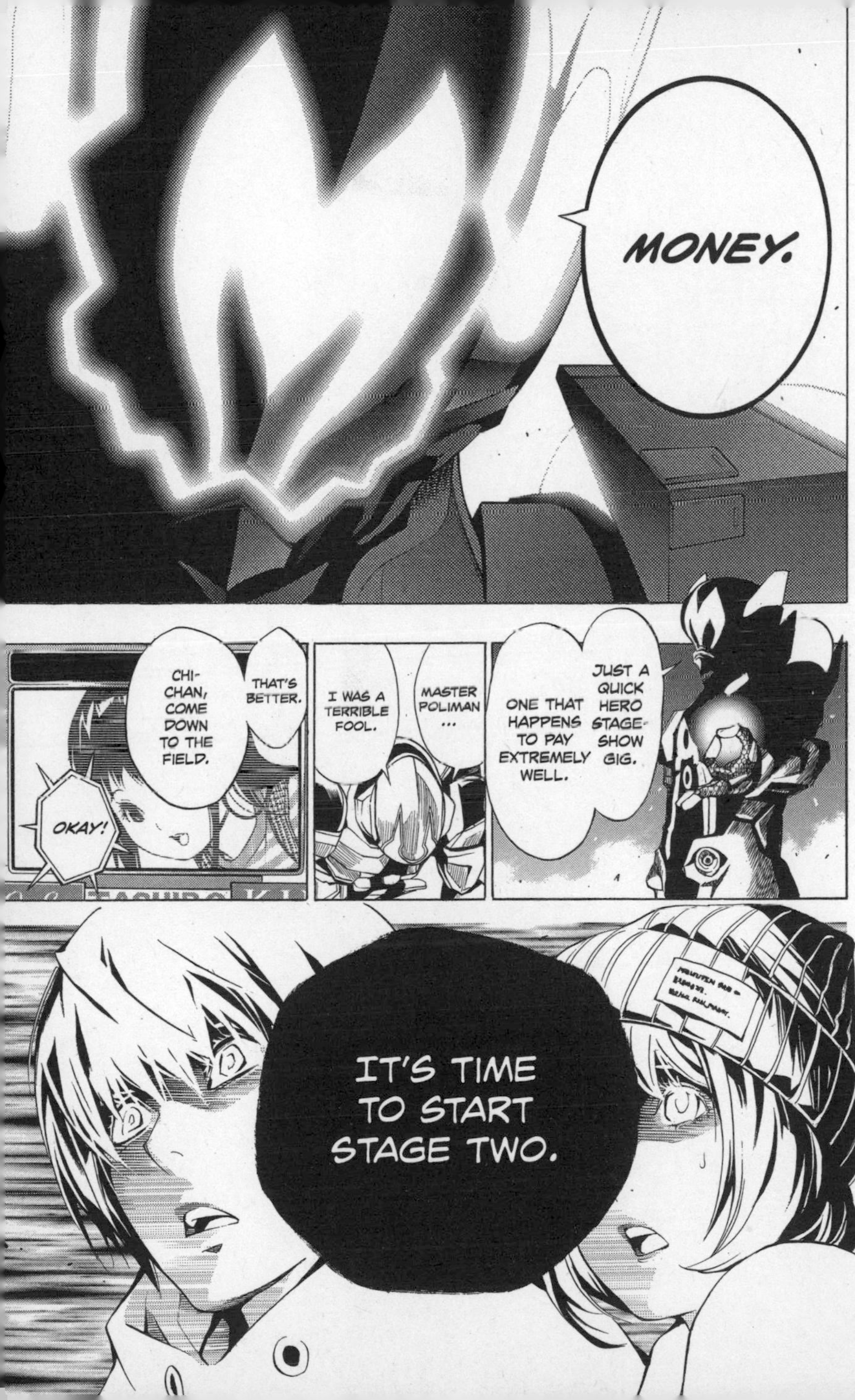
MONEY.
JUST A QUICK HERO STAGE-SHOW GIG.
ONE THAT HAPPENS TO PAY EXTREMELY WELL.
MASTER POLIMAN...
I WAS A TERRIBLE FOOL.
THAT'S BETTER.
CHI-CHAN, COME DOWN TO THE FIELD.
OKAY!
IT'S TIME TO START STAGE TWO.

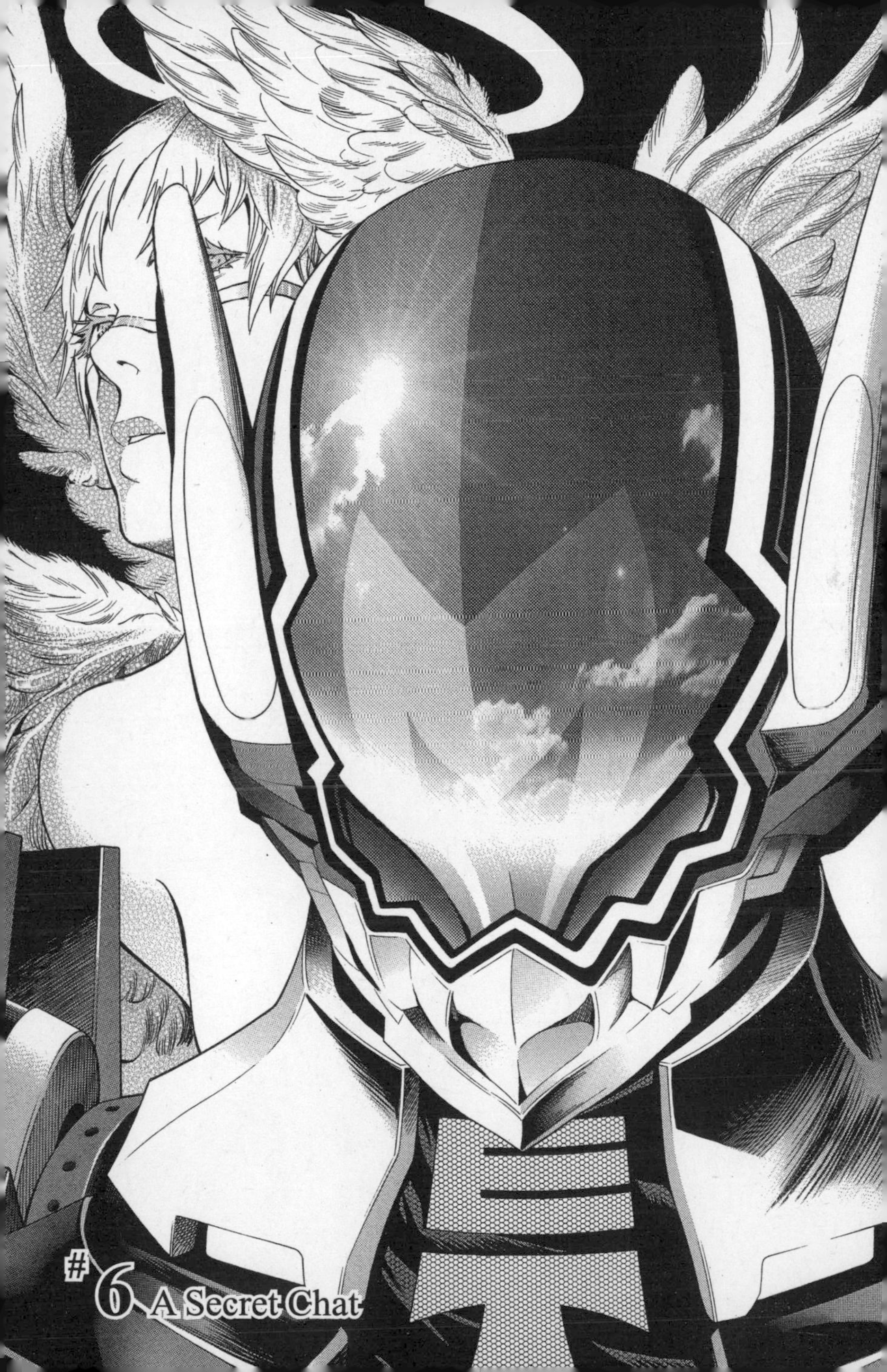
#6 A Secret Chat

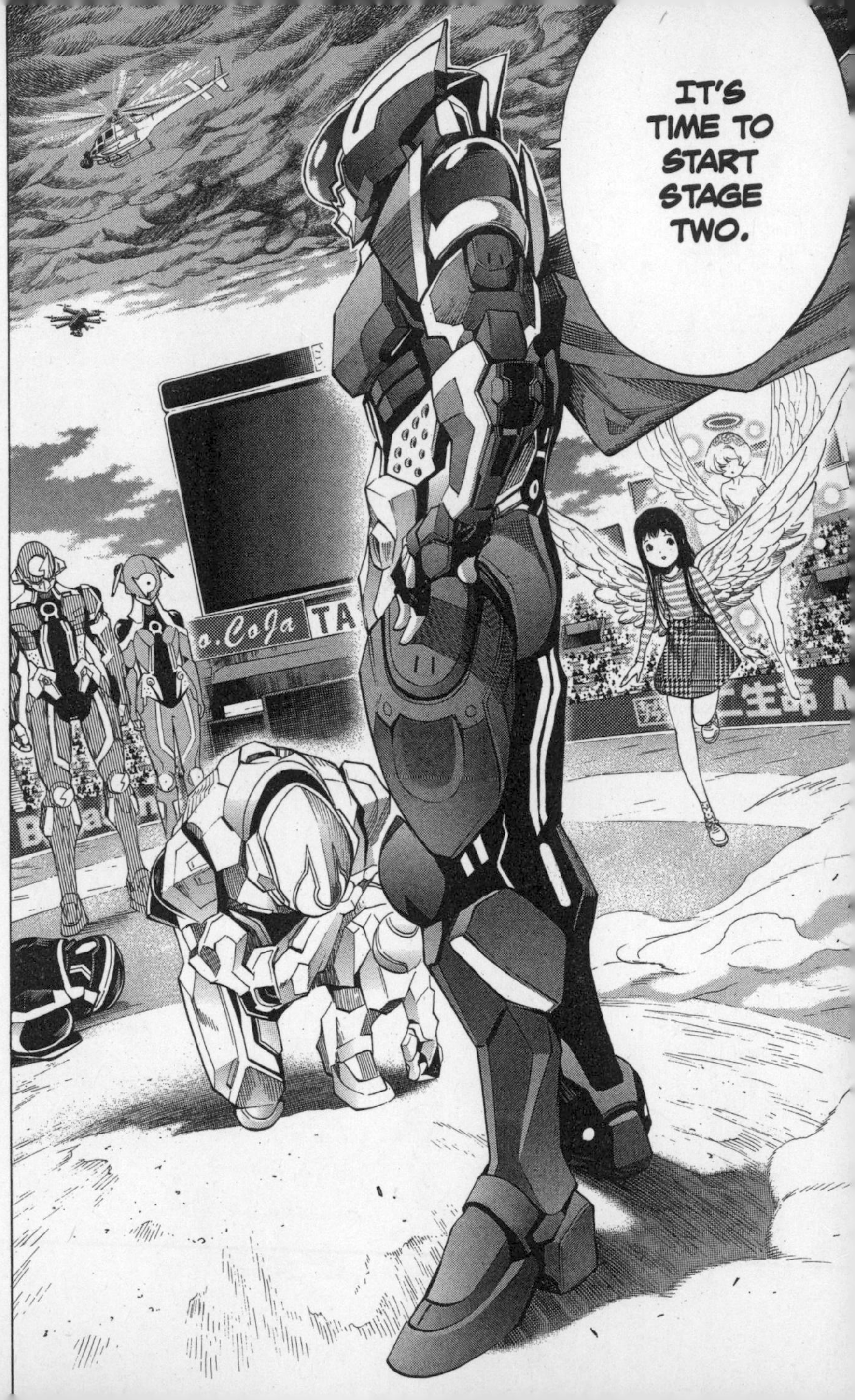
IT'S TIME TO START STAGE TWO.

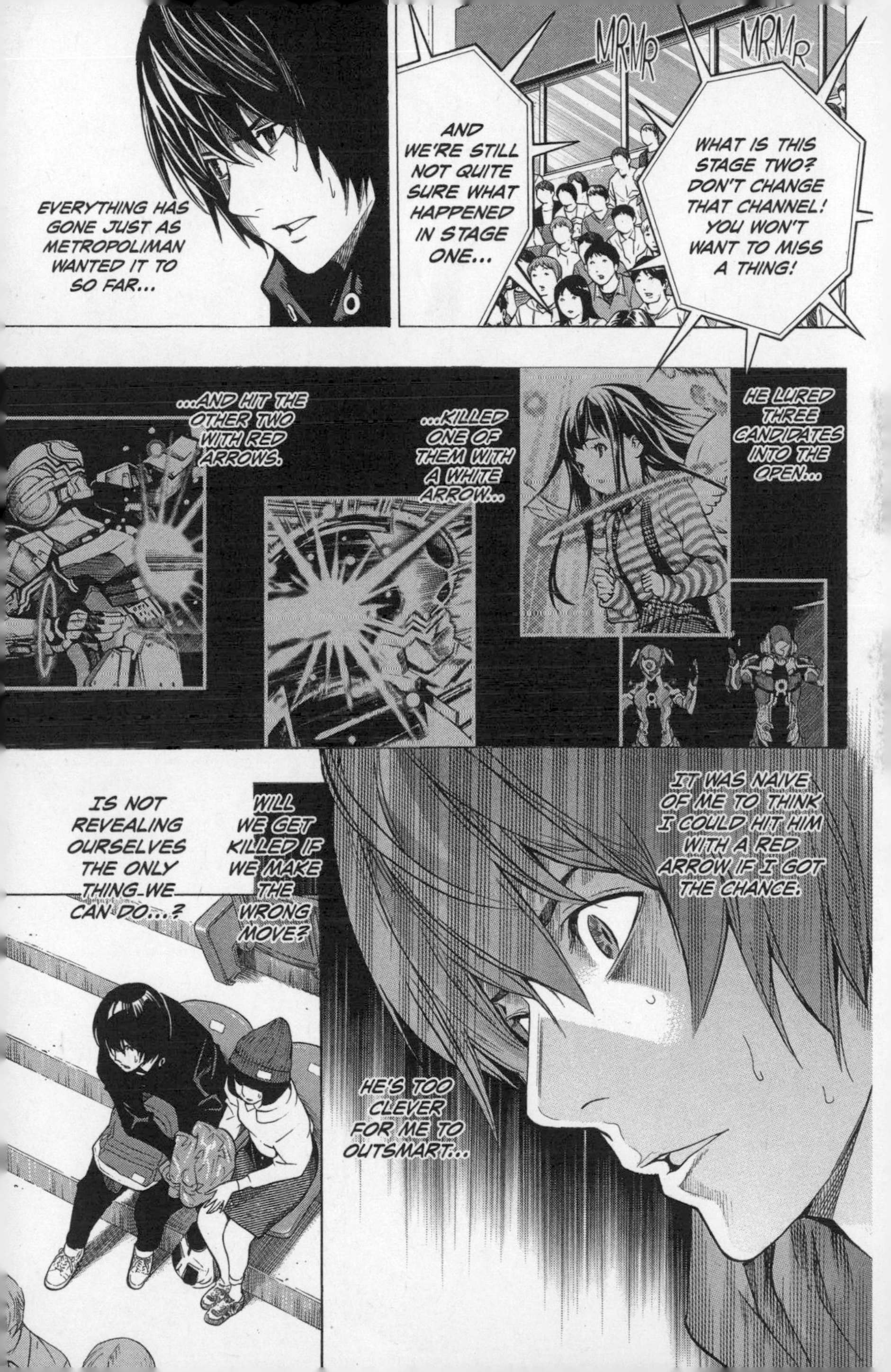
MRMR
MRMR
WHAT IS THIS STAGE TWO? DON'T CHANGE THAT CHANNEL! YOU WON'T WANT TO MISS A THING!
AND WE'RE STILL NOT QUITE SURE WHAT HAPPENED IN STAGE ONE...
EVERYTHING HAS GONE JUST AS METROPOLIMAN WANTED IT TO SO FAR...
HE LURED THREE CANDIDATES INTO THE OPEN...
...KILLED ONE OF THEM WITH A WHITE ARROW...
...AND HIT THE OTHER TWO WITH RED ARROWS.
IT WAS NAIVE OF ME TO THINK I COULD HIT HIM WITH A RED ARROW IF I GOT THE CHANCE.
HE'S TOO CLEVER FOR ME TO OUTSMART...
WILL WE GET KILLED IF WE MAKE THE WRONG MOVE?
IS NOT REVEALING OURSELVES THE ONLY THING WE CAN DO...?

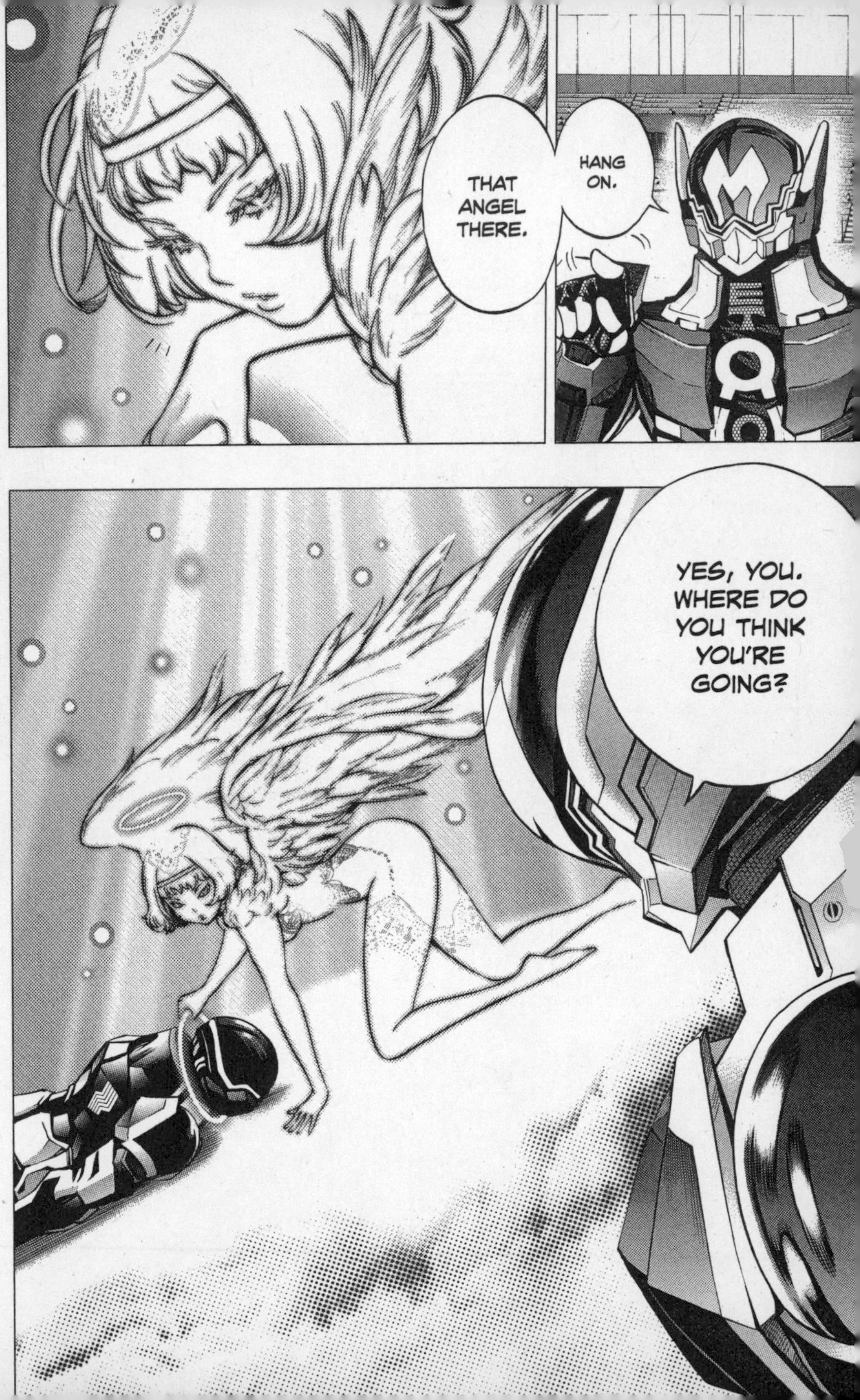
HANG ON.
THAT ANGEL THERE.
YES, YOU. WHERE DO YOU THINK YOU'RE GOING?

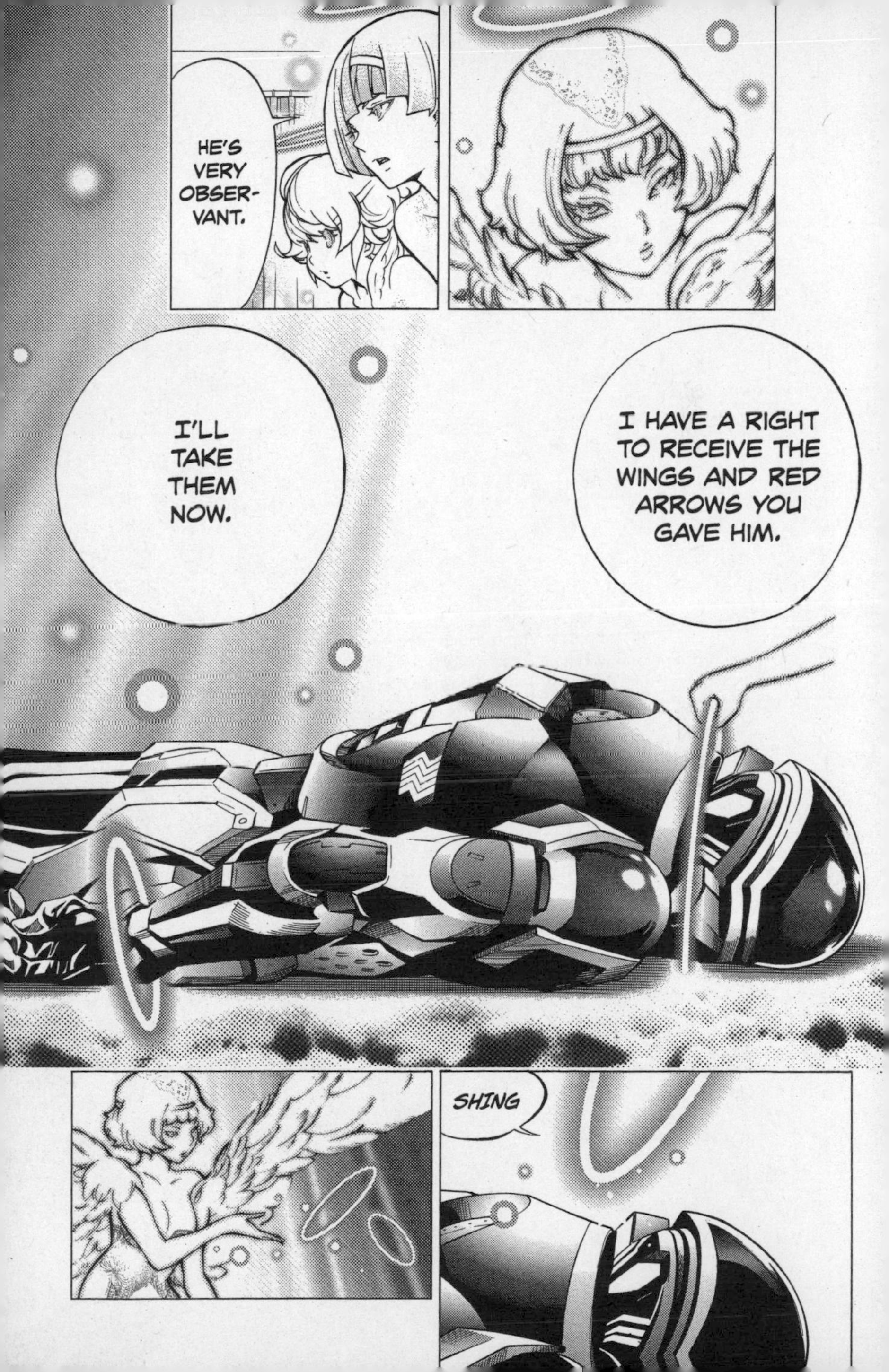
HE'S VERY OBSERVANT.
I HAVE A RIGHT TO RECEIVE THE WINGS AND RED ARROWS YOU GAVE HIM.
I'LL TAKE THEM NOW.
SHING

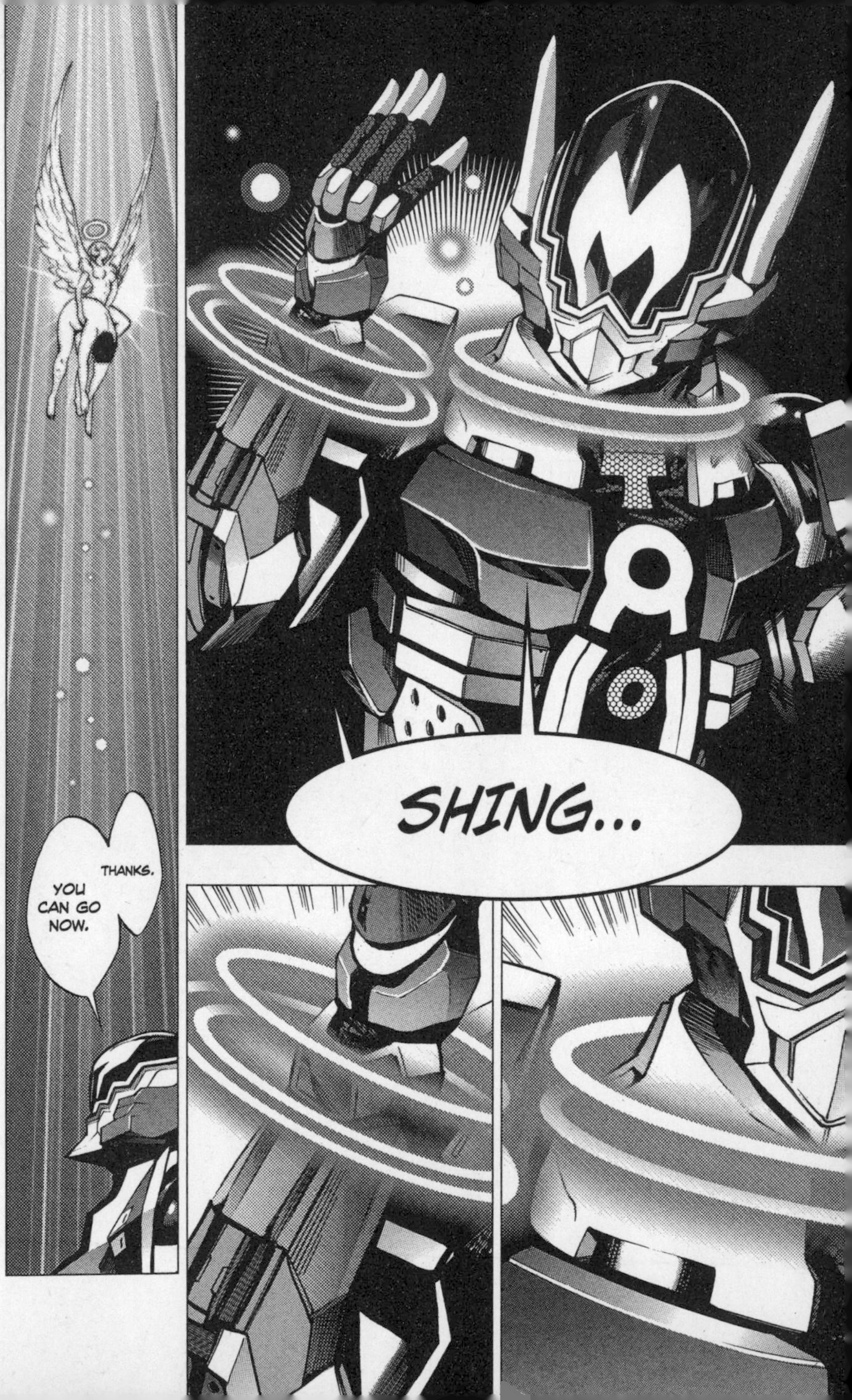
SHING...
THANKS. YOU CAN GO NOW.

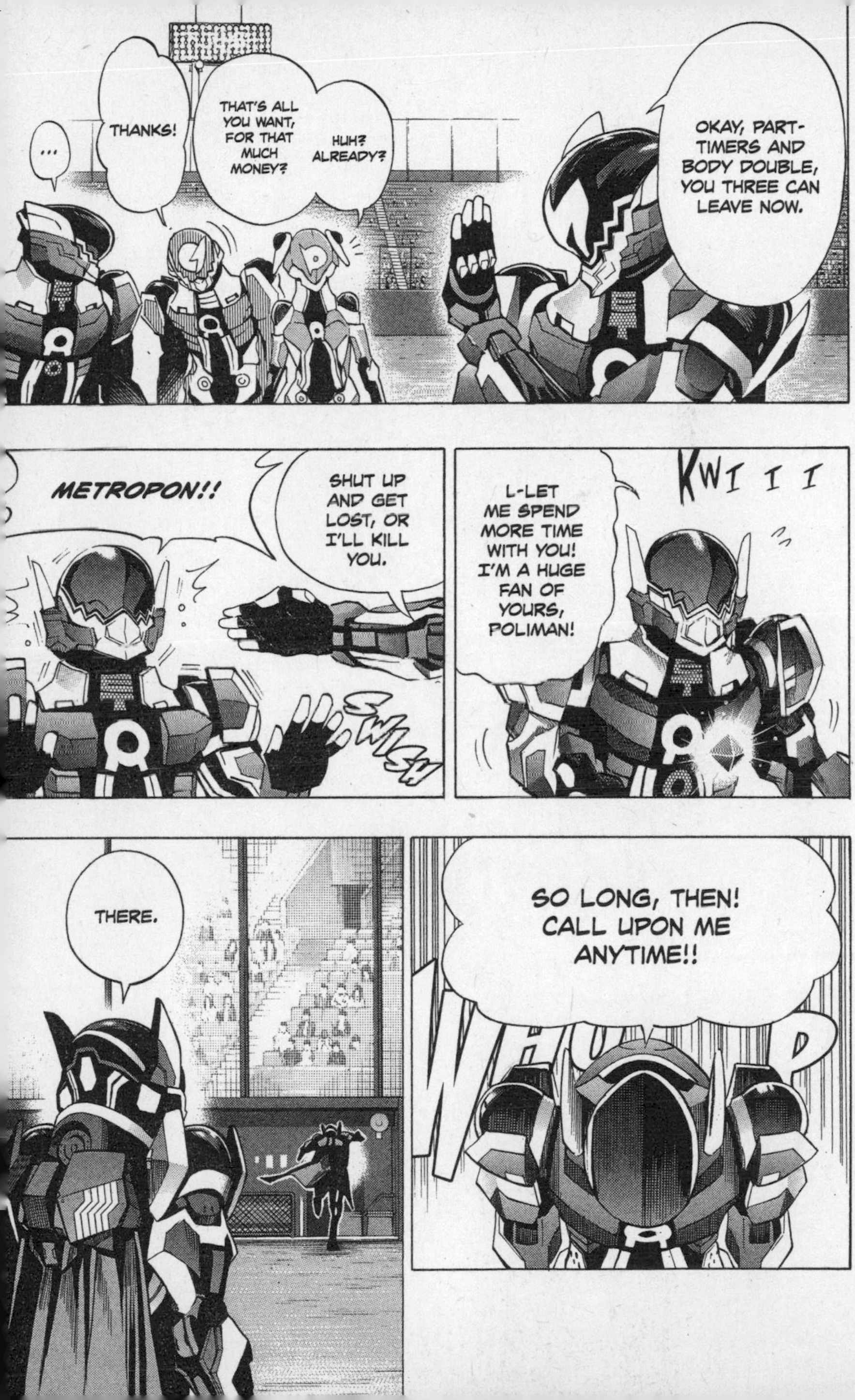
OKAY, PART-TIMERS AND BODY DOUBLE, YOU THREE CAN LEAVE NOW.
HUH? ALREADY?
THAT'S ALL YOU WANT, FOR THAT MUCH MONEY?
THANKS!
...
KWIIII
L-LET ME SPEND MORE TIME WITH YOU! I'M A HUGE FAN OF YOURS, POLIMAN!
SHUT UP AND GET LOST, OR I'LL KILL YOU.
METROPON!!
SWISH
SO LONG, THEN! CALL UPON ME ANYTIME!!
THERE.

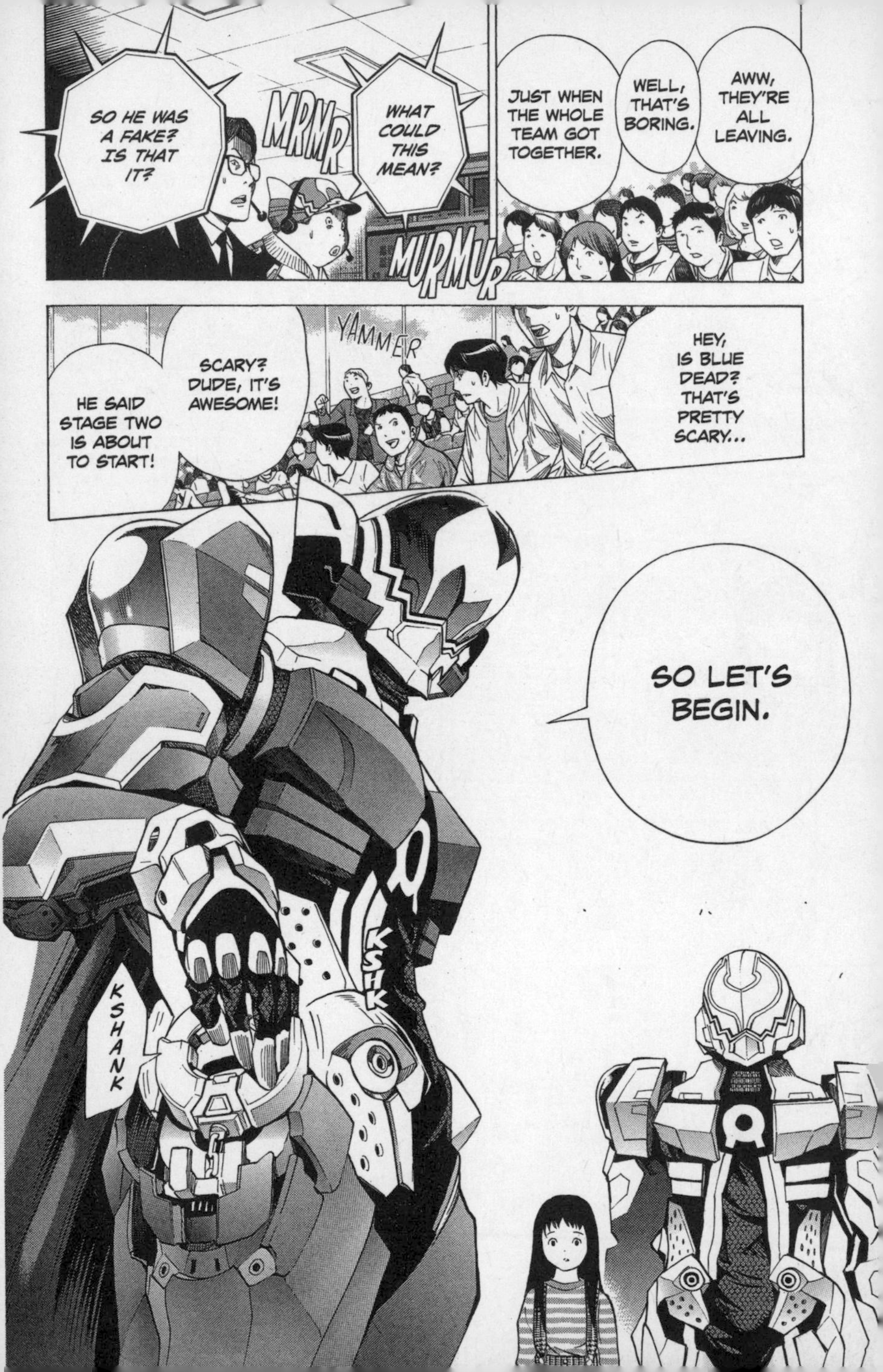
AWW, THEY'RE ALL LEAVING.
WELL, THAT'S BORING.
JUST WHEN THE WHOLE TEAM GOT TOGETHER.
MURMUR
WHAT COULD THIS MEAN?
MRMR
SO HE WAS A FAKE? IS THAT IT?
HEY, IS BLUE DEAD? THAT'S PRETTY SCARY...
YAMMER
SCARY? DUDE, IT'S AWESOME!
HE SAID STAGE TWO IS ABOUT TO START!
SO LET'S BEGIN.
KSHK
KSHANK

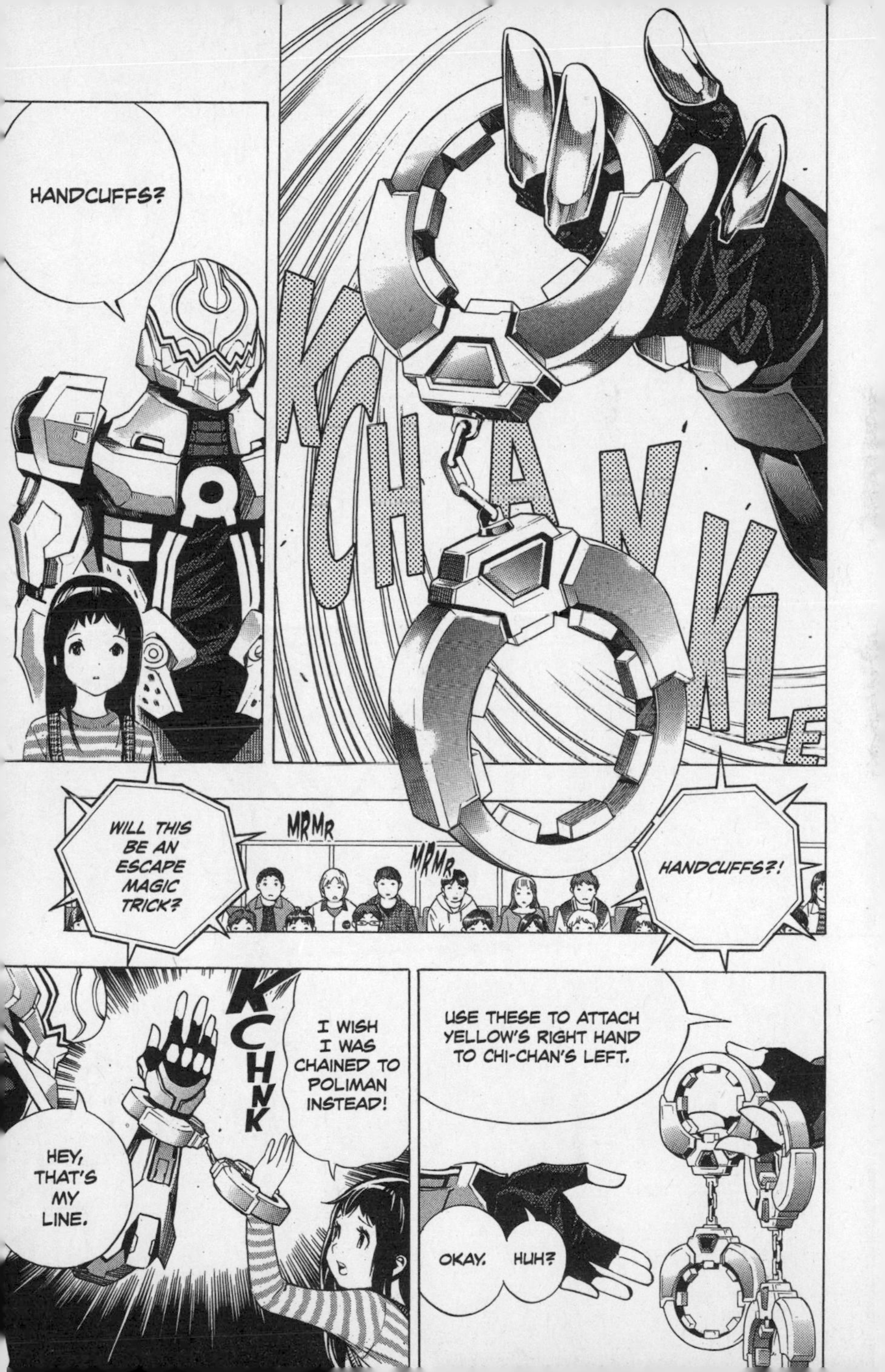
KCHANKLE
HANDCUFFS?
HANDCUFFS?!
MRMR
MRMR
WILL THIS BE AN ESCAPE MAGIC TRICK?
USE THESE TO ATTACH YELLOW'S RIGHT HAND TO CHI-CHAN'S LEFT.
HUH?
OKAY.
KCHNK
I WISH I WAS CHAINED TO POLIMAN INSTEAD!
HEY, THAT'S MY LINE.

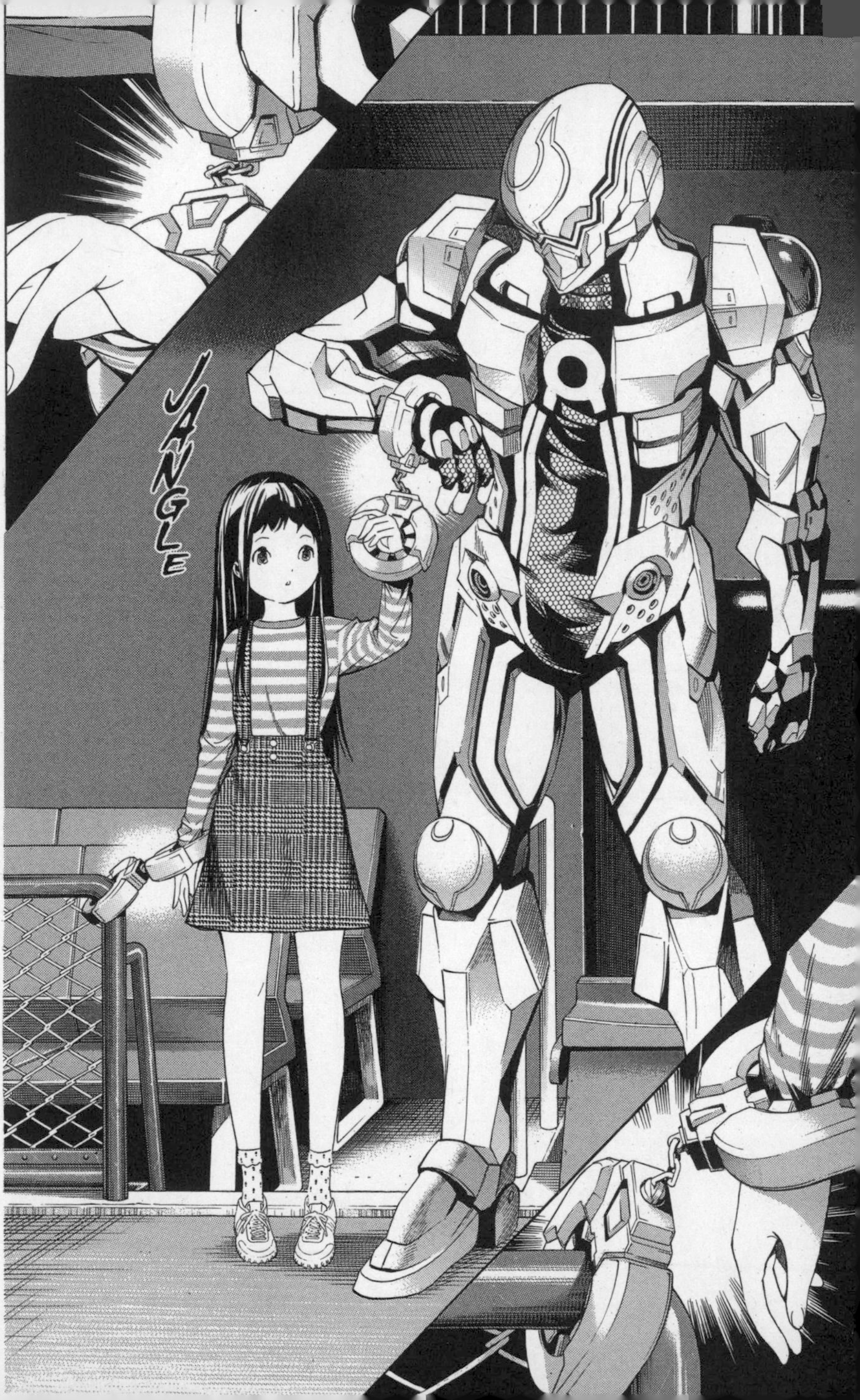
JANGLE

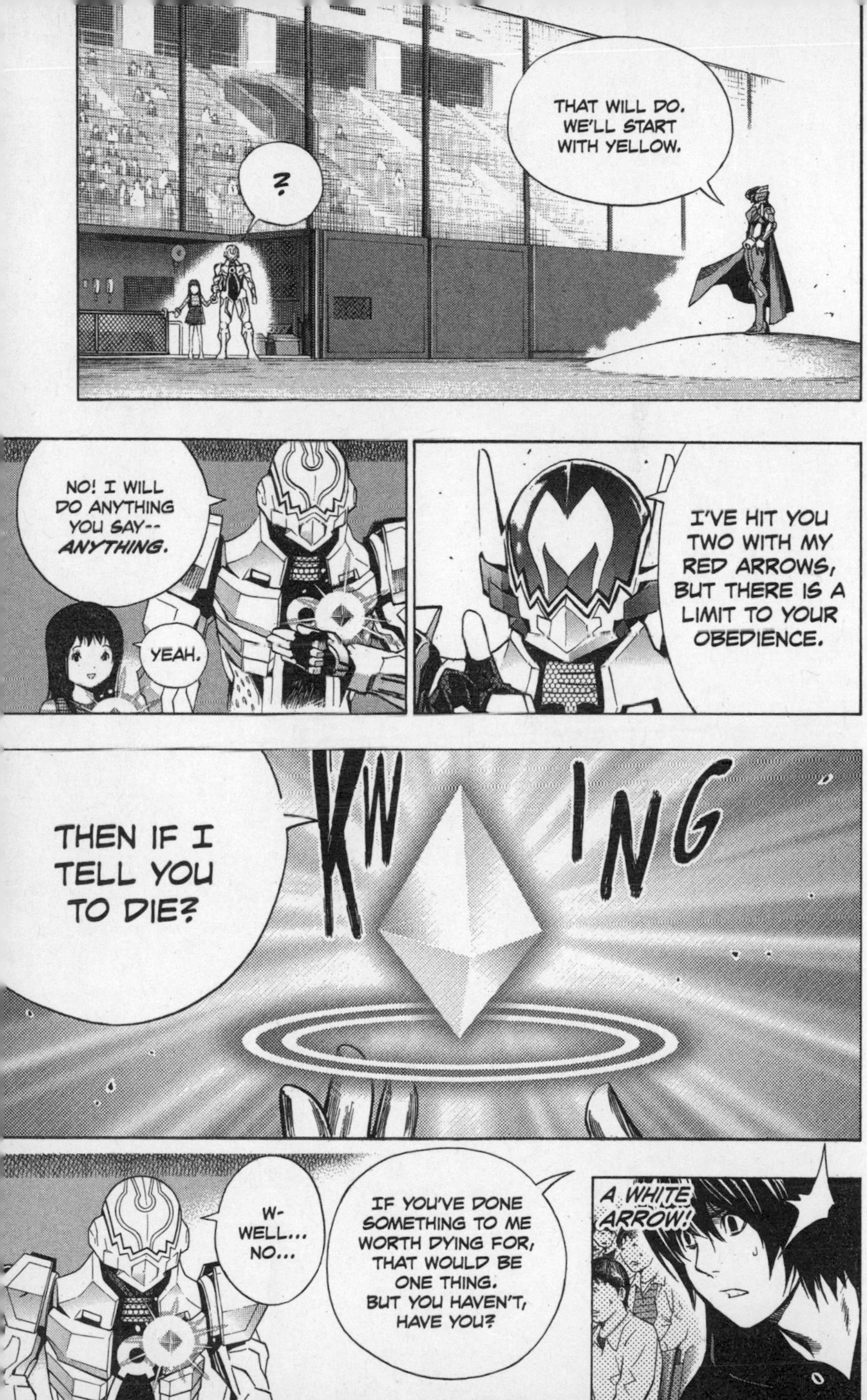
THAT WILL DO. WE'LL START WITH YELLOW.
?
I'VE HIT YOU TWO WITH MY RED ARROWS, BUT THERE IS A LIMIT TO YOUR OBEDIENCE.
NO! I WILL DO ANYTHING YOU SAY-- *ANYTHING*.
YEAH.
KWING
THEN IF I TELL YOU TO DIE?
A WHITE ARROW!
W-WELL... NO...
IF YOU'VE DONE SOMETHING TO ME WORTH DYING FOR, THAT WOULD BE ONE THING. BUT YOU HAVEN'T, HAVE YOU?

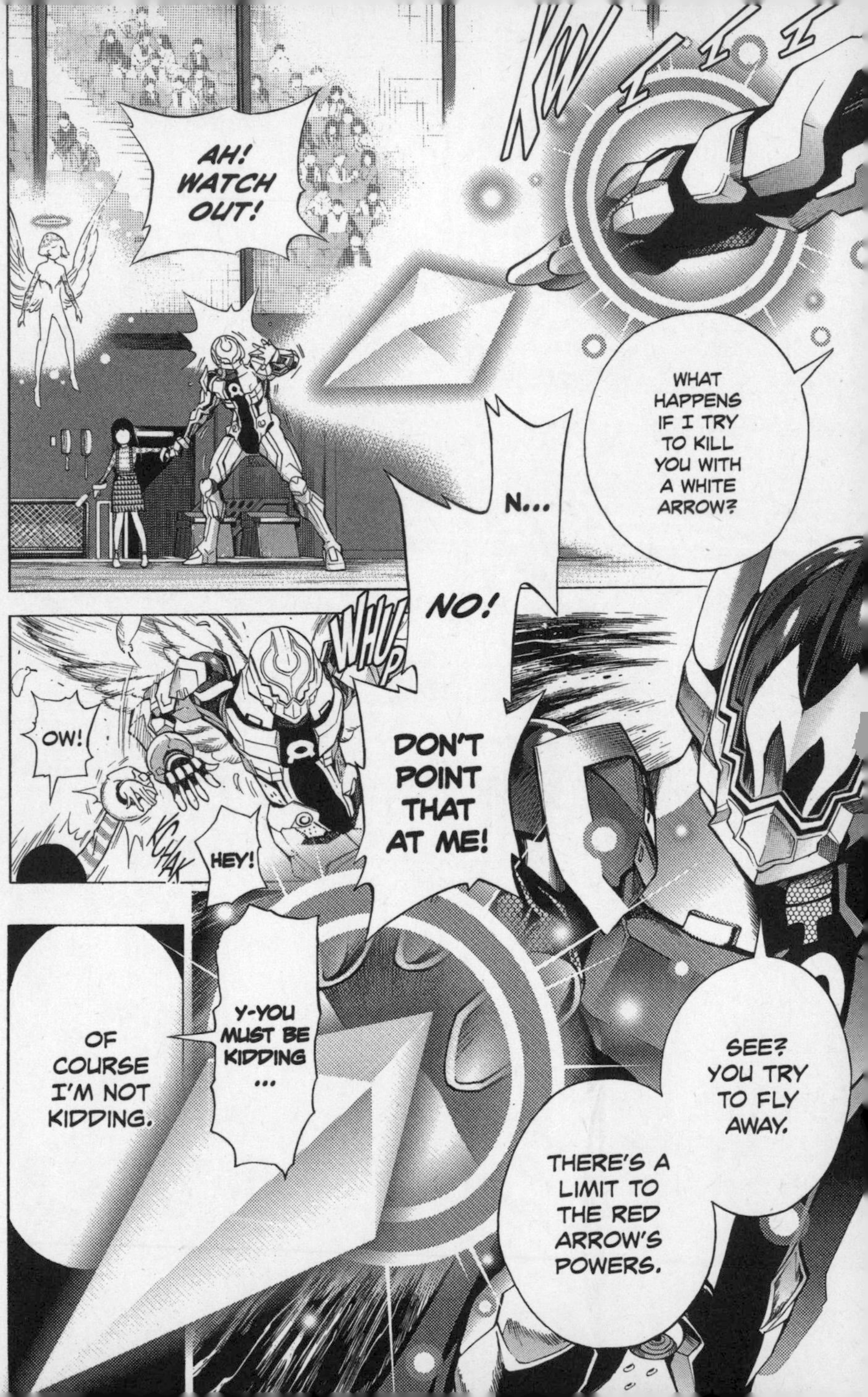

KWIIII
WHAT HAPPENS IF I TRY TO KILL YOU WITH A WHITE ARROW?
N...
NO!
DON'T POINT THAT AT ME!
AH! WATCH OUT!
WHUP
OW!
HEY!
KCHAK
SEE? YOU TRY TO FLY AWAY.
THERE'S A LIMIT TO THE RED ARROW'S POWERS.
Y-YOU MUST BE KIDDING...
OF COURSE I'M NOT KIDDING.

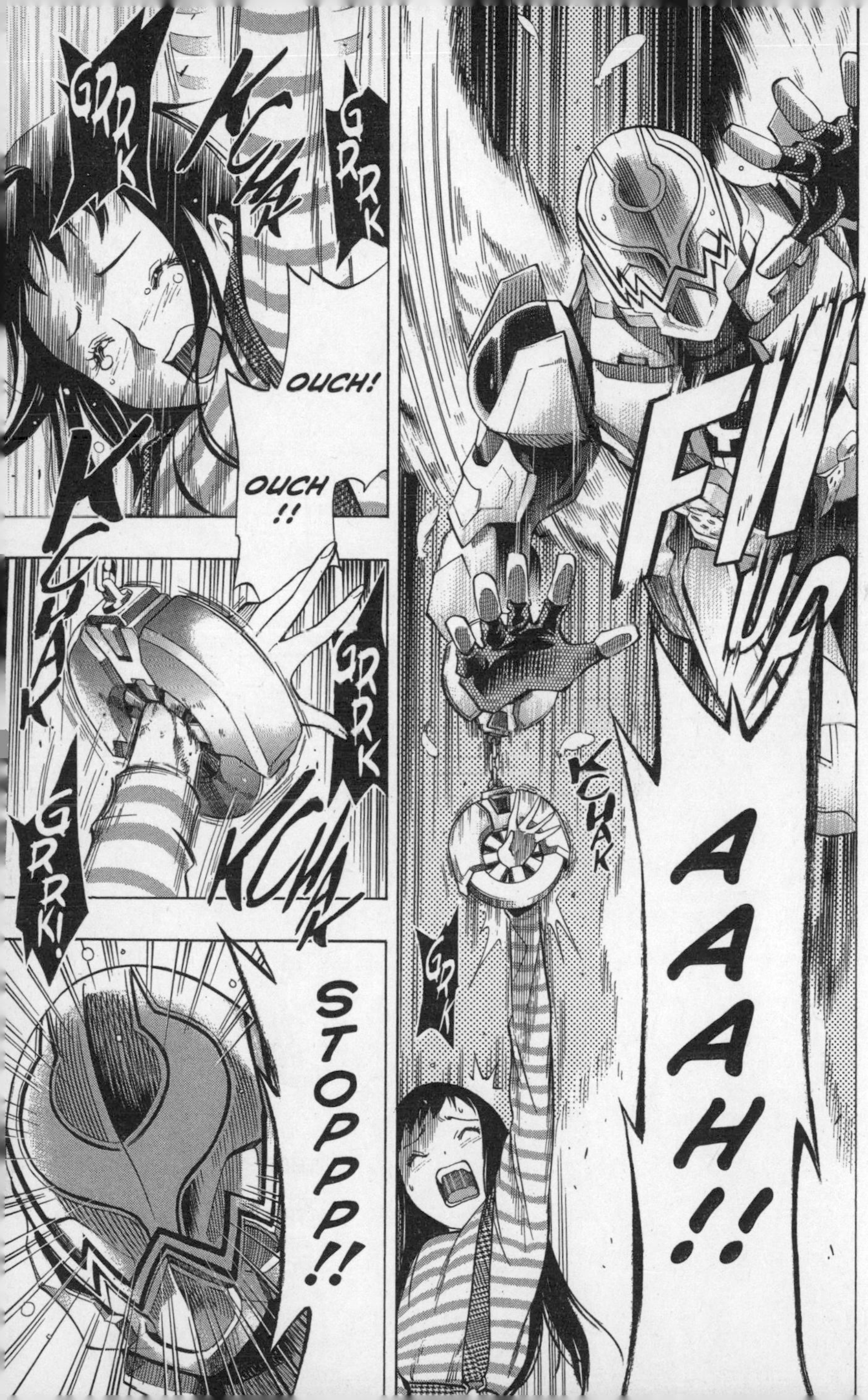
AAAH!!
KCHAK
GRK
GRRK
KCHAK
GRRK
OUCH!
OUCH!!
GRRK
KCHAK
KCHAK
GRRK!
STOPPP!!

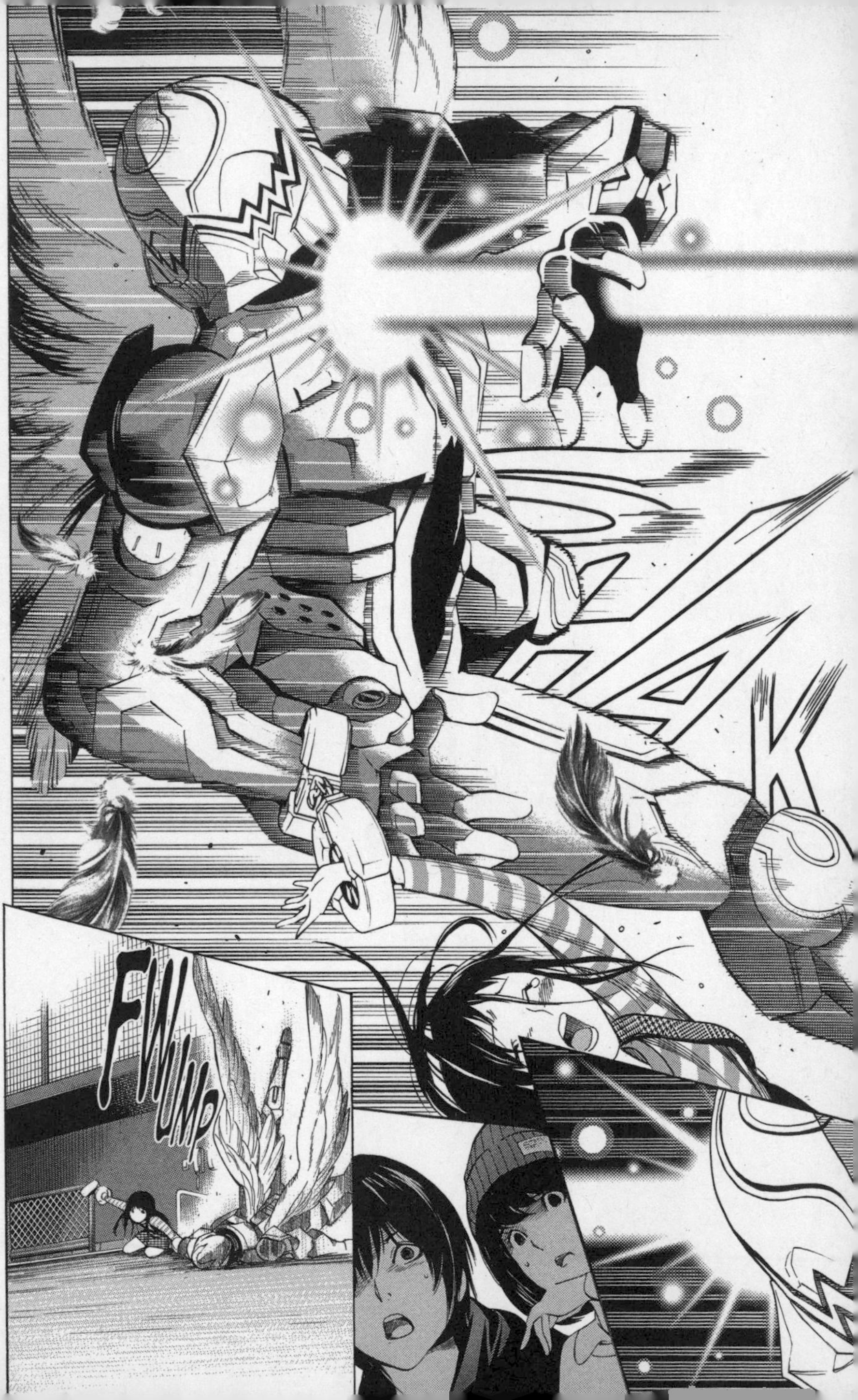
FWUMP

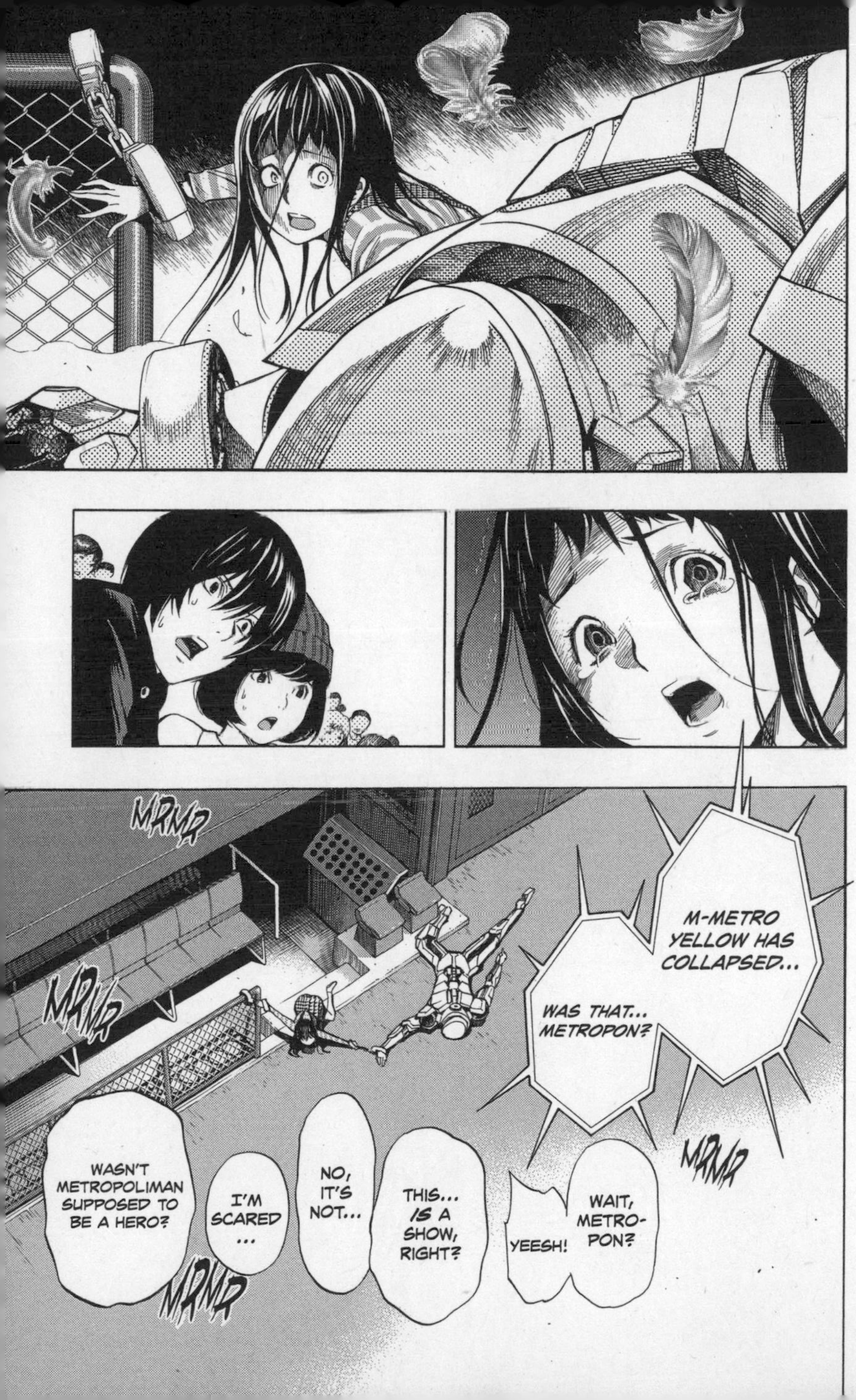
M-METRO YELLOW HAS COLLAPSED...
WAS THAT... METROPON?
MRMR
WAIT, METRO-PON?
YEESH!
THIS... IS A SHOW, RIGHT?
NO, IT'S NOT...
I'M SCARED...
WASN'T METROPOLIMAN SUPPOSED TO BE A HERO?
MRMR
MRMR
MRMR

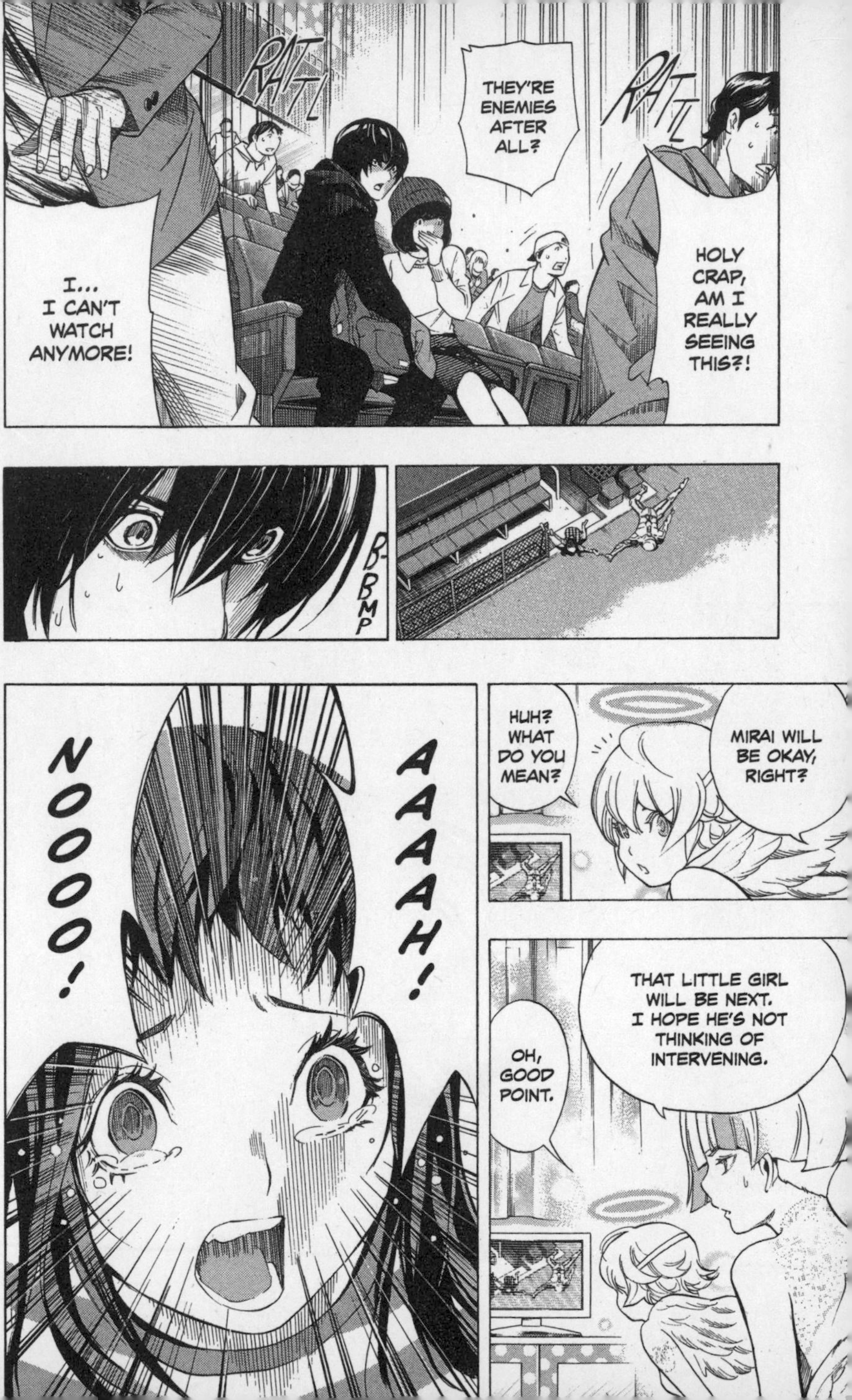
RATTL
THEY'RE ENEMIES AFTER ALL?
RATTL
HOLY CRAP, AM I REALLY SEEING THIS?!
I... I CAN'T WATCH ANYMORE!
R-BBMP
MIRAI WILL BE OKAY, RIGHT?
HUH? WHAT DO YOU MEAN?
THAT LITTLE GIRL WILL BE NEXT. I HOPE HE'S NOT THINKING OF INTERVENING.
OH, GOOD POINT.
AAAAAH!
NOOOOO!

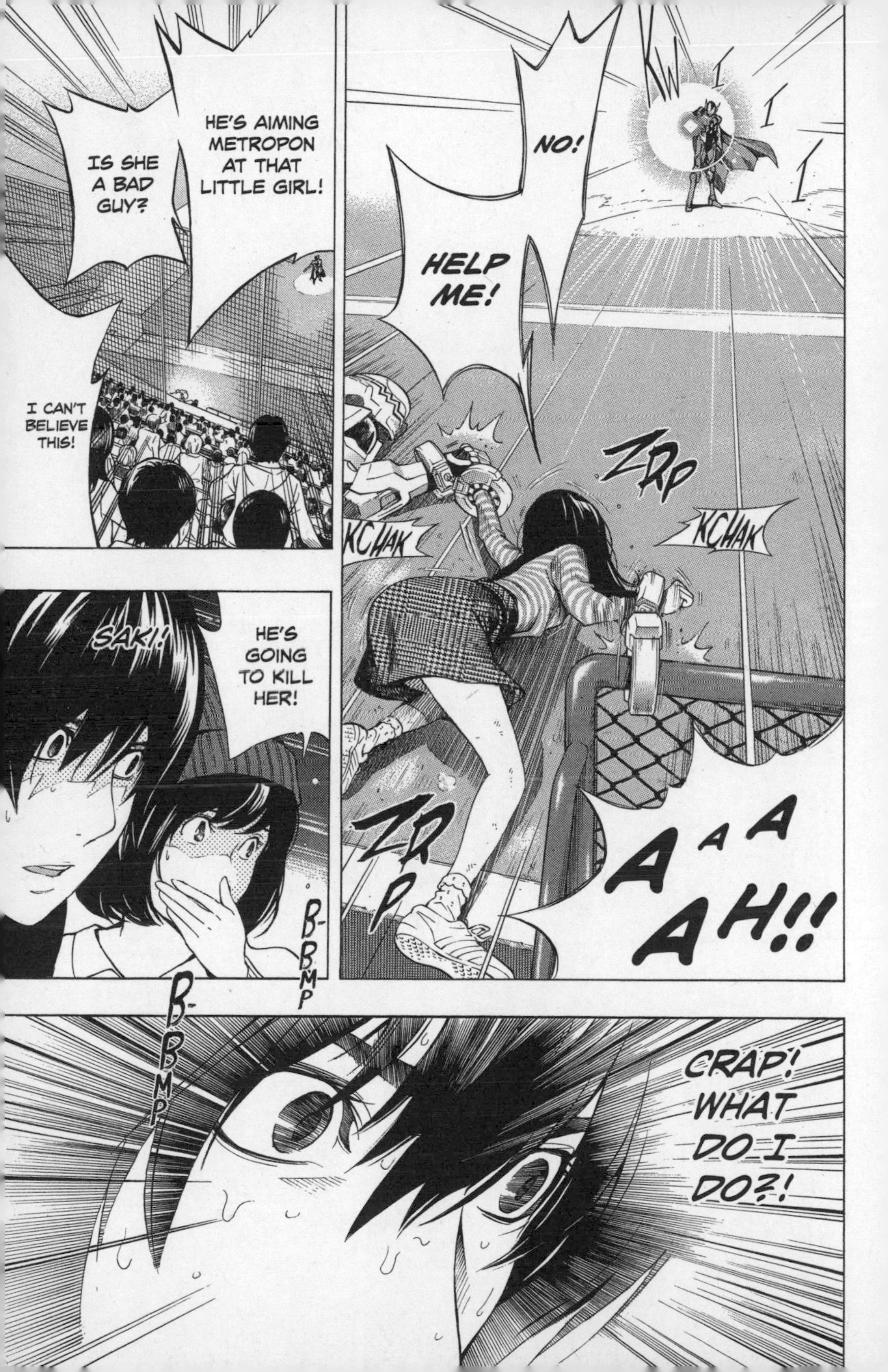
KWIIII
NO!
HELP ME!
ZRP
KCHAK
KCHAK
ZRP
AAAAAH!!
HE'S AIMING METROPON AT THAT LITTLE GIRL!
IS SHE A BAD GUY?
I CAN'T BELIEVE THIS!
HE'S GOING TO KILL HER!
SAKI!
B-BMP
B-BMP
CRAP! WHAT DO I DO?!

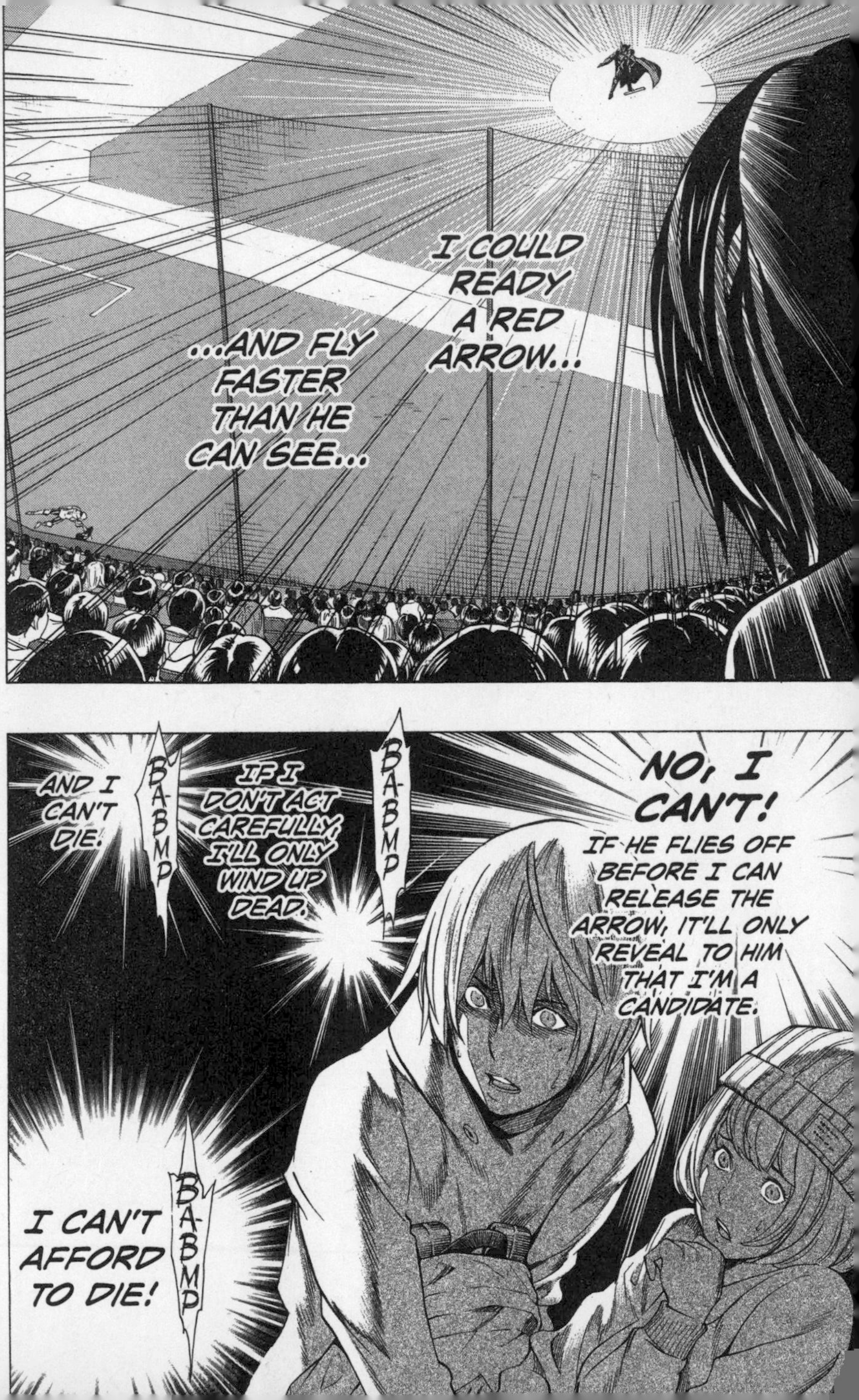
I COULD READY A RED ARROW...
...AND FLY FASTER THAN HE CAN SEE...
NO, I CAN'T!
IF HE FLIES OFF BEFORE I CAN RELEASE THE ARROW, IT'LL ONLY REVEAL TO HIM THAT I'M A CANDIDATE.
BA-BMP
IF I DON'T ACT CAREFULLY, I'LL ONLY WIND UP DEAD.
BA-BMP
AND I CAN'T DIE.
BA-BMP
I CAN'T AFFORD TO DIE!

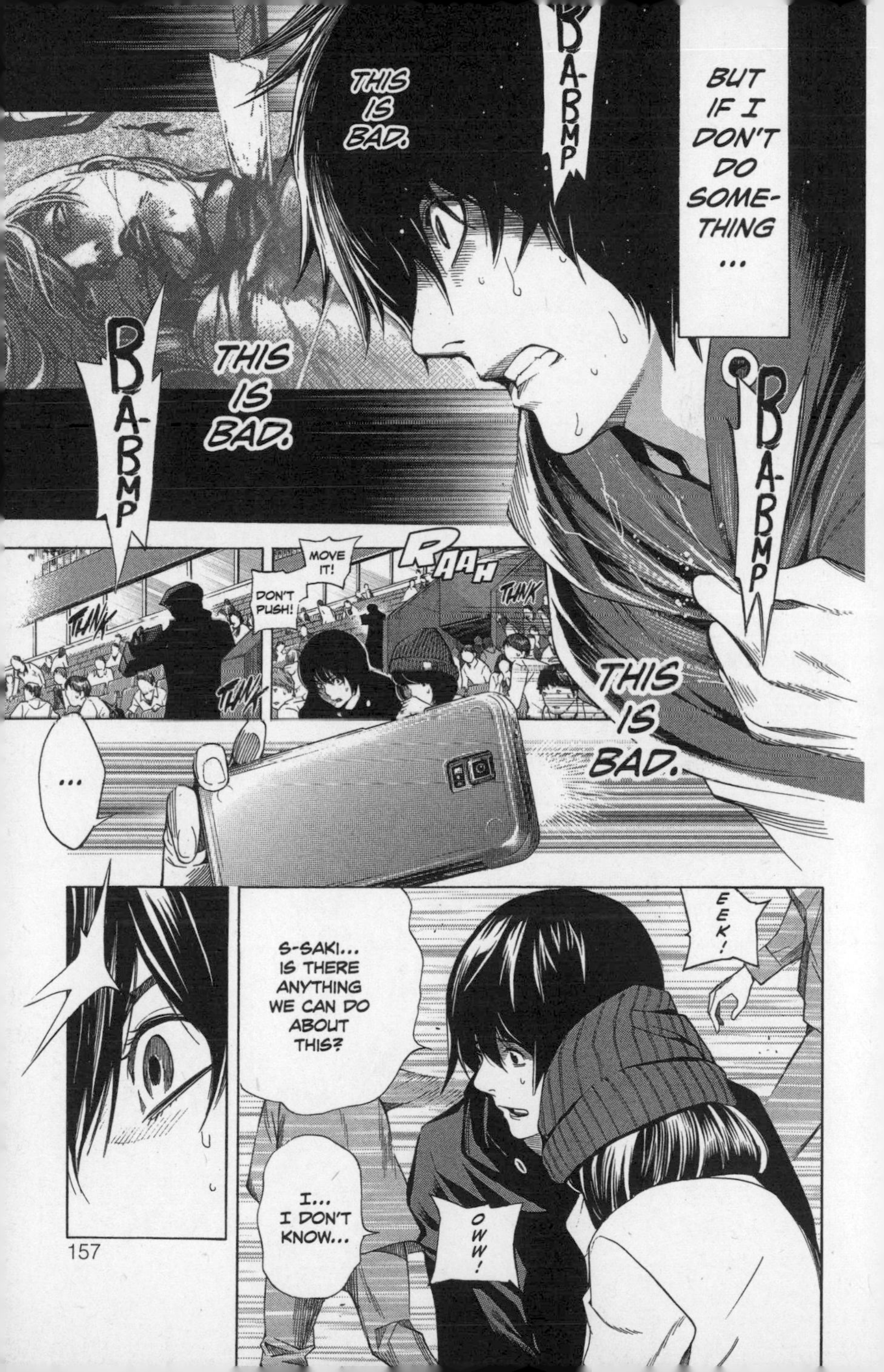
BUT IF I DON'T DO SOME-THING...
BA-BMP
THIS IS BAD.
BA-BMP
THIS IS BAD.
BA-BMP
RAAH
MOVE IT!
DON'T PUSH!
THNK
THNK
THNK
THIS IS BAD.
...
EEK!
S-SAKI... IS THERE ANYTHING WE CAN DO ABOUT THIS?
OWW!
I... I DON'T KNOW...

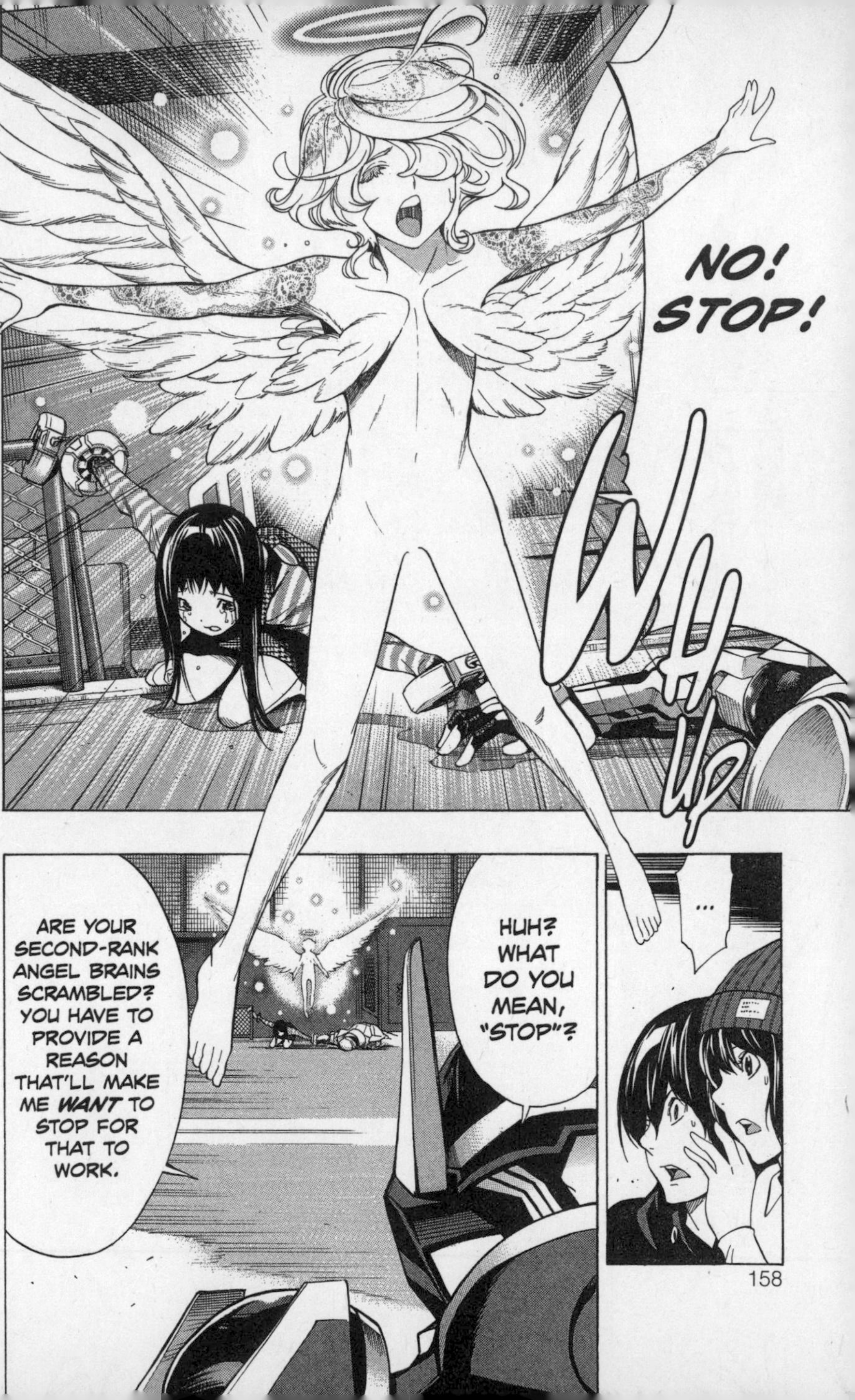
NO! STOP!
WHUP
...
HUH? WHAT DO YOU MEAN, "STOP"?
ARE YOUR SECOND-RANK ANGEL BRAINS SCRAMBLED? YOU HAVE TO PROVIDE A REASON THAT'LL MAKE ME *WANT* TO STOP FOR THAT TO WORK.

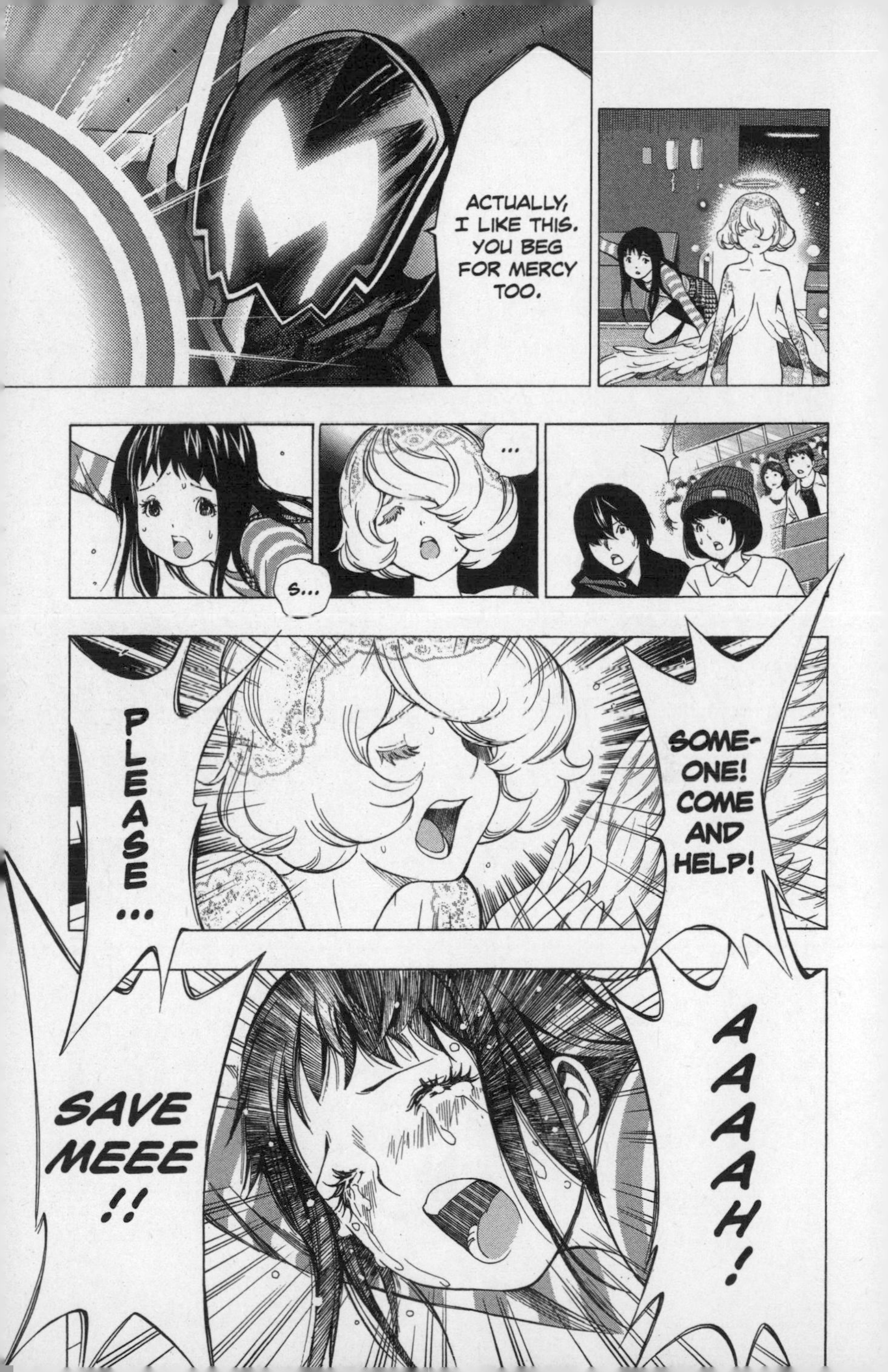
ACTUALLY, I LIKE THIS. YOU BEG FOR MERCY TOO.
...
S...
SOME-ONE! COME AND HELP!
PLEASE...
AAAAAH!
SAVE MEEE!!

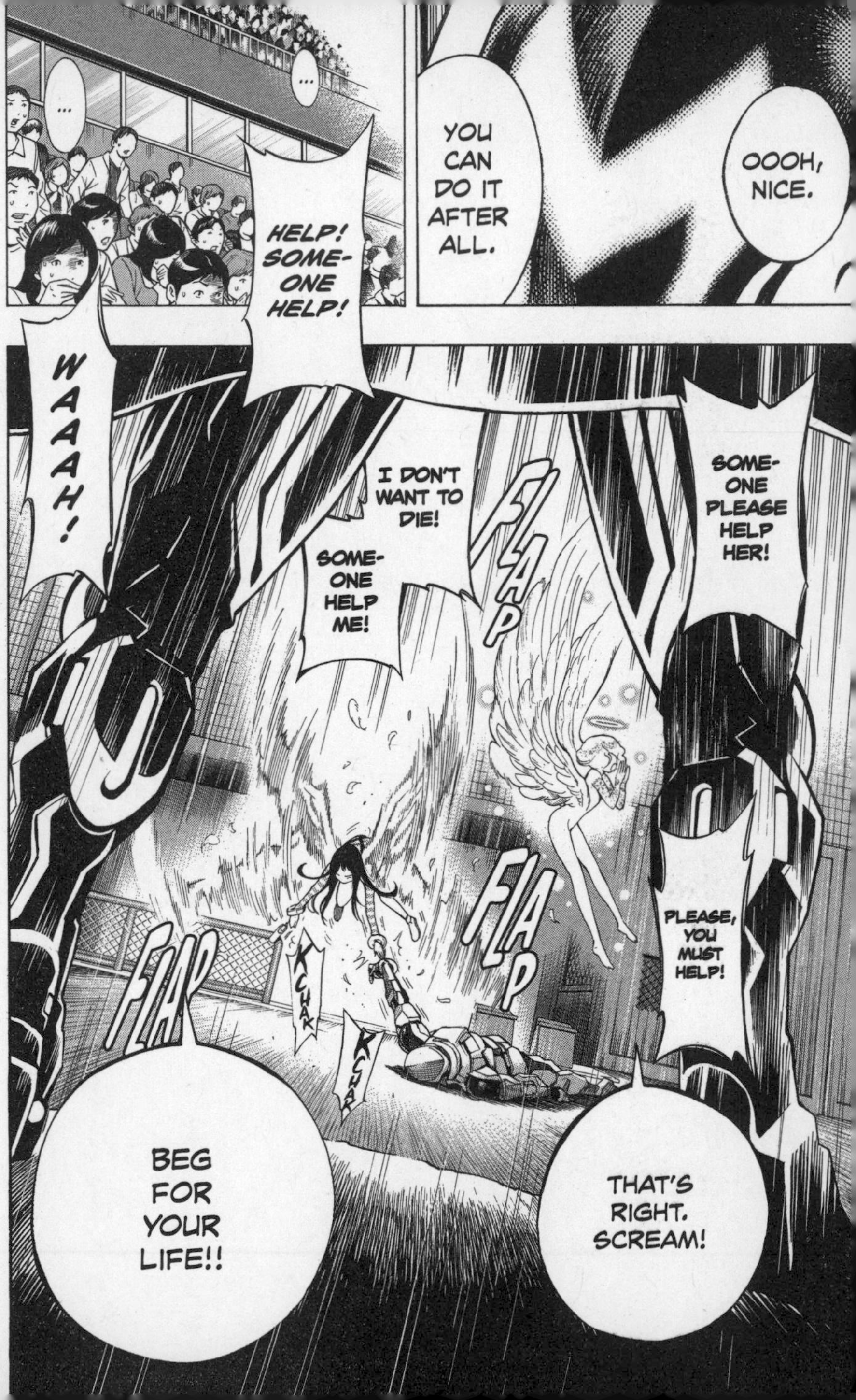

OOOH, NICE.
YOU CAN DO IT AFTER ALL.
...
...
HELP! SOMEONE-ONE HELP!
SOME-ONE PLEASE HELP HER!
FLAP
I DON'T WANT TO DIE!
SOME-ONE HELP ME!
WAAAAH!
PLEASE, YOU MUST HELP!
FLAP
KCHAK
KCHAK
FLAP
THAT'S RIGHT. SCREAM!
BEG FOR YOUR LIFE!!

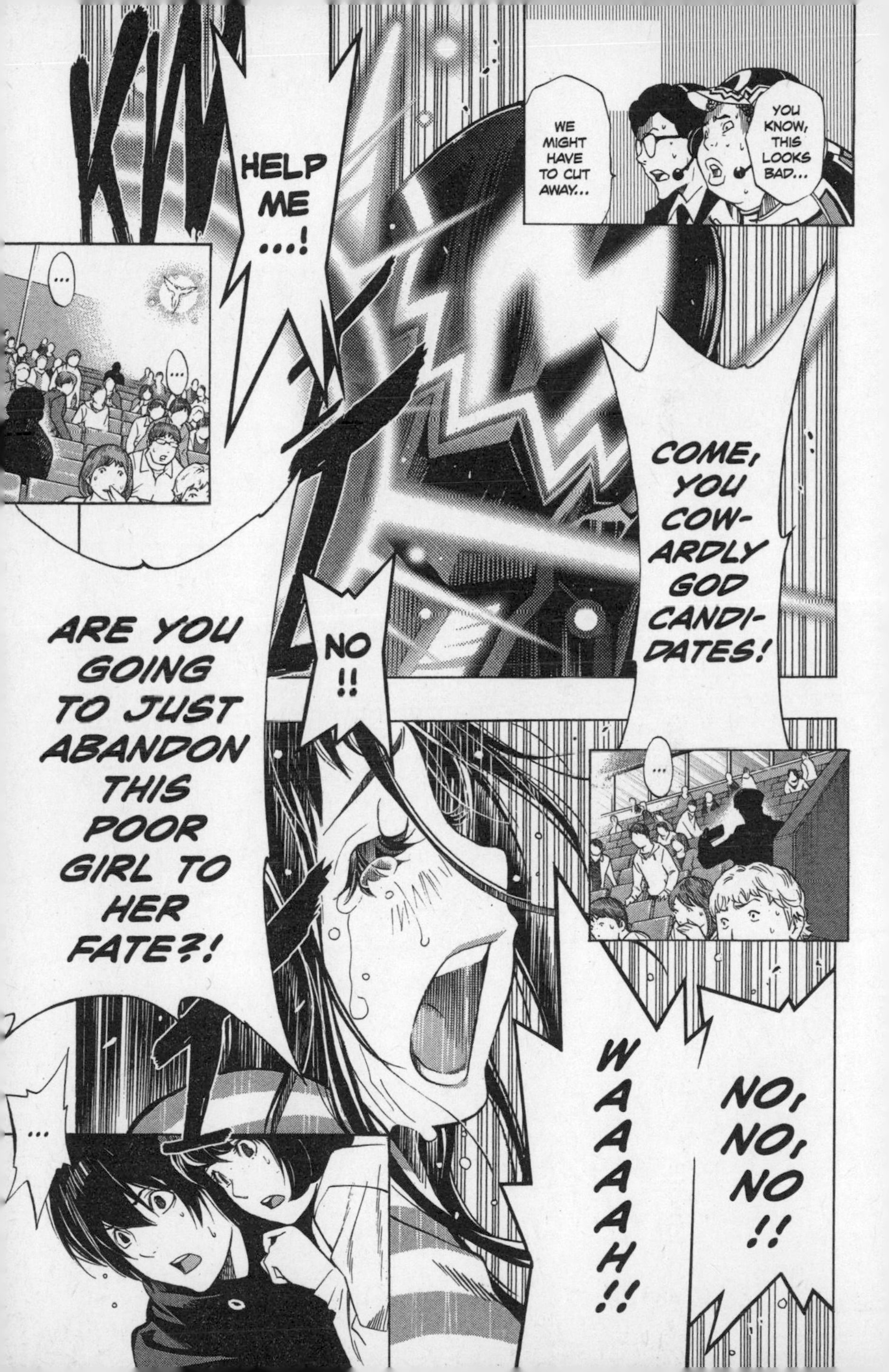
YOU KNOW, THIS LOOKS BAD...
WE MIGHT HAVE TO CUT AWAY...
HELP ME...!
...
...
COME, YOU COW-ARDLY GOD CANDI-DATES!
NO!!
ARE YOU GOING TO JUST ABANDON THIS POOR GIRL TO HER FATE?!
...
NO, NO, NO!!
WAAAAAH!!
...

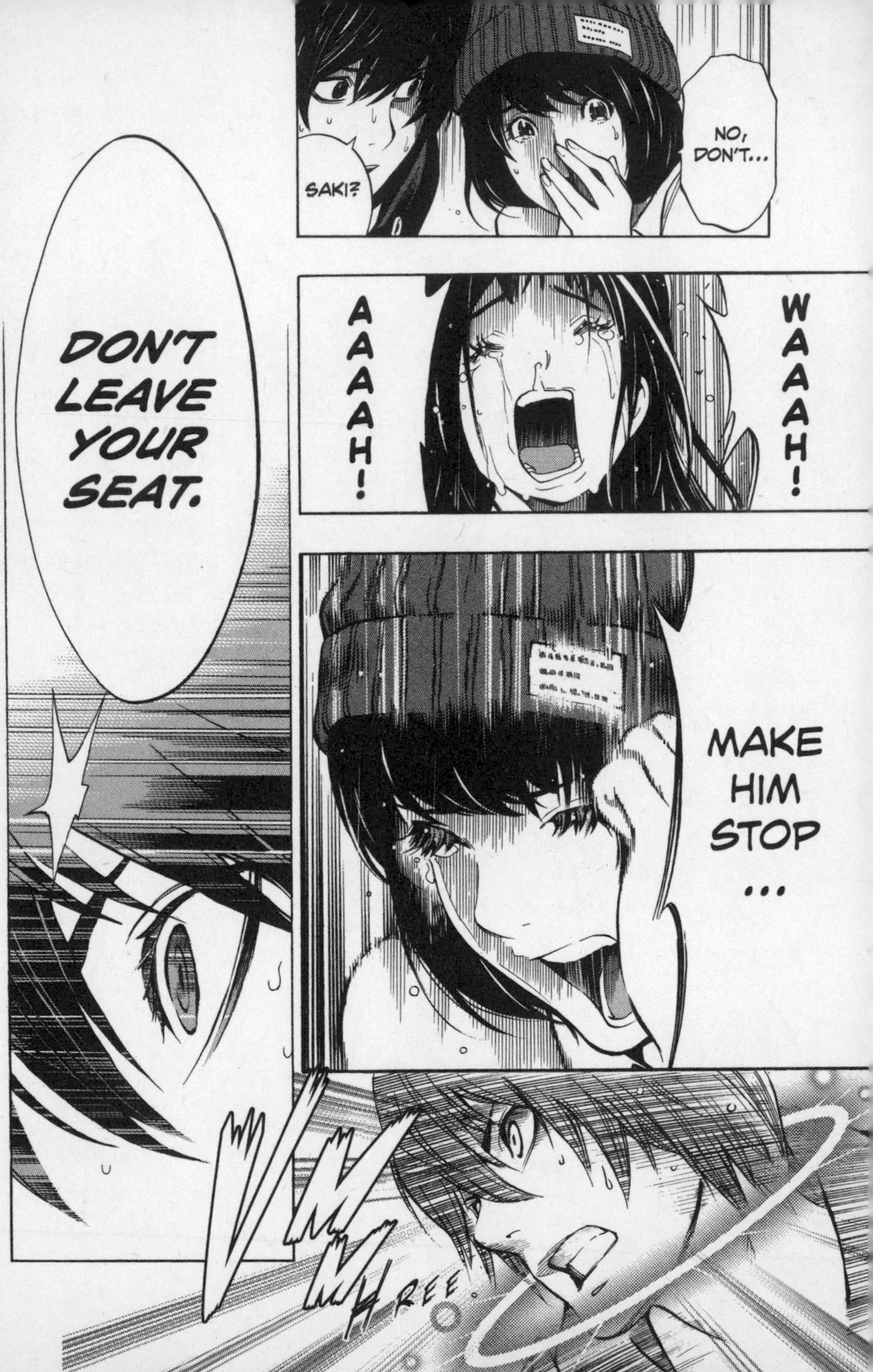

NO, DON'T...
SAKI?
WAAAAH!
AAAAH!
MAKE HIM STOP ...
DON'T LEAVE YOUR SEAT.
WMMHREE

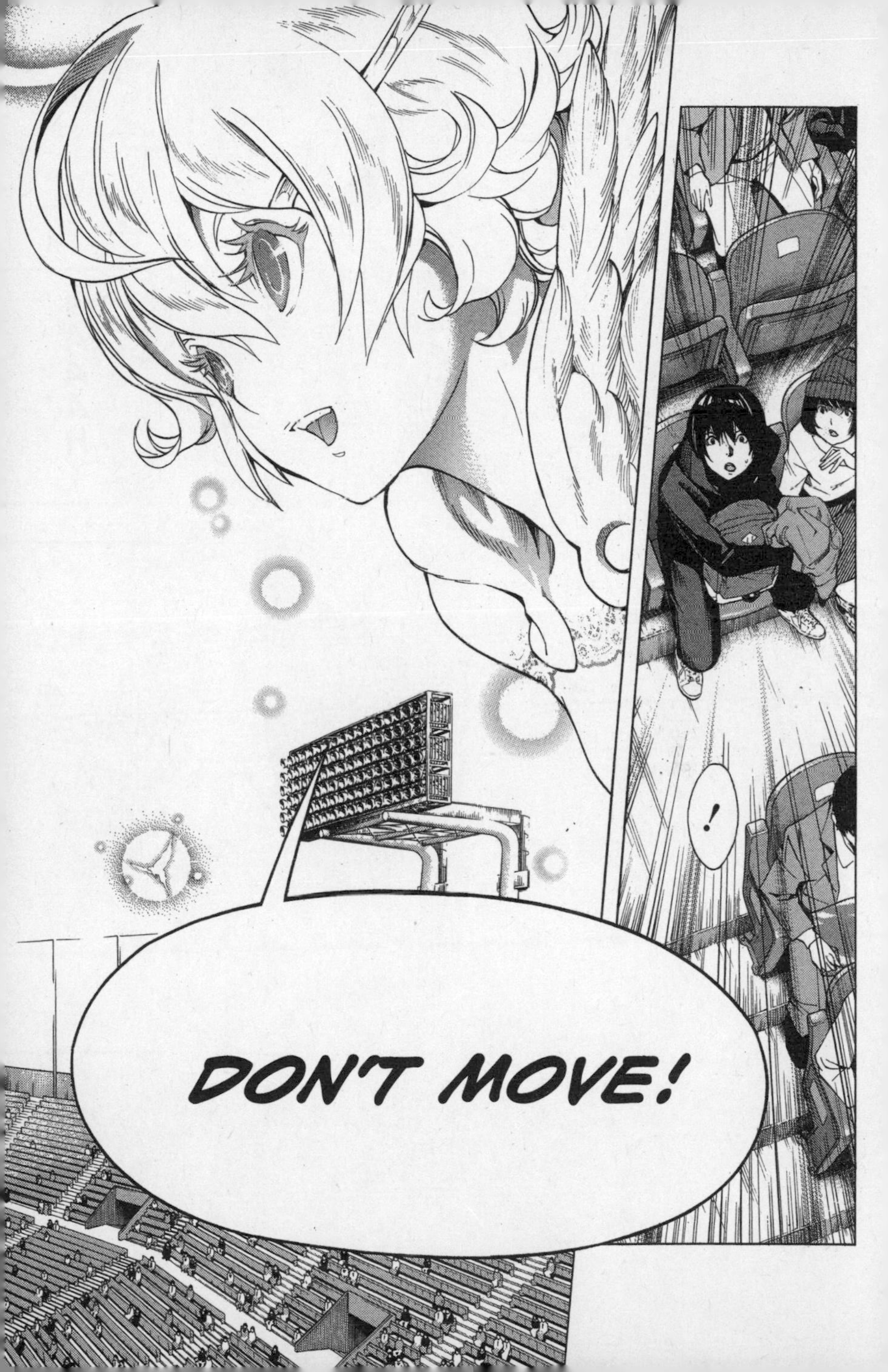
!
DON'T MOVE!

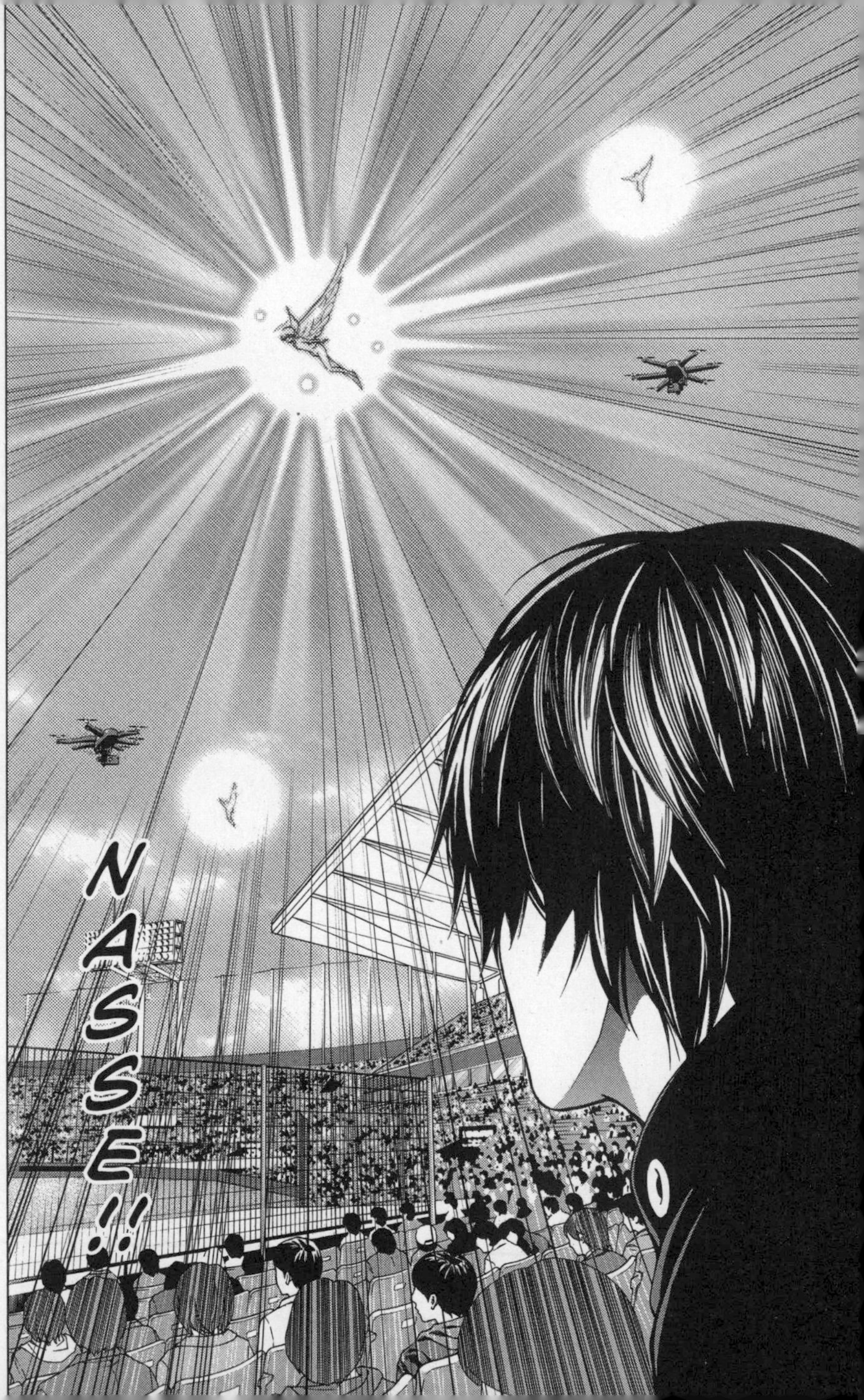
NASSE!!

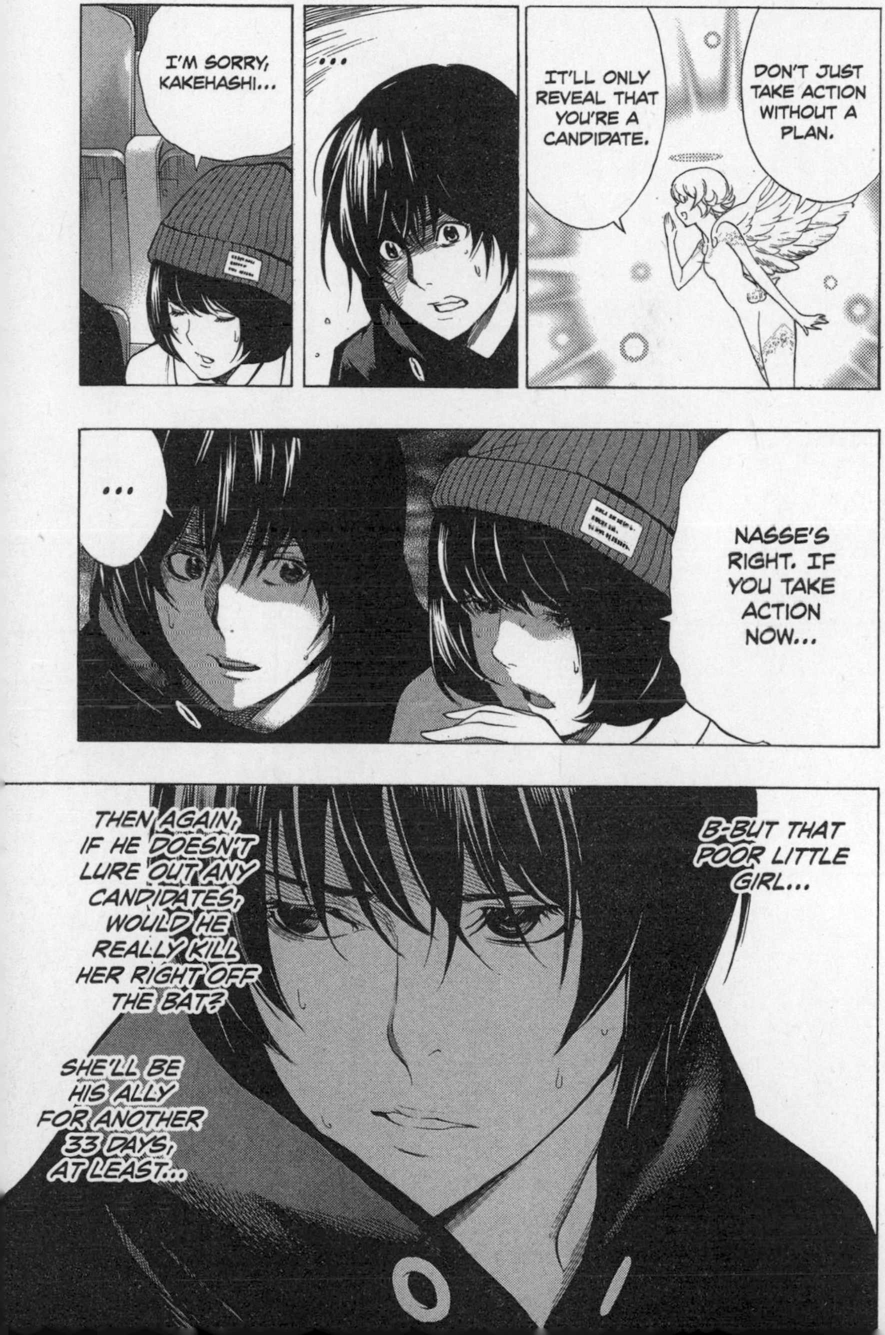
DON'T JUST TAKE ACTION WITHOUT A PLAN.
IT'LL ONLY REVEAL THAT YOU'RE A CANDIDATE.
...
I'M SORRY, KAKEHASHI...
NASSE'S RIGHT. IF YOU TAKE ACTION NOW...
...
B-BUT THAT POOR LITTLE GIRL...
THEN AGAIN, IF HE DOESN'T LURE OUT ANY CANDIDATES, WOULD HE REALLY KILL HER RIGHT OFF THE BAT?
SHE'LL BE HIS ALLY FOR ANOTHER 33 DAYS, AT LEAST...

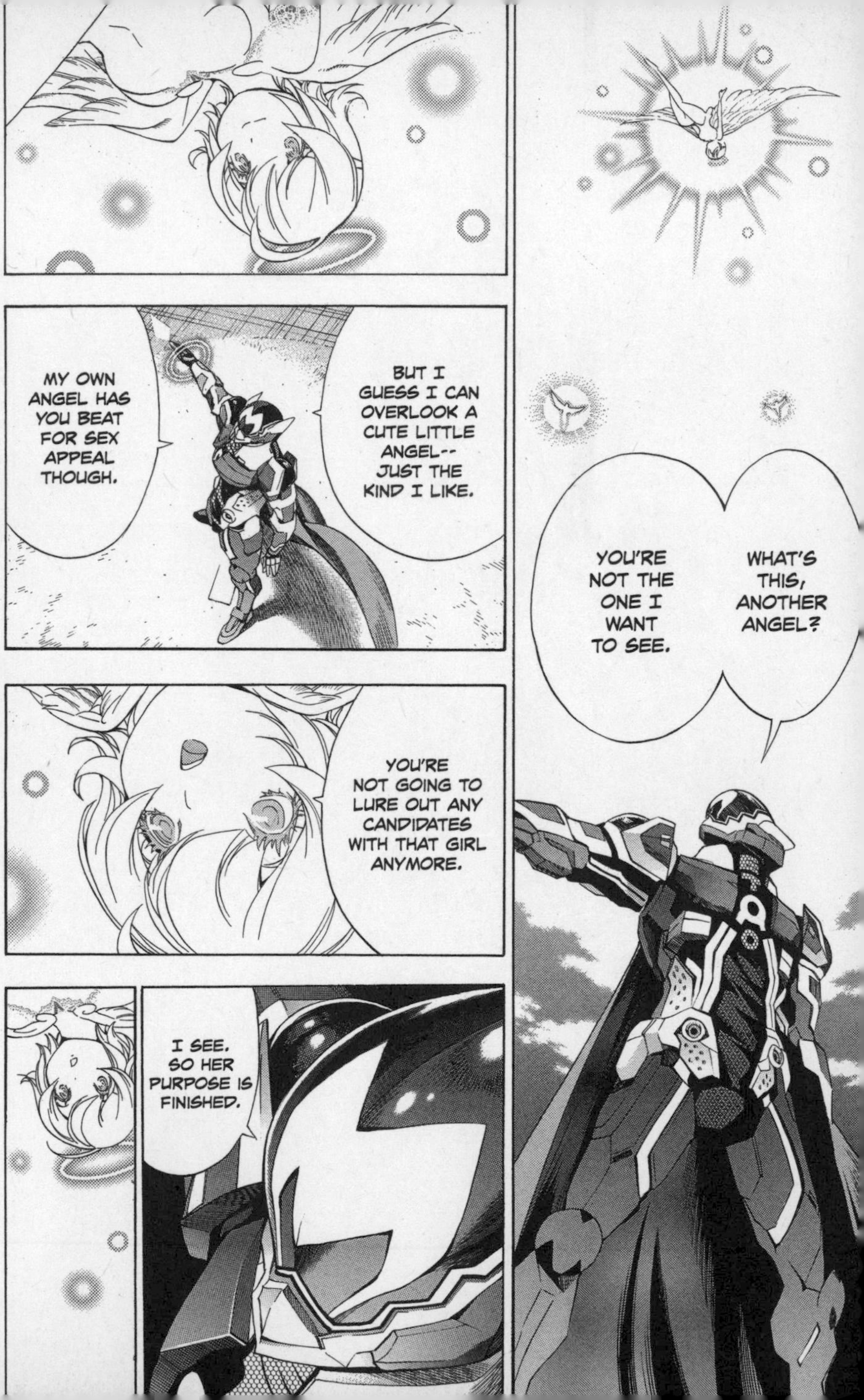
WHAT'S THIS, ANOTHER ANGEL?
YOU'RE NOT THE ONE I WANT TO SEE.
BUT I GUESS I CAN OVERLOOK A CUTE LITTLE ANGEL-- JUST THE KIND I LIKE.
MY OWN ANGEL HAS YOU BEAT FOR SEX APPEAL THOUGH.
YOU'RE NOT GOING TO LURE OUT ANY CANDIDATES WITH THAT GIRL ANYMORE.
I SEE. SO HER PURPOSE IS FINISHED.

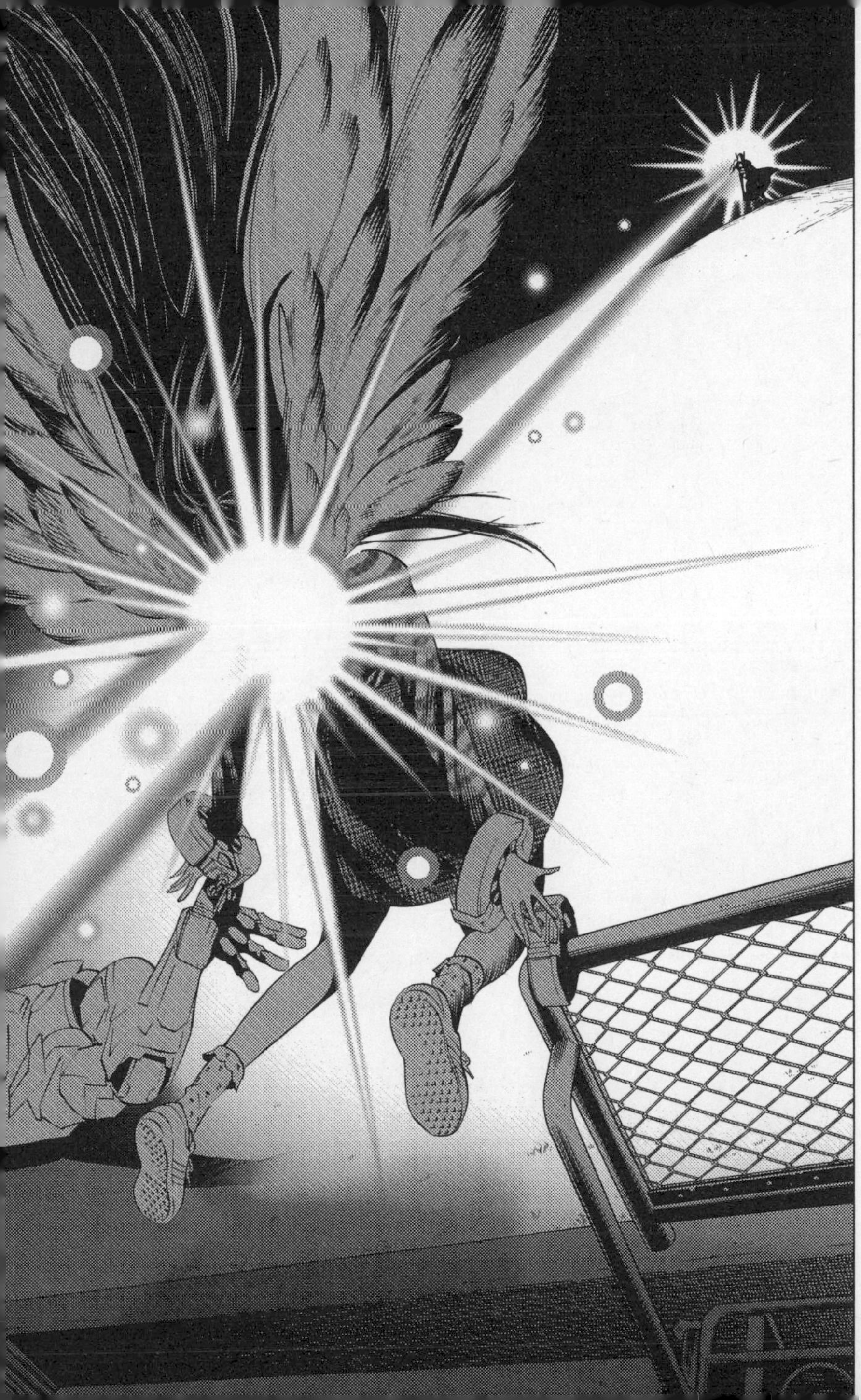

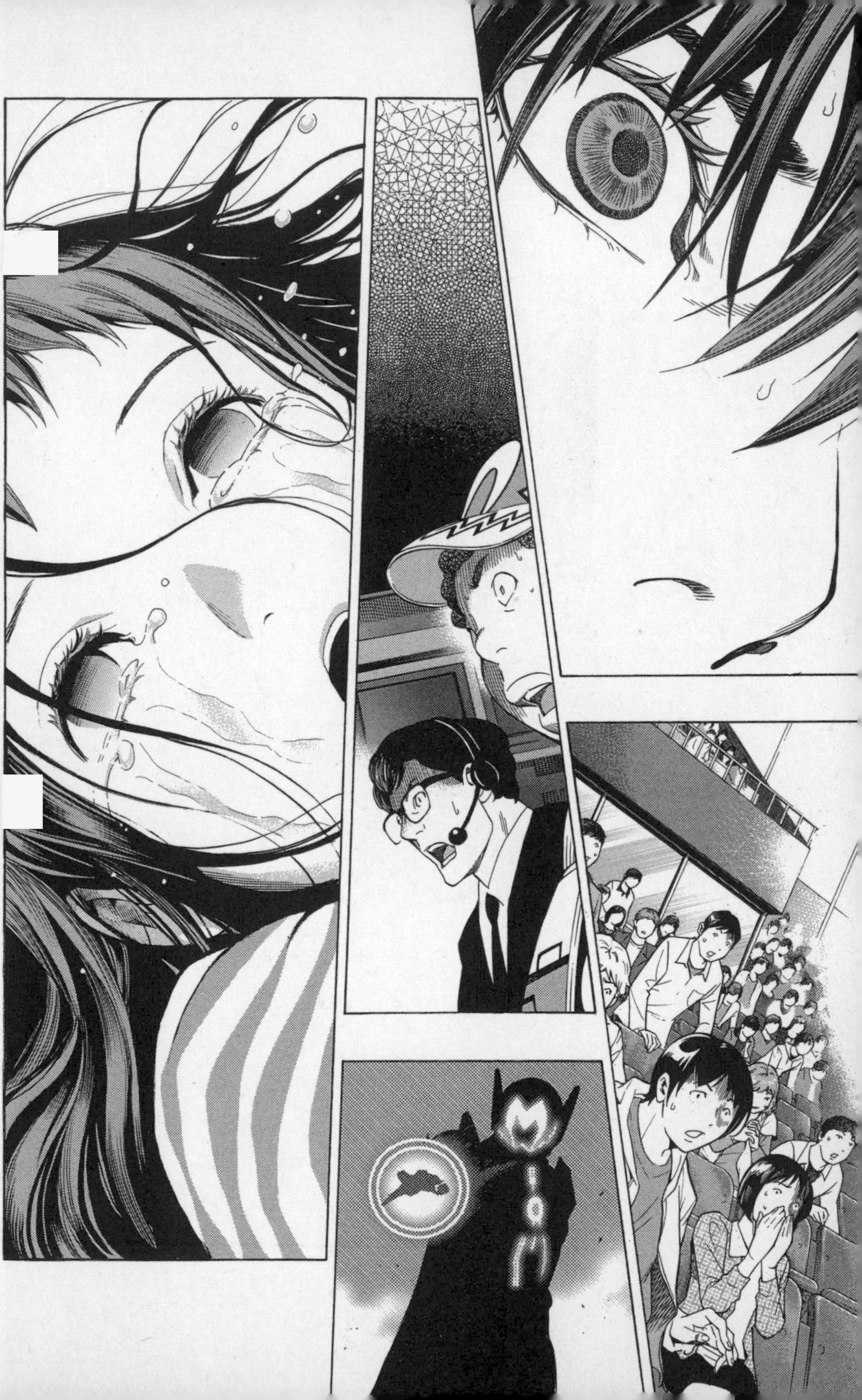

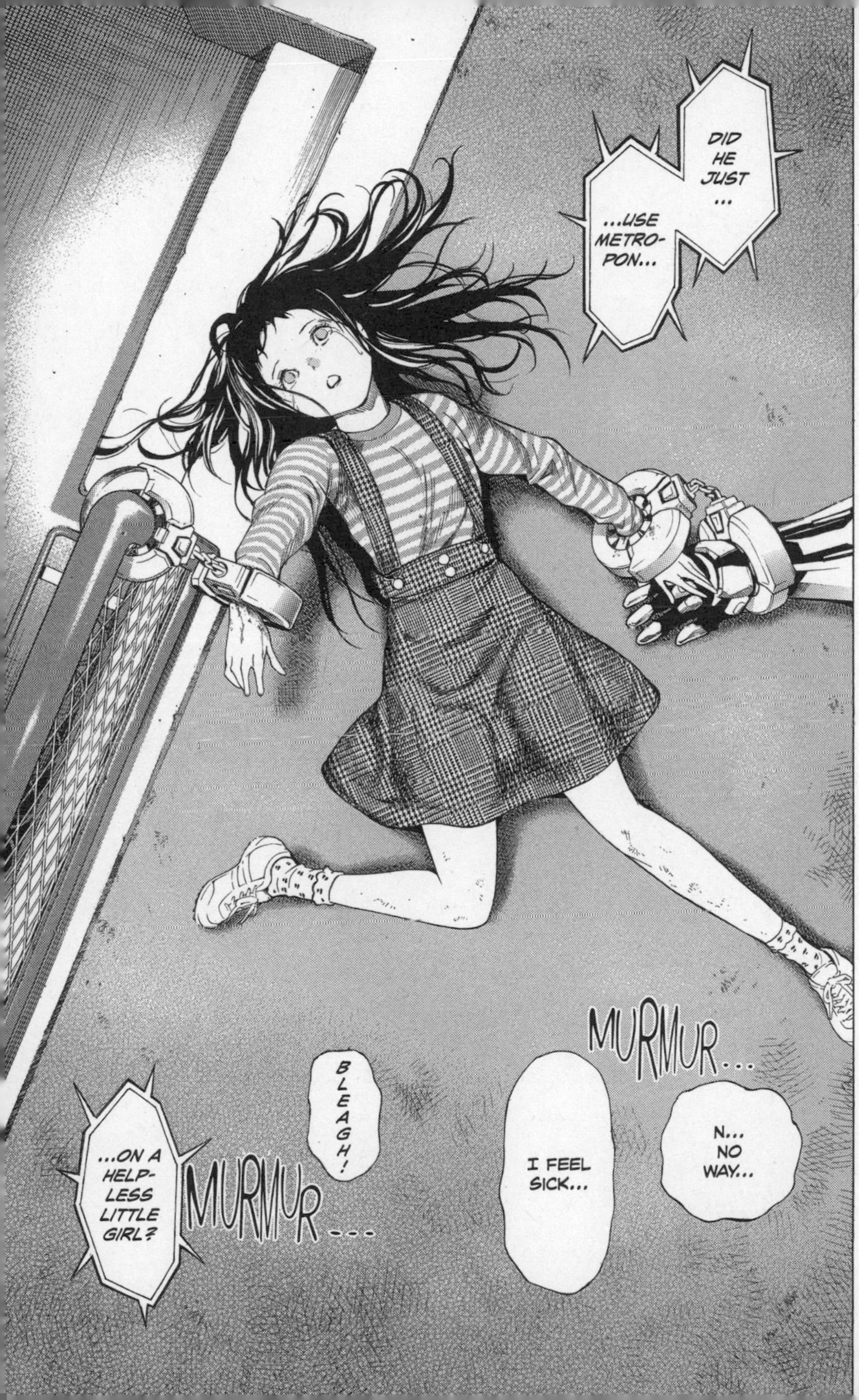
DID HE JUST...
...USE METROPON...
MURMUR...
N... NO WAY...
I FEEL SICK...
BLEAGH!
MURMUR...
...ON A HELPLESS LITTLE GIRL?

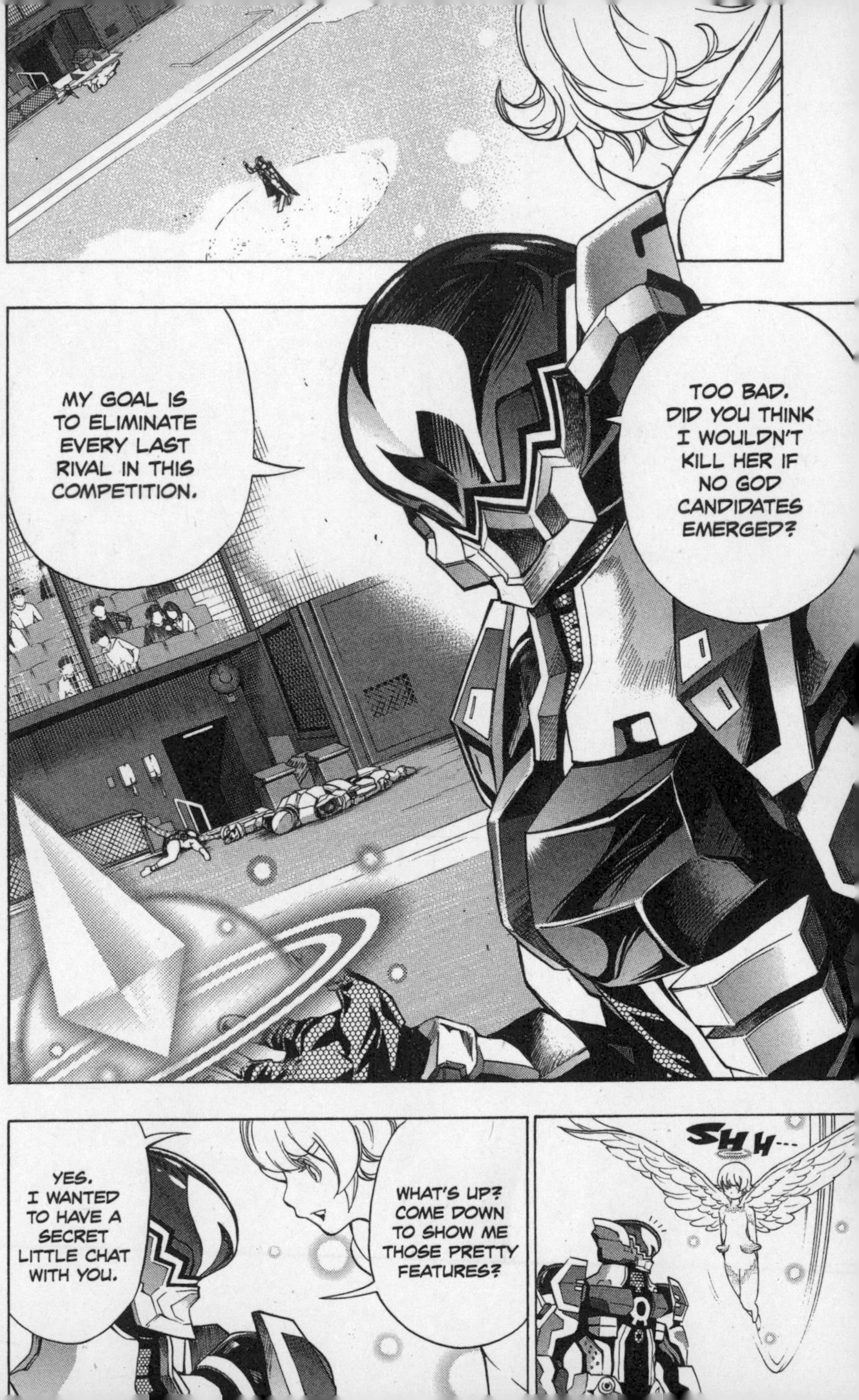
TOO BAD. DID YOU THINK I WOULDN'T KILL HER IF NO GOD CANDIDATES EMERGED?
MY GOAL IS TO ELIMINATE EVERY LAST RIVAL IN THIS COMPETITION.
SHH...
WHAT'S UP? COME DOWN TO SHOW ME THOSE PRETTY FEATURES?
YES. I WANTED TO HAVE A SECRET LITTLE CHAT WITH YOU.

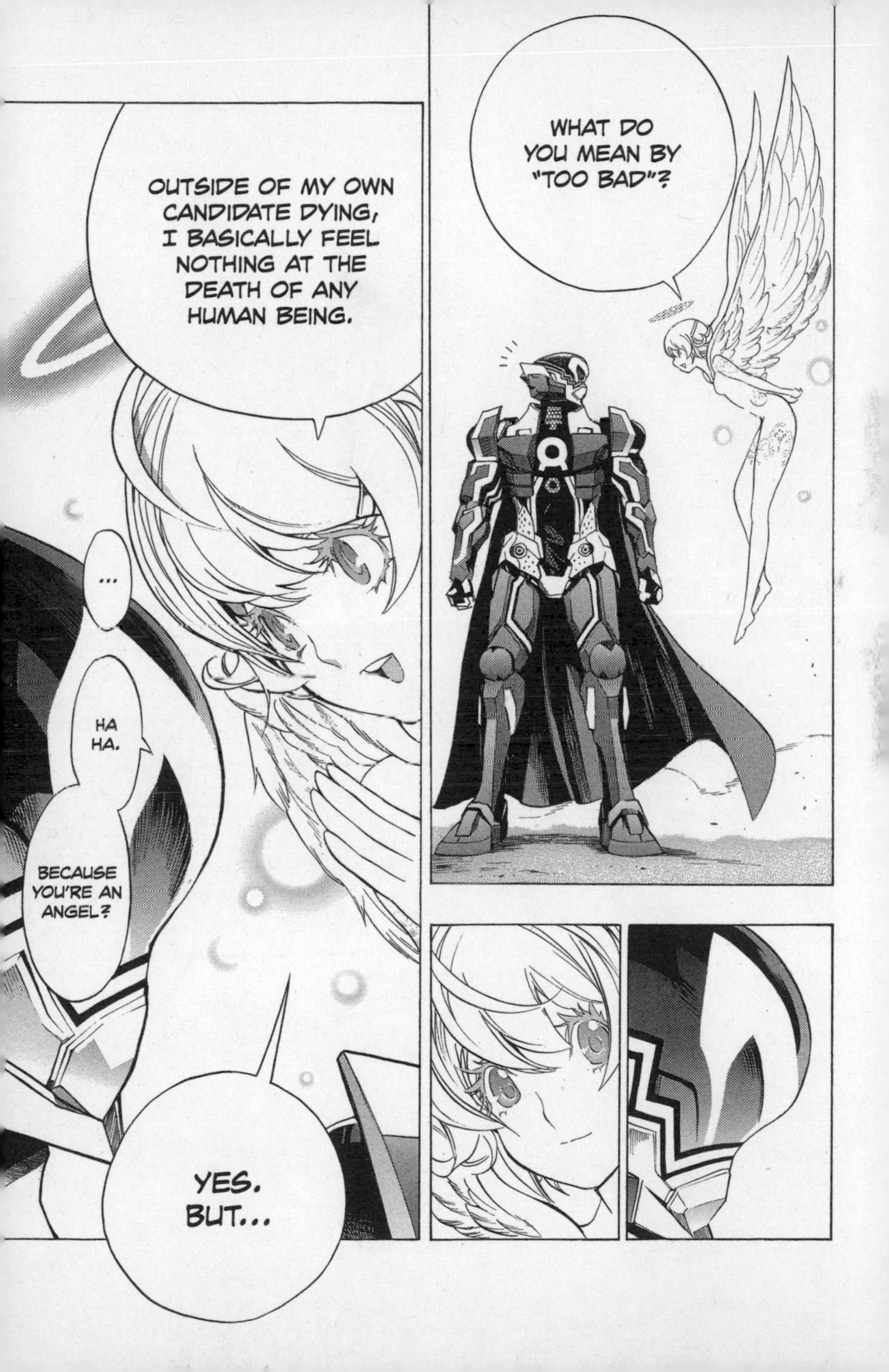
WHAT DO YOU MEAN BY "TOO BAD"?
OUTSIDE OF MY OWN CANDIDATE DYING, I BASICALLY FEEL NOTHING AT THE DEATH OF ANY HUMAN BEING.
...
HA HA.
BECAUSE YOU'RE AN ANGEL?
YES. BUT...

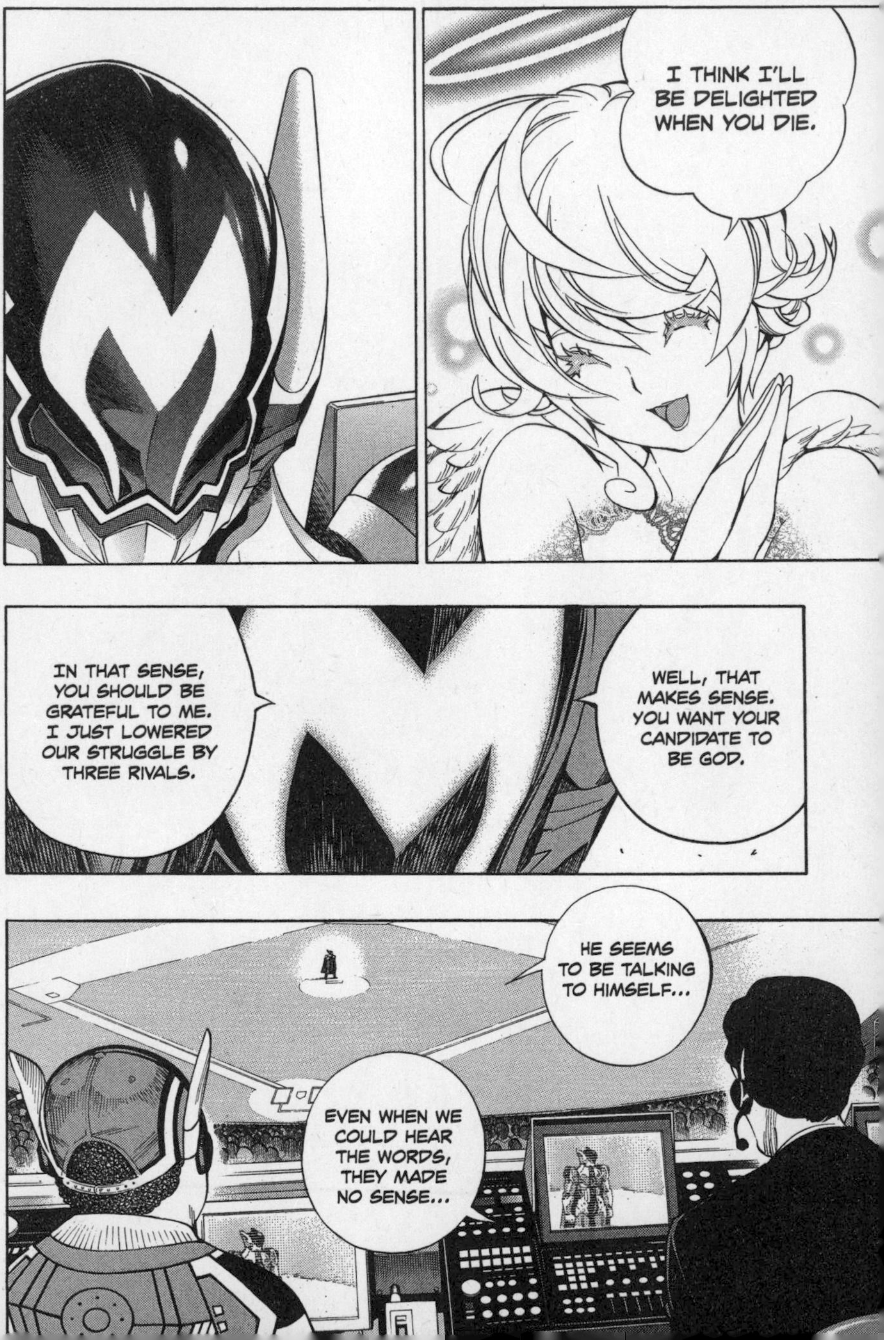
I THINK I'LL BE DELIGHTED WHEN YOU DIE.
WELL, THAT MAKES SENSE. YOU WANT YOUR CANDIDATE TO BE GOD.
IN THAT SENSE, YOU SHOULD BE GRATEFUL TO ME. I JUST LOWERED OUR STRUGGLE BY THREE RIVALS.
HE SEEMS TO BE TALKING TO HIMSELF...
EVEN WHEN WE COULD HEAR THE WORDS, THEY MADE NO SENSE...

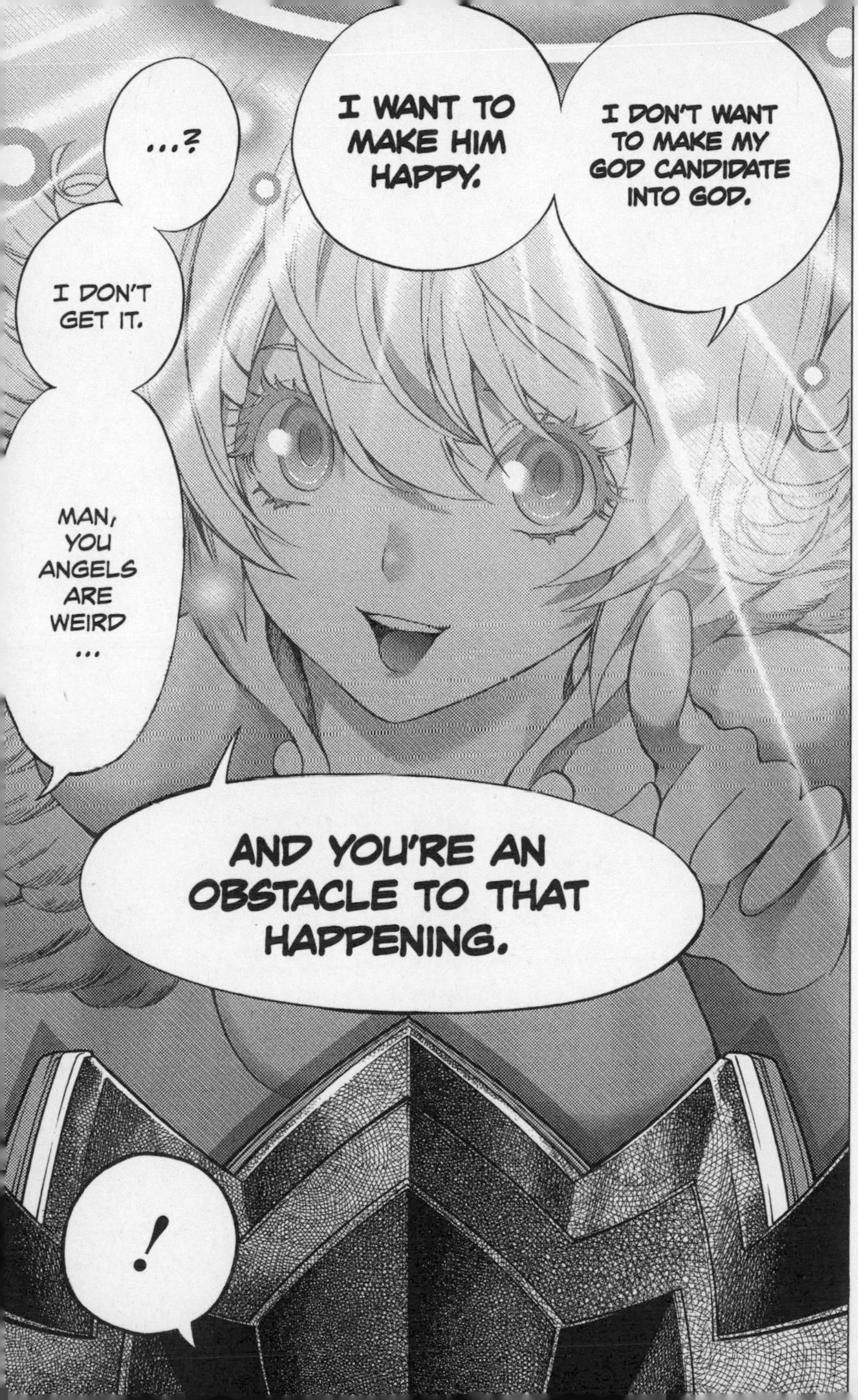
I DON'T WANT TO MAKE MY GOD CANDIDATE INTO GOD.
I WANT TO MAKE HIM HAPPY.
...?
I DON'T GET IT.
MAN, YOU ANGELS ARE WEIRD...
AND YOU'RE AN OBSTACLE TO THAT HAPPENING.
!

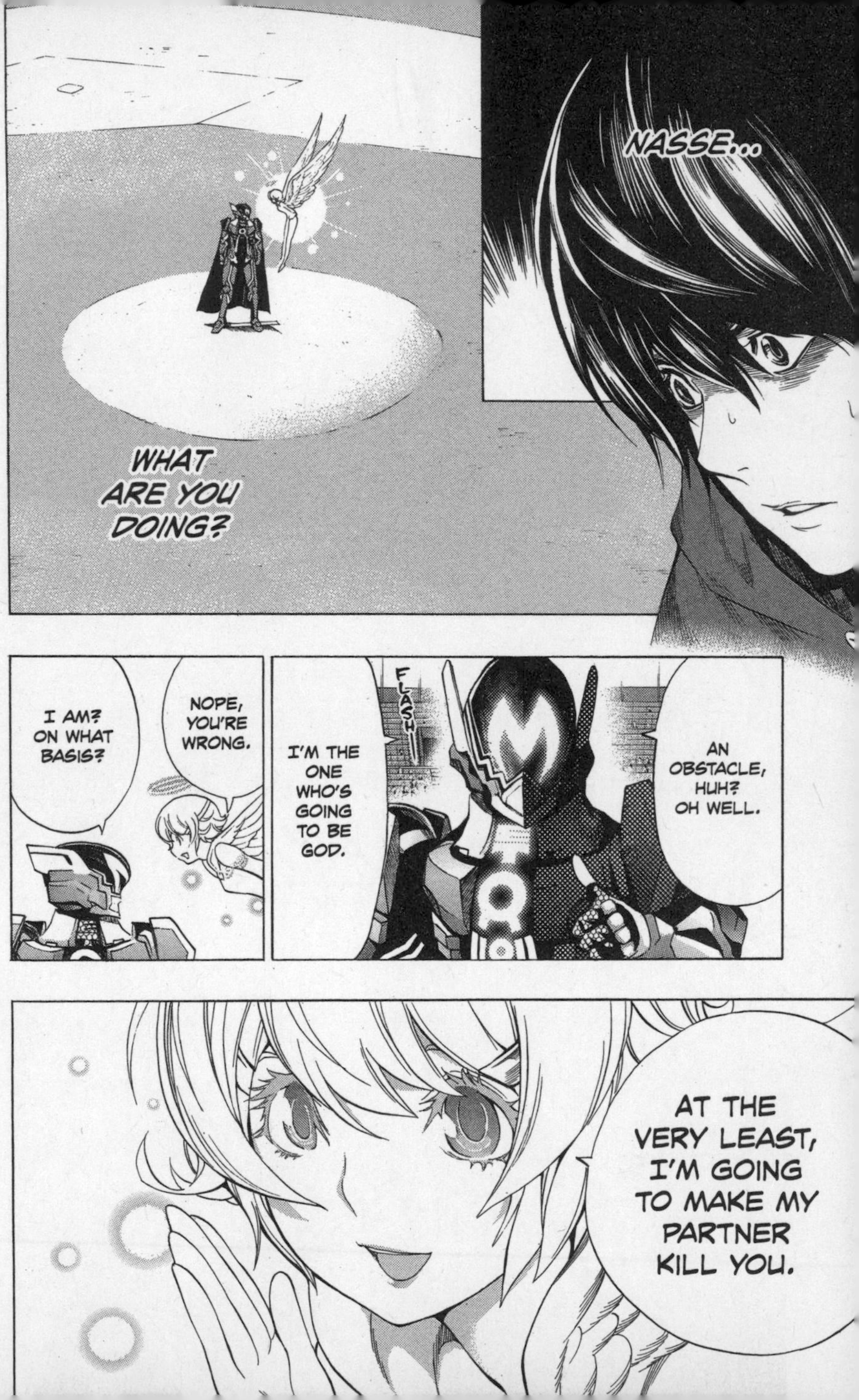
NASSE...
WHAT ARE YOU DOING?
AN OBSTACLE, HUH? OH WELL.
FLASH
I'M THE ONE WHO'S GOING TO BE GOD.
NOPE, YOU'RE WRONG.
I AM? ON WHAT BASIS?
AT THE VERY LEAST, I'M GOING TO MAKE MY PARTNER KILL YOU.

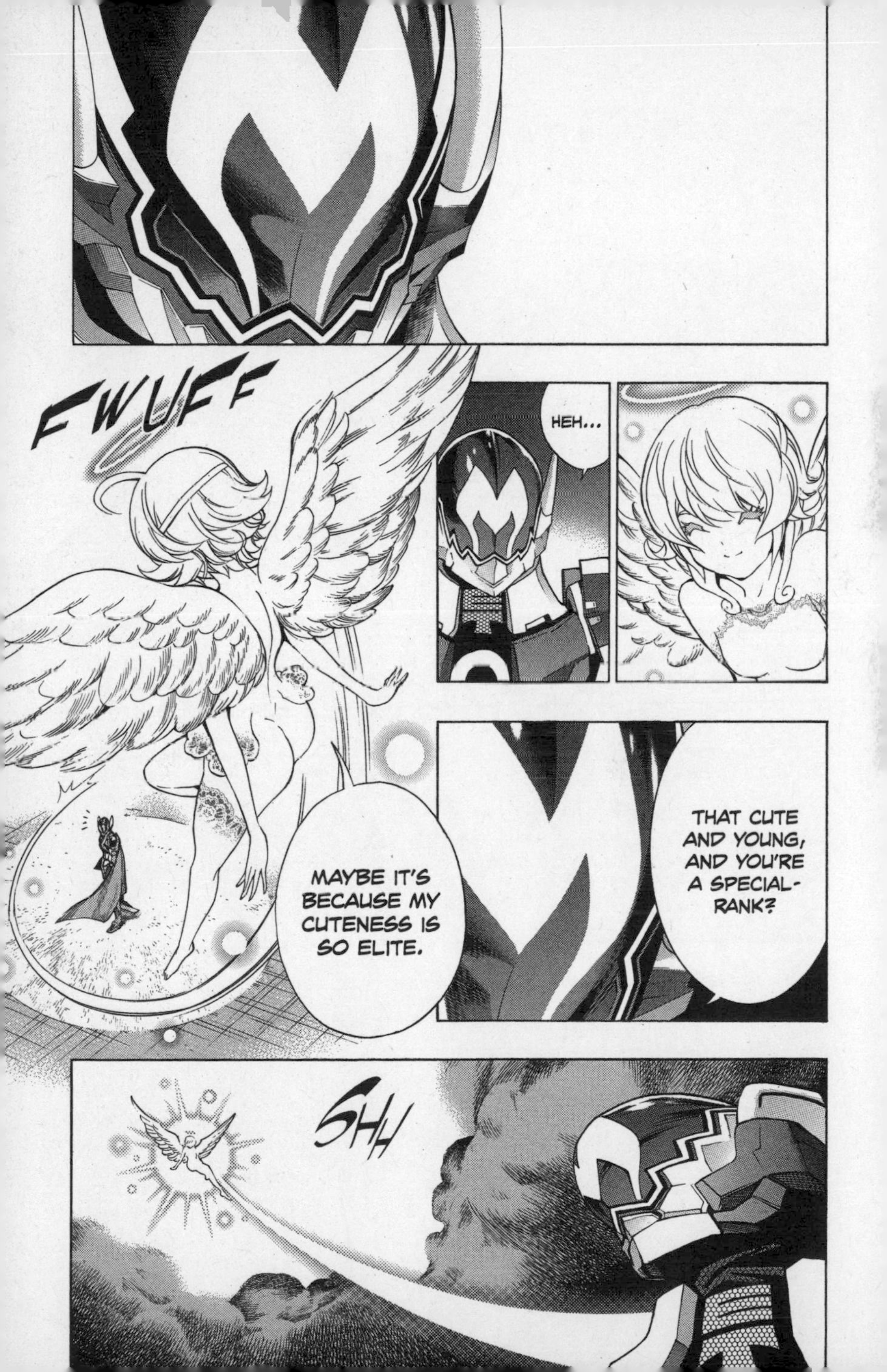
HEH...
THAT CUTE AND YOUNG, AND YOU'RE A SPECIAL-RANK?
FWUFF
MAYBE IT'S BECAUSE MY CUTENESS IS SO ELITE.
SHH

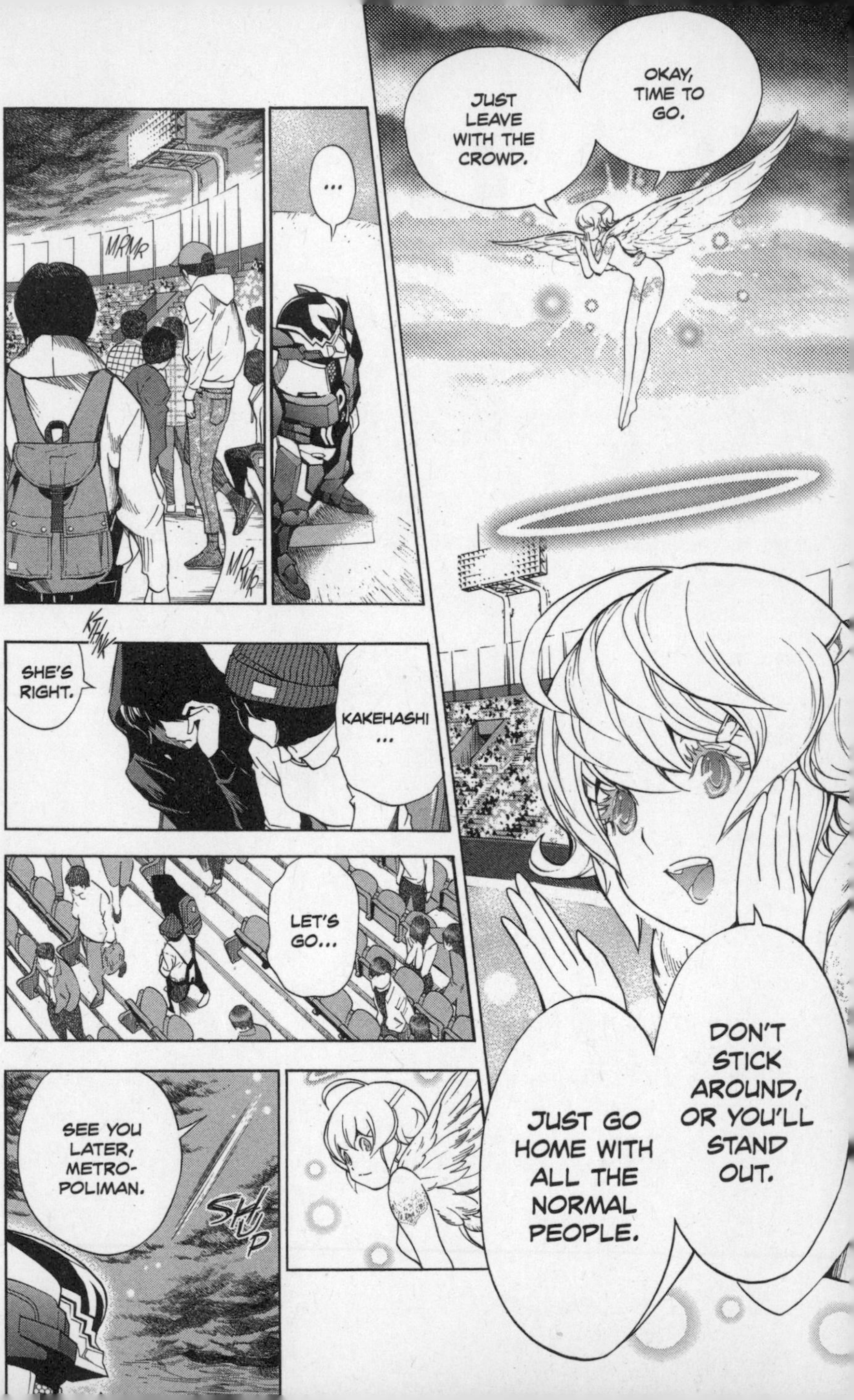
OKAY, TIME TO GO.
JUST LEAVE WITH THE CROWD.
DON'T STICK AROUND, OR YOU'LL STAND OUT.
JUST GO HOME WITH ALL THE NORMAL PEOPLE.
...
MRMR
MRMR
KTHNK
KAKEHASHI ...
SHE'S RIGHT.
LET'S GO...
SEE YOU LATER, METRO-POLIMAN.
SHUP

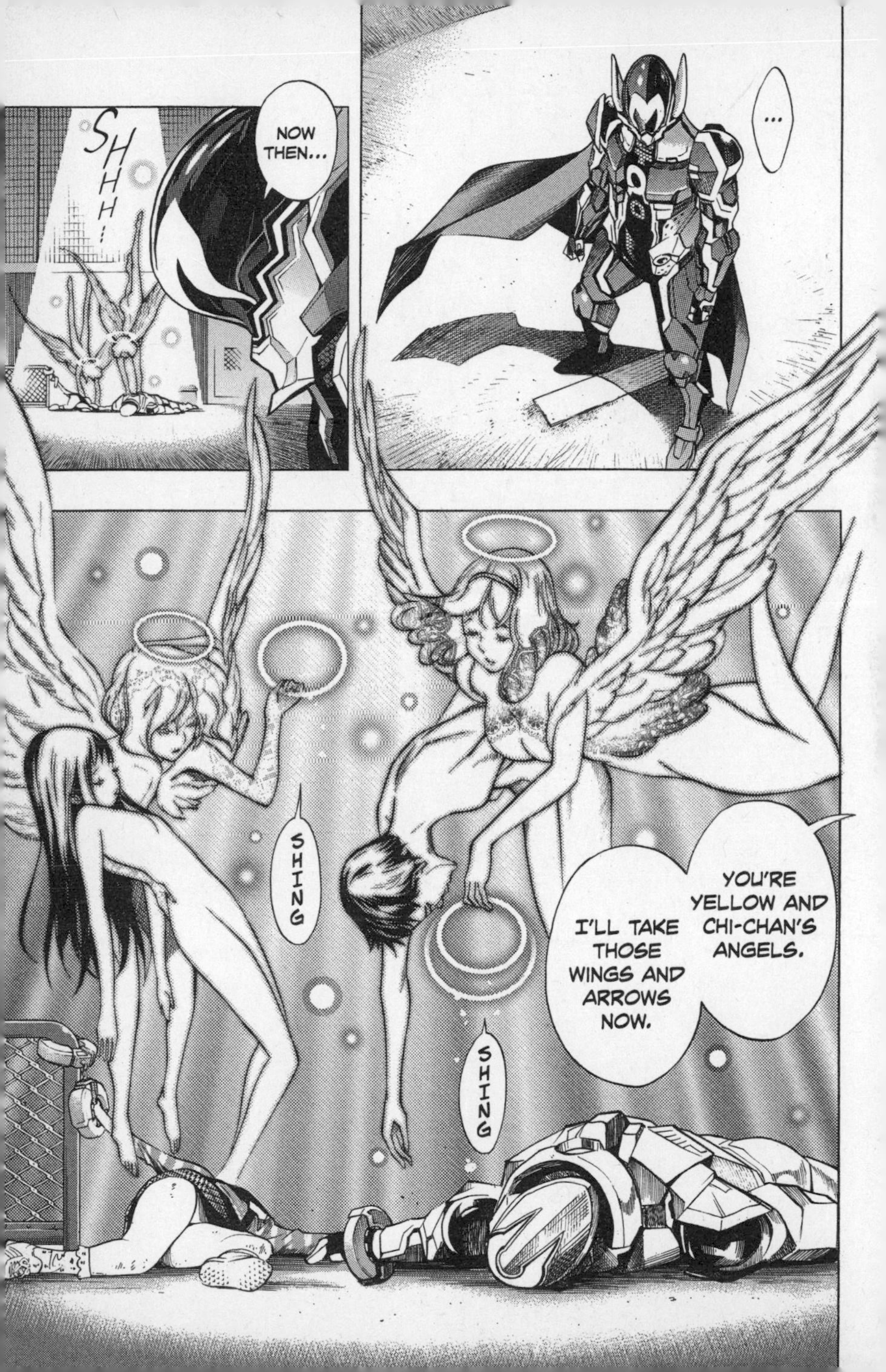
...
NOW THEN...
SHHH!
YOU'RE YELLOW AND CHI-CHAN'S ANGELS.
I'LL TAKE THOSE WINGS AND ARROWS NOW.
SHING
SHING

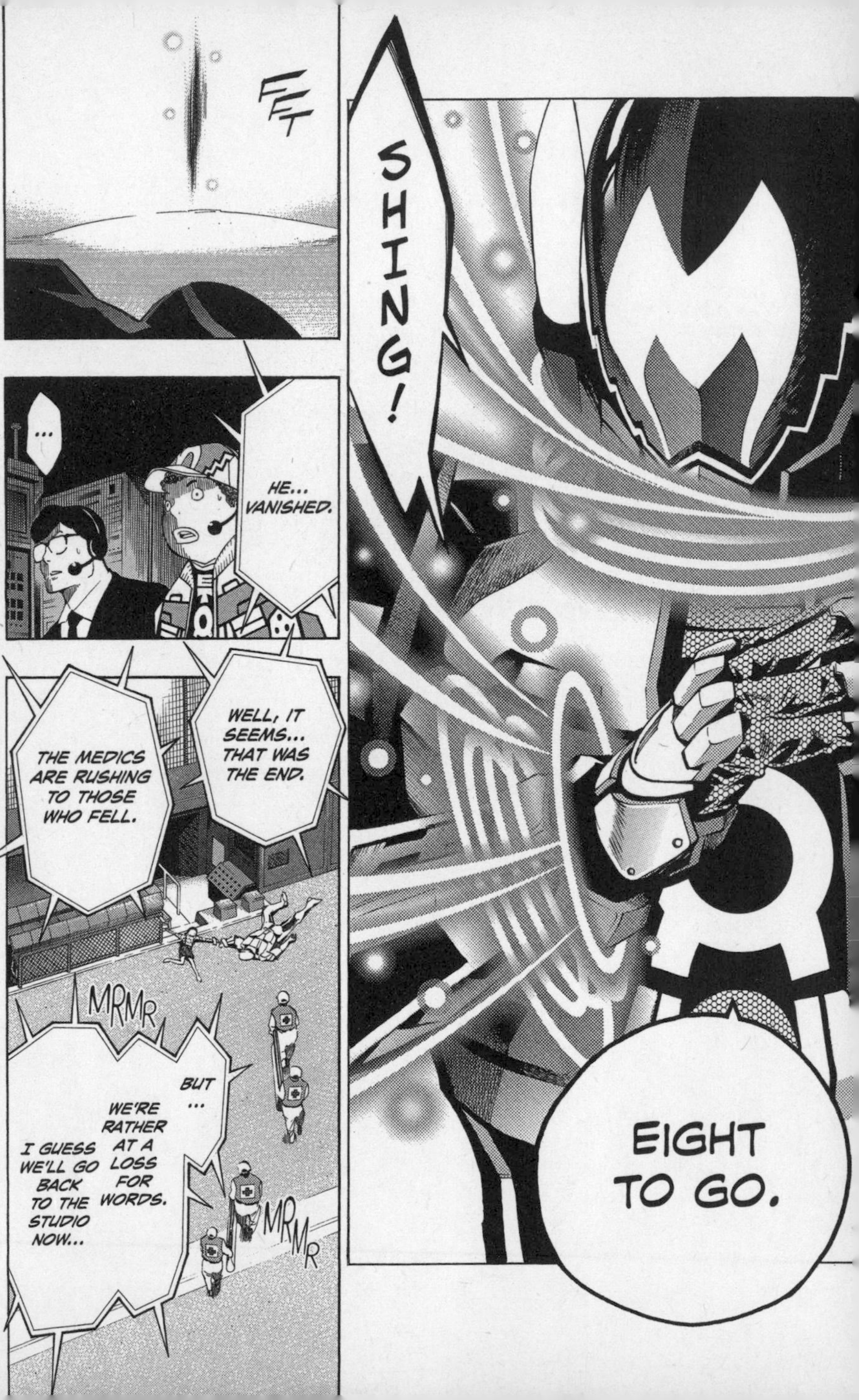
SHING!
EIGHT TO GO.
FFT
...
HE... VANISHED.
WELL, IT SEEMS... THAT WAS THE END.
THE MEDICS ARE RUSHING TO THOSE WHO FELL.
MRMR
BUT...
WE'RE RATHER AT A LOSS FOR WORDS.
I GUESS WE'LL GO BACK TO THE STUDIO NOW...
MRMR

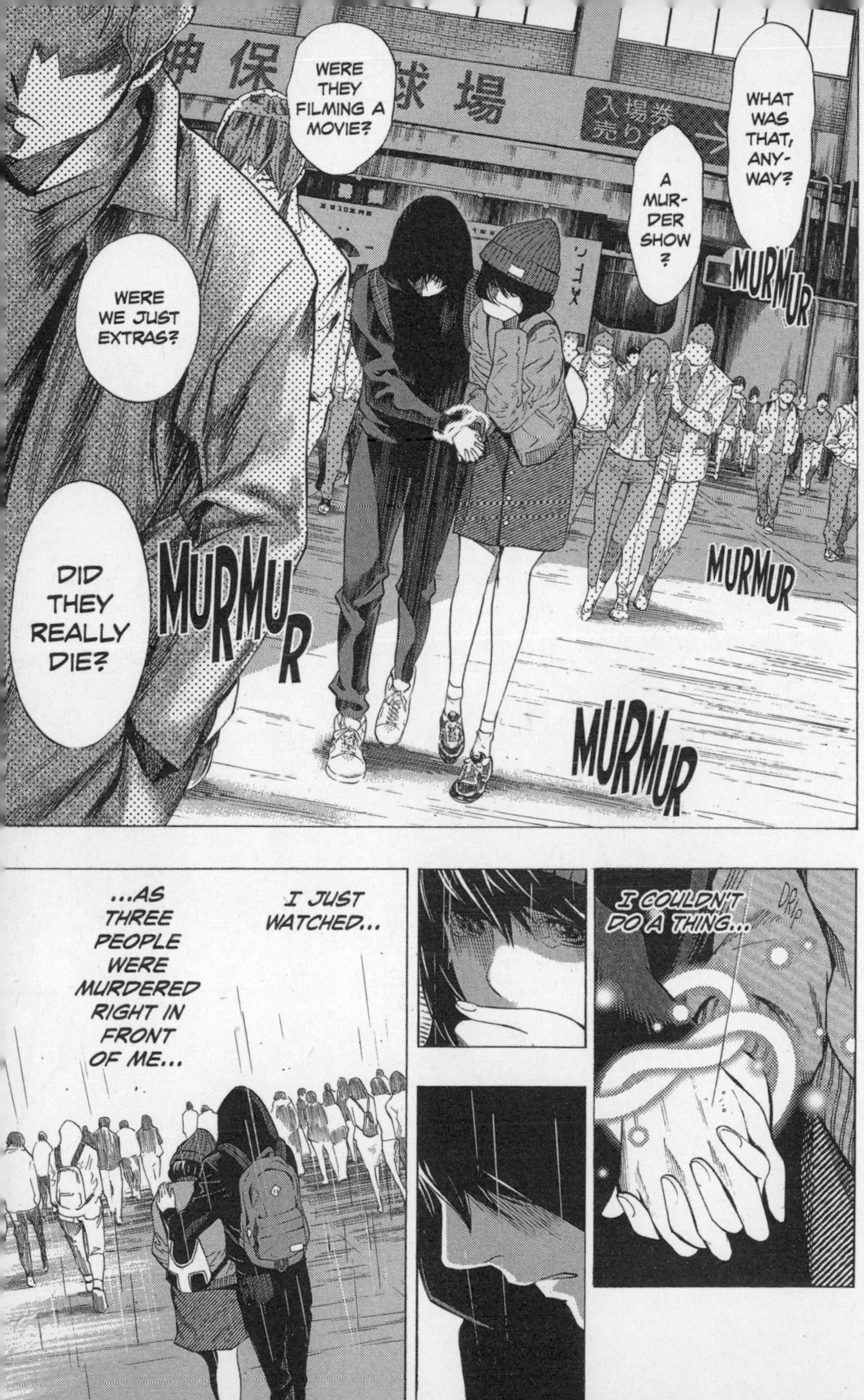
WHAT WAS THAT, ANYWAY?
A MURDER SHOW?
MURMUR
WERE THEY FILMING A MOVIE?
WERE WE JUST EXTRAS?
MURMUR
DID THEY REALLY DIE?
MURMUR
MURMUR
DRIP
I COULDN'T DO A THING...
I JUST WATCHED...
...AS THREE PEOPLE WERE MURDERED RIGHT IN FRONT OF ME...

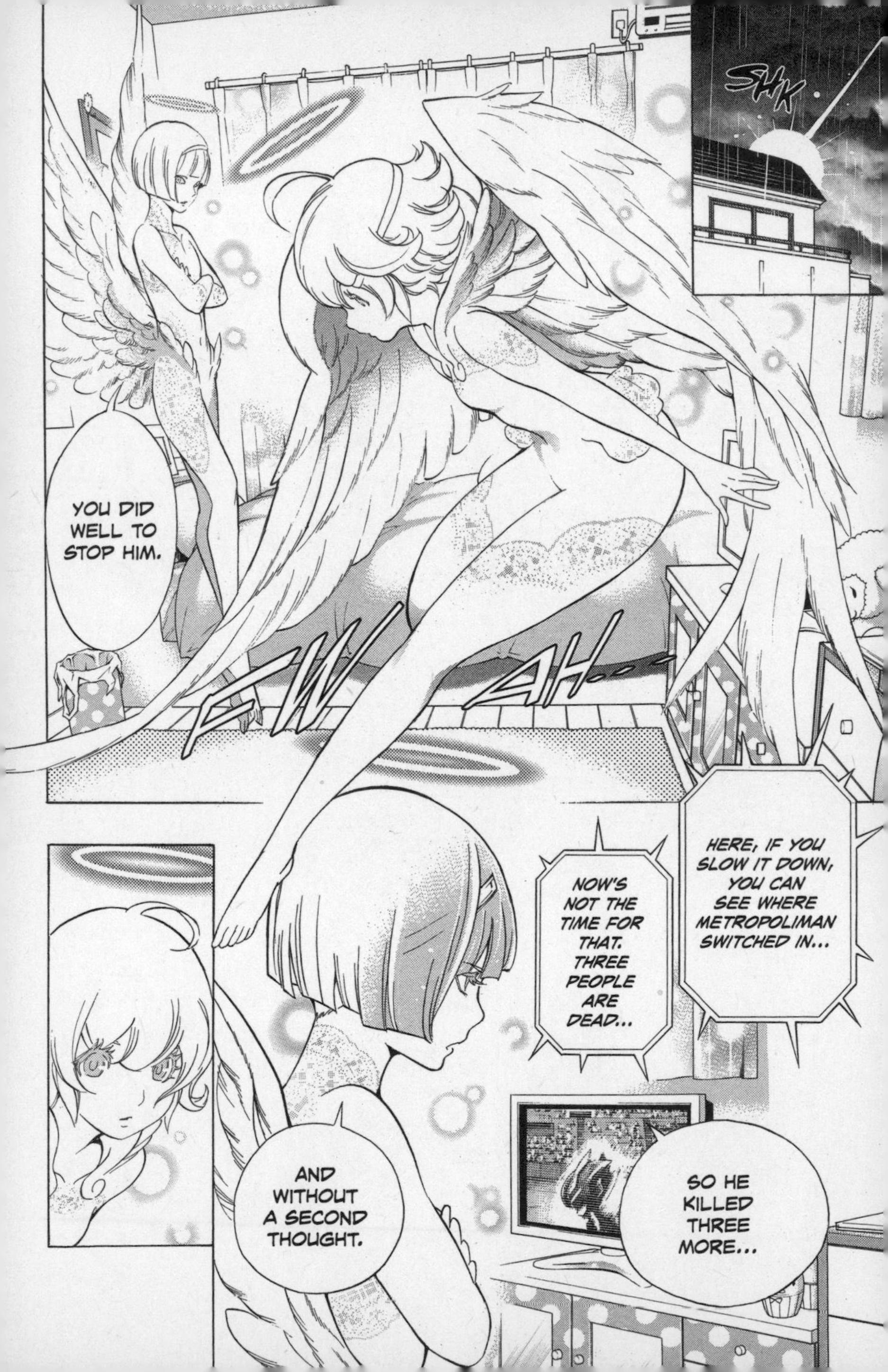
SHK
AW
AH...
YOU DID WELL TO STOP HIM.
HERE, IF YOU SLOW IT DOWN, YOU CAN SEE WHERE METROPOLIMAN SWITCHED IN...
NOW'S NOT THE TIME FOR THAT. THREE PEOPLE ARE DEAD...
SO HE KILLED THREE MORE...
AND WITHOUT A SECOND THOUGHT.

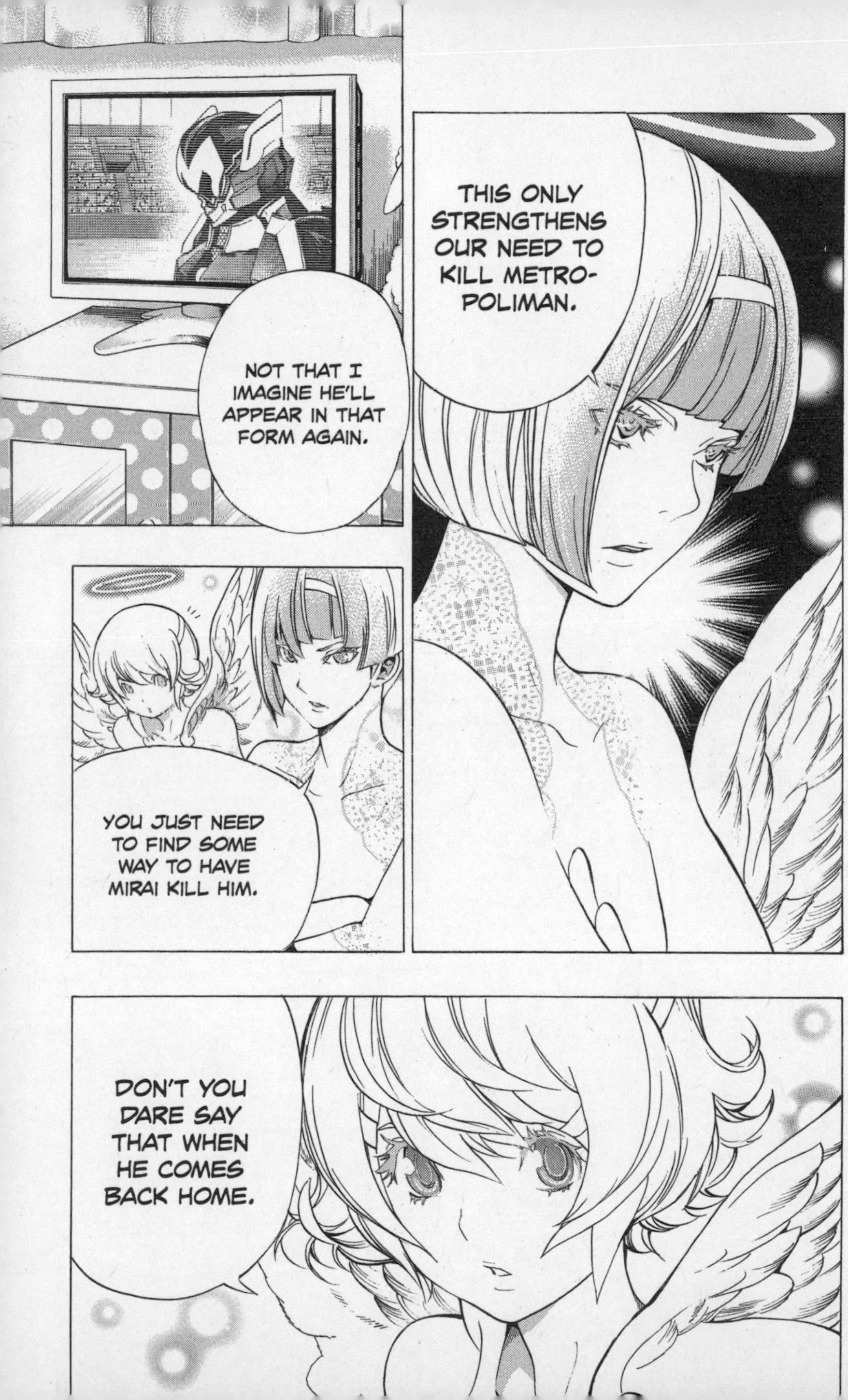
THIS ONLY STRENGTHENS OUR NEED TO KILL METRO-POLIMAN.
NOT THAT I IMAGINE HE'LL APPEAR IN THAT FORM AGAIN.
YOU JUST NEED TO FIND SOME WAY TO HAVE MIRAI KILL HIM.
DON'T YOU DARE SAY THAT WHEN HE COMES BACK HOME.

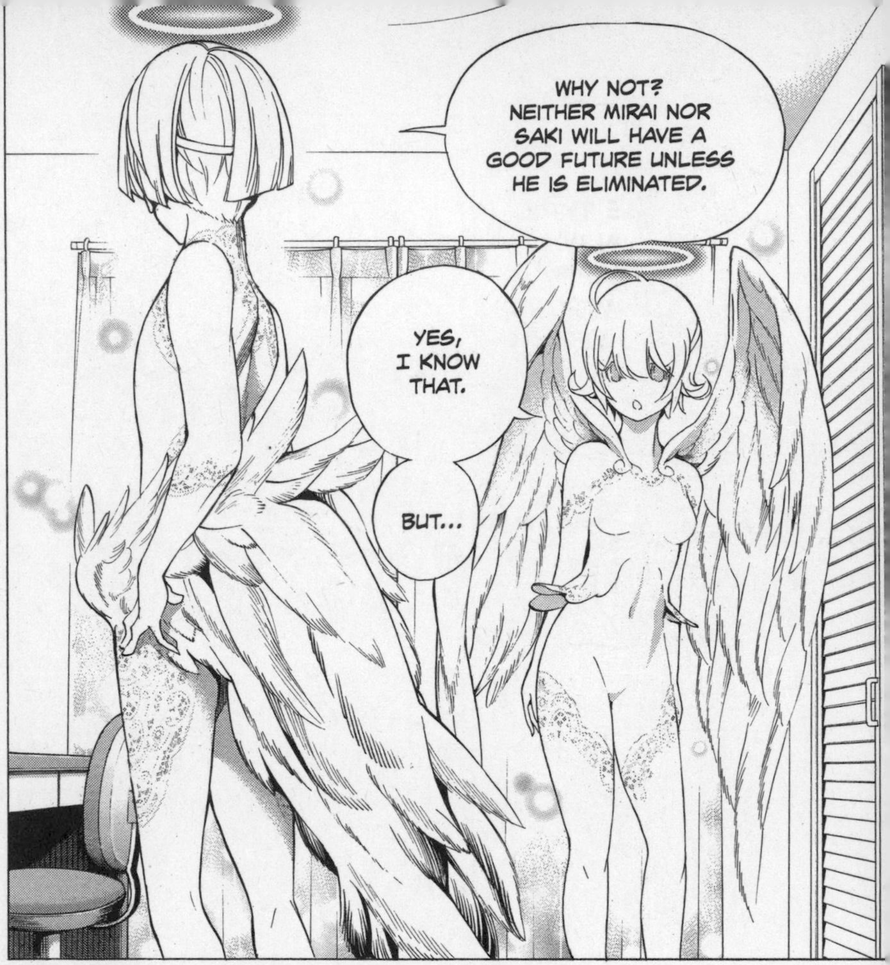
WHY NOT? NEITHER MIRAI NOR SAKI WILL HAVE A GOOD FUTURE UNLESS HE IS ELIMINATED.
YES, I KNOW THAT.
BUT...

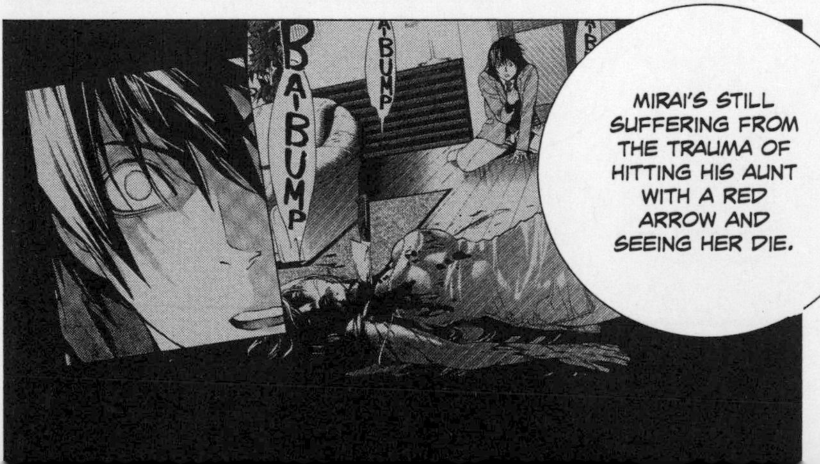
MIRAI'S STILL SUFFERING FROM THE TRAUMA OF HITTING HIS AUNT WITH A RED ARROW AND SEEING HER DIE.
BA-BUMP
BA-BUMP

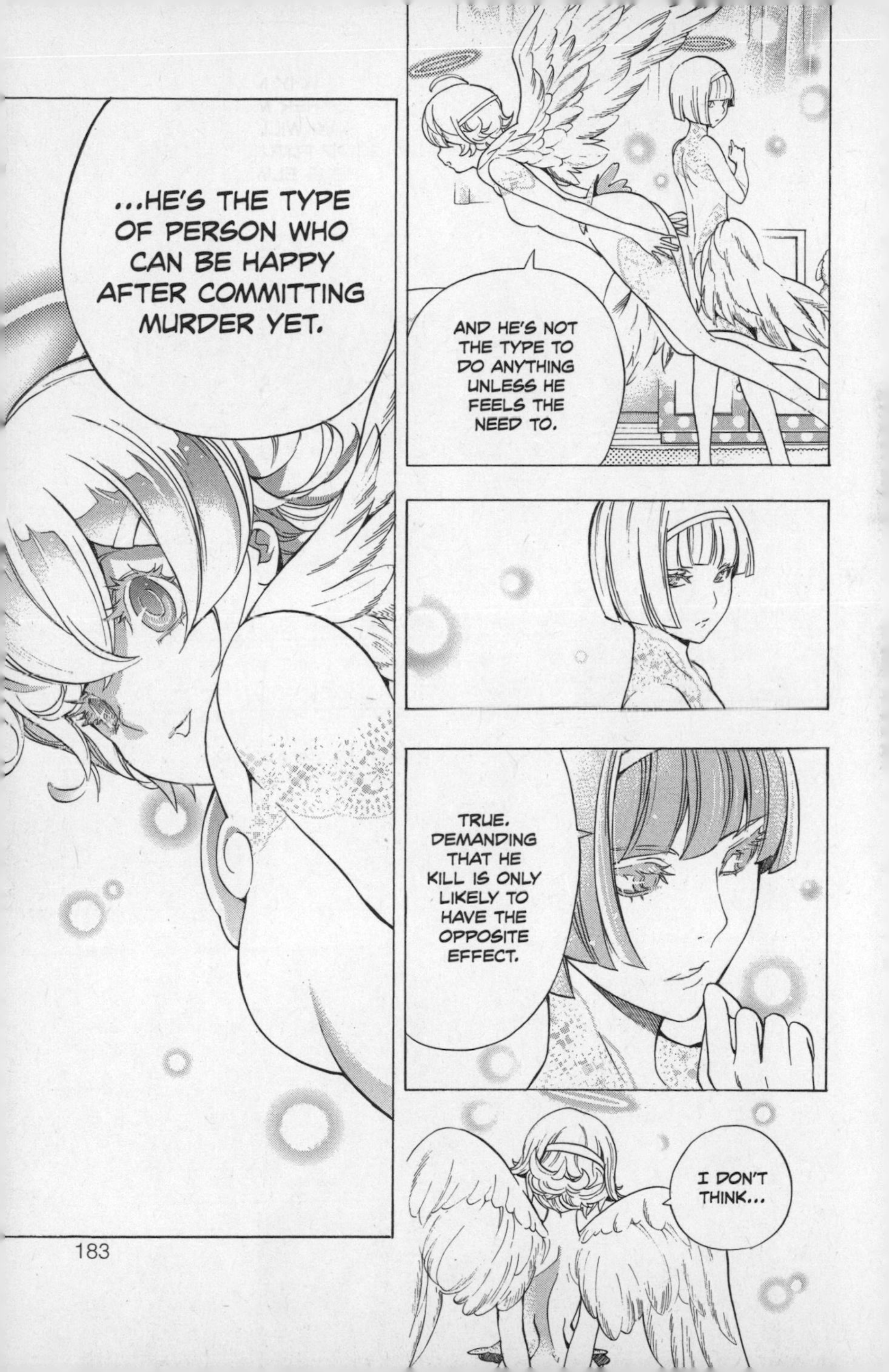
AND HE'S NOT THE TYPE TO DO ANYTHING UNLESS HE FEELS THE NEED TO.
TRUE. DEMANDING THAT HE KILL IS ONLY LIKELY TO HAVE THE OPPOSITE EFFECT.
I DON'T THINK...
...HE'S THE TYPE OF PERSON WHO CAN BE HAPPY AFTER COMMITTING MURDER YET.

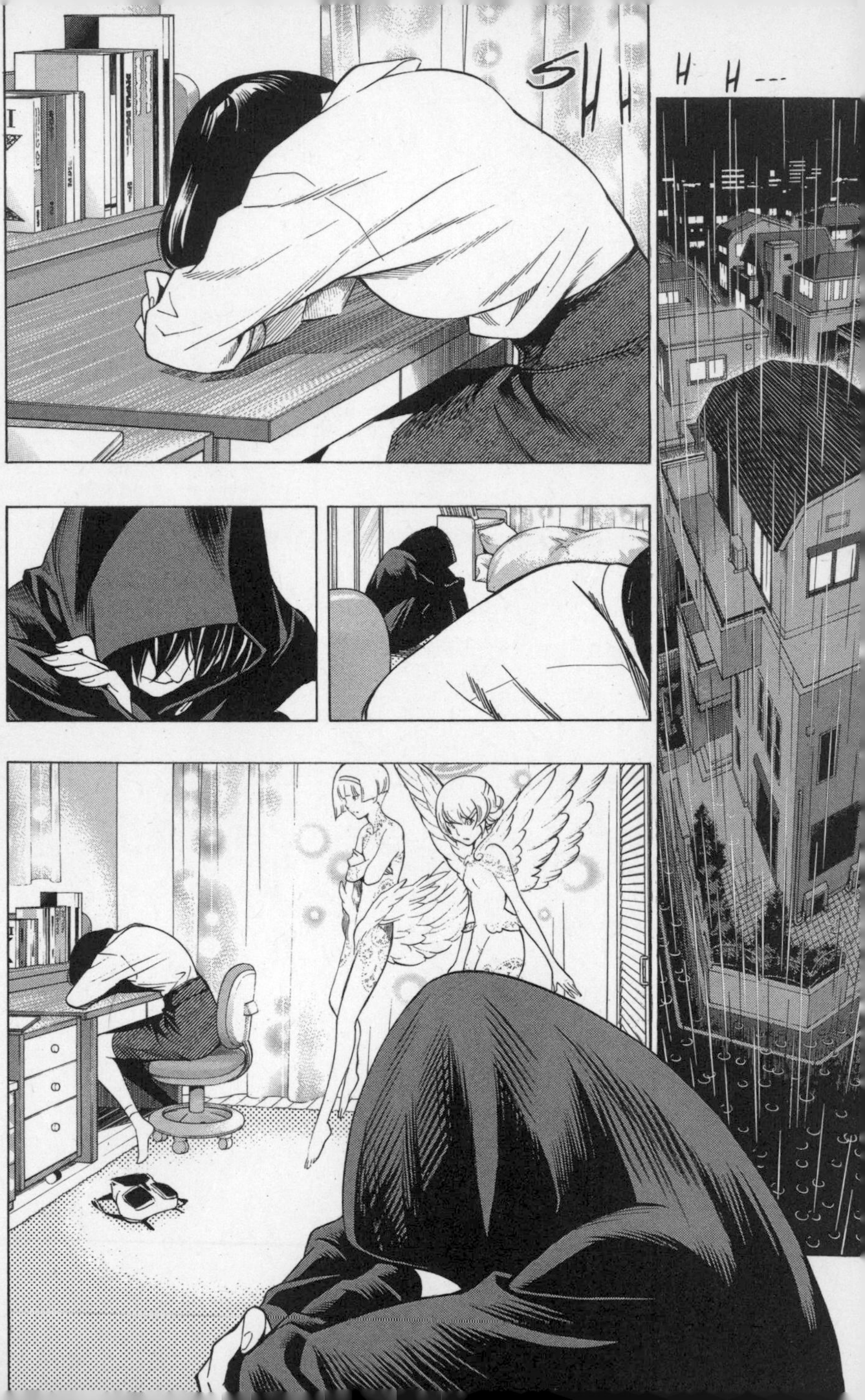
SHHHH---

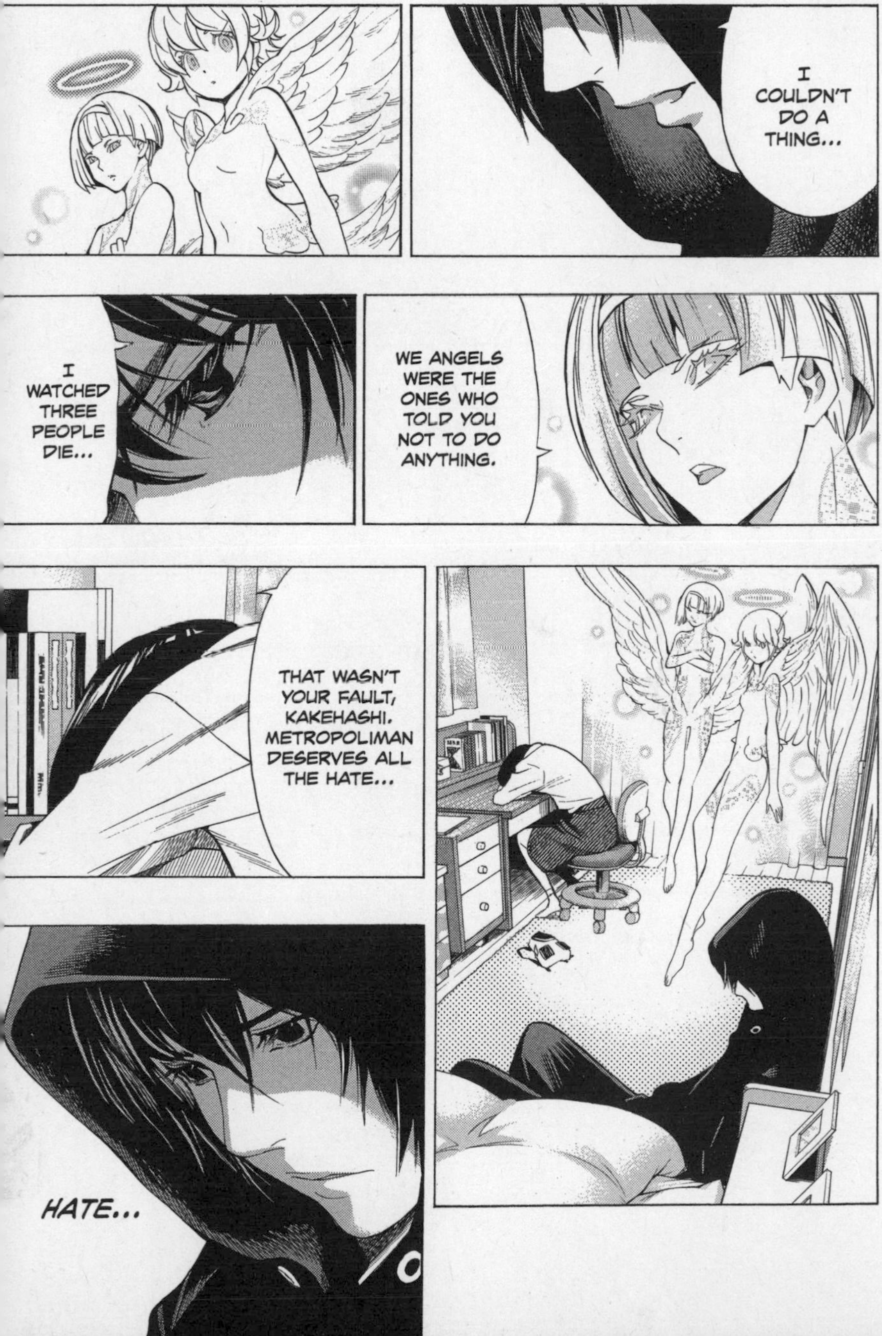
I COULDN'T DO A THING...
WE ANGELS WERE THE ONES WHO TOLD YOU NOT TO DO ANYTHING.
I WATCHED THREE PEOPLE DIE...
THAT WASN'T YOUR FAULT, KAKEHASHI. METROPOLIMAN DESERVES ALL THE HATE...
HATE...

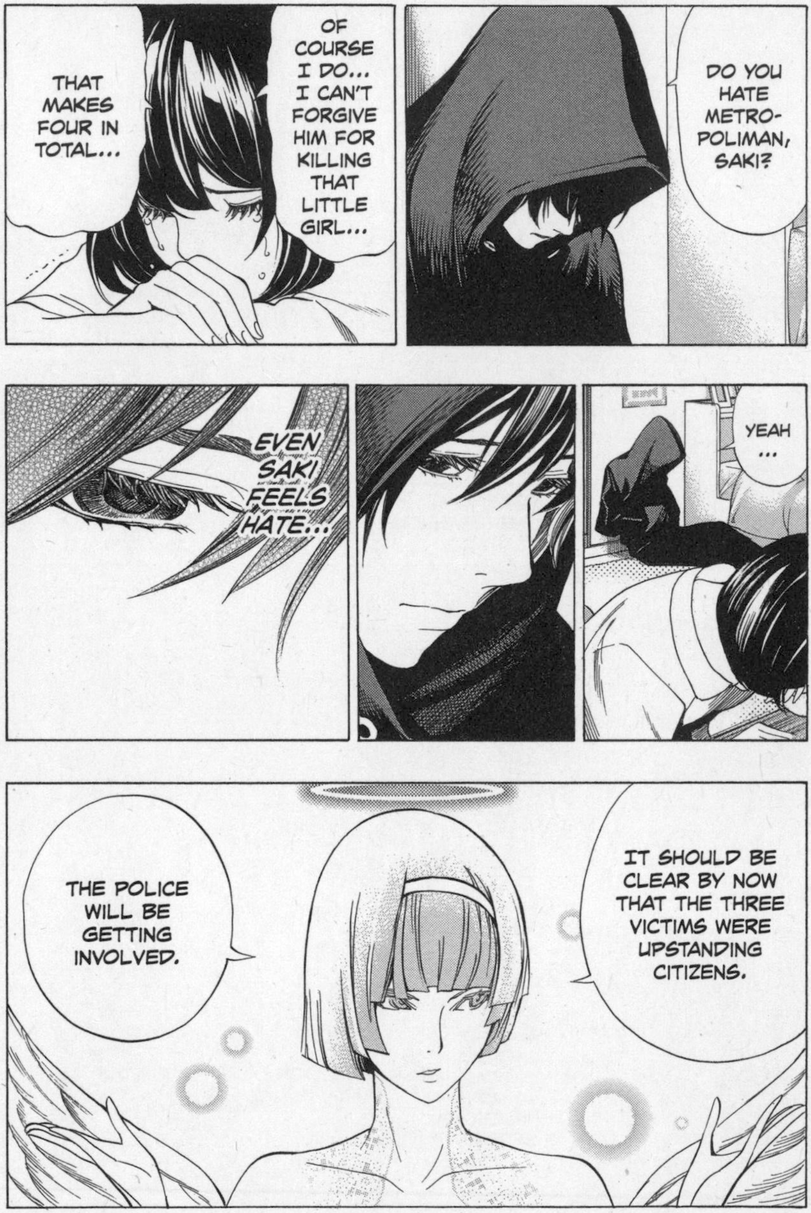
DO YOU HATE METRO-POLIMAN, SAKI?
OF COURSE I DO... I CAN'T FORGIVE HIM FOR KILLING THAT LITTLE GIRL...
THAT MAKES FOUR IN TOTAL...
YEAH ...
EVEN SAKI FEELS HATE...
IT SHOULD BE CLEAR BY NOW THAT THE THREE VICTIMS WERE UPSTANDING CITIZENS.
THE POLICE WILL BE GETTING INVOLVED.

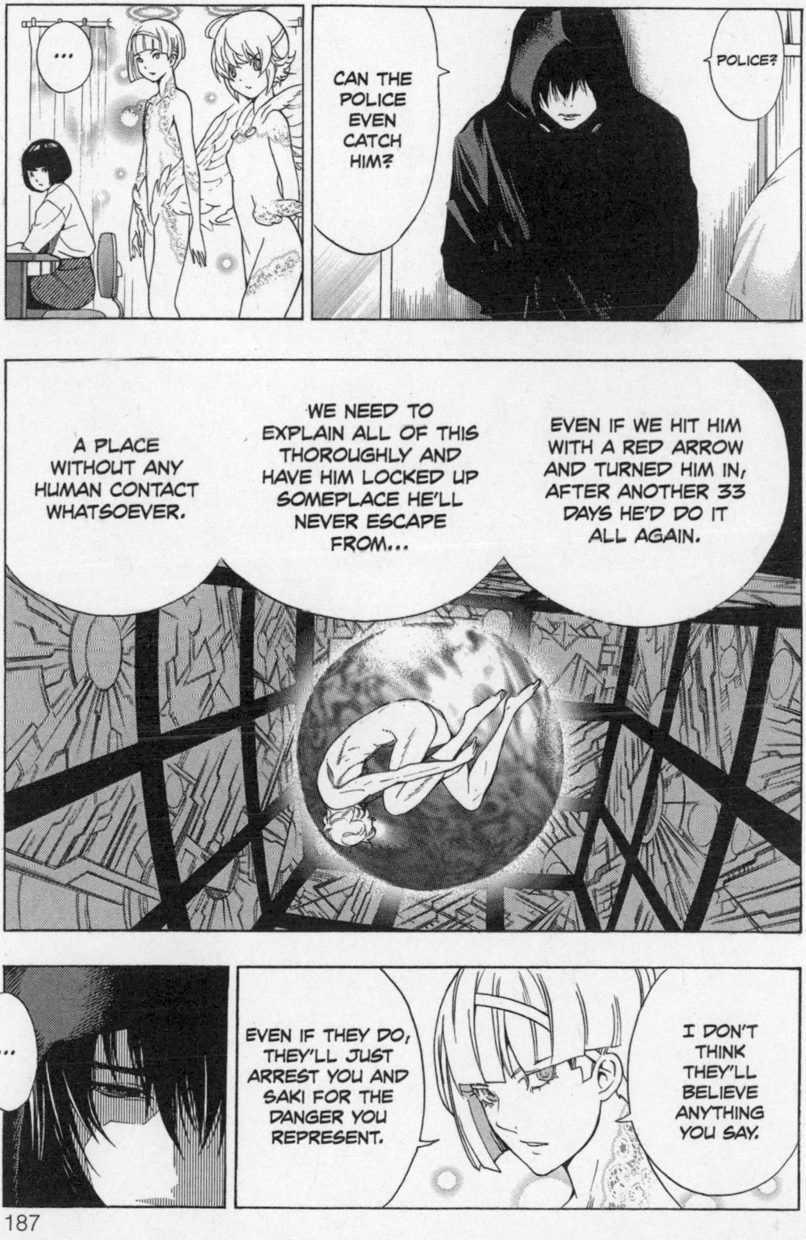
POLICE?
CAN THE POLICE EVEN CATCH HIM?
...
EVEN IF WE HIT HIM WITH A RED ARROW AND TURNED HIM IN, AFTER ANOTHER 33 DAYS HE'D DO IT ALL AGAIN.
WE NEED TO EXPLAIN ALL OF THIS THOROUGHLY AND HAVE HIM LOCKED UP SOMEPLACE HE'LL NEVER ESCAPE FROM...
A PLACE WITHOUT ANY HUMAN CONTACT WHATSOEVER.
I DON'T THINK THEY'LL BELIEVE ANYTHING YOU SAY.
EVEN IF THEY DO, THEY'LL JUST ARREST YOU AND SAKI FOR THE DANGER YOU REPRESENT.
...

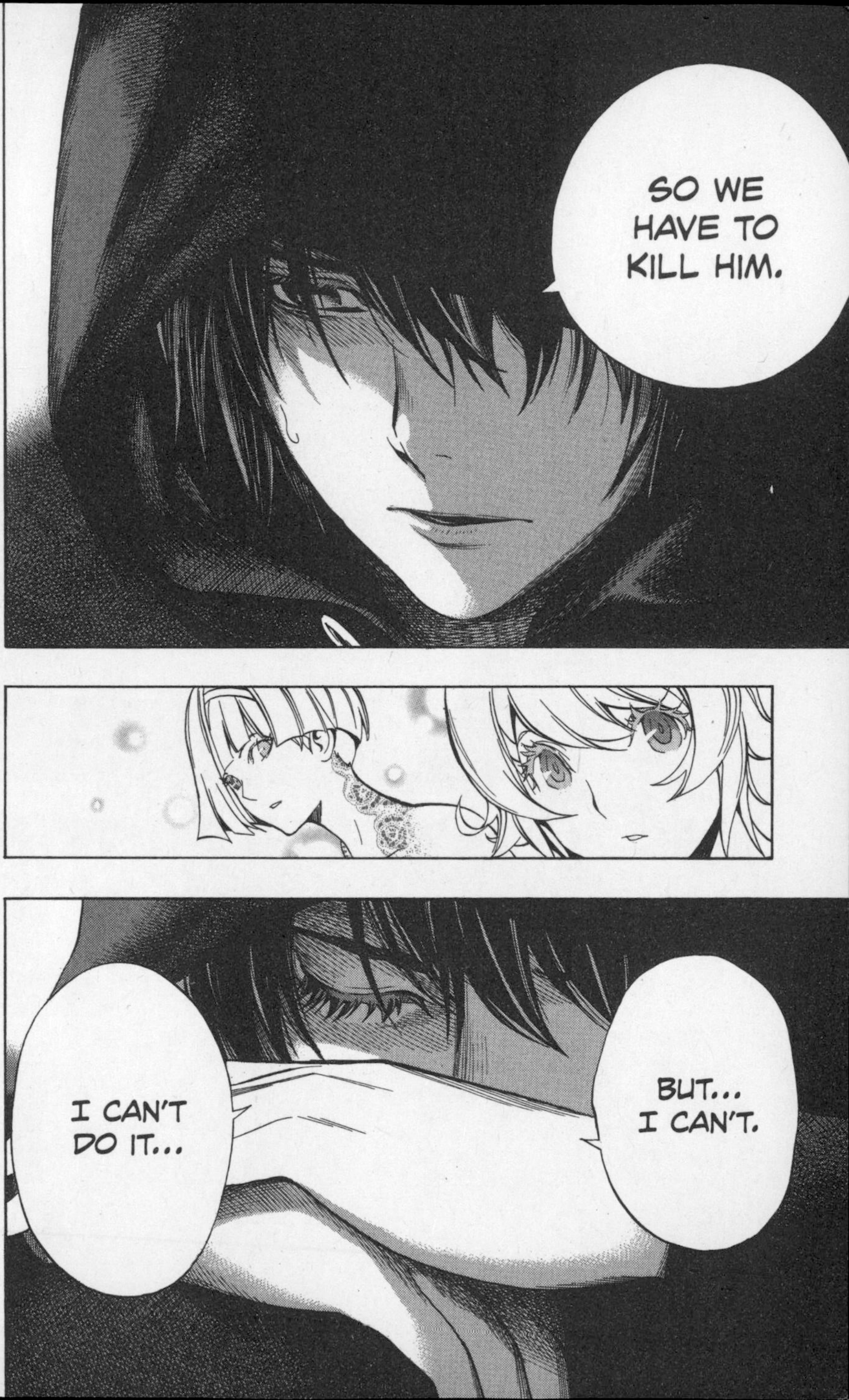
SO WE HAVE TO KILL HIM.
BUT... I CAN'T.
I CAN'T DO IT...

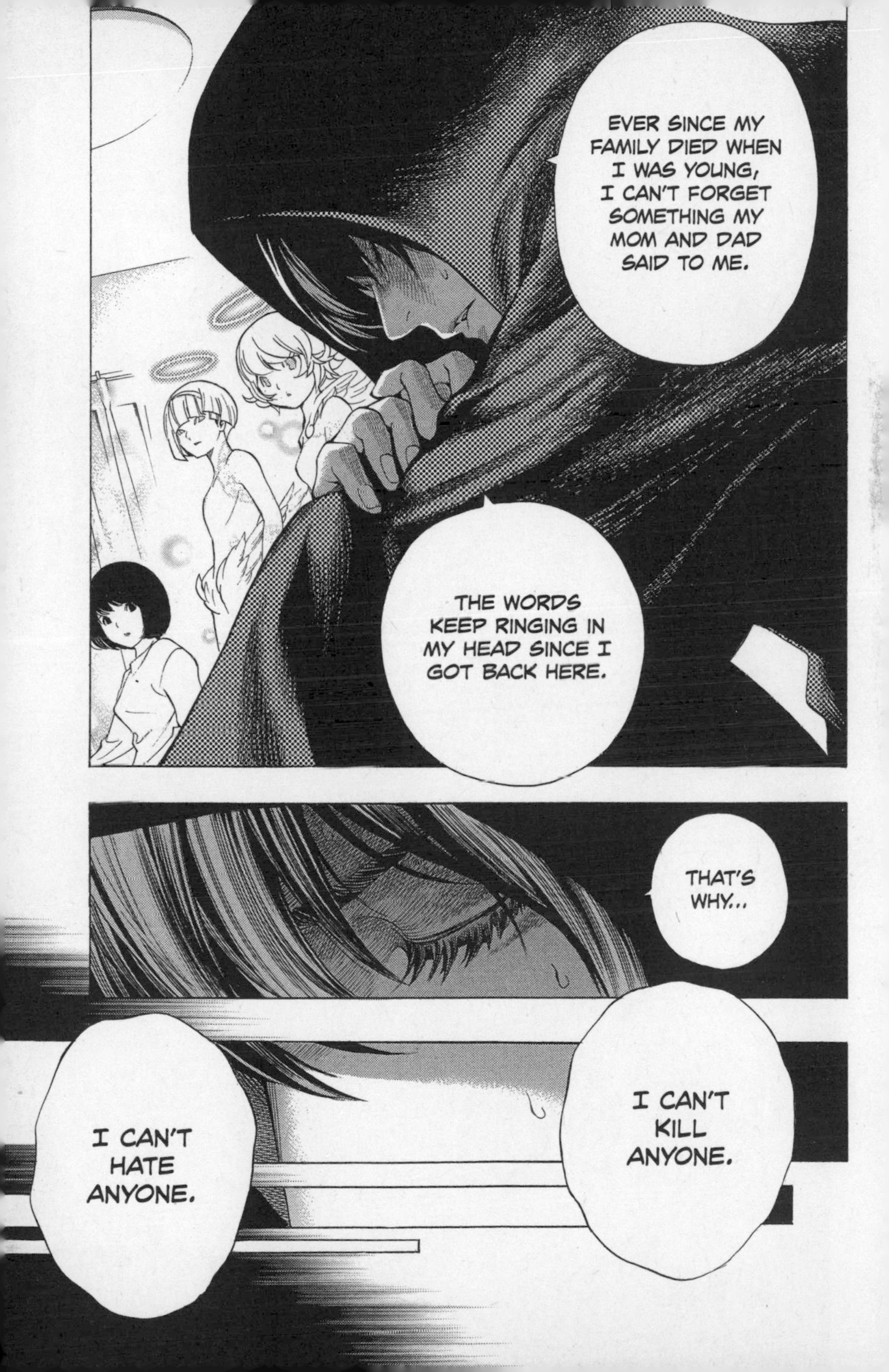
EVER SINCE MY FAMILY DIED WHEN I WAS YOUNG, I CAN'T FORGET SOMETHING MY MOM AND DAD SAID TO ME.
THE WORDS KEEP RINGING IN MY HEAD SINCE I GOT BACK HERE.
THAT'S WHY...
I CAN'T KILL ANYONE.
I CAN'T HATE ANYONE.

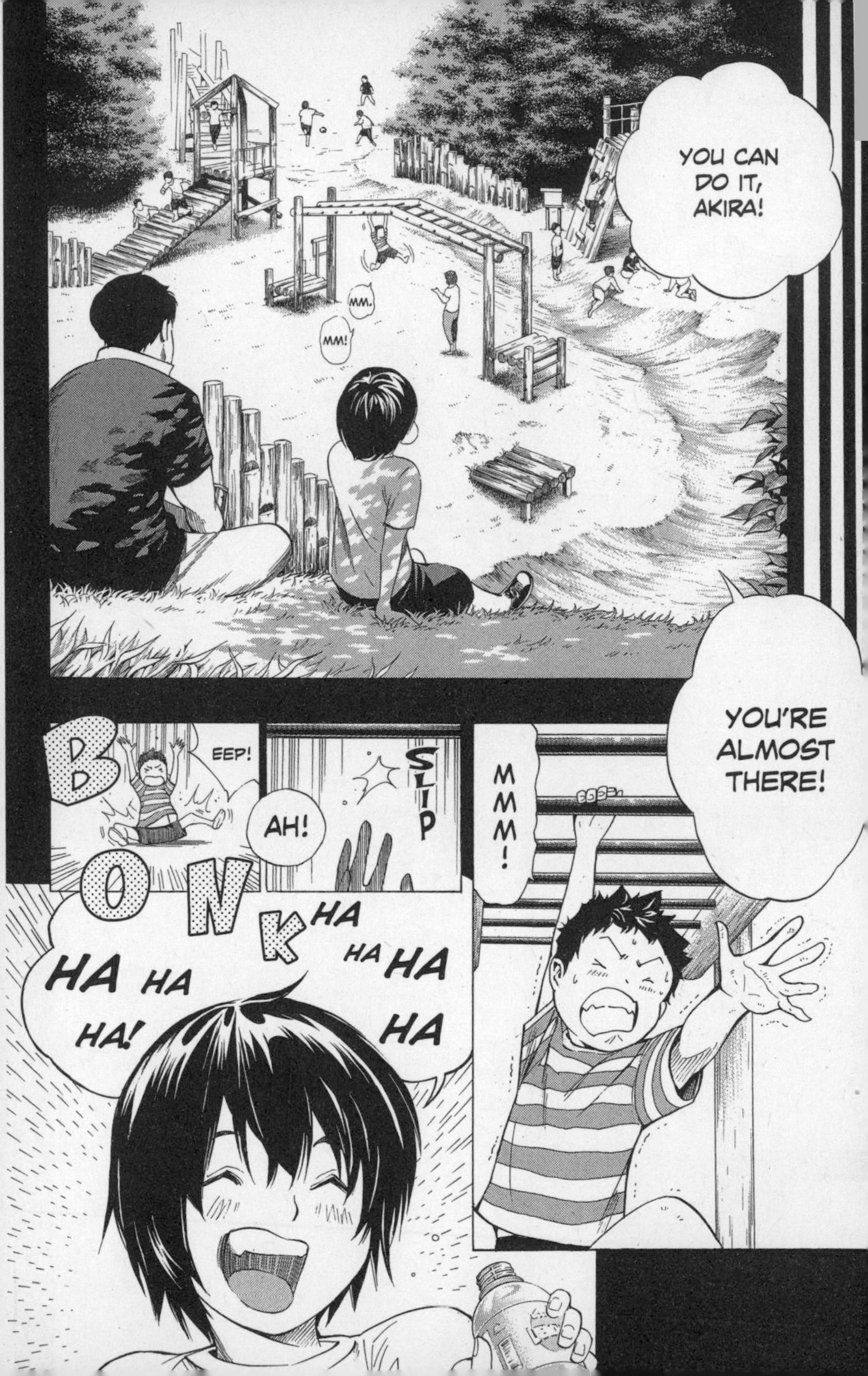
YOU CAN DO IT, AKIRA!
MM.
MM!
YOU'RE ALMOST THERE!
MMM!
SLIP
AH!
EEP!
BONK
HA HA HA HA HA HA HA!

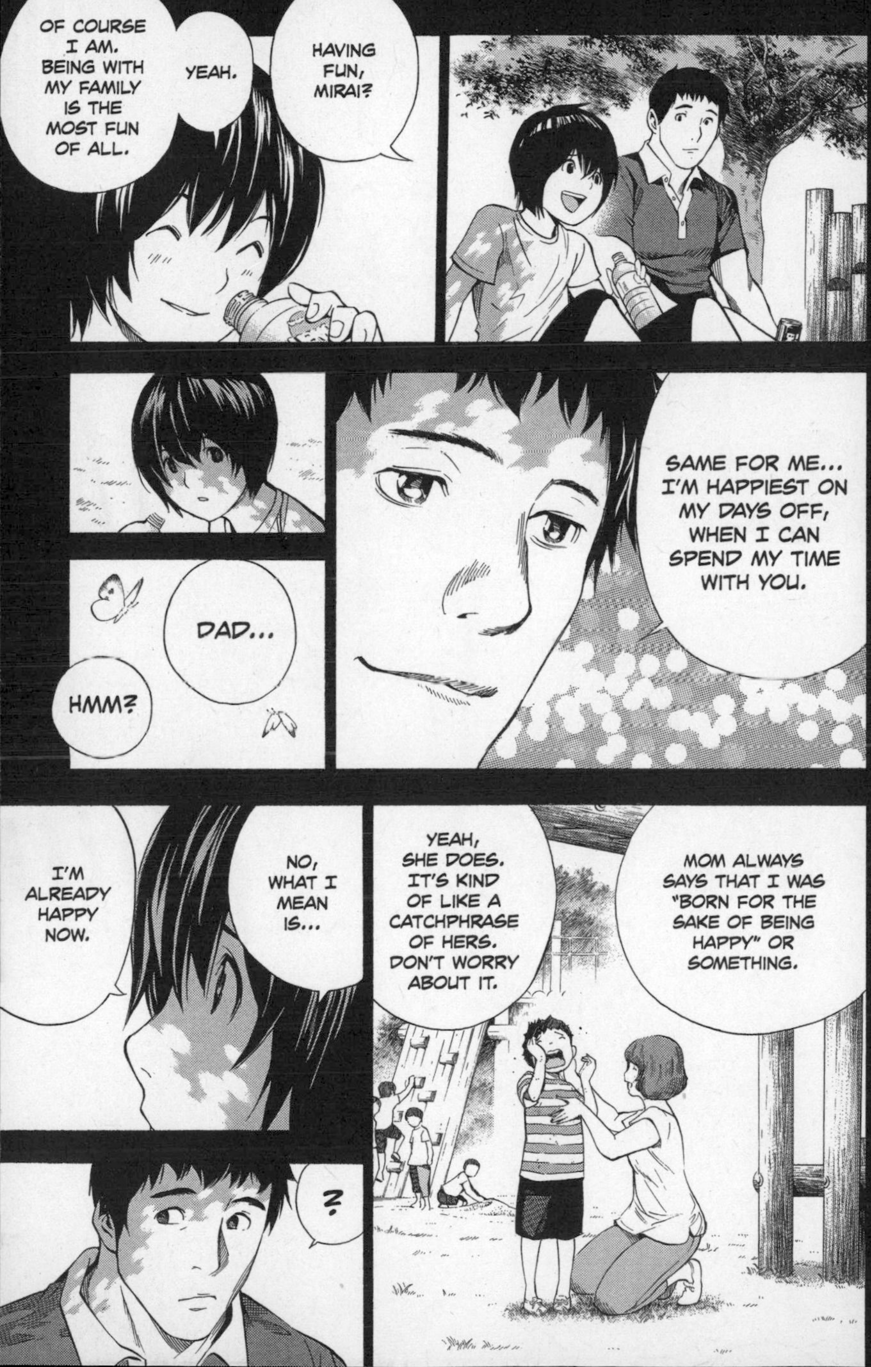
HAVING FUN, MIRAI?
YEAH.
OF COURSE I AM. BEING WITH MY FAMILY IS THE MOST FUN OF ALL.
SAME FOR ME... I'M HAPPIEST ON MY DAYS OFF, WHEN I CAN SPEND MY TIME WITH YOU.
DAD...
HMM?
MOM ALWAYS SAYS THAT I WAS "BORN FOR THE SAKE OF BEING HAPPY" OR SOMETHING.
YEAH, SHE DOES. IT'S KIND OF LIKE A CATCHPHRASE OF HERS. DON'T WORRY ABOUT IT.
NO, WHAT I MEAN IS...
I'M ALREADY HAPPY NOW.
?

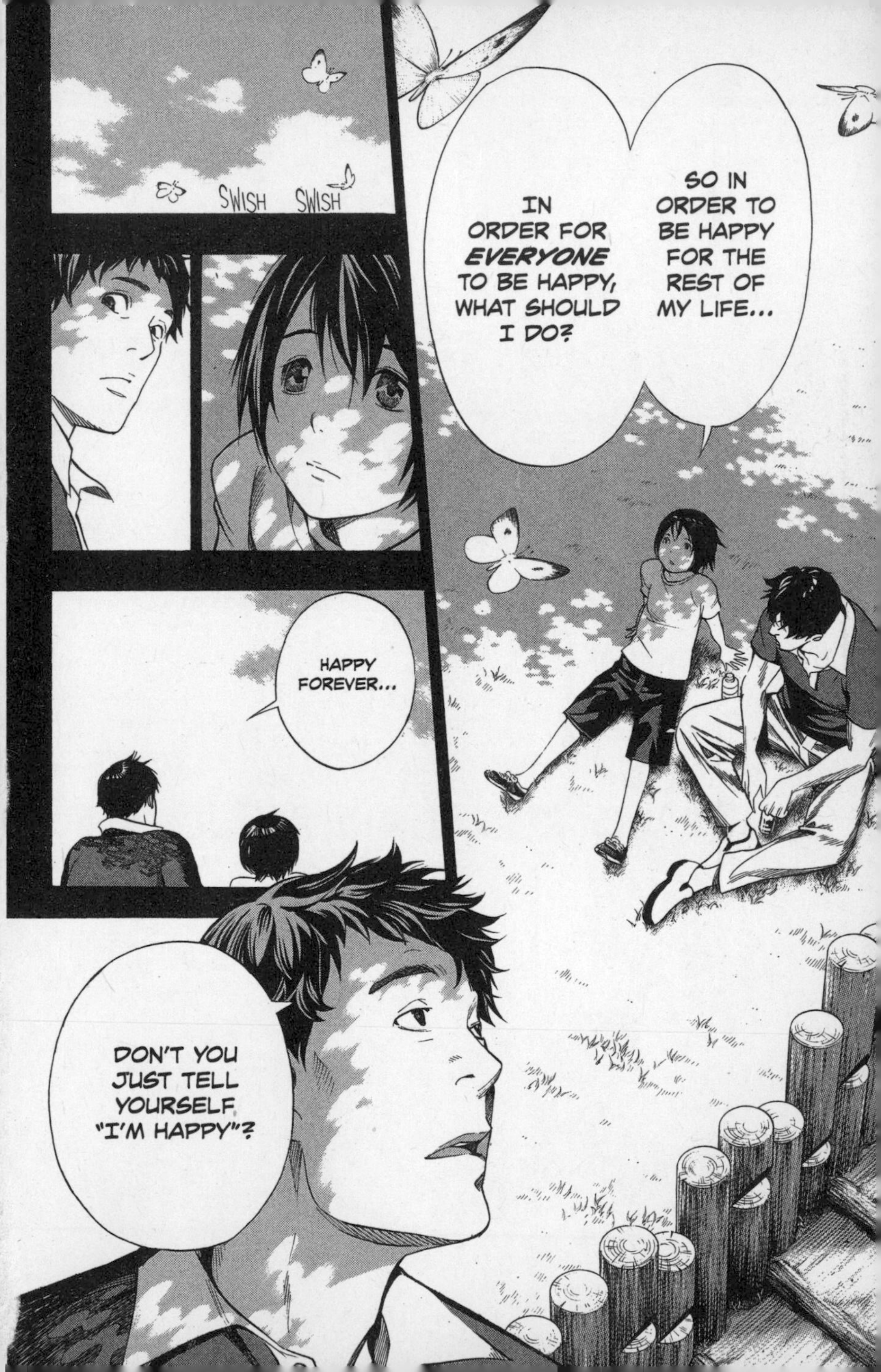
SO IN ORDER TO BE HAPPY FOR THE REST OF MY LIFE...
IN ORDER FOR *EVERYONE* TO BE HAPPY, WHAT SHOULD I DO?
SWISH SWISH
HAPPY FOREVER...
DON'T YOU JUST TELL YOURSELF "I'M HAPPY"?

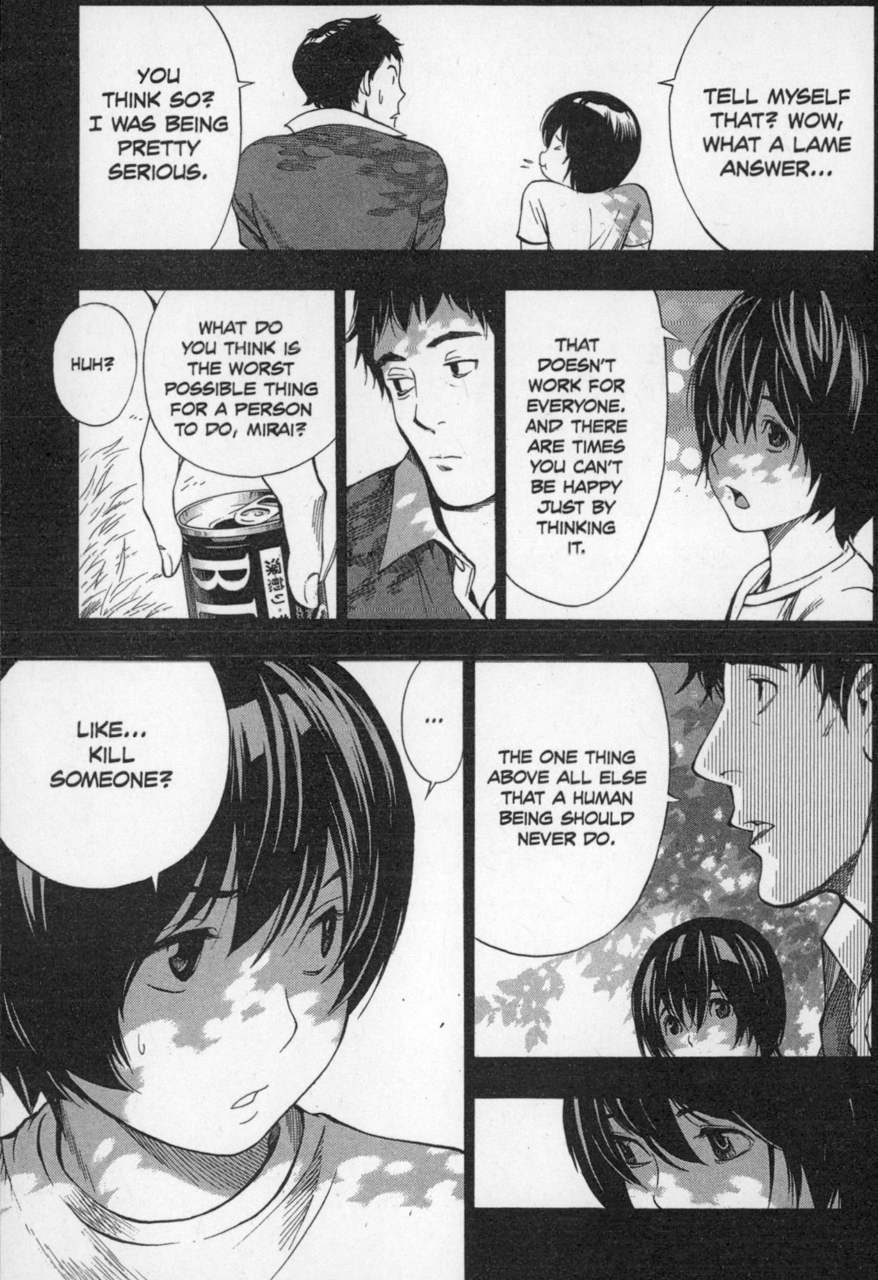
TELL MYSELF THAT? WOW, WHAT A LAME ANSWER...
YOU THINK SO? I WAS BEING PRETTY SERIOUS.
THAT DOESN'T WORK FOR EVERYONE. AND THERE ARE TIMES YOU CAN'T BE HAPPY JUST BY THINKING IT.
WHAT DO YOU THINK IS THE WORST POSSIBLE THING FOR A PERSON TO DO, MIRAI?
HUH?
THE ONE THING ABOVE ALL ELSE THAT A HUMAN BEING SHOULD NEVER DO.
...
LIKE... KILL SOMEONE?

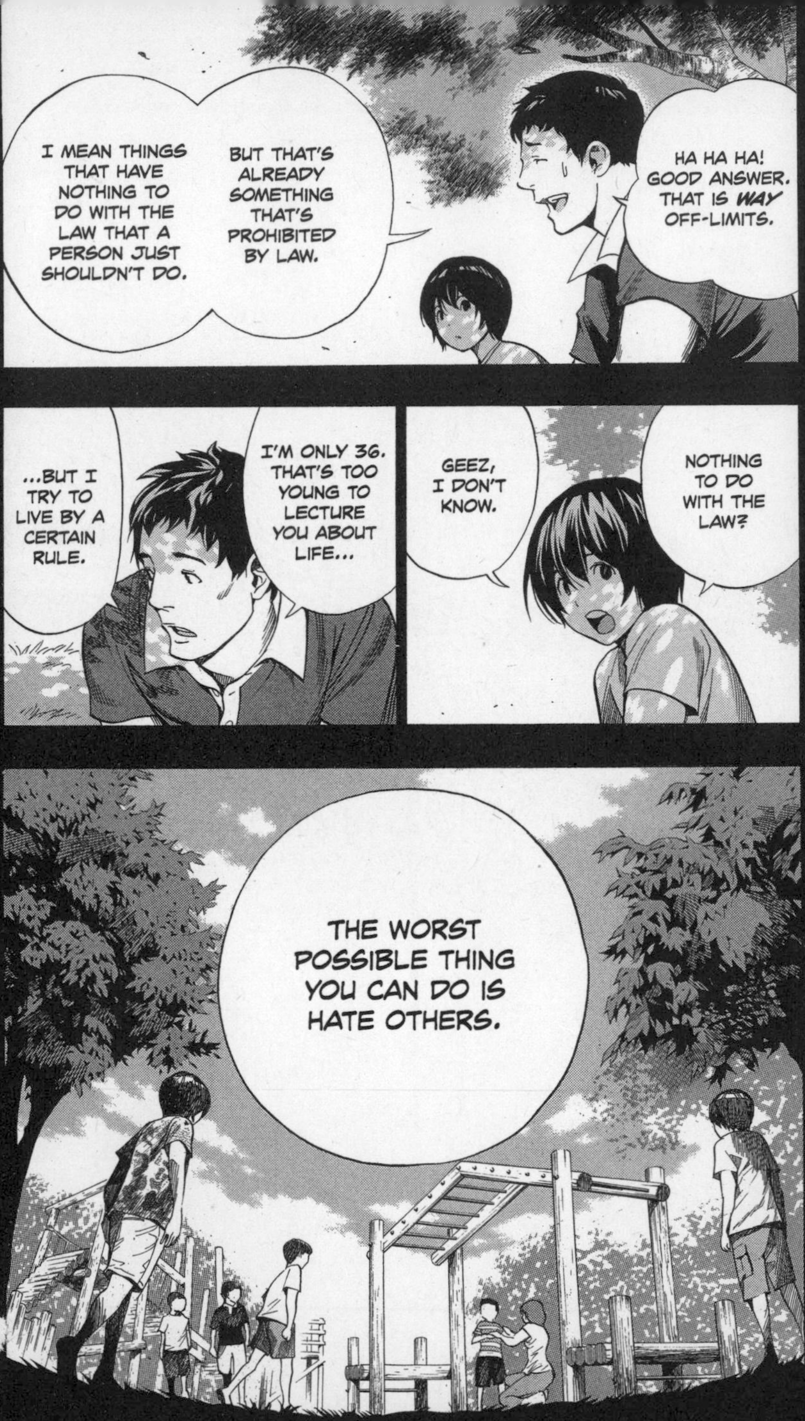
HA HA HA! GOOD ANSWER. THAT IS *WAY* OFF-LIMITS.
BUT THAT'S ALREADY SOMETHING THAT'S PROHIBITED BY LAW.
I MEAN THINGS THAT HAVE NOTHING TO DO WITH THE LAW THAT A PERSON JUST SHOULDN'T DO.
NOTHING TO DO WITH THE LAW?
GEEZ, I DON'T KNOW.
I'M ONLY 36. THAT'S TOO YOUNG TO LECTURE YOU ABOUT LIFE...
...BUT I TRY TO LIVE BY A CERTAIN RULE.
THE WORST POSSIBLE THING YOU CAN DO IS HATE OTHERS.

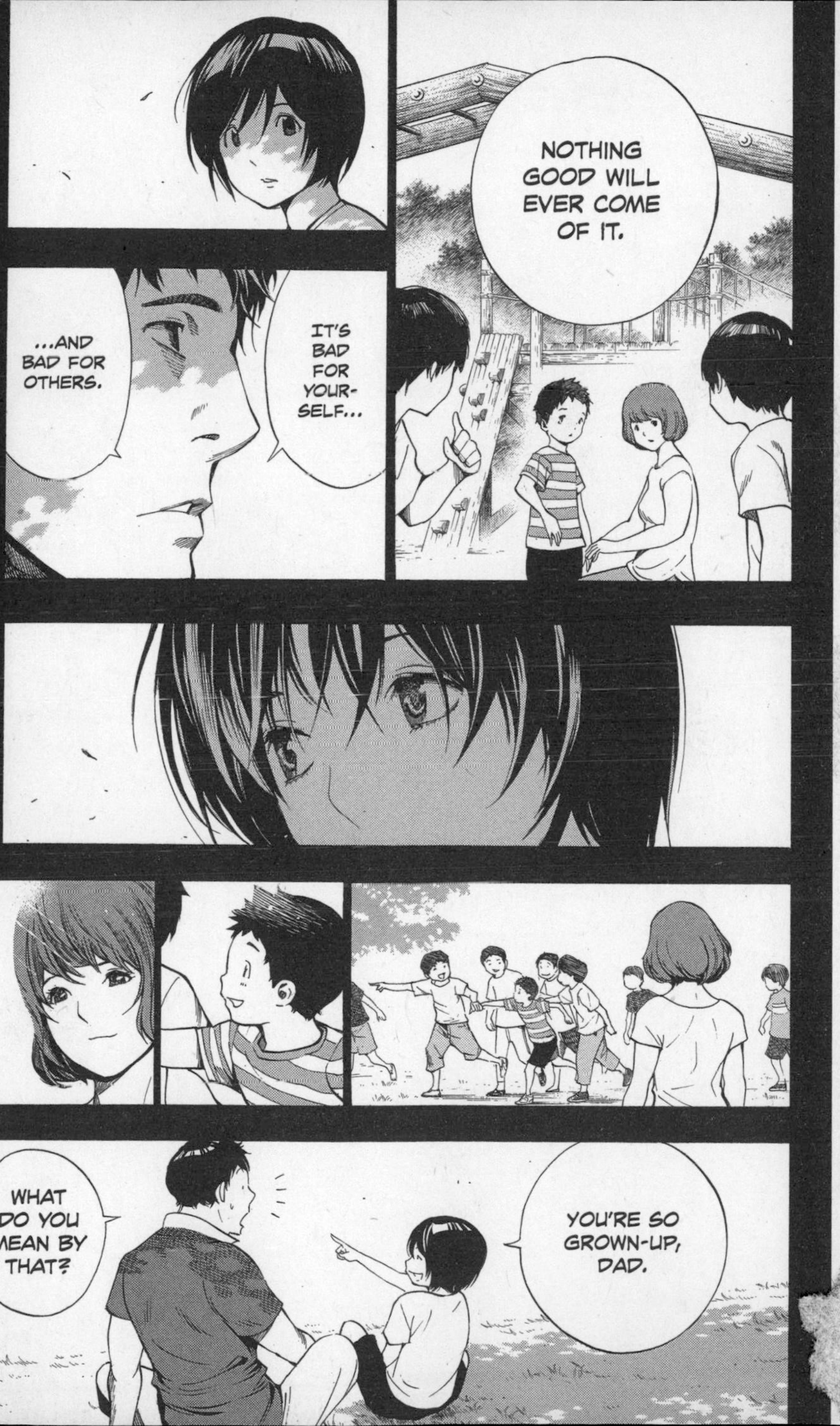
NOTHING GOOD WILL EVER COME OF IT.
IT'S BAD FOR YOUR-SELF...
...AND BAD FOR OTHERS.
YOU'RE SO GROWN-UP, DAD.
WHAT DO YOU MEAN BY THAT?

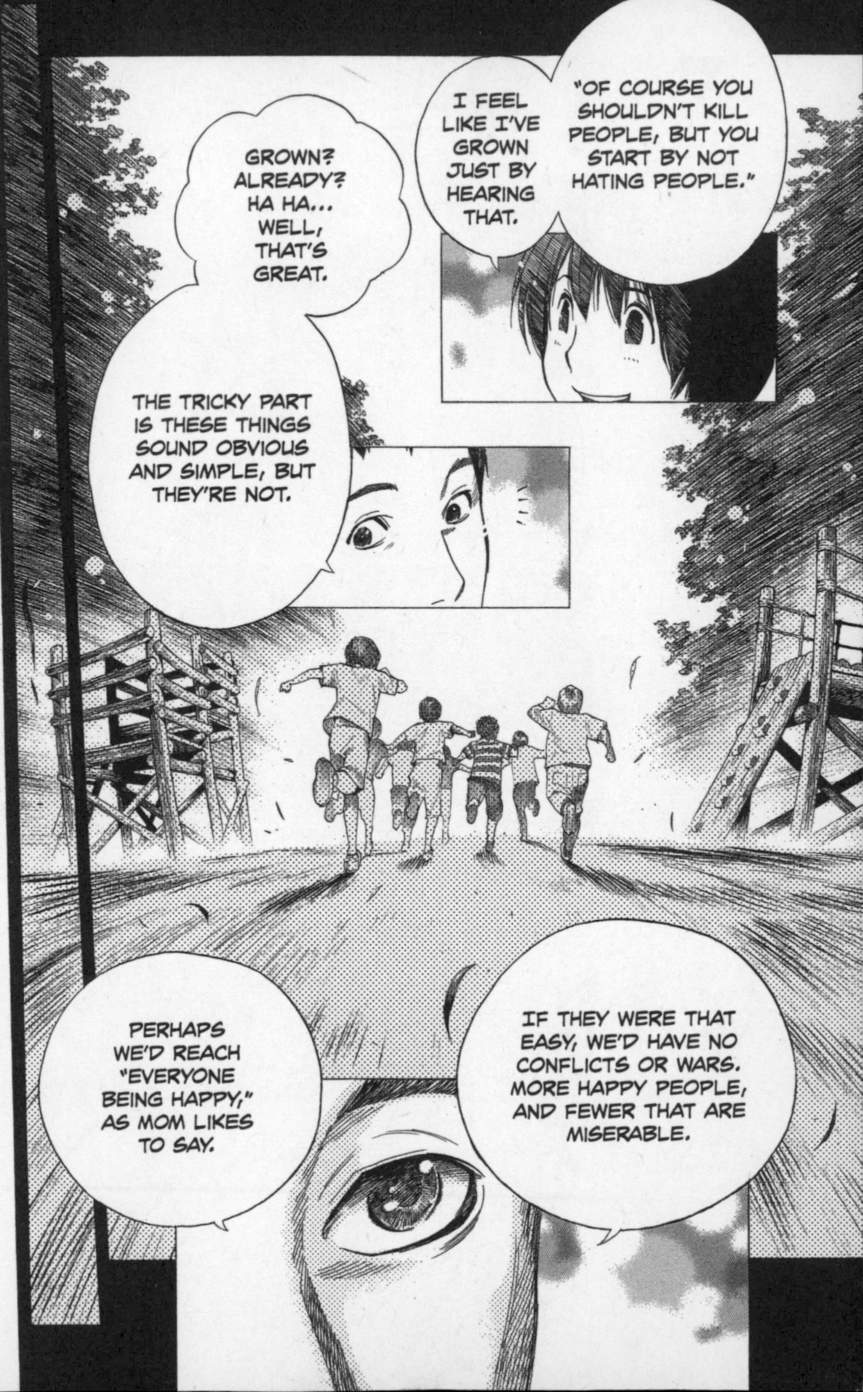
"OF COURSE YOU SHOULDN'T KILL PEOPLE, BUT YOU START BY NOT HATING PEOPLE."
I FEEL LIKE I'VE GROWN JUST BY HEARING THAT.
GROWN? ALREADY? HA HA... WELL, THAT'S GREAT.
THE TRICKY PART IS THESE THINGS SOUND OBVIOUS AND SIMPLE, BUT THEY'RE NOT.
IF THEY WERE THAT EASY, WE'D HAVE NO CONFLICTS OR WARS. MORE HAPPY PEOPLE, AND FEWER THAT ARE MISERABLE.
PERHAPS WE'D REACH "EVERYONE BEING HAPPY," AS MOM LIKES TO SAY.

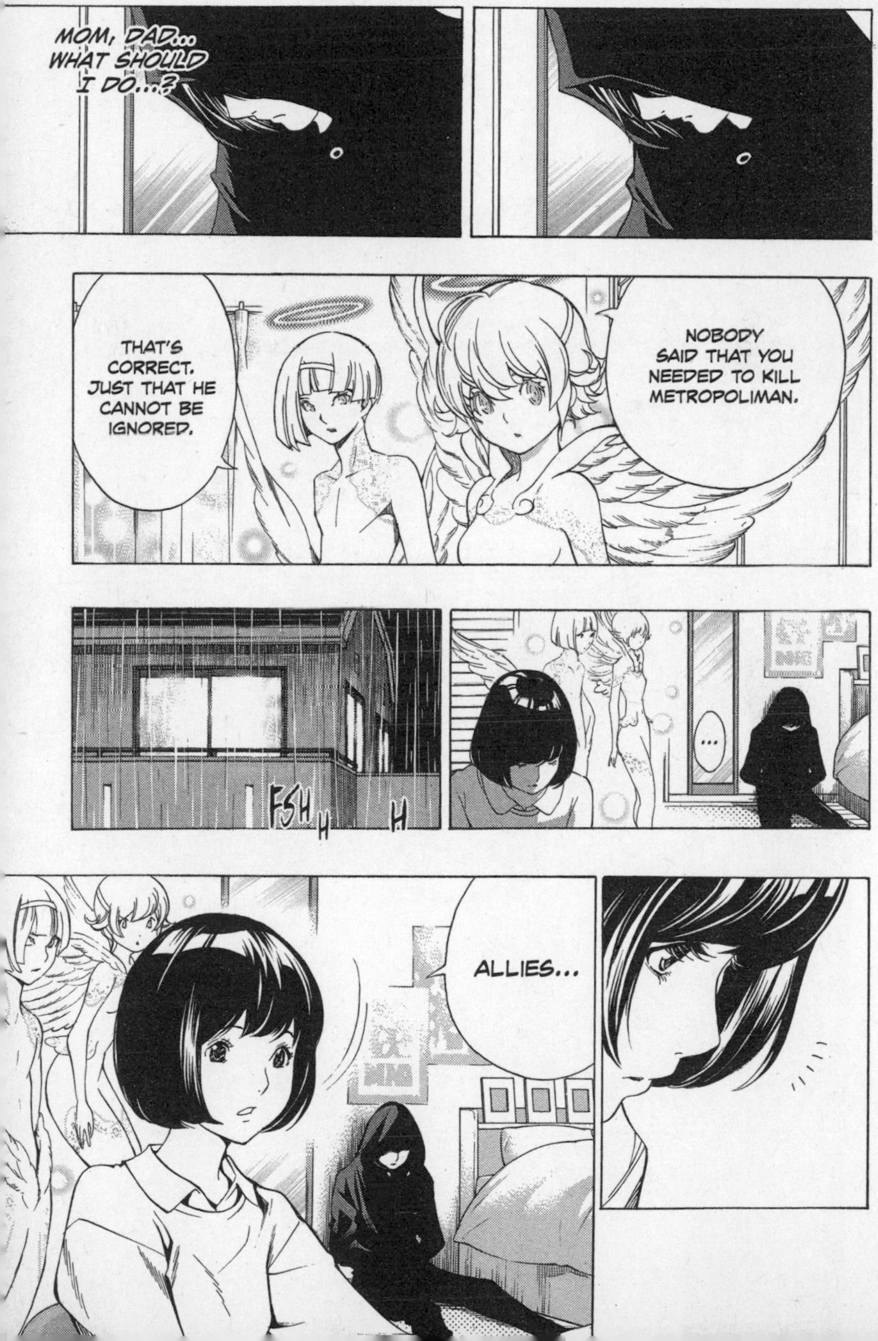
MOM, DAD... WHAT SHOULD I DO...?
NOBODY SAID THAT YOU NEEDED TO KILL METROPOLIMAN.
THAT'S CORRECT. JUST THAT HE CANNOT BE IGNORED.
...
FSHHH
ALLIES...

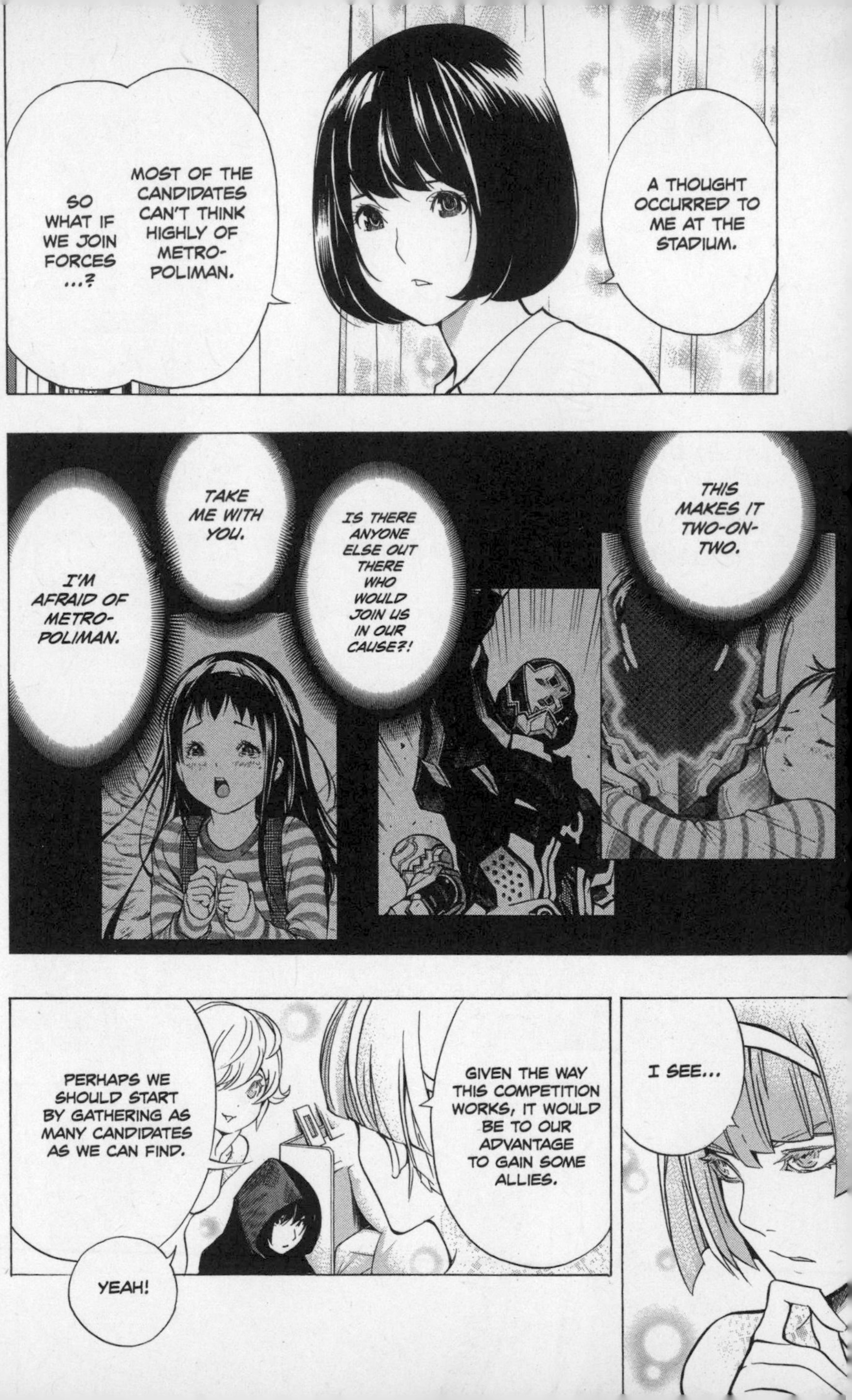
A THOUGHT OCCURRED TO ME AT THE STADIUM.
MOST OF THE CANDIDATES CAN'T THINK HIGHLY OF METRO-POLIMAN.
SO WHAT IF WE JOIN FORCES ...?
THIS MAKES IT TWO-ON-TWO.
IS THERE ANYONE ELSE OUT THERE WHO WOULD JOIN US IN OUR CAUSE?!
TAKE ME WITH YOU.
I'M AFRAID OF METRO-POLIMAN.
I SEE...
GIVEN THE WAY THIS COMPETITION WORKS, IT WOULD BE TO OUR ADVANTAGE TO GAIN SOME ALLIES.
PERHAPS WE SHOULD START BY GATHERING AS MANY CANDIDATES AS WE CAN FIND.
YEAH!

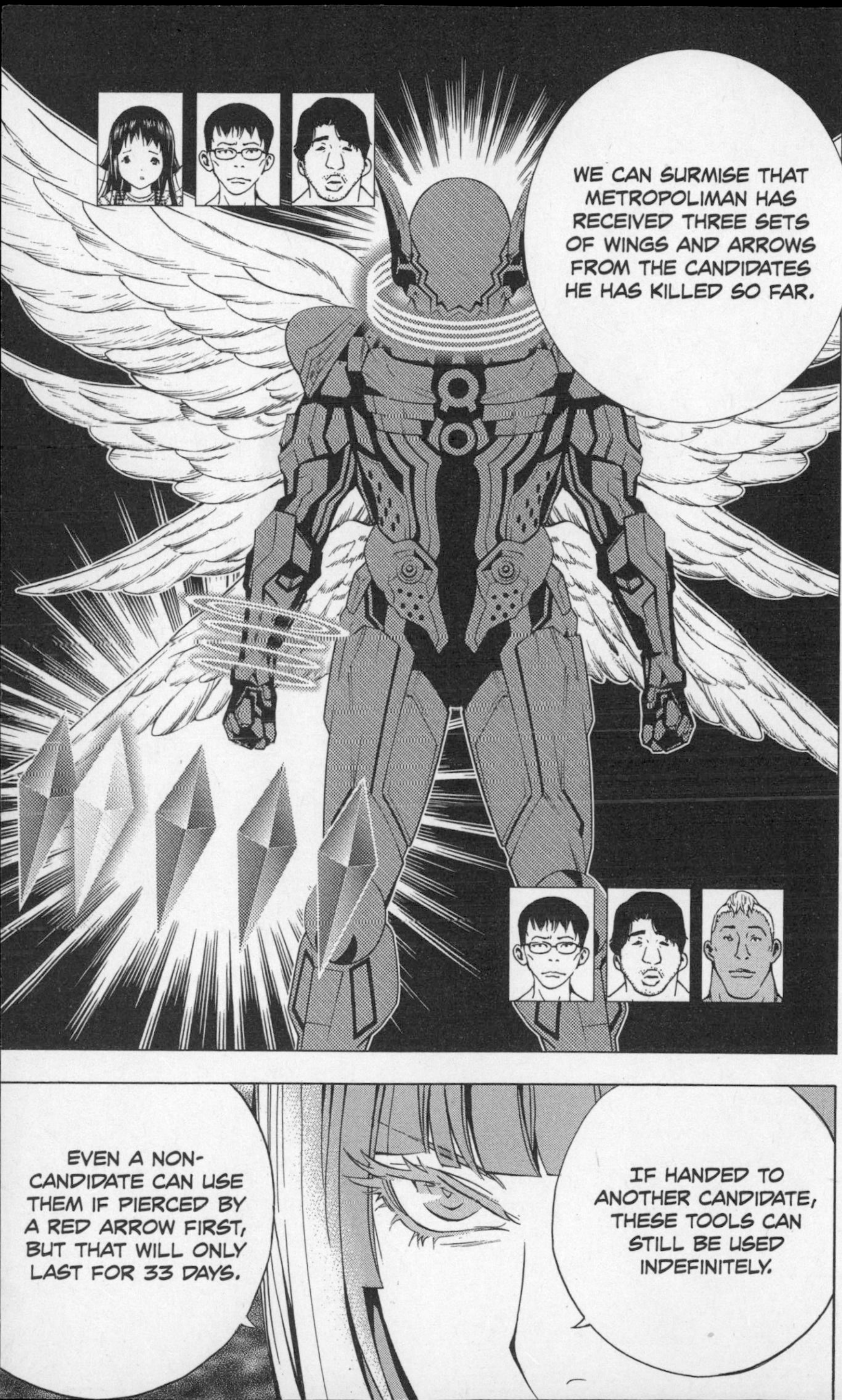
WE CAN SURMISE THAT METROPOLIMAN HAS RECEIVED THREE SETS OF WINGS AND ARROWS FROM THE CANDIDATES HE HAS KILLED SO FAR.
IF HANDED TO ANOTHER CANDIDATE, THESE TOOLS CAN STILL BE USED INDEFINITELY.
EVEN A NON-CANDIDATE CAN USE THEM IF PIERCED BY A RED ARROW FIRST, BUT THAT WILL ONLY LAST FOR 33 DAYS.

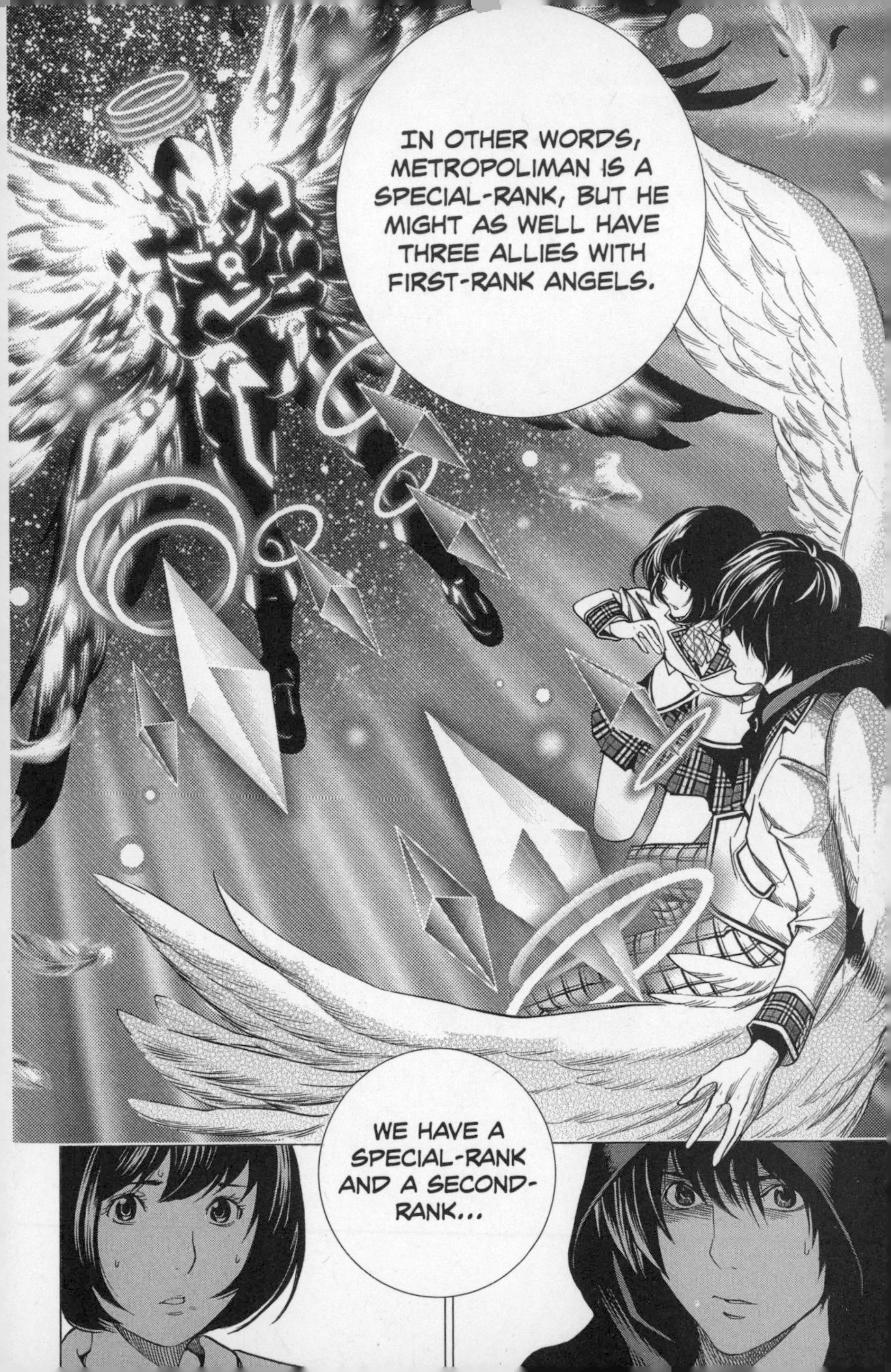
IN OTHER WORDS, METROPOLIMAN IS A SPECIAL-RANK, BUT HE MIGHT AS WELL HAVE THREE ALLIES WITH FIRST-RANK ANGELS.
WE HAVE A SPECIAL-RANK AND A SECOND-RANK...

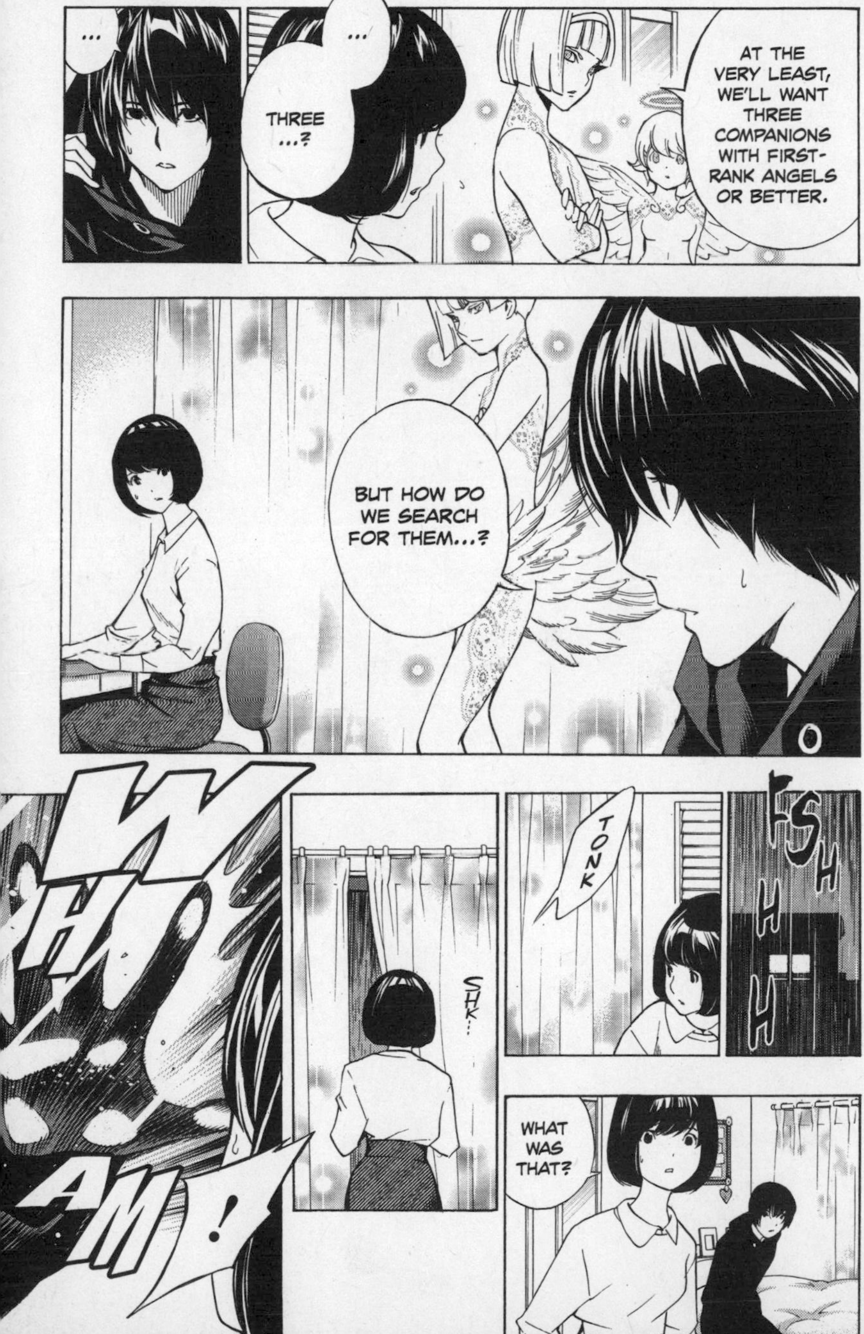
AT THE VERY LEAST, WE'LL WANT THREE COMPANIONS WITH FIRST-RANK ANGELS OR BETTER.
...
THREE ...?
...
BUT HOW DO WE SEARCH FOR THEM...?
FSHHHH
TONK
WHAT WAS THAT?
SHK...
WHAM!

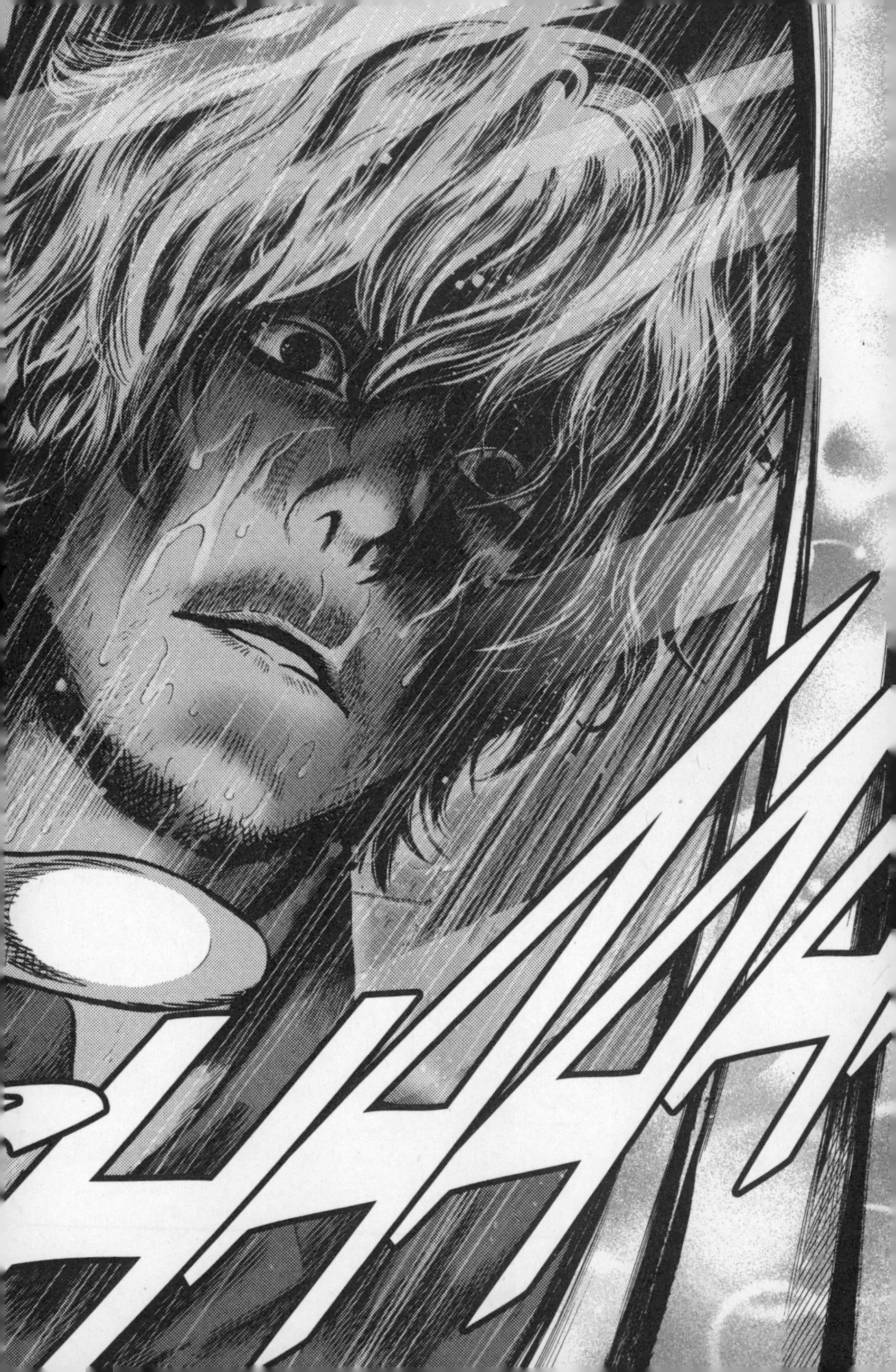

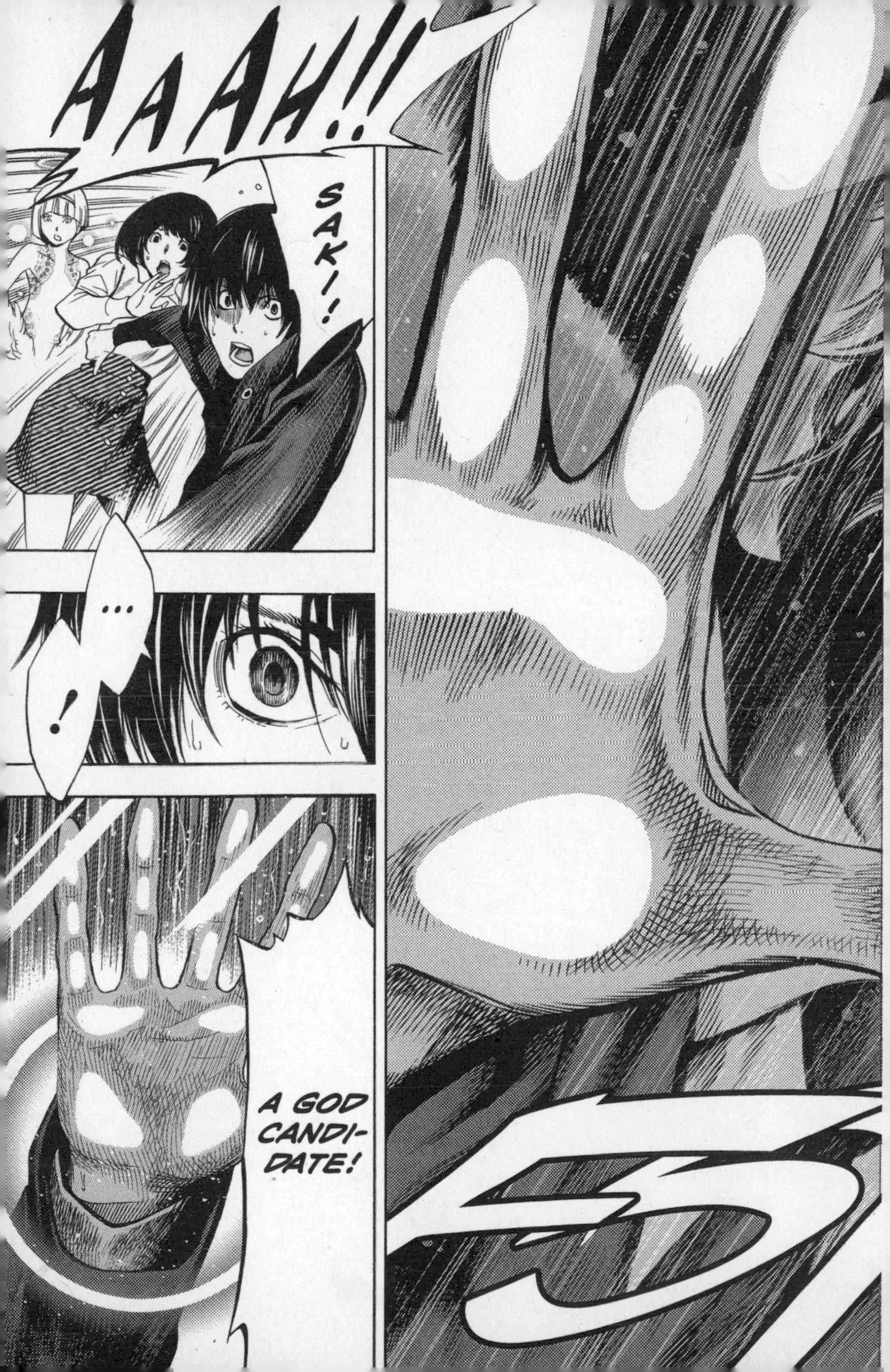
AAAH!!
SAKI!!
...
!
A GOD CANDI-DATE!

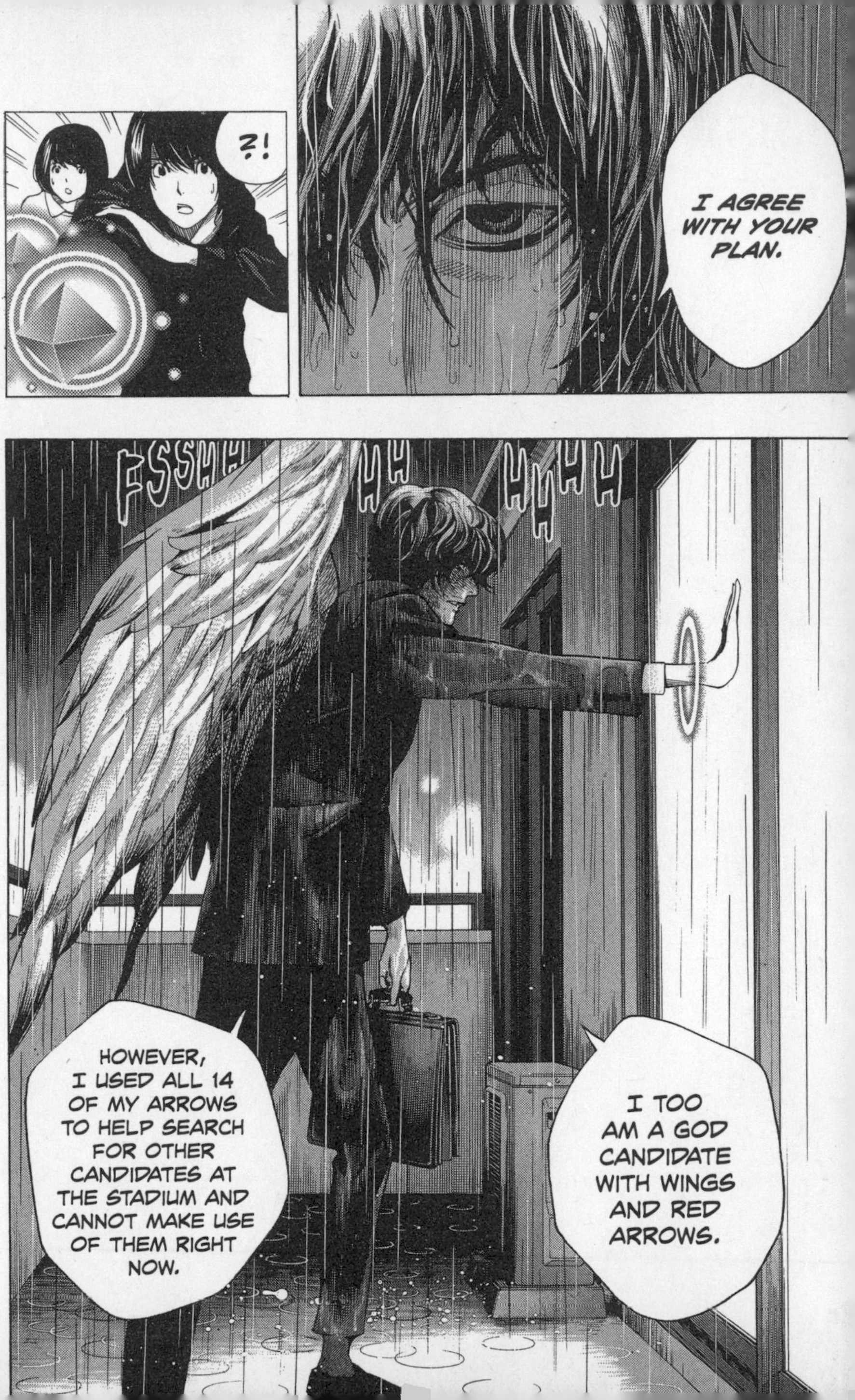
I AGREE WITH YOUR PLAN.
?!
FSSHHHHHHHH
I TOO AM A GOD CANDIDATE WITH WINGS AND RED ARROWS.
HOWEVER, I USED ALL 14 OF MY ARROWS TO HELP SEARCH FOR OTHER CANDIDATES AT THE STADIUM AND CANNOT MAKE USE OF THEM RIGHT NOW.

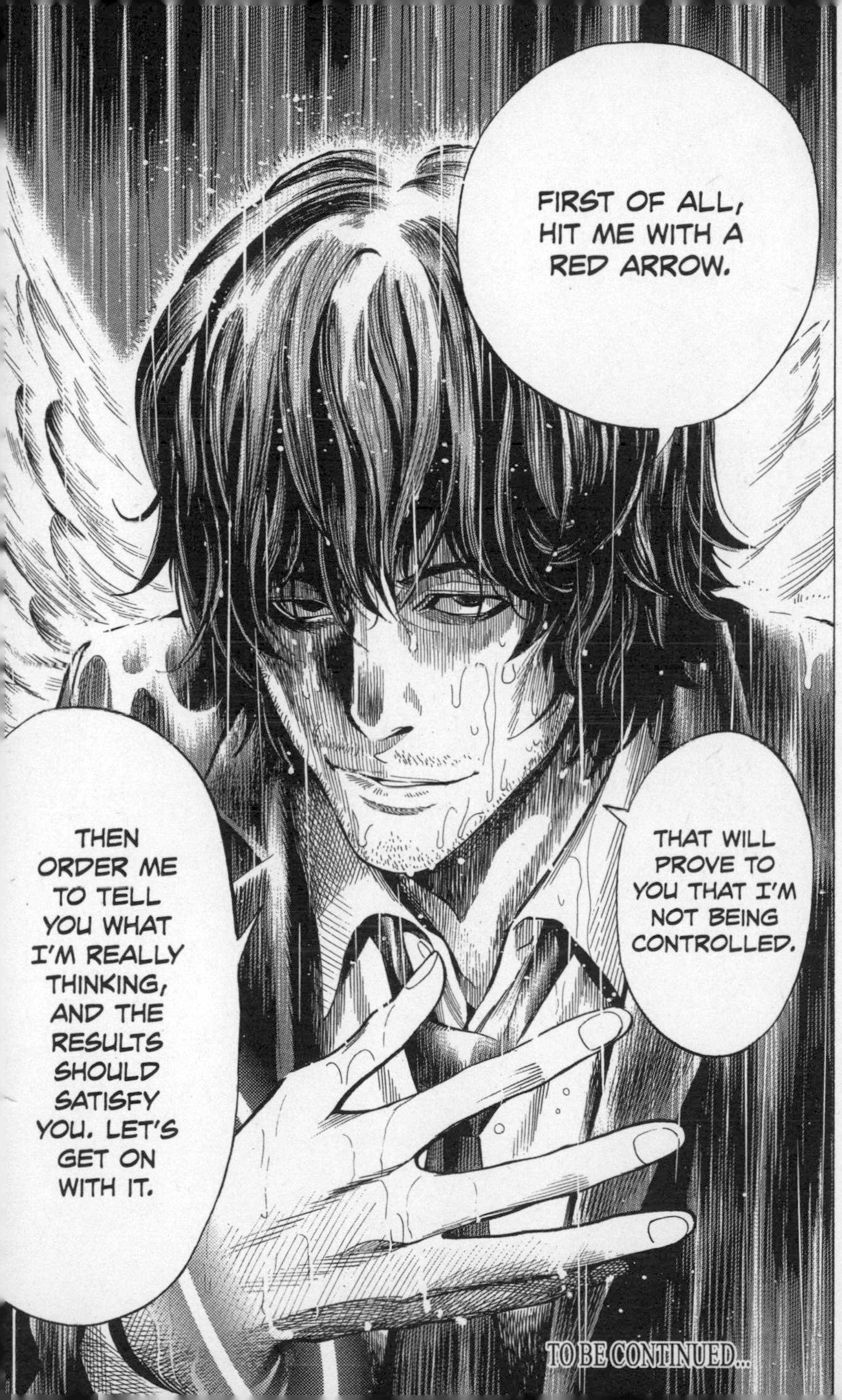
FIRST OF ALL, HIT ME WITH A RED ARROW.
THAT WILL PROVE TO YOU THAT I'M NOT BEING CONTROLLED.
THEN ORDER ME TO TELL YOU WHAT I'M REALLY THINKING, AND THE RESULTS SHOULD SATISFY YOU. LET'S GET ON WITH IT.
TO BE CONTINUED...

T s u g u mi **Oh** b **a**

°

Born in Tokyo, Tsugumi Ohba is the author
of the hit series *Death Note* and *Bakuman*。.

°

°

°

°

Ta **k** e s **h** i O b a **ta**

°

Takeshi Obata was born in 1969 in Niigata,
Japan, and first achieved international
recognition as the artist of the wildly popular
Shonen Jump title *Hikaru no Go*, which won the
2003 Tezuka Osamu Cultural Prize: Shinsei
"New Hope" Award and the 2000 Shogakukan
Manga Award. He went on to illustrate the smash
hit *Death Note* as well as the hugely successful
manga *Bakuman*。 and *All You Need Is Kill*.